No Best Way

*An Evolutionary Perspective
on Human Resource Management*

Stephen M. Colarelli

PRAEGER

Westport, Connecticut
London

Library of Congress Cataloging-in-Publication Data

Colarelli, Stephen M., 1951–
    No best way : an evolutionary perspective on human resource management /
Stephen M. Colarelli.
      p. cm.
    Includes bibliographical references and index.
    ISBN 0–275–95739–X (alk. paper)
    1. Personnel management. 2. Psychology, Industrial. I. Title.
HF5549.C5615   2003
658.3—dc21   2002033383

British Library Cataloguing in Publication Data is available.

Library of Congress Catalog Card Number: 2002033383
ISBN: 0–275–95739–X

First published in 2003

Praeger Publishers, 88 Post Road West, Westport, CT 06881
An imprint of Greenwood Publishing Group, Inc.
www.praeger.com

Printed in the United States of America

∞™

The paper used in this book complies with the
Permanent Paper Standard issued by the National
Information Standards Organization (Z39.48–1984).

10 9 8 7 6 5 4 3 2 1

Copyright Acknowledgments

Extracts from Campbell, D.T., On the conflicts between biological and social evolution
and between psychology and moral tradition, *American Psychologist*, 30, 1975: 1103–
1126, are used by permission of American Psychological Association.

Figure 3.5, copyright ©1997 by the American Psychological Association. Reprinted with
permission.

The writing of this book was supported in part by a grant from the Earhart Foundation.

To
Social engineers, everywhere

One of the first things a child is taught when learning the piano is to play a C-major scale. We always begin with the simple fingering 1 2 3 1 2 3 4 5, and we are shown how to exploit the special character of the human hand and the mobile thumb by crossing the thumb under the third finger as we play the scale. . . . This is a basic part of piano technique as it is conceived in conservatories the world over. Nevertheless, it is a mark of the extraordinary variability of approaches to playing the piano that this fundamental practice is not as useful for some pianists as piano teachers think. A pupil of the late Dinu Lipatti, one of the most interesting pianists of this century, told me that Lipatti once remarked: "You know, it has been at least ten years since I last crossed my thumb under the third finger."

I was pleased to hear this, because I too have discovered that this position is in fact very uncomfortable. . . . Everything depends, of course, on the shape of the hand, and it must be stressed that there is no type of hand that is more suited to the piano than another.

—Charles Rosen (1999, October 21).
On playing the piano. *New York Review of Books*, 49–54.

Contents

Acknowledgments   ix

Introduction   xi

1. Clocks, Caves, and Utopias
   The Mechanical Design Perspective   1

2. Storms, Pilots, and Byzantium
   The Evolutionary Perspective   45

3. Splinters in the Mind
   Methods of Hiring People   109

4. Alternatives to Jigsaw Puzzle and Spray Paint Utopias   185
   Evolutionary Approaches to Hiring People

5. Look! We're Modern
   Training People   245

Conclusion   315

Index   323

Acknowledgments

My good friend and colleague Peter Koper edited the early drafts of the manuscript. His broad knowledge, powerful intellect, and well-turned phrases enriched and enlivened the book. Working with Peter was the kind of intellectual engagement a scholar thrives on. It was all the more enjoyable because we were *d'accord* on many issues and because, on a few, we were not—which, combined with cups of black coffee, sparked many animated conversations. Several colleagues read and commented on the manuscript or portions of it, and I am grateful for their generosity. Kingsley Browne and Richard Wielkiewicz read the entire manuscript and helped me to rethink and clarify a number of issues. David Geary, Gary Johns, Owen Jones, and Richard Redding read portions of the manuscript and provided invaluable feedback. My editor at Praeger, Debora Carvalko, was encouraging and patient as the manuscript evolved. Becky Hays helped cheerfully and professionally with everything from reworking and polishing tables and figures to correspondence and formatting. Guangrong Dai, Padmapriya Ranganath, Chulguen Yang, Geeta D'Souza, and Jeffrey Labrador were research assistants *par excellence*.

As an apostate in industrial and organizational psychology, I would like to thank those stalwart colleagues who were supportive of my view that industrial and organizational psychology could benefit by incorporating an evolutionary perspective. I am particularly grateful to Rick Price for his encouragement. I owe a debt of gratitude to many friends, too, for providing enjoyable respites from writing. A sabbatical leave from Central Michigan University and a grant from the Earhart Foundation gave me what an author needs most: unencumbered time to think and write. I am immeasurably grateful for that support. Ingrid Merikoski of the Earhart Foundation was especially gracious and encouraging throughout all phases of this project. My wife, Margaret, and daughters, Catherine and Julia, have their own rich and interesting lives, so home life did not revolve around the writing of this book. We enrich and give meaning to each other's lives, and that provides sustenance for our vocations.

Introduction

How can evolutionary theory influence and alter the ways we think about, conduct research on, and practice human resource management (HRM)?[1] Although evolutionary theory has been a theoretical bedrock of the life sciences for a century, only recently—primarily within the last decade—has it made inroads into organizational theory and psychology. With few exceptions, ideas from evolutionary theory are absent from scholarship and practice in HRM. This book is an attempt to get the evolutionary ball rolling. Both the general paradigm of evolution by natural selection—and specific ideas from sociocultural evolution and evolutionary psychology—can make important contributions to the ways we think about, design, and practice HRM.

Other than to provide occasional background, the present volume does not discuss the literature on traditional approaches in HRM. Rather, my goals are: (1) to present an evolutionary framework for thinking about HRM practices; (2) to describe examples of HRM practices based on an evolutionary perspective; and (3) to stimulate further research and pragmatic policies and practices from an evolutionary perspective so that they become integrated into everyday thinking about human resource management. This book offers something for both the theoretically minded scholar and the thoughtful manager.

The seeds for this work were planted early in my career. While serving as a consultant, I noticed that organizations rarely used the state-of-the-art human resource practices that I learned about in graduate school.

Moreover, I noticed that HR practitioners rarely adopted the new practices that studies in scientific journals claimed were effective. In one medium-sized, family-owned firm, the human resource manager I worked with prided himself on his knowledge of statistics and modern personnel-selection testing methods. He had earned a Ph.D. and was trained as an industrial/organizational (I/O) psychologist. Yet when it came to hiring, tradition prevailed. Rather than using professionally developed tests or conducting studies of validity, he interviewed candidates. The organization did not even train managers to conduct "proper" standardized, structured interviews. In another organization (a Fortune 100 company), I worked with a management development manager (also trained as an I/O psychologist) who was in charge of management training. We used few state-of-the-art training practices. The department normally did not base training programs on an analysis of needs, and it frequently used the latest training fads. I cannot recall that we ever evaluated our training programs to determine whether they worked. These problems were not unique to my experience, but they have plagued the fields of human resource management and I/O psychology for years (Johns, 1993).

This problem is confined neither to organizations in the United States nor to business organizations in the private sector. As it turns out, organizations in Britain and Europe also use HRM practices for which HRM scholars have found little or no scientific validity. One of the most widely used selection tests in France is graphology (handwriting analysis), yet studies have found no relationship between handwriting characteristics and subsequent job performance (Ben-Shakhar, Bar-Hillel, Bilu, Ben-Abba, & Flug, 1986; Bruchon-Schweitzer & Ferrieux, 1991). Ironically, the problem occurs in universities, too—and among I/O psychologists who teach there. When I began my career as a professor, I noticed that professors of I/O psychology would use traditional procedures rather than the "best practice" techniques that they taught to their students. We taught our students to use structured interviews, yet we did not use them ourselves when hiring new faculty. We advised our students that letters of recommendation were unreliable, yet we required them from all candidates for faculty jobs and applicants to our graduate programs. I remember one faculty member in particular. He was critical of traditional personnel methods, heaping scorn on ignorant personnel managers who did not use the latest scientific HRM techniques. Yet when involved in hiring a new faculty member, he hung on every word of a letter of recommendation, not hesitating to reject a candidate whose letter contained just one unflattering phrase. We also told our students about new training technologies; yet most of us continued to use traditional lecture-and-discussion methods in our own teaching. Was this just the everyday, garden variety of "resistance to change," commonly encountered with any attempt to innovate? Or was this inconsistency unique to HRM? I had the uneasy feeling that, although innovations typically meet with resistance, the deep reluctance to innovate in HRM reflected a real problem with modern HRM rather than just habitual resistance to change.[2]

The HRM literature has been around since the middle of the twentieth century, and the origin of many commonly used HRM interventions (IQ tests, work sample tests, job analysis, employee training, pay for performance) goes back to the beginning of the twentieth century. Technologies that have been in existence for a much shorter time are widely accepted and used by organizations (and individuals) throughout the world. Personal computers were introduced commercially in the 1980s, and the Internet was introduced several years later. By 1998, less than two decades later, 42 percent of adults said they had personal computers in their homes. Sixty-five percent of them reported they had access to the Internet. In 1993, less than 3 percent of U.S. classrooms were connected to the Internet; by 1998, over half had Internet access (Hall & Visgaitis, 1998). Most of the people who develop or sell technologies use what they make or sell. Microsoft co-founder Bill Gates has a reputation for frequently using e-mail, even answering messages from just about any Microsoft employee who sends him one (Gates, 1999). Most Americans would find it absurd if they learned that Mr. Gates used a typewriter (rather than a word processing program) to compose business correspondence or a calculator (rather than a spreadsheet program) to analyze financial plans. Similarly, because of the credibility of scientific research that links smoking to lung cancer and heart disease, we would find it absurd if most physicians were heavy cigarette smokers. The same can hardly be said about HRM practitioners and scholars who often do not use the technologies they develop.[3]

Some modern social technologies, however, are widely used in *some* sectors—principally in public sector organizations. Although standardized tests see limited use in the private sector, government organizations, the military, and universities use them extensively (Wigdor & Garner, 1982). Almost every student who applies to college must take the SAT or ACT (Lemann, 1999). Although only about 11 percent of companies use formal training programs to train their nonmanagement employees (Labor Letter, 1991), the military uses them extensively. The use of formal performance appraisal is another conundrum. Although hundreds of articles on performance appraisal have been published by academic psychologists, and some academic psychologists argue that the economic utility of state-of-the-art performance appraisal is high, many organizations do not act as if performance appraisal is important.

> "At some places the PA [performance appraisal] process is a joke—just a bureaucratic thing that the manager does to keep the IR (industrial relations) people off his back." If organizations really believed that valid performance appraisal could lead to savings in the millions, they would hardly treat performance appraisal in such a cavalier fashion and would not tolerate executives who regarded appraisal as a joke. (Murphy & Cleveland, 1995, p. 308)

Yet performance appraisal is widely used, implemented carefully, taken seriously, and relied upon for promotions and firing decisions in college and professional sports. Copious and accurate performance records are a hallmark of collegiate and professional sports. Almost any book on any sport or the sports pages of a daily newspaper contain columns of appraisal statistics (batting averages, passes completed, race times to the one-hundredth of a second). Virtually any nine-year-old boy in the United States—and almost certainly any nine-year-old in San Francisco or St. Louis—knows which baseball player holds the record for the most home runs in a season. The name of the ballplayer, the number of home runs, the year of the record, the ballplayer who is in second place, and his home run performance are common knowledge (mainly, but not exclusively, among baseball fans).[4] Performance appraisal is not a joke in sports.

The issue of *use* seemed to me a—perhaps *the*—critical problem for HRM. We need to understand why organizations use the practices that they do and under what circumstances. We need to learn why the methods recommended in the HRM literature are used so infrequently in so many organizations. We know little about why traditional practices are used as much as they are and what accounts for their remarkable staying power. People are reluctant to give up traditional practices and are also hesitant to use newer ones. But we do not know why. I found it puzzling that there has been little research on the use of HRM interventions (for exceptions, see Johns, 1993; Terpstra & Rozell, 1997). Of 63 articles on training published in five of the top scholarly journals related to HRM between 1983 and 1994, only three examined factors that affected the use of training. Other than passing comments on the economic utility of employment tests, the chapter on personnel selection in the most recent edition (1991) of the *Handbook of Industrial and Organizational Psychology* mentions no factors that affect the use of selection procedures.

What theoretical framework might be useful for explaining the utilization of HR interventions? As my research and theoretical work moved to these questions, I began to develop an evolutionary perspective because the questions of use and function were fundamental to evolutionary theory. Evolutionary biologists regularly ask why this or that feature of an animal (or plant) developed and what its function might be. If a trait is common in a species, the evolutionary biologist endeavors to discover *why* it exists. Certainly, such logic could also apply to the use of human resource practices.

Two seminal works had a profound effect on my thinking and on the subsequent course of my work. The first was Donald T. Campbell's 1975 article, "On the Conflicts Between Biological and Social Evolution and Between Psychology and Moral Tradition." Campbell argued that concepts from evolutionary theory can apply to social practices. Just as adaptation and speciation in organisms occurred through evolution by natural selection, the development and change of organizations and societies, social customs, and organizational practices can be understood as a process of sociocultural evolution by natural selection. In sociocultural evolution, *acquired* characteristics—such as values—are socially selected and retained through cultural means, through a process of variation, selection, and retention. Campbell also argued that social practices which developed and came to be used through social evolution are often more effective than the practices developed by social scientists. Although the great majority of psychologists and social scientists believed that the social and behavioral sciences held the key to improving human happiness and welfare, here was one of the field's most distinguished scholars arguing that many of the traditional customs that evolved over the years—marriage, religion, and moral codes—were better bets (Campbell, 1975). The article was Campbell's presidential address to the American Psychological Association. It is all the more remarkable because of Campbell's reputation as a hard-headed methodologist. He was well known for his work on experimental design and the application of scientific methodology to social problems. Yet here he was suggesting that there were good *scientific* reasons to believe that social practices resulting from sociocultural evolution were often more effective than those developed through *a priori* design. As I read more about social evolution, I came increasingly to view social and organizational practices in Campbell's terms.

The second work that convinced me of the value of this line of thinking for HRM was Boyd and Richerson's (1985) classic book, *Culture and the Evolutionary Process*, which presented a formal theory of cultural evolution. This work helped me to think more deeply about cultural evolution, particularly about the mechanisms by which cultural evolution occurs—such as imitation, trial-and-error learning, and guided variation through the application of science—and the cultural units that vary and are transmitted. Boyd and Richerson present formidable mathematical evidence to support Campbell's thesis. In addition to their treatment of cultural evolution, they introduce the topic of co-evolution, the connection between cultural and biological evolution.

Those two classic works re-calibrated my compass, and my reading began to uncover scholars in a variety of disciplines who were using an evolutionary perspective to explain a variety of social and technical phenomena. Henry Petroski (1993) wrote a delightful book about the evolution of the pencil. Used by millions of people throughout the world, the pencil is a product of hundreds of years of technical evolution. George Basalla (1988) applied the general paradigm of variation–selection–retention to the development of technology. In the realms of organization theory and economics, the evolutionary perspective has been applied to understanding how organizations are created, persist, and ultimately wither away (Hannan & Freeman, 1989; Nelson & Winter, 1982).

In the early 1990s, I encountered the emerging field of evolutionary psychology, and I attended my first meeting of the Human Behavior and Evolutionary Society in 1994. Evolutionary psychologists argue that many human behaviors—particularly those related to survival and reproduction—are a product of biological evolution and are instantiated in the brain in psychological mechanisms. That is, just as the nature of human physiology and morphology can be explained by natural selection, so too can many of our cognitive and behavioral tendencies. This opened up new possibilities for thinking about HRM practices, particularly for understanding forces that drive their appeal (or lack of it) and use (or lack of it). Evolutionary psychology accounts for the infrequent use of scientific personnel technologies compared to traditional methods: modern selection technologies contain features that are incompatible with humans' evolved preferences for information about other people (Moore, 1996). People prefer to assess and make decisions about people based on information gathered from face-to-face interaction (e.g., an employment interview), or if that is not possible, from narrative information (letters of recommendation, talking to personal references). On the other hand, most people have an aversion to using statistical information to make decisions about people and therefore use scientifically based personnel selection methods less frequently (Terpstra & Rozell, 1997). That the interview continues to be used, despite the protestations of personnel psychologists that it is unreliable and does not predict job performance well, has been called the "black hole" of personnel selection research. However, this is not surprising within the context of evolutionary psychology.

Humans and their information processing demands evolved during the Pleistocene era. During the 1.8 million years of the Pleistocene, people lived and worked in small hunter-gatherer bands. Under these conditions, the principal sources of information about other people were face-to-face interaction and narrative dialogue. If we were to compress all of human evolution up to the present into 24 hours, the amount of time that people have used paper-and-pencil tests and statistical information would amount to about the last second of our evolution.[5] Human cognitive architecture for processing information about people, therefore, is still adapted to the conditions under which *Homo sapiens* evolved. The change from living in small hunter-gatherer bands to mass societies has been too recent for our cognitive architecture to adapt biologically. Our neurocognitive systems developed to utilize information about people delivered from other people in the rich form of everyday language and gesture. We are far less likely to be responsive to abstract, scientific, and numerical forms of information—precisely the types of information about people that are common in the modern employment tests—than face-to-face interaction and narrative. An evolutionary perspective was an obvious framework for thinking about the use of HRM practices. Yet, with rare exceptions (Nicholson, 2000; Studd & Gattiker, 1991), there has been little scholarship linking evolutionary psychology to HRM. The evolutionary perspective seemed to offer critical theoretical insight into cracking the problem of use.

I was initially bewildered at the contempt that so many HRM scholars had for traditional practices. However, increasingly I came to see the contempt as a mixture of technocratic hubris, vanity, and veiled self-interest. It would be a severe blow to the HRM experts' prestige if they were to admit that traditional practices were as good as their methods. Their unwillingness to look at the possible merits of traditional practices has a religious fervor to it. One I/O psychologist, for example, uses the terms *whim and prejudice* when describing how organizations typically make hiring decisions. I'll never forget a dinner conversation I had with a newly minted Ph.D. some years ago. When the topic turned to hiring practices, we lamented the fact that few managers used methods based on research conducted by industrial psychologists. He shook his head and said mockingly that managers still think they can "sniff 'em out." He was sarcastically referring to managers' misguided (in his opinion) belief that they could accurately spot talent without the aid of expert personnel psychologists and their employment tests. That remark was particularly ironic because this newly minted industrial psychologist was at a job interview when he made the comment—where another colleague and I were sniffing him out, so to speak, to assess whether he would be offered a job.

I found that many of my graduate students in I/O psychology were also contemptuous of traditional methods. To counter this attitude, I began posing the following question in my graduate seminars when we studied employment tests:

> Assume that a test has been developed to match couples' interests, backgrounds, and marital compatibility. Studies have shown that couples who score high on the *Marital Compatibility Test* also score, on average, higher on a measure of marital satisfaction. Would you be willing to forego traditional dating and courtship, and choose your spouse through the use of this standardized test?

Uniformly, their answer was "no." They preferred to stick to traditional methods, but they were at a loss to explain why. I also posed a similar question in classes where most of the students were older and likely to have children:

> Assume that a test has been developed for selecting baby-sitters, the *Baby-sitting Aptitude Test*. Studies have shown that there is a positive relationship between scores on the *Baby-sitting Aptitude Test* and baby-sitting performance. Would you be willing to forego personal interviews with baby-sitter applicants, recommendations from other parents, your "gut instinct" reaction to baby-sitter applicants, and instead hire a baby-sitter, unseen, based solely on her test scores?

Again, the answer was uniformly no. Both of these questions are particularly significant. They deal with issues that, on a personal level, involve more important stakes than hiring an employee and trying to predict moderate differences in productivity on the job: mating, reproduction, and the safety of one's children. Our strong desire to evaluate potential mates and people who care for our children through face-to-face interaction is probably hardwired (Buss, 1999).

The hubris of I/O psychologists about the merits of HRM interventions is unjustified for a specific reason: they have no historical record of tangible accomplishment. The historical record is not flattering to HRM, particularly in comparison with the historical record of other technologies developed recently. HRM achievements pale in comparison to technological achievements in transportation, communications, and medicine. Technology, for example, has changed the speed of travel. For most of human history, we could travel only as fast as we could run;

we began to travel a bit faster with the use of domestic animals and wind-powered ships. In the nineteenth century, the speed of transportation increased exponentially. With the invention of the steam-powered trains, people began to travel up to and beyond 50 miles per hour, surpassing the speed and endurance of animal travel. In the twentieth century, with the inventions of the automobile and aircraft—and the infrastructures to support them—people would routinely travel at 60 miles per hour on the ground and at 600 miles per hour in the air. Spacecraft now enable humans to travel well over 15,000 miles an hour.

Yet commensurate changes have not occurred in human organizational capabilities. Many of the human resource challenges of centuries past were resolved as well as they are today, and in some cases, better. The army of the ancient Roman Empire, in the second century A.D., defended an empire of about 50 million people living in the Mediterranean Basin and did so efficiently. The Roman army excelled on the battlefield. Its *esprit* and excellence came from, as Ferrill (1986) points out, "tactical organization and training." Along with the nineteenth century French historian Ardant du Picq, Ferrill argues that the Roman system of tactical organization and discipline was "the most effective in the history of the world" (p. 29). To make a comparison in a way that is meaningful to today's organizations, we can look at how much organizational output one could purchase using roughly similar units of purchasing power. Although comparisons with today's currency and technology are not equivalent, Ferrill suggests that a general comparison can be made of the length of time an army could be supported by the fortunes of wealthy individuals:

> A recent estimate puts the annual military budget of the Roman Empire in the second century at 450,000,000 to 500,000,000 sesterces. . . . There were *individual* Romans in the first century who had private fortunes of nearly this amount. . . . The wealthiest individuals in the United States today could not come close to supporting the US military for a year! (Ferrill, 1986, p. 26; emphasis in original)

If an army in ancient Rome could be one of the most effective and efficient in history—largely because of its administrative, organizational, and training procedures—then what does this say about the "advances" alleged to have been made in human resource management practices in the twentieth century? At best, the advances are small; at worst, they are illusory.

This book reflects my belief that the problems of theoretical coherence, utilization, and effectiveness of HRM practices can be best addressed by an evolutionary perspective. I use the term *evolutionary perspective* in a broad sense to include sociocultural evolution and evolutionary psychology. My evolutionary perspective also incorporates thinking from neoclassical economics, organization theory, and complexity theory. Like species in an ecosystem, HRM practices are embedded in complex organizations, which in turn are embedded in complex environments. HRM actors and activities in organizations can be viewed as elements in complex ecosystems or economies. These ecosystems involve thousands of transactions among individuals, each pursuing his or her own interests; some of those transactions involve human resource activities. Trainers provide instruction in this or that skill in exchange for some form of compensation related to their self-interest. Employees take training courses because they perceive it to be in their interest to do so. Many I/O psychologists and HRM academics seem to think that people engage (or *should* engage) in HRM activities for "the good of the organization." This is equivalent to thinking that ants mulch grass and that worms aerate the soil for "the good of the forest," or that businesses sell Honduran cigars and Kentucky bourbon—or baby diapers or anything else, for that matter—for "the good of the economy or of society." As Adam Smith theorized—and as later empirical and historical analyses have shown—robust economies are more likely to emerge when individuals are reasonably free to pursue their own interests, within parameters of evolved cultural standards and human proclivities. The same is true of human resource activities and organizations. Robust organizations are more likely to emerge when organizational members are reasonably free to pursue their self-interest, within parameters of evolved organizational standards and human proclivities.[6]

Organizational life does not follow a master plan, driven by a "top-down" bureaucracy; rather, it evolves through natural (social) selection. Outcomes are not preordained or planned. Prescriptions (means) that are presumed to be *the* "best" way to do things and outcomes (ends) that are presumed to be *the* only appropriate ends regularly produce unintended consequences. Over time, there is no "one best way" to run an organization. Fixed means and ends over the long term result in organizational rigidity at best and totalitarianism at worst. This does not imply relativism. General rules constrain possibilities. They allow freedom within particular parameters and include traditions that evolved in social systems over many years (Burke, 1790/1964; Campbell, 1975); in human decision making rules, preferences, and emotions (Buss, 1995); and in processes of exchange, interaction, and emergence in complex organizations (Holland, 1995; Samuelson, 1976). This is akin to the general guidelines that genes follow for constructing the protein-based building blocks of the body. They provide parameters and constraints but allow freedom for variations within those parameters.[7] *Level of analysis* is a critical issue here. At what level are variability and independent decision making functional? At what other levels are they dysfunctional, levels where consistency and third-party decision making become functional? I believe, and argue in this book, that the same general principles that apply to national (or global) economies are relevant to organizations. Excessive centralized control in organizations, excessive centralized planning, excessive restrictions on individual freedom of choice, and third-party decision making are likely to be detrimental to organizational viability, just as they are to national and global economies.

Most economists nowadays argue that free markets result in the greatest overall economic prosperity. Although capitalist, liberal democracies are by no means perfect, recent history has shown that they work considerably better (with respect to economic growth, innovation, overall wealth, the distribution of wealth, health, and the distribution of creature comforts) than centralized governments with command economies (Fukuyama, 1992). The basic idea is that people pursuing their own interests—free to make, buy, and sell—will produce the best for the whole. Given the diverse needs, innovations, and transactions of thousands or millions of individuals, it is impossible to devise a centralized plan that takes into account and can handle the complexity of all those interactions. Centrally planned economies cannot efficiently meet the interests of millions of people. It is beyond the capability of a centralized authority to invent, produce, distribute, and price goods and services to meet the needs of a large and diverse population. If this is true at the level of societies, then it is probably also true at the level of complex organizations. If the same basic principles of complexity and evolution show that centralized planning and third-party decision making are ruinous to modern nation states, they are also probably ruinous to large, complex organizations.

This book is an integrative and, to some extent, a speculative work. My aims are to show that the widely accepted mechanical perspective in HRM—which assumes that interventions designed by experts will produce precise, intended effects—has outlived its usefulness; to suggest that an evolutionary perspective offers a more realistic and potentially more useful approach to thinking about and designing HRM practices; and to develop some preliminary practical applications of an evolutionary approach to HRM. There is no shortage of theory and basic research with an evolutionary flavor to draw from in psychology, economics, and organization studies. Unfortunately, this is not the case when it comes to practical applications. There is little work that theorizes about or tests hypotheses about *applications* derived from sociocultural evolution or evolutionary psychology (for exceptions see Browne, 2002; Colarelli, 1996; Colarelli & Montei 1996; Jones, 1997; Nicholson, 1997, 2000; Posner, 1992). There are relatively few of us—so far, at least—laboring in this vineyard. However, I am optimistic. If the applications in the life sciences are any indication, the tide will turn; it is just a matter of time. For now, however, more tinkering, research, and trial-and-error will be needed to find the evolutionary-based HRM practices that are most helpful.

When I initially set out to write this book, I hoped to analyze and suggest new practices for a wide range of HRM practices—hiring, training, performance appraisal, supervisory practices, work group and team management, and organizational design. However, as I began writing, it became apparent that this would take much longer than I had expected. So I narrowed my focus to cover more intensively a smaller number of topics. The first two chapters of the book present the theoretical arguments—the mechanistic model of HRM and the theoretical underpinnings of the evolutionary approach. For readers who want to get directly to the applications of the evolutionary perspective of HRM, they should skim Chapters 1 and 2 to get some basic background and then proceed directly to Chapter 3. Chapters 3, 4, and 5 address the practical problems and practices of personnel selection and training. Although they can serve as paradigms for evolutionary approaches to other areas of HRM, an exposition of other areas must await further books. For now my hope is that this book opens up new ways of thinking about HRM and stimulates the development and use of HRM interventions that are in tune with evolutionary processes.

NOTES

1. Human resource management involves those activities, in formal organizations, directed toward the acquisition, transformation, utilization, and elimination of human resources. Typical human resource management activities include: recruiting and hiring, training and development, evaluating and controlling, group and organizational design, and terminations and retirement.

2. A note on terminology is appropriate here. I will use the term *intervention* in a general way to refer to social technologies that are intended to produce specific social or administrative outcomes in social studies. I will refrain from using the term *social technology* because *technology* has the connotation of physical artifacts. Modern technology, moreover, connotes physical artifacts based on knowledge from the natural sciences. To be precise, however, a *technology*—whether physical or social—is a design or process to reduce cause-effect uncertainty in achieving an intended effect (Rogers, 1983). For example, selec-

tion technologies are processes for predicting the behavior of job applicants. *Method* refers to a general class of technology. For example, the interview would be one method for hiring people, while paper-and-pencil tests would be another. *Technique* refers to a variation within a given method. The structured interview is one type of interview technique, while an unstructured interview is another technique. *Practice* is a method or technique that an organization uses routinely.

3. Although I have yet to come across a survey on the extent to which I/O psychologists practice what they preach, an article by York and Cranny (1989) advises new I/O psychologists looking for jobs in university psychology departments that the primary hiring practices they will encounter are letters of recommendation and unstructured interviews. Professional newsletters and job ads reflect a similar protocol. Almost every professional job advertisement requires applicants to submit several letters of recommendation. An interesting study would ask I/O psychologists about which hiring methods they use and why they use them.

4. Even some aesthetes, such as myself, who prefer Bach and Haydn to spectator sports, know that Barry Bonds of the San Francisco Giants holds the record for the number of home runs in a season, at 73, set in the 2001 season and that, in the 1998 season, Mark McGuire of the St. Louis Cardinals set the record at 70 home runs.

5. Standardized paper-and-pencil psychological tests emerged within the last 100 years and statistics within about the last 200 years.

6. For a contemporary view that argues against the idea that people pursuing self-interest will result in the good of the whole, see Allen, Stelzner, and Wielkiewicz (1998).

7. Other than constraints on fair trade, safe working conditions, and the like, the rule of law does not provide detailed rules on who can or cannot engage in commerce, how a business should be run, what products it produces, how it manages its employees and so on. With broad guidelines, people are more or less free to engage in whatever commercial activities they choose.

REFERENCES

Allen, K. E., Stelzner, S. P., & Wielkiewicz, R. M. (1998). The ecology of leadership: Adapting to the challenges of a changing world. *The Journal of Leadership Studies, 5,* 62–82.

Basalla, G. (1988). *The evolution of technology.* New York: Cambridge University Press.

Ben-Shakhar, G., Bar-Hillel, M., Bilu, Y., Ben-Abba, E., & Flug, A. (1986). Can graphology predict occupational success? Two empirical studies and some methodological ruminations. *Journal of Applied Psychology, 71,* 645–653.

Boyd, R., & Richerson, P. J. (1985). *Culture and the evolutionary process.* Chicago: University of Chicago.

Browne, K. R. (2002). *Biology at work: Rethinking sexual equality.* New Brunswick, NJ: Rutgers University Press.

Bruchon-Schweitzer, M., & Ferrieux, D. (1991). Une enquete sur le recrutement en France. *European Review of Applied Psychology, 41*, 9–17.

Burke, E. (1790/1964). *Reflections on the revolution in France*. London: Dent.

Buss, D. (1999). *Evolutionary psychology*. Boston: Allyn & Bacon.

Buss, D. M. (1995). Evolutionary psychology: A new paradigm for psychological science. *Psychological Inquiry, 6*, 1–30.

Campbell, D. T. (1975). On the conflicts between biological and social evolution and between psychology and moral tradition. *American Psychologist, 30*, 1103–1126.

Colarelli, S. M. (1996). Establishment and job context influences on the use of hiring practices. *Applied Psychology: An International Review, 45*, 153–176.

Colarelli, S. M., & Montei, M. S. (1996). Some contextual influences on training utilization. *Journal of Applied Behavioral Science, 32*, 306–322.

Ferrill, A. (1986). *The fall of the Roman Empire: The military explanation*. New York: Thames & Hudson.

Fukuyama, F. (1992). *The end of history and the last man*. New York: Avon.

Gates, B. (1999, March 22). Bill Gates' new rules. *Time*, 72–84.

Hall, C., & Visgaitis, G. (1998, October 20). PC homes by income. *USA Today*, p. D1.

Hannan, M. T., & Freeman, J. H. (1989). *Organizational ecology*. Cambridge, MA: Harvard University Press.

Holland, J. H. (1995). *Hidden order*. Reading, MA: Helix.

Johns, G. (1993). Constraints on the adoption of psychology-based personnel practices: Lessons from organizational innovation. *Personnel Psychology, 46*, 569–592.

Jones, O. D. (1997). Evolutionary analysis in law: An introduction and application to child abuse. *North Carolina Law Review, 75*, 1117–1242.

Labor letter. (1991, October 22), *Wall Street Journal*, p. A1.

Lemann, N. (1999). *The big test*. New York: Farrar, Straus and Giroux.

Moore, R. F. (1996). Caring for identified versus statistical lives: An evolutionary view of medical distributive justice. *Ethology and Sociobiology, 17*, 379–401.

Murphy, K. R., & Cleveland, J. N. (1995). *Understanding performance appraisal*. Thousand Oaks, CA: Sage Publications.

Nelson, R. R., & Winter, S. G. (1982). *An evolutionary theory of economic change*. Cambridge, MA: Belknap.

Nicholson, N. (1997). Evolutionary psychology: Toward a new view of human nature and organizational society. *Human Relations, 50*, 1053–1078.

Nicholson, N. (2000). *Executive instinct*. New York: Crown.

Petroski, H. (1993). *The pencil*. New York: Alfred A. Knopf.

Posner, R. A. (1992). *Sex and reason*. Cambridge, MA: Harvard University Press.

Rogers, E. M. (1983). *Diffusion of innovations* (3rd ed.). New York: Free Press.

Samuelson, P. A. (1976). *Economics* (10th ed.). New York: McGraw-Hill.

Studd, M. V., & Gattiker, U. E. (1991). The evolutionary psychology of sexual harassment in organizations. *Ethology and Sociobiology, 12,* 249–290.

Terpstra, D. E. & Rozelle. J. (1997). Why some potentially effective staffing practices are seldom used. *Public Personnel Management, 26,* 483–495.

Wigdor, A. K., & Garner, W. R. (Eds.) (1982). *Ability testing: Uses, consequences, and controversies, Part II: Documentation Section.* Washington, DC: National Academy Press.

York, K. M., & Cranny, C. J. (1989, May). Job hunting and applicant recruiting: Expectations in the interview process and suggestions for improvement. *The Industrial-Organizational Psychologist, 26,* 19–23.

CHAPTER 1

Clocks, Caves, and Utopias
The Mechanical Design Perspective

[There will be] great gain, both to the employers and employés (*sic*) . . . from the substitution of scientific for rule-of-thumb methods. . . . There is always one method . . . which is quicker and better than any of the rest. And this one best method . . . can only be discovered or developed through a scientific study. . . . In almost all of the mechanic arts the science which underlies each act of each workman is so great . . . that the workman who is best suited to actually doing the work is incapable of fully understanding this science, without the guidance and help of those who are working . . . over him.
                                    —Frederick W. Taylor (1911/1967, pp. 24–26)

I share with some of my colleagues the conviction that the social sciences could contribute more effectively than they have to managerial progress with respect to the human side of enterprise. There are, of course, many reasons why improvement has been slow. Some have to do with the social sciences themselves: they are still in their adolescence in comparison with the physical sciences; their findings are piecemeal and scattered; they lack precision; many critical issues are still in controversy. . . . [However], the position of the manager vis-à-vis the social sciences will one day be no different than that of the engineer vis-à-vis the physical sciences or the doctor vis-à-vis chemistry or biology.
                                    —Douglas McGregor (1960, p. 5)

Fortunately, research and practice are leading to solutions that appear promising. I have organized this knowledge in a theoretical framework that predicts what is likely to happen and that can be used to reverse the counterproductive trends.

—Chris Argyris (1990, p. xiv)

ORGANIZATIONAL PROBLEMS

A casual survey of organizational problems reported in the newspapers during the weeks that I wrote the first draft of this chapter indicates that harmonious human relations and clockwork efficiency are still a long way off.[1,2] The teachers of the Detroit public schools went on strike, and the faculty of Wayne State University threatened to go on strike. Educational reformers called for a fundamental restructuring of American educational institutions—from K–12 schools through universities. A book by a best-selling journalist lamented that the postindustrial workplace has robbed average American men of meaningful work and their masculinity. A court ordered a major brewery to pay a fired male supervisor $1.4 million in damages for wrongful discharge after a female employee had accused him of sexual harassment. Affirmative action and diversity programs at American universities were under serious attack for being ineffective and discriminatory. All of this occurred at a time of unprecedented economic prosperity.[3]

Organizational problems, however, are nothing new. For as long as there have been complex organizations, there have been organizational problems. In the fourth century A.D. the Roman emperor Constantine perceived—as did others in his court—that the Empire faced increasing external threats from barbarian forces (Ferrill, 1986). In Renaissance Italy, Machiavelli regarded poor leadership and destructive feuds between principalities as serious problems. During the industrial revolution in America, "muckrakers," such as Upton Sinclair, chronicled widespread abuses in the emerging industrial economy, revealing everything from the selling of unsafe products to poor labor conditions (Hofstadter, 1972). At the same time, Frederick Taylor inveighed in his book, *Scientific Management*, against the inefficiencies caused by traditional rule-of-thumb work practices. In the 1950s, William Whyte complained in his best-seller, *The Organization Man*, of the overly conformist tendencies of American middle managers. The 1970s and 1980s witnessed problems in organizational productivity and efficiency, with fears that organizations in the United States would lose to the more efficient Japanese and German organizations, as Lester Thurow (1992) predicted in *Head to Head*. In the early 1990s, Robert Reich (1991) worried, in *The Work of Nations*, that productivity and our standard of living would decline unless organizations and the nation paid more attention to developing human resources.

When organizational leaders or influential outsiders perceive organizational problems, they usually respond by proposing an intervention— a new strategy, new organizational structures, new personnel, and so on. Yet, attempts to solve organizational problems have a mixed record. Constantine's attempt to repel the barbarian threat to the Roman Empire's frontiers, by using a strategy of defense-in-depth, had devastating consequences. Ferrill contends that "the grand strategy of Constantine took a terrible toll in military efficiency and *esprit de corps*" (1986, p. 50). He makes the case that the increasingly ineffective military was responsible for the fall of the Empire in the fifth century A.D. Fifteen hundred years later, the record of efforts to solve *organizational* problems still does not inspire confidence. Organizations do not seem to be any more successful. Anywhere from one-third to one-half of all new firms will be out of operation after five years. Of the 5.5 million small businesses that existed in the United States in 1990, over 34.5 percent went out of business and about 24.5 percent contracted by 1995, a time of remarkable economic expansion (U.S. Small Business Administration, 1999). Even most large firms cannot maintain market dominance. One index is the turnover of corporations listed on *Fortune* magazine's annual list of the largest U.S. companies. Only 187 of the 500 companies listed in 1955 remained on the list of 1986 (Shanklin, 1986). By 1995, no fewer than 1,318 different companies had appeared on the list at least once (Loomis, 1995). Almost half of the firms on the list in 1980 were not listed in 1990 (Bartley, 1992, p. 140; cited in Sowell, 1995, p. 66).[4] Attempts at solving organizational problems in education and social policy have been equally lackluster (Gillon, 2000; Glazer, 1988; Lagemann, 2000; Moynihan, 1996; Ravitch, 2000).

Yet the advice industry has blossomed. One estimate puts the amount of money organizations spent on management consultants in 1996 at $43 billion (Chadderdon, 1998). The number of advice books for managers—management and leadership how-to books—also blossomed. In 1996, more than 1,700 business books were published (Chadderdon, 1998). Formal business education is booming. The number of business and management graduates with bachelor degrees increased from 51,076 in 1960 to 226,663 in 1997. During the same period, those earning master degrees increased from 4,643 to 97,619, and the number of graduates with doctoral degrees in business and management increased from 135 to 1,336. In the academic year of 1995–1996, there were 2,949,000 students enrolled in business schools in postsecondary education (*Digest of Education Statistics*, 1999). By 1992, there were 39,928 full-time instructors in business schools and 34,679 part-time instructors (National Center for Education Statistics, *Digest of Educational Statistics*, 1999).[5]

Despite continuing attempts to solve organizational problems and despite the stream of advice from consultants and scholars, we have improved only modestly since Constantine, 1,500 years ago. Arguably, a major reason so little progress has been made in solving organizational problems is that organizational interventions have not worked particularly well. The difference in effectiveness between social science interventions and technologies stemming from the natural sciences is huge. The natural sciences and allied fields in technology have produced substantial advances in knowledge and technology. They have lurched forward in a cumulative and directional way. The speed of transportation has steadily increased. Bridges are larger and sturdier. Astronomers know more about the nature of the universe, and biologists have cracked the human genome. Although the impact of the natural sciences and technology on human well-being remains somewhat ambiguous (Basalla, 1985; Fukuyama, 1992), there can be little doubt about their power. Many technological and scientific problems have been solved. Progress in the social sciences, on the other hand, has been unremarkable, especially "considering their track record in comparison with the resources placed at their command" and in comparison with the natural sciences, which have made dramatic progress both theoretically and practically (Wilson, 1998, p. 181). Progress in the social sciences is, at best, scattered, noncumulative, lacking in any clear historical direction, and technologically anemic.

Many organizational improvement programs have their intellectual roots in what I call the *mechanical design perspective*. It goes as far back as Plato, and it is out of step with advances in our understanding of human nature and social systems. A large part of the reason that organizational improvement programs, and applied social science in general, have produced such disappointing results is that they are based on the mechanical design perspective. To the extent that a perspective is at odds with how people and organizations function, interventions based on that perspective are unlikely to meet expectations. My goals in this chapter are to provide a historical sketch of the development of the mechanical design perspective, to describe its basic assumptions, and to discuss its limitations. This sets the stage for Chapter 2, where I discuss the development and assumptions of the evolutionary perspective, a perspective that is more compatible with human nature and the nature of social systems.

THE VALUE OF AN HISTORICAL PERSPECTIVE

The social sciences—particularly the applied social sciences—tend to be ahistorical. One reason for this is that the social sciences did not emerge until the nineteenth century, with the applied social sciences following shortly thereafter.[6] Social scientists presumed that they were starting from scratch and building a new edifice of knowledge about human behavior (Hale, 1980). Yet, old beliefs about human nature and organizations did not disappear with the advent of social science and social scientists. Social science and social scientists were not separate from the historical, cultural, and intellectual traditions passed on over the centuries. They did not wipe the slate clean and begin with fresh beliefs about human nature, organizations, and society. The questions they asked, the assumptions they held, and the studies they conducted were influenced by a long intellectual history (Nisbett, Peng, Choi, & Norenzayan, 2001).

Many fields in the sciences and humanities—for example, mathematics, astronomy, physics, biology, geography, literature, music, and art—have vibrant and well-chronicled intellectual histories going back hundreds of years. Understanding the history of a field is important for understanding the evolution of its principles and how changing cultural and economic milieus have influenced its development. Art history explains how representation evolved as artists learned to incorporate perspective into painting, and how belief systems—religious and secular—influenced the content of art during different historical periods. The history of mathematics shows how concepts that we now take for granted—such as the Hindu-Arabic numeral system, the zero, basic operations such as multiplication and division, and statistics—evolved over years of intellectual labor. A historical perspective teaches how contemporary ideas and artifacts owe debts to the past. The division of musical tones in the common scale used in almost all European and American music began over 2,500 years ago with Pythagoras's investigations of tone and vibrations. In chronicling the evolution of the pencil, Petroski (1993) shows how this simple, useful, and inexpensive artifact is the product of hundreds of years of technical evolution. On the other hand, much of what is common today was uncommon in the past. Today, probability theory and statistics are common tools in financial analysis, scientific research, and survey methodology. Yet modern statistical theory is only about 200 years old (Bernstein, 1996).

A historical perspective reveals the ebb and flow of change and a sense of progress in a field. Only 150 years ago, one common scientific view about the origin of species was that they developed spontaneously ("spontaneous generation"). God designed every minute detail of every living creature. This was a view that had not changed much for the 2,000 years preceding Darwin. Yet in the latter half of the nineteenth century, the theory of evolution by natural selection was born with the publication of Darwin's *The Origin of Species* and Gregor Mendel's pea-breeding experiments. In 1953 Watson and Crick discovered the double helical structure of DNA. In 1966, the genetic code was cracked, showing how DNA provides the instructions to make proteins. By 2000, the human genome was mapped. What is state of the art at one point in time is soon vestigial. A sense of history increases the probability that scholars will see their own field from an anthropological perspective—that is, to see the mix of novelty, imitation, originality, similarity, and repetition in their current situation.

A New Organizational Context

A historical perspective also helps us see how the context of organizations changes over the years. By the beginning of the twentieth century, scholars and advice-givers started directing their attention to private organizations. Since Plato, analysis attended to political and military organizations. The twentieth century also saw the ascendancy of questions about how to manage large organizations and solve social problems. These questions began to take center stage among many practical-minded intellectuals because of major economic and political transformations. The twentieth century witnessed the transformation of most Western nations (and Japan) from agricultural to industrial economies. Prior to the twentieth century, large organizations were rare.[7] For most of human history, humans lived in small hunter-gatherer bands, probably rarely exceeding 100 people (Diamond, 1999; McGeary, 1995). The development of agriculture allowed societies to support increasing numbers of nonfood-producing specialists (e.g., rulers, administrators, soldiers, artisans, and priests). Yet, until the industrial revolution, the production of food and goods was done primarily on a small scale. Peasants and serfs working in family units were the primary food producers, and goods were produced by craft organization (McNeil, 1971). There was large-scale food production in a few places. A few large construction organizations arose that produced great public displays and public works—the Egyptian Pyramids, the road and canal systems of the Roman Empire, the Great Wall of China, and the great medieval European cathedrals. And, of course, there were large armies. But these were relatively rare in the larger scheme of things. They often involved slavery and were directed by government or religious bureaucracies.

The seeds for the growth and variety of large organizations began in the Middle Ages with the advent of capitalism and individualism (Coleman, 1974). People's belief systems changed from viewing themselves as extensions of an inclusive social order to agents free to amass and exchange resources in pursuit of their own ambitions. The subsequent industrial revolution that took hold in the nineteenth century unleashed new forms of energy, such as the steam engine, production, and social organization that increased people's ability to develop large organizations as instruments to pursue their ambitions. The industrial revolution ushered in large concentrations of unskilled wage labor with technology to mass-produce industrial and consumer goods. The economic and technological center of gravity shifted from craft shops and small farms to large factories. As large private and public businesses became common, the beginning of the twentieth century saw the emergence of a new middle class of "technicians and salaried professionals, clerical workers, salespeople, and public-service personnel" (Hofstadter, 1972, p. 215). The number of large corporations increased steadily. By the mid-1970s, 46 percent of all people employed in the United States worked in organizations with 100 or more individuals (Bureau of the Census, 1975/1976). By the year 1988, 60 percent of all employees in United States worked in firms with 100 or more individuals. In the year 1998, the corresponding figure was 63.32 (U.S. Census Bureau, n.d.).

With greater numbers of people being employed in large organizations, with the number of large organizations increasing, and with large organizations being used for a greater variety of purposes, new problems arose. Although organizations made exponential leaps in productivity in the early part of the century, labor was perceived as inefficient (Rabinbach, 1990). Organizations had to develop systems for hiring workers who had no experience and for quickly training them. Factory owners complained that workers became too easily fatigued. Large-scale labor unrest also became a problem. Unions developed in response to management policies that workers perceived as harmful to their interests and well-being. The new context brought problems associated with government regulation, competition from other organizations, and continually changing technologies. These dramatic changes and the problems they created increased the need for administrative solutions.

At the advent of the twentieth century, for some people science appeared to offer a new approach to organizational (and social) problems that accompanied these massive social changes. This had its roots in the change in the intellectual climate after the Renaissance. The power of science and the scientific method to understand nature was clear, and many hoped that this power would extend to human nature. The scientific discoveries about the physical and natural world overthrew thousands of years of previous beliefs. Copernican astronomy, Newtonian mechanics, the circulation of the blood, Boyle's law, and the theory of germs and disease were revolutionary. Major advances in technology, though not always direct applications of science, were broadly based on the scientific *weltanschauung* and produced observable results. Weaving looms, steam engines, new chemicals, telegraphs and telephones, flight, the internal combustion engine, electrical engines, and repeating rifles were powerful evidence of the power of natural science.

Social science arose as an effort to apply the methods of natural science to social phenomena. The successes of natural science suggested to some that it was only a matter of time until social science generated social technologies as significant as the technologies of natural science. The profound changes occurring in the social fabric of industrializing societies gave impetus to the quest for new understandings of organizations. Thrust from agrarian into industrial society, people were ripe for explanations of their condition and for programs and people to lead them to a better life. As the historian Matthew Hale has written: "Psychology promised power—over self and others—in years when men and women felt increasingly powerless to control their own lives, and it offered an explanation for the irrational behavior that seemed more and more to dominate public life" (Hale, 1980, p. ix).

MECHANICAL DESIGN AND ITS ASSUMPTIONS

Attempts to solve organizational problems involve assumptions about people, systems, and change. When consultants propose a training program to reduce conflict between warring factions in an organization, they are assuming that conflict is dysfunctional, that some other pattern of behavior would be an improvement, that some expert knows what the better state is, and that the people involved in the conflict will change their behavior. The care given to the selection of leaders reflects an assumption that leaders' decisions are important. Meticulous planning assumes that planners can envision future conditions, that they have sufficient knowledge to devise adaptive strategies, and that their strategies can be implemented. Lurking behind these assumptions is the further assumption that organizations involve predictable sequences of causation—that they are in some ways like machines and that, like machines, they have designs that can be readily changed to accomplish specific purposes. Most contemporary HR interventions bear the stamp of these assumptions about mechanical design. HR interventions or philosophies that initially seem quite different—ranging from rational-

technocratic to organizational development to diffusion of innovation—
are often similar in their mechanistic assumptions.

Contemporary HR Interventions

Rational-technocratic system design assumes that effective HR interventions are based on scientific knowledge (de Wolff, 1993).[8] The degree
to which HR interventions work is assessed by rigorous scientific
analysis, and their value to organizations, cannot be presumed until they
have undergone such an analysis. Decision makers either understand or
do not understand the value of HR interventions. If they do, they will
use them. If not, their decisions will be based on ignorance or error; they
will often use ineffective interventions. HR interventions are designed
and installed to attain specific, manifest goals. The context in which HR
interventions operate is seldom relevant because interventions based on
scientific knowledge are effective in nearly all situations. HR interventions are "surgically" installed and are not expected to have strong interactions with other components of an organization (Colarelli &
Stumpf, 1990). Knowledge and education generate change in patterns
of utilization, and scientists are expected to educate HR gate keepers
about the benefits of valid interventions. Time is not a significant factor
in utilization. Once a valid technology is installed, it should produce its
intended outcomes quickly.

Organization development (OD) also assumes that effective HR interventions stem from scientific knowledge and that scientific studies determine whether OD interventions work (Porras & Robertson, 1992).
However, OD stresses the psychological factors in resistance to change;
furthermore, it assumes that managers do not always have a clear understanding of their problem or have clear goals (Schein, 1969). Therefore,
it assumes that utilization is influenced by both the nature of social interventions and the processes for implementing them. OD assumes that
social interventions serve their intended functions. The psychological
context of perceptions, emotions, and role expectations influence acceptance and implementation. However, OD should work across most situations when they are managed according to OD prescriptions. OD places
little emphasis on the larger social and environmental context (Johns,
1993). Change occurs when experts collaborate with managers in diagnosis, planning, and implementation. This involves gathering valid data
and using valid interventions to build commitment to new programs,
as well as educating HR gate keepers about OD. The implementation
of OD interventions typically takes a period of months to several years
because of the lengthy processes of diagnosis, planning, and persuasion.

A third approach to interventions comes from the literature on the diffusion of innovation (Johns, 1993; Rogers, 1983). HR interventions arise from a variety of sources including, but not limited to, science. The criterion of value for a technology is its efficiency—that is, its comparative capacity to transform inputs into desired outputs (Rogers, 1983).[9] Efficiency by itself is not sufficient to influence utilization. Context plays a key role (Rogers, 1983). Three significant contextual factors are communication channels, a system's norms and values, and time (Rogers, 1983). This focus assumes that HR interventions are designed and installed to attain specific goals. Unanticipated consequences may accompany the introduction of an innovation; however, they are regarded more as perturbations (Rogers, 1983). Changes in utilization patterns require changes in social, political, or institutional contexts (Johns, 1993). Strategies for change involve political influence, encouraging imitation, and developing communication networks (Johns, 1993).

Assumptions

The mechanical design perspective assumes that organizational problems recur because of the design of organizations; that people who run organizations do not have an adequate understanding of how organizations work; and that the analysis of organizations by experts will reveal a set of logical organizational principles.[10] Once those principles have been discovered, experts can develop interventions to solve organizational problems. This is similar to the paradigm of natural science and technology. Just as we have been able to use physical principles to develop increasingly sophisticated technologies (heavier than air flight, antibiotics, open-heart surgery, plastics, the internal combustion engine, and so on), so too can we develop increasingly sophisticated social interventions by understanding the logic of organizations.[11]

Organizations resemble clocks, but they are not well-running clocks. They were designed and assembled by people without a deep understanding of how clocks work and without skill in assembling sophisticated, well-running, and accurate clocks. Managers are analogous to clockmaking children. Understanding how organizations work and how to properly design them are beyond the reach of ordinary people, such as managers and children. They are like Plato's cave dwellers who can only see the shadows of ideas. To understand and improve the world, ordinary people need the assistance of experts who have ventured outside the cave. The proper application of the correct principles of organizational design, however, will lead to harmony and efficiency, creating organizational utopias or near-utopias—hence, the title of this chapter: clocks, caves, and utopias.

Clocks

The mechanical design perspective views systems as collections of parts that relate to one another in a direct and consistent manner—like clocks (Gharajedaghi & Ackoff, 1984). *If* the parts are assembled properly, a system should function effectively, with the parts working in a coordinated fashion to achieve the system's goals. The "if" is critical. If organizations are not assembled properly, they will not function well. Plato's writings evidence one of the earliest and certainly one of the most influential versions of this view (see Popper, 1966, p. 35). Plato's *theory of forms* proposes an underlying reality—an orderly system—beneath the chaos, change, and instability of everyday life. Popper (1966, p. 31) uses the term *methodological essentialism* to describe Plato's view and that of many of his followers. Methodological essentialism holds that "it is the task of pure knowledge or 'science' to discover and to describe the true nature of things, i.e. their hidden reality or essence."

The idea of an underlying, "clocklike" order to things, including the social world, reappears and is more explicitly articulated in the idea of *mechanism* in the era of Newton. Mechanism was a revolutionary idea that was crucial in the development of modern science. It assumed that we can take things apart, including biological and chemical phenomena, and figure out from known physical principles what makes them work. It replaced the doctrine of vitalism, which assumed that nonmaterial or supernatural forces operated the machinery (Williams, 1996). Many philosophers and scientists also thought that mechanism applied equally well to social phenomena, and it had a strong influence on the development of the social sciences well into the twentieth century (Schneer, 1960, p. 157). Mechanism is part and parcel of modern natural science and technology. Physical cause and direct action are real in many phenomena. Unfortunately, the idea that mechanism applied to *social* phenomena was accepted before there was any evidence that social phenomena operated in this manner. Mechanism has three distinguishing characteristics: (1) reductionism, (2) denial of action at a distance, and (3) determinism.

Mechanists believe that phenomena are reducible to irreducible elements (Schneer, 1960; Westfall, 1971). Ultimately, we can only understand nature by reducing phenomena to their most basic elements. This involves viewing systems primarily in terms of their constituent parts. Understanding and manipulating systems is best accomplished by defining the elements in a system and understanding how they combine to form a whole. Like Newton's view of the universe as a celestial clock, HR management tends to view organizations as large machines (Colarelli & Stumpf, 1990; Gharajedaghi & Ackoff, 1984). From its beginnings, it had a markedly reductionist orientation. Frederick Taylor's "scientific management" is a highly reductionistic idea. He maintained that "perhaps the most prominent single element in modern scientific management is the task idea" (Taylor, 1911/1967, p. 39). Hugo Münsterberg, who along with Frederick Taylor was one of the founding fathers of industrial psychology, "did not abandon his youthful enthusiasm for a reductionist science in which the laws of mechanics could account for all appearances, both in nature and human society" (Hale, 1980, pp. 70–71). To this day, the reductionist spirit of scientific management shapes the scope of much of HRM and applied psychology (Dunnette, 1976; Sackett, 1986), as well as much of traditional American management practices (Commission on the Skills of the American Workforce, 1990). In personnel psychology, there is still a tendency to reduce people and jobs to their smallest elements. Most methods of job analysis involve understanding whole jobs by breaking them down into parts. Many personnel selection methods regard job applicants as collections of discrete skills and personality characteristics, and theorists of organizations regard organizational cultures as constellations of core values. Methods for analyzing the economic utility of personnel programs focus on how the abilities of individuals combine to influence organizational productivity.

A second feature of mechanism is that it denies "action at a distance." The denial of action at a distance means that phenomena can be explained only by the *direct action* of one element (or variable) on another (Toulmin, 1990; Westfall, 1971). Since any phenomenon is made up of a number of elements that are connected with one another, then any variation or change in one element has a specific effect on other elements in the system. Mechanistic theories are uncomfortable with the notion of indirect action through "fields" and with the probabilistic nature of the activity of elements in a field (Schneer, 1960). A denial of action at a distance is implicit in much of applied social science, particularly in personnel psychology. It is axiomatic in personnel psychology that individual differences in knowledge, skills, and abilities influence job and organizational performance through direct action. Stable individual attributes are assumed to exist in some quantity. These attributes affect individual behavior, which in turn influences job performance, which influences organizational outcomes.

Schneider (1987) makes one of personnel psychology's most explicit mechanistic arguments, although he does not use the word "mechanism." Schneider's thesis is that "the attributes of people, not the nature of the external environment, or organizational technology, or organizational structure, are the fundamental determinants of organizational behavior" (p. 437). He maintains that organizational structures, processes, culture, climate, and interventions are a direct function of the types of individuals in an organization. Change the mix of traits and organizations change. Obviously, this line of thinking has some merit. If an organization was initially composed of bumpkins and they were gradually replaced with aesthetes, it is probable that the organization would change, if only in the beauty of office décor and quality of lunch conversation. The problem, however, is the questionable mechanistic assumption that organizational processes, structures, and outcomes can be predicted from knowledge of attributes of the people in the organization. This is tantamount to asserting that the whole equals the sum of its parts.

The linkage of individual attributes and organizational performance can be seen in the literature on utility analysis—specifically, the work that addresses the economic utility of personnel programs (for an overview, see, e.g., Boudreau, 1991). A common theme in most personnel psychologists' work on utility is that individual attributes have an *additive* effect on organizational performance—that is, organizational performance is the sum of individual parts. The work on the utility of personnel selection programs generally makes explicit mathematical connections between individual attributes, job performance, and organizational performance (Schmidt, Hunter, McKenzie, & Muldrow, 1979). Increases in organizational performance—resulting from improved personnel selection methods—are considered a direct, additive function of the effects of individual ability.

The idea that the whole equals the sum of the parts is characteristic of mechanistic thinking (Gharajedaghi & Ackoff, 1984). Most personnel and applied psychologists, therefore, do not seem to acknowledge the phenomenon of emergence. Emergence is the idea that wholes make up something fundamentally different than the sum of their parts—primarily because of interactions among the parts. It is rarely acknowledged that the relationships between individual differences and outcomes vary depending on the organizational forces impinging on individual differences (Colarelli & Boos, 1992). Yet organizational influences—such as reward systems—often impinge on the relationship between individual attributes and individual performance (Schmidt & Hunter, 1983). The same is true for communication patterns, which often influence the relationship between individual attributes and group or organizational performance (Colarelli & Boos, 1992; Snyder & Morris, 1984). This suggests that there is not a fixed, direct correspondence between individual attributes and outcomes; rather, fields or forces affect the interplay between individual attributes and outcomes (Lewin, 1951). Just as talking about fields was a *facon de parler* among early twentieth-century physicists, talking about "processes," "organizational forces," or "general patterns" is a *facon de parler* in personnel psychology. The idea that performance is a function of processes (such as communication or problem solving) is foreign to personnel psychologists (Argyris, 1976).

A third feature of mechanism is determinism. Mechanism argues that all elements in a system are not only connected, but they relate to one another in specified ways. This being the case, any movement or adjustment to one element has a predictable effect on other elements. As Westfall (1971, p. 1) points out, "the mechanical philosophy... concerned itself with the causation of individual phenomena." The parts in a system are generally assumed to influence one another in a *tightly coupled* manner (cf. Orton & Weick, 1990; Toulmin, 1990; Westfall, 1971). This suggests that the nature of the relationships among parts and outcomes are stable and that the strength of the relationships is consistent over time. The elements in a system relate to one another in ways that can be specified. Therefore, given sufficient knowledge, one could predict the behavior of elements in a system, and one could use social interventions to achieve intended effects by adding or manipulating parts in a specified manner. That a determinist universe allows prediction is a basic tenet of mechanism. In some natural sciences, such as astronomy and chemistry, a high degree of prediction can be achieved. Early successes in the natural sciences led some to think that the same degree of determinism was possible with social phenomena. As physicist Stephen Hawking writes:

> The success of... Newton's theory of gravity... led the French scientist Marquis de Laplace at the beginning of the nineteenth century to argue that the universe was completely deterministic. Laplace suggested that there should be a set of scientific laws that would allow us to predict everything that would happen in the universe, if only we knew the complete state of the universe at one time. For example, if we know the positions and speeds of the sun and planets at one time, then we could use Newton's laws to calculate the state of the Solar System at any other time.... Laplace went further to assume that there were similar laws governing everything else, including human behavior. (1988, p. 53)

Later in the nineteenth century, positivism went a step further and argued that the "*fundamental task* [of science] is to predict phenomena in order to utilize them" (Abbagnano, 1967, p. 415, emphasis added).

Indeed, the contemporary scientific objectives of "prediction and control" stem, in large part, from the positivist orientation. The emphasis on prediction reflects positivism's orientations toward essentialism, mechanism, and determinism. The positivist approach assumes that science can (and will) evolve to the point where specific events can be predicted with accuracy and precision. Prediction is useful not only to test hypotheses, but to guide social action. Comte phrased this as an aphorism: "science whence comes prediction; prediction whence comes action" (cited in Abbagnano, 1967, p. 415).

The prediction of behavior is still a major part of industrial psychology (and much of psychology in general). One might argue, in fact, that the *raison d'etre* of industrial psychology is to predict the behavior of individuals in organizations. Long before industrial psychology was concerned with general laws, it was concerned with prediction. Since the days of Hugo Münsterberg (see Münsterberg, 1914, p. 354), industrial psychology has been oriented toward predicting specific, intended effects produced by psychological interventions. The primary goal of personnel selection is still the prediction of the behavior of job applicants.

> [A major] function of science is prediction. Researchers [in industrial/ organizational psychology] try to predict which employees will be productive, who are likely to quit, and who will be dissatisfied. This information is then used to select applicants who would be better employees. (Muchinsky, 2000, p. 24)

Zedeck and Cascio urge the faithful onward to do even better, asking:

> Will the field again freeze and discourage attempts to develop new and better predictors? At best, individual validities may reach .4 or .5 while composites may reach .6; i.e. at most, 36% of criterion variance is accountable—*more can be explained.* (1984, p. 488; emphasis added)

Although scientific models in applied research typically imply that variables *influence* rather than *determine* outcomes, suggestions about applications of psychological interventions often imply that they should produce (i.e., they are predictive of) specific results. Realistic job previews are expected to lower turnover, goal setting is expected to increase motivation, and proper training and selection are expected to increase productivity.

The belief in a hierarchy of goals that is common in much of human resource management also reflects a clocklike conception of deterministic systems. It presumes that the purpose of organizations is to achieve overarching goals. The overarching goals spawn a hierarchy of subgoals designed to facilitate the attainment of the overarching goals. The subgoals cascade downward and become absorbed by departments, groups, and individuals. As these lower levels attain subgoals, the results compound back up through the organization, leading to the attainment of the overarching goals (e.g., Campbell, McCloy, Oppler & Sager, 1993). Hierarchies of goals minimize conflict and incompatibility among the components of the system (Colarelli & Stumpf, 1990). Because of its concern with how specific interventions advance a stated goal, this perspective emphasizes the intended outcomes of goals and gives almost no attention to unintended consequences or incompatibilities among goals.

Caves

The mechanical design perspective assumes that, with the proper application of *expert* knowledge, existing organizational problems can be solved. Moreover, experts can design organizations so that the imperfections of organizations can be significantly reduced or virtually eliminated (Colarelli, 1998; Popper, 1966; Sowell, 1995). Experts and expert knowledge are key. The mechanical design perspective assumes that the reason for the existence of so many organizational problems in the first place is that ordinary people have been left to their own devices. Like Plato's cave dwellers, ordinary people will tend to make poor decisions. And like enlightened philosophers, social scientists are best able to understand how organizations work and how organizations should be designed.

In addition to designing organizations and societies, the mechanical design perspective advocates that scientific and other cognitive elites should play a central role in organizing and managing society. Because laypeople's beliefs, decisions, and actions are based on common sense and custom and because laypeople do not have the mental horsepower to manage complex institutions, they are likely to err in their methods and goals. John Stuart Mill argued that progress and well-being depend on "the most cultivated intellects in the country . . . those who have been in advance of society in thought and feeling" (cited in Sowell, 1995, p. 114). Thomas Jefferson believed that the country should be ruled by a "natural aristocracy." Those from the natural aristocracy should be "raked from the rubbish" and cultivated for positions of leadership.

With the advent of modern ability-testing methods, mechanical designers believed they had an efficient rake with which to sort geniuses from the rubbish, and they went at it with a fervor. Lancelot Ware and Roland

Berrill founded Mensa (originally called The High-IQ Club) in Britain in 1946 so that the British government could have ready access to the best minds in the country. Ware and Berrill believed that Britain (and the world) should be run neither by hard-working ordinary people nor by the well-born nor by the well-connected, but by an aristocracy of the bright (Scott, 2001). Two years later, the British Education Act was passed (1948), and among its provisions was the testing of British school children to sort them by cognitive abilities. At about the same time, James Bryant Conant and Henry Chauncey began their long battle to make the Scholastic Aptitude Test (SAT) the standard by which American students were selected for college. While Mensa is now little more than a social and dating club, and while Ware and Berrill's plan for staffing the British government by a high-IQ elite never materialized, the rule of the cognitive elite is a reality. It is commonplace in America that the "best and brightest" are identified with tests and channeled into elite educational institutions and then to the professions, business management, and government (Herrnstein & Murray, 1994; Lemann, 2000; Reich, 1991).

The Reign of Experts in Human Affairs—From Plato to Positivism

The wise shall lead and rule, and the ignorant shall follow.
—Plato

A critical factor in the mechanical design perspective is third-party decision making—removing decision making from ordinary people and placing it in the hands of experts. Because ordinary people are incapable of accurately apprehending reality and making informed judgments, organizations and society will function more effectively if decisions are left to experts (Sowell, 1995). Advocates of the mechanical design perspective argue that there are proper and improper ways to organize organizations (and society). Proper programs solve problems. Since experts are capable of more rational decisions and have more accurate perceptions of reality than the benighted, they can design organizations that will operate more efficiently and effectively than when the design of organization is left to custom and ordinary social evolution. Thus, the primary and most appropriate orientation to reality is scientifically verifiable knowledge (Cronbach, 1986; Toulmin, 1977). Action based on anything but such knowledge is based on either ignorance or error, and it is unlikely to achieve intended effects. Popper (1966) argues that Plato's ideas about the importance of experts and the fallibility of laypeople held sway among utopian social thinkers for two and a half millennia. He refers to this as "the spell of Plato." This perspective was part of the intellectual tapestry of Mill, Comte, and Marx in the nineteenth century, of the applied psychology of Taylor, Münsterberg, Scott, and Yerkes in the early twentieth century, and it is still prominent in applied psychology and management today (Eastman & Bailey, 1994; Kanigel, 1997). The preeminence of the scientist-practitioner in applied psychology and the applied psychologists' distrust of traditional recipes for living and working reflect this view (Campbell, 1975; Eastman & Bailey, 1994; O'Sullivan & Quevillon, 1992).

In Plato's analogy of the cave, ordinary people were like permanent cave dwellers, unable to leave the cave. True reality, the true essence of things and ideas, existed outside of the cave. The cave dwellers could not see the true essence of things; they could only see the shadows—imperfect representations—of true essences that appeared on the cave's walls. However, some people were better at comprehending the true nature of things from the shadows than others. These were the philosophers. Because of their greater ability and education, philosophers had expert knowledge of the true nature of things. Plato believed that only those who had undergone a rigorous philosophical education should be in charge. Plato regarded philosophers as critical to the development of an ideal state. The ideal of justice and its earthly approximation in the appropriate organization of the city-state was due to philosophical reasoning. When people are assigned to their places in society according to their talents, society (and organizations) will run smoothly and efficiently. When people and positions are mismatched, society will descend into chaos. Plato's society is static; people are born into their castes—whatever their parents were, they will be. It's not clear how people were assigned to castes initially, although one presumes it was done by philosophers. "[Plato's] Ideal State depends both for its creation and for its preservation upon its kings being philosophers or philosophers being its kings. For they know and only they know wherein the public weal consists" (Ryle, 1967, p. 331).

Almost 2,500 years later, we find this same belief in contemporary HR management. Society and organizations will work ideally when people's talents are properly matched with jobs. Although this notion reflects the utopian aspect of the mechanical design perspective, it also reflects the importance of expert decision making: we need experts and expert knowledge to determine which people are placed in which jobs. Guion's view is typical:

> It is both wasteful and immoral to deny qualified people desirable and available employment for invalid reasons, including some whims known as "company policies." Tests and test technology used in employment pro-

cedures can markedly reduce the frequency and degree of wasteful selection errors. The employing organization has a responsibility to itself and to the society that supports it to be sure that it uses these tools competently and wisely. (1965, p. 5)

Here, the aptitude tester is philosopher and the manager is king.

Francis Bacon (1561–1626) is the father of the modern empirical, cumulative, and collegial view of science. In his writings on the human mind and on social organization, Bacon had little faith in tradition and in the ability of people to accurately perceive reality and to make important decisions regarding organizational life (see Popper, 1966, Vol. II, p. 378). Bacon was an empiricist and believed that progress in knowledge, particularly scientific knowledge, was possible through the scientific method. Although an empiricist—and hence human perception of reality plays a critical role in his method—Bacon "discerned certain general tendencies in the human mind that needed to be corrected if knowledge was to be advanced" (Cranston, 1967, p. 237). He called these tendencies the four Idols—the Idols of the Tribe, Den, Market Place, and Theater. However, ordinary people were unaware of the Idols, and thus their ability to perceive reality was severely limited. The Idols of the Tribe are errors based on human biological limitations. People's perceptual faculties are like "false mirrors" distorting true reality. The Idols of the Den are errors based on variations in individual experience and education. The Idols of the Market Place refer to errors that arise from commerce between people, particularly the difficulties that arise with the ambiguities inherent in language. Finally, the Idols of the Theater refer to errors in people's thinking that arise from erroneous philosophical systems and dogmas. Bacon's new methods for science are the basis for the techniques designed to compensate for these errors.

Bacon developed a formal program so that society and organizations could benefit from science, although it does not appear that the institutions themselves were to be structured according to scientific principles. Scientists were clearly more important than ordinary people in the utopian society called Bensalem, described in *New Atlantis*. Unlike Sir Thomas Moore's *Utopia*, which emphasized the roles of the social system, the family, and religion, Bacon's *New Atlantis* concentrated on one institution, Solomon's House—a center for scientific discovery and activity. A scientist-priest and the elders of Solomon's House ruled Bensalem. Science played a central role in Solomon's House, and it was, in Bacon's words, "the very eye of the kingdom." The purpose of Solomon's house "is the knowledge of causes, the secret motions of things; and the enlarging of the human Empire, to the effecting of all things possible." It is composed of elders who spend their time in pursuit of knowledge, conducting experiments and gathering data. Solomon's House is completely independent from the state. The Elders of Solomon's House decide which scientific discoveries will be made public and which will not; it also decides when to make discoveries public.

> Those inventions approved for general public consumption are announced during circuits of the principal cities. In the course of these journeys, the Elders perform good works in preventive medicine and in mitigating the effect of such disasters as they can predict. (Manuel & Manuel, 1979, p. 258)

Scientists' roles vis-à-vis the state and the masses are essentially based on Christian charity. Ordinary people benefit from science, but they are dependent on the Elders for improvements to their lives. Bacon considered the masses of ordinary people "the heart of dark superstition" (Manuel & Manuel, 1979, p. 252).

> The priest-scientist elite in Bensalem can be likened to the nobles free to lead lives of contemplation in Patrizi's *Citta Felice* and to the priest-rulers of Campanella's *City of the Sun*. Ordinary persons are treated with varying degrees of contempt or condescension. (Manuel & Manuel, 1979, p. 259)

Positivism is another ingredient in the mechanical design perspective. It is one of the most explicit philosophical statements about the importance of experts and expert knowledge—and their superiority to ordinary people and custom—for understanding and organizing society. Positivism is both a philosophy of science and a philosophy of society. It became a broad and influential philosophical movement in the Western world during the latter half of the nineteenth century and the early part of the twentieth century. Like mechanism, positivism assumed that systems operate in a deterministic fashion and that the prediction of natural and social phenomena is possible once sufficient knowledge is accumulated. The central tenet of positivism is its rejection of metaphysics and common-sense understanding. From a positivist perspective, science is the only significant mechanism for encountering reality (Parsons, 1937). Accordingly, positivism suggests that scientifically verifiable knowledge is the only appropriate basis to reality. Like mechanism, positivism is reductionistic, atomistic, and deterministic. Positivism holds that knowledge, *as well as the structure of social organization*, should be based on information verifiable by scientists. For the positivist, "Scientifically verifiable knowledge of the situation becomes the only *significant orienting medium* in the action system. . . . Positive science

constitutes man's sole possible significant cognitive relation to external
. . . reality" (Parsons, 1937, p. 61; emphasis in the original).

This is a dramatic and false claim, but it is the origin of much of the
HR literature. The appropriate means to achieve an end in a social system is to use scientifically valid knowledge, and only positively verified
information is considered scientifically valid. We see this attitude mani-
fested in a number of ways in the HR literature. One, of course, is the
professionally accepted doctrine that the practicing I/O psychologist
should follow the model of the scientist-practitioner (Muchinsky, 2000).
This model of professional practice holds that psychological interventions be validated *before* they are used in organization and evaluated
by experts *after* they are implemented (Belar & Perry, 1992; Society for
Industrial and Organizational Psychology, 1987). An intervention should
be used *only* when *expert evidence* indicates that it is likely to work; its
continued use should be based on expert evidence that the intervention
is achieving intended goals. Lest I be accused of arguing against the scientific method, let me be clear about the meaning of my critique of the
scientist-practitioner model. I am *not* suggesting that all interventions
be accepted at face value or that there is no need to evaluate social programs. The problem with the scientist-practitioner model and its prog-
eny is the overzealous application of scientism.[12] It needlessly denigrates
the common sense that most of us get by on every day, and it over-
estimates the capacity of social science for making accurate and useful
predictions about complex social phenomena. The scientist-practitioner
model assumes that studies with the trappings of science inevitably lead
to practical knowledge about social systems that is superior to traditional
structures that have withstood the test of time.

Another manifestation of positivism is the consternation that I/O psychologists express when their work is ignored. In commenting on the
use of the employment interview, Arvey and Campion state: "Perhaps
the glaring 'black hole' in all previous reviews and in the current literature concerns the issue of why use of the interview persists in view of
the evidence of its relatively low validity, reliability, and its susceptibility
to bias and distortion" (1982, p. 314). Interventions that are not based
on the positive approach are considered inappropriate (Society for Industrial and Organizational Psychology, 1987) and based on ignorance
or error (Muchinsky, 2000).

One consequence of positivism is the emergence of a scientific elite
to manage social and organizational life. Because science is the only significant mechanism for orienting to reality, scientists are the only individuals who possess sufficient knowledge of the means for ordering
society to achieve desired ends and goods. Unlike those scientists,

laypeople's beliefs, decisions, and actions are based on common sense, religion, and custom. Therefore, laypersons, according to positivists, do not have adequate knowledge to properly organize society. Frederick Taylor (1911) argued that the design of work should be based on time and motion and efficiency studies, not on tradition. Taylor expected engineers and time and motion experts to have more authority in the design of jobs and organizations than workers or employers. In fact, the goal of his classic book, *The Principles of Scientific Management*, was to "attempt to show the enormous gains which would result from the substitution by our workmen of scientific for rule-of-thumb methods" (1911, p. 16). Tayor's approach to management reduced managers' authority and discretion. According to Bendix, scientific management "questioned [employers'] good judgment and superior ability which had been the subject of public celebration for many years" (1956, p. 280). Münsterberg agreed with Taylor that the design of the work in organizations was properly in the domain of experts, not workers or employers. He believed that the expert should have a leading role in the organization of society and work (Hale, 1980).

The work of modern personnel psychologists continues to state or imply that: (1) personnel interventions in organizations designed by nonexperts or that evolved through tradition are generally inefficient and ineffective; and (2) personnel psychologists, through scientific research, can design more effective personnel interventions than nonexperts or than personnel practices that have evolved through tradition. Commenting to and about industrial psychologists, Frank Schmidt states:

> We are the experts in human resources. No other group has as much to offer. During my eleven years in Washington, I was repeatedly struck by the fact that, in comparison to other groups intervening in HR issues and policy debates, we have much more solid usable knowledge than they do. We have the wherewithal and the obligation to tackle really big questions . . . on which the future of this country depends. (1993, p. 500)

Here Schmidt also demonstrates that he has no serious experience of Greek tragedy.

Positivists also assume that appropriate or useful courses of action can be determined only through rational decision making. Choices not based on explicit rational algorithms must, according to positivists, be based on either ignorance or error (Parsons, 1937). Rationality for positivists involves understanding one's current situation and then predicting its future development (Parsons, 1937). A more recent view of rationality in the positivistic spirit is the Bayesian model of rational choice, which argues that rational choice has two aspects: utility and subjective probability (see Boyd & Richerson, 1985, p. 87). Utility is the numerical value of an outcome. Subjective probability is the estimated likelihood that a decision will result in a particular outcome. Rational behavior, then, involves assigning numerical utilities and probabilities to outcomes of decisions and then choosing the alternative that results in the highest expected utility (Savage, 1954). The literature on personnel interventions emphasizes rational decision making. One of the best examples of this is the literature on the utility of personnel selection methods (Boudreau, 1991). A desired outcome is identified (usually job performance), and economic values are placed on levels of job performance. One or more employee selection methods (e.g., cognitive ability tests, interviews) are identified as possible courses of action that can lead to increased job performance. What is believed to be valid scientific knowledge is then used to estimate the probabilities that valued outcomes will occur when different courses of action are chosen.

Utopias

The mechanical design perspective views the implementation of expert knowledge as progress toward ideal, rational social systems. Such progress is the "true role" of social institutions in the march of history (Popper, 1966). Social engineering is the proper means to bring about ideal institutions. Adherents to the mechanical design perspective are what Popper (1966) calls *utopian social engineers*. Utopian social engineers begin with the premise that rational action needs an ultimate goal. What distinguishes *utopian* social engineering from everyday efforts to be happy is its emphasis on ultimate ends. This idea is so pervasive among adherents to the mechanical design perspective that they can be called *constructive utopians*. Constructive utopians believe that if the proper design is followed, then a considerably better state of affairs will result. The early Greek approaches to utopia addressed people's personal, social, and political relations. During the Middle Ages, utopias were more concerned with people's relationship with God than with fellow humans. Beginning in the Renaissance and continuing into the modern age, utopian visions returned to human relations and the need for experts to direct people to an ideal state of affairs (Passmore, 1970, p. 169).

What Is an Organizational Utopia?

A utopia is an ideal social organization in which negative qualities have been eliminated and positive qualities are present; the nature of the utopian social organization sustains positive qualities; and the utopian organization is regarded as a final or ultimate state of affairs. Change is no longer necessary once the utopian ideal has been achieved. The values of a utopia's designer are usually the basis for defining negative and positive qualities. Three models of organizational utopias are evident in the human resource management literature: (1) good fit, (2) personal potential, and (3) committed submission.

The first model dates back to Plato. In Plato's ideal society, the good was justice, which in turn would lead to happiness. Plato's conception of justice was based on his notions of essentialism and ideal types. An ideal society had a prescribed order based on proper functioning of particular roles—administration, internal security, production, defense, and so on. People had different essences or qualities. Some were natural leaders, while others were natural soldiers or farmers. Justice and the ideal society occur when people are properly matched to their roles (Plato, 1968; see also Popper, 1966, Vol. I, p. 169). Some industrial psychologists have similar versions of this ideal. The following quotes from former presidents of the Society of Industrial and Organizational Psychology reflect the Platonic notion that properly fitting people to jobs leads to ideal organizations.

> In an *idealized* world, our aim would be to place all persons on jobs perfectly suited to them and to society. (Dunnette, 1966, p. 2; emphasis added)

> In an *idealized* existence our goal would be to assess each individual's aptitudes, abilities, personality, and interests, to profile these characteristics, and then to place all individuals in jobs perfectly suited to them and to society. (Cascio, 1998, pp. 2–3; emphasis added)

> [We have described] the stages of an *ideal* staffing program [placing people in jobs for which they are perfectly suited]. . . . Obviously every organization will not be able to carry out all of these steps for every job. . . . [However], it is important to keep [the ideal] in mind when *not* doing the optimal so that the tradeoffs in circumventing the ideal can be made explicit. (Schneider & Schmitt, 1986, p. 415; first emphasis added)

Taylor (1911) presents a similar but more encompassing model based on his philosophy of scientific management. His organizational ideal starts with selecting the right person for the job. However, fitting people to jobs is only part of a total system to maximize efficiency, the ultimate goal of Taylor's utopia. Taylor's system includes prescribed methods for designing jobs, training workers in proper methods, and rewarding them to ensure continued motivation and morale—all of which help to ensure a proper fit between people and jobs.

The fulfillment of personal potential is an ideal associated primarily with organizational psychology. Organizational psychologists typically view the ideal organization as one that fosters the personal potential of its members. In this ideal organization, people are involved and empowered; work offers the opportunity for personal growth. Supervisors listen to (and often act upon) their employees' suggestions; people are treated with dignity and respect; work is satisfying and interesting; people work collaboratively; and communication is authentic. The following quotes from organizational psychologists epitomize this view:

> The challenge is to indicate the need for a new and larger view of the world as well as a look at the quality of worklife it reflects. The idea is that the improving of the place, the organization and the nature of work can lead to a better work performance and a better quality of life in our society.... [There is the need] for the redesign of work with attention to human factors rather than to plant factors only. (Meltzer & Wickert, 1976, p. 6)

> The capacities of the average human being for creativity, for growth, for collaboration, for productivity (in the full sense of the term) are far greater than we have recognized.... And, if we can learn how to realize the potential for collaboration inherent in the human resources of industry, we will provide a model for governments and nations which mankind sorely needs. (McGregor, 1960, pp. 245–246)

This ideal of organizations is similar to Karl Marx's conception of an ideal society, where people are no longer burdened by meaningless work and where they are free to pursue activities that allow them to reach their full human potential. "The kingdom of freedom actually begins only where drudgery, enforced by hardship and by external purposes, ends" (Marx, cited in Popper, 1966, Vol. II, p. 104).

> Marx can fairly be regarded as subscribing to the perfectibility of man. ... Man will finally become what he has it in himself to be, not a superman but a "true" man, not a mere functionary, dedicated to the pursuit of technical perfection but an all-round human being, living in a society from which "the enslaving subordination of the individual to the division of labour, and therewith, also the antithesis between mental and physical labour, has vanished".... It will be, too, a free society. Negatively, it will be free of oppression, positively, it will be so organized that men can express their own nature in their labour and in their social relationships. (Passmore, 1970, p. 237)

The third type of organizational utopia is committed submission. It originated primarily from management consultants and management professors in American business schools, who took an empirical, reverse engineering approach to organizational utopias. The typical procedure would be to identify existing, exemplary organizations based on the criteria of long-term profitability, exceptional financial returns, and high status. The organizations are analyzed to determine their distinguishing characteristics, and the characteristics they find are the ones they recommended as ideals. Many of these studies suggest that talented employees, who are committed to the organization, and who share its core values are the key ingredients of sustained organizational profitability, high financial returns, and high status. These organizations have a clear set of values and a strong organizational culture. They recruit people who have similar values and then intensely socialize them into the organization's values. People whose values do not match the organization's values leave voluntarily or are terminated. Employees are rewarded for their submission because the organization shows a high concern for human resources. It also provides employees with exceptional training and development. Because employees share the organization's values, they become personally identified with the organization and are personally committed to its success. They are willing to work very hard and sacrifice for the good of the organization. The following quotes illustrate the flavor of ideal committed submission:

> The vision presented by the core group committed to the organization establishes a climate which encourages people to participate in the decisions affecting them, and personally commit to profit, productivity, and growth objectives for the business. (Beer, Eisenstat, & Spector, 1990, p. 74)

> The critical variable is not the content of a company's ideology, but how deeply it *believes* its ideology and how consistently it lives, breathes, and expresses it in all that it does. Visionary companies do not ask, "What should we value?" They ask, "What do we *actually* value deep down to our toes?" (Collins & Porras, 1994, pp. 1, 8; emphases in original)

> The point of smallness is that it induces manageability and, above all, commitment. (Peters & Waterman, 1982, p. 271)

Views of Human Nature

Since people are the raw material of utopias, constructive utopians need a theory of human nature. Interestingly, constructive utopians do not share similar assumptions about human nature. Some, like Plato and his modern-day intellectual descendants, assume that a person's personality and intellectual capacities are fixed, either inborn or acquired early in life (although they may not be expressed until adolescence or adulthood). At the other extreme are Locke and his intellectual descendants who assume that the mind is a blank slate—a person's experiences determine personality and abilities. The good fit model shares the Platonic assumption about fixed individual differences; the personal potential model shares the Lockean assumptions about the malleability of human nature; and the committed submission model falls somewhere in between.

Despite this range of assumptions among constructive utopians, the three models of organizational utopias have two common assumptions. First, each assumes that *differences among people are important*—both inherently and because of their effects on organizations and society. The Platonic view is preoccupied with the stability of differences, how to assess them, the consequences of those differences, and what to do with people of different temperaments and abilities. The Lockean view is preoccupied with how the environment shapes differences, the best methods for creating differences, what differences to create and in whom, and how to allocate people to various difference-creating institutions. Second, each regards differences among people as *instrumental to attaining policy goals*. The Platonic view assumes that people with different inborn abilities and temperaments are better at some tasks than others. Thus, the attainment of (utopian) social or organizational goals requires that people with different abilities be sorted and matched to appropriate roles. The Lockean view, on the other hand, assumes that given the proper circumstances, people can develop a wide range of abilities, skills, or temperaments. Thus, the attainment of goals requires the development of social structures and educational policies that will produce requisite abilities, skills, and temperaments.

Historical Inevitability

The mechanical design perspective is wedded to the idea of progress. Common among its adherents is a belief that society and organizations evolve from lower to higher forms. Comte (1855/1974) suggested that this evolution occurs in three stages. The first and most primitive stage is the theological; the second is the metaphysical; the third and most advanced stage is the scientific or positive stage. Marx viewed society as progressively evolving toward an ideal state of communism, occurring as part of the inevitable working out of history. The theorists of mechanical design have a less articulated historicist vision, but they do convey a sense that organizations pass through stages toward a final ideal. Frederick Taylor implied this notion when he wrote: "in the past the man has been first. In the future the System must be first" (1911, p. 7). Rensis Likert (1961, p. 1), who had a very different vision of ideal organizations than Taylor, also implies a historical inevitability: "important forces and resources are accelerating . . . the process of pointing the way to an appreciably more effective system of management than now exists." Pfeffer (1994) is fairly pessimistic about organizational change but still assumes an ideology of progress. McGregor evidences a belief in progress when he writes that "it is possible that the next half century will bring the most dramatic social changes in human history. . . . The possible result could be developments . . . with respect to the human side of enterprise comparable to those that have occurred in technology during the past half century" (McGregor, 1960, pp. 245–246). Kanter (1983) invokes the coming of a "corporate Renaissance" where "the spirit of enterprise could be reborn" (p. 353).

The classical positivists argued that science is the engine driving society from a state of disorder and conflict to one of order and harmony. An ideal society is possible because there are general laws of society, and science provides the means for the discovery and application of these laws (Parsons, 1937; Rabinbach, 1990). As modern science assembles its stores of facts and theories, uncovering nature's secrets and gaining control over its resources, humanity ascends the ladder of progress. The progressive driving spirit of science will transform human activity (cf. Basalla, 1988, p. 132). Others, and here I would include most human resource scholars in the mechanical design camp, view science as an ancillary force. It provides managers with the tools to improve organizational responses to technological, social, and economic forces. These forces exert pressure on organizations to change, and social science helps to manage the change. Likert (1961) argues that these forces include increased competition, changes in social values, and rising expectations. Pfeffer (1994) also emphasizes the role of global competition and the ease with which technology and capital can flow across national borders. Argyris (1976, 1990) suggests that rising expectations and the conflict between actual human nature and the limited view of human nature on which most organizational design is premised are powerful forces.

Experts and Organizational Utopias

Historical and social forces do not produce ideal organizations unless aided by experts. Organizational experts—people who can provide advice on how organizations should be designed—are a critical ingredient for the development of ideal organizations. Proponents of mechanical design believe that organizational improvements will not occur indirectly, through social processes such as competition in the market-place, trial and error, or progress in the natural sciences which stimulate new interventions and economic activity.[13] Left to their own devices, organizations are unlikely to reach an ideal state of affairs. Recall that Plato regarded philosophers as critical to the development of an ideal state. Although Bacon did not evidence much interest in the lot of ordinary people, he too believed that they would benefit from experts through a trickle-down effect. Scientists could help ordinary people become better off by developing inventions and periodically making them available to the masses. It could also warn of impending disasters. Bacon was concerned with the applications of *natural* science for improving the lot of humankind. By giving scientists a key position in society, by allowing them to work freely and independently to pursue knowledge, and by trusting their wisdom, society would improve the lot of ordinary people.[14] A scientific elite was also essential to Comte's utopian ideal. The overarching goals of his utopian society were order and stability based on inevitable laws. Order, in any society, was established when all (or most) members of society held similar opinions. In his ideal society, opinions would be based on true social knowledge. Once science had discovered true social knowledge, there would be little to fight over, since the truth would be established. A scientific elite assumed a priestly role in society. It was their job to unify society by teaching people the inevitable laws of nature and society.

That experts are crucial ingredients of organizational utopias is a common theme in the human resource management literature of the twentieth century. Experts are necessary for discovering scientific laws about human behavior in organizations, translating that knowledge into interventions, and communicating that knowledge to managers. For Taylor and Münsterberg in the early twentieth century, the goal of organizational efficiency could only be obtained when experts taught managers how to apply the newly discovered scientific principles of management to their organizations. B. F. Skinner and others in the behaviorist tradition (such as James B. Watson) saw behaviorism as the ticket to utopia in the twentieth century on a grand scale. In his utopian novel, *Walden Two*, Skinner describes a utopian community in which social engineers use behaviorist principles to shape the environment to eliminate evil and produce individual happiness and harmonious social relations. Thirty years after the publication of *Walden Two*, Skinner was still echoing his abiding faith that behaviorism could cure the world's ills:

> We need to make vast changes in human behavior. . . . It is not enough
> to "use technology with a deeper understanding of human issues," or to

"encourage technologists to look at human problems." Such expressions imply that where human behavior begins, technology stops. . . . What we need is a technology of behavior. We could solve our problems quickly enough if we could adjust the growth of the world's population as precisely as we adjust the course of a spaceship. (1971, p. 5)

The current crop of social engineers is more vague about what utopia will look like. They talk about "making the world a better place" and the "wisest and most humane use of its human resources." But they share the belief of their predecessors that it will take experts to determine these uses. Argyris views experts (i. e., professors and consultants who understand and use his theory) as critical to helping people in organizations become more authentic.

> We are losing the battle against designed ignorance. . . . The most fundamental assumption of the underground managerial world is that truth is a good idea when it is not embarrassing or threatening—the very conditions under which truth is especially needed.
>   Fortunately, research and practice are leading to solutions that appear promising. I have organized this knowledge in a theoretical framework that predicts what is likely to happen and that can be used to reverse the counter productive trends. (Argyris, 1990, pp. xiii–xiv)

Says Muchinsky,

> I can think of few other fields of work that are as critical to human welfare as I/O psychology. . . . As our society faces increasing problems of economic productivity, the field of I/O psychology continues to contribute to making our world a better place in which to live. (2000, p. 22)

According to Cascio, "Society can and should do a better job of making the wisest and most humane use of its human resources. . . . Personnel psychology holds considerable potential for improving the caliber of personnel management in organizations" (1998, p. 3).

THE LIMITATIONS OF THE MECHANICAL DESIGN PERSPECTIVE

The mechanical design perspective has led to a number of unrealistic expectations about the *application* of psychology. It expects applied psychology to produce intended effects in organizations. This expectation goes back at least to Münsterberg (1914) and his early discussion of the aims of applied psychology:

We may use the word psychotechnics for that practical application which *aims toward the realization of certain concrete ends.* . . . Psychotechnics is really a technical science related to causal psychology as engineering is related to physics. Psychotechnics necessarily refers to the future. (1914, p. 354; emphasis added)

Yet, after a century's worth of social interventions, it is abundantly clear that social interventions are problematic. They do not consistently produce intended effects. More often they produce unintended effects (Colarelli, 1998; Gillon, 2000).

The mechanical design perspective also has the silly assumption that progress will be rapid. People have come to expect that psychological interventions can be installed to fix organizational problems, in much the same way as new parts can be installed to repair a machine. This leads to a belief that psychological interventions can provide quick fixes to ameliorate organizational problems. The literature in applied psychology leaves one with the impression that realistic job previews will lower turnover in a few months (Wanous, 1980), that goal setting will quickly increase productivity (Locke & Latham, 1990), and that cognitive ability tests to screen job applicants will increase productivity within months (Ree & Earles, 1992). But reviews and analyses of these methods indicate that their effects are inconsistent than expected (Hartigan & Wigdor, 1989; Hollenbeck & Klein, 1987; Phillips, 1998).

Another expectation in mechanical design is that process—the series of events that lead to an outcome after the use of psychological interventions—can be ignored. It emphasizes the characteristics of the intervention and minimizes processes, such as multiple interactions among system components, feedback, fine-tuning, and later incremental improvement (Colarelli, 1998). By viewing organizations as machines and people and psychological interventions as parts, it suggests that it is a simple matter to replace or fix a part. Little attention, therefore, is paid to the sequence of events involved in replacing the part. An organization need not be concerned with interventions as they evolve (Gharajedaghi & Ackoff, 1984). It is assumed that the internal processes of an organization remain constant. This being the case, changes in input directly influence outputs. This line of reasoning, though often implicit, is common in selection research and practice. Selection research has focused and continues to focus on how changes in inputs (e.g., the abilities of job applicants) influence outputs (typically, job performance), while ignoring the organizational processes that mediate between the individual abilities and output, and that also influence output (Colarelli & Boos, 1992). We also see this in the training literature that focuses on the content or technology of the training method, while ignoring the social or psychological context in which training occurs.

It Doesn't Work

Mechanical designs do not work in complex systems. Expectations for them have been high, but the results have been poor. Throughout the twentieth century, policymakers called upon social scientists to help solve social and organizational problems. This was particularly apparent in education, the War on Poverty, civil rights, and management. Until the 1960s, social scientists were confident that they were up to the task. At a symposium in 1954 to commemorate the twenty-fifth anniversary of the University of Chicago's Social Science building, social scientists saw themselves on the brink of scientific and political coups. Yet 25 years later, at a symposium to honor its fiftieth anniversary, the tone of the papers had changed dramatically. The symposium "had the flavor more of a wake than of a celebration" (Converse, 1986, p. 42). From school integration policies to educational reforms and management techniques, progress in applications of psychology and social science has been disappointing (Beer & Walton, 1990; Lindblom & Cohen, 1979; Moynihan, 1996; Ravitch, 2000). In a massive review of the organizational development literature, summarizing 14 years worth of research, Porras and Robertson (1992, p. 786) reported that less than half of the studies found positive organizational change. Roberts, Hulin, and Rosseau (1978) were not any more sanguine about the effects of elaborate personnel selection interventions.

> Organizational scientists engaged in personnel-selection research are responsive to both low levels of predictability of behavior by means of psychological tests and our lack of progress over the span of sixty years. Numerous suggestions are offered as panaceas. . . . Most of these approaches are little more than minor tinkerings with the elements of the basic selection paradigm. . . . Every few years our attention moves from one new approach to a different new approach. . . . Whatever approach is in vogue, it is normally fitted out with more elaborate statistical procedures than those preceding it, and results are produced that initially appear to justify the use of the new methods. Unfortunately, the next wave of research frequently indicates that the clothing of the new emperor is just as transparent as that of the previous one. (Roberts, Hulin, & Rosseau, 1978, p. 118)

The *popularity* of social interventions reflects these dismal appraisals. Eighty-nine percent of American corporations offer no formal training to nonmanagement employees (Labor Letter, 1991). Most organizations do not analyze training needs or evaluate training programs, and few organizations in Europe, Britain, or the United States use the personnel selection practices recommended by the HR literature (Levy-Leboyer, 1994; Saari, Johnson, McLaughlin, & Zimmerle, 1988; Terpstra & Rozell, 1997). The amount of money spent on formal psychological interventions, relative to other organizational programs, is very small. For example, American firms spend more on "coffee breaks, lunch, and other paid rest time for their employees than on formal training" (Office of Technology Assessment, 1990, p. 129). The allocation of research money also reflects a pessimistic view of the value of social interventions. The social sciences receive considerably less funding than the other branches of science at the National Science Foundation. In 1999, for example, the National Science Foundation's budget included $392 million for biological sciences, $299 million for computer and information science and engineering, $370 million for engineering, $478 million for geosciences, $734 million for mathematical and physical sciences, but only $142 million for the social, behavioral, and economic sciences (National Science Foundation, 2000). Organizational science and human resource management have little currency with and impact on government policymakers. There is a President's Council of Economic Advisors, but no official council of human resource management advisors.

Equally revealing is the decline in the academic prestige of applied psychology during the latter half of the twentieth century. Howard Gardner (2002, p. B8) refers to industrial psychology as "that exile from the university." During the first half of the twentieth century, psychology departments at many top-tier American universities—including Chicago, Yale, Cornell, Stanford, Princeton, Northwestern, and Pennsylvania—offered graduate programs in industrial psychology. Of the 25 universities that offered Ph.D. programs in industrial psychology in 1946 (Sears, 1946), 19 were in top-tier research universities. In the 1954–1955 academic year, 31 universities had Ph.D. programs in industrial psychology (Moore, 1954), 16 of which were in top-tier universities. By 2000, no Ivy League universities offered Ph.D.s in the field, and only 7 of these programs were at the top 50 national universities. Most Ph.D. programs in I/O psychology are now housed in second-tier through fourth-tier universities. In schools of business, human resource management programs have remained a poor stepchild to disciplines such as finance, accounting, and marketing. Human resource programs are the least well funded and have the smallest number of faculty. A search for MBA websites using Peterson's Education Center shows that 404 of the 960 business schools in the database provide MBA concentrations in accounting, 371 provide concentrations in finance, 357 have marketing concentrations, 418 have general management concentration, but only 245 schools have concentrations in human resource management. Of the business schools ranked by *US News & World Report* (*US News*, 2001) only 10 in the top 50 have MBA or Ph.D. programs in human resource management.[15]

Perhaps the largest schools using applied social science in American universities are the schools of education. Yet the science of education continues to remain elusive. The practical results of much educational research have been dismal, and these schools attract the least academically gifted students (Browne, 2002; Lagemann, 2000; Ravitch, 2000). Indeed, confidence in social programs has become so low that it is significant news to find one that works. This was epitomized by a book recently published with the title, *Social Programs That Work* (Crane, 1998). The book is based on papers from a conference titled "Social Programs That Really Work." These titles imply that most social programs do *not* work and that it is news to find some that do.

A mechanical design perspective has resulted in useful engineering applications from the natural sciences. However, in most cases it is inappropriate for the social sciences and social interventions. Compared to complex human organizations, the natural sciences deal with situations where there are more controls, fewer interactions, and generally fewer variables (Wilson, 1998). The objects chemists study and manipulate are not willful and conscious. The process of reduction → analysis → reassembly works with, say, plastics, polymers, and hip replacements— but not with complex organizations and social interventions (Colarelli, 1998; Diamond, 1999).

NOTES

1. *Organizations* are human groupings constructed for a purpose. Organizational participants—while understanding the value of the organization as a resource and its general purpose—pursue multiple and conflicting interests, often at odds with the organization's stated purpose. Organizational subunits are interdependent, and they interact with and are dependent on the organization's environment (Scott, 1998). Armies, state bureaucracies, religious orders, and modern manufacturing and service firms are all examples of organizations. The Dow Chemical Company, the Hoover Institution, and the University of Chicago are organizations, and so were the Roman Empire's army, the medieval Catholic Church, and perhaps even Renaissance principalities. Families, clans, informal groups, and nations, on the other hand, are not organizations by my definition.

2. An *organizational problem* is the perception that some aspect of the current state of affairs in an organization is unsatisfactory. What one person perceives as a problem is not necessarily perceived as such by others. Situations that typically receive attention as problems are those that organizational leaders or influential outsiders perceive as problems. The perceived seriousness of a problem—again by organizational leaders or influential outsiders—affects whether attempts will be made to solve it and the amount of time and resources it will receive. Situations in organizations may be viewed as unsatisfactory for a variety of reasons. Most critically, a situation may be perceived as threatening the immediate or long-term survival of the organization, such as a dramatic drop in customers or the emergence of a powerful competitor. Leaders or influential outsiders also tend to regard the existence of norms or values they disapprove of as a problem (Sowell, 1995).

3. August and September 1999.

4. While individual organizations continue to fail at high rates and large organizations predictably get bumped from the dominant market perches, manufacturing and service organizations *as industries* became more productive during the twentieth century. Worker accident rates decreased and overall economic output increased. The occupational injury and illness incidence rate per 100 full-time workers in 1973 was 11; the corresponding figure was 6.3 in 1998 (U.S. Department of Labor Occupational Safety and Health Administration, n.d./ 2001). The fatal workplace injury incidence rate per 100,000 full-time workers in 1974 was 9.8. In 1991, this rate decreased to 4.3 (U.S. Department of Labor, Occupational Safety and Health Administration, n.d./2001). In the private business sector, multifactor productivity increased from 51.5 in 1948 to 103.5 in 1999. In private nonfarm businesses, multifactor productivity increased from 56.3 in 1948 to 103.0 in 1999 (U.S. Department of Labor, Bureau of Labor Statistics, n.d./2001). While problems with individual schools and teaching methods continue unabated, the overall level of literacy and education in advanced industrial democracies has steadily increased (Fukuyama, 1992).

5. The success of business education in general is still open to question. Porter and McKibbin (1988) reported four criticisms of business school graduates: overly high expectations, lack of organizational loyalty, poor communication and interpersonal skills, and lack of leadership skills. Shipper (1999) compared the managerial skills of middle managers with MBAs and non-MBAs. This comparison failed to find that MBAs have a significant advantage in managerial skills.

6. Although social theories and speculations about the causes and effects of human behavior have been around at least since the ancient Greeks, the use of scientific methods (the systematic collection of data, testing theories empirically, experimentation, and replication) to study social phenomena did not emerge until the late nineteenth century.

7. What is considered *large* is a somewhat arbitrary question, but scholars suggest that an organization is large when the number of people in the organization is so great that they do not all know one another (Diamond, 1999; Nicholson, 2000). This means that organizations are large when they exceed

about 100 people. As organizations increase in size, they also increase in complexity: small units become responsible for different tasks, subunits increase in size, and administrative functions and personnel increase (Scott, 1998).

8. For a good general description of the rational-technocratic approach and its limitations, see Boyd and Richerson (1985, pp. 87 ff.).

9. Although technical efficiency ("relative advantage") is important, other characteristics of an intervention also affect adoption: complexity, trialability, and observability (Rogers, 1983, pp. 16–17). I would also add immediacy—how quickly the effects occur.

10. In previous writings I have referred to these design assumptions as "traditional" and "mechanistic" (Colarelli 1998; Colarelli & Stumpf, 1990). For the sake of consistency, and to avoid confusion with terms used by other authors (e.g., Morgan, 1997; Scott, 1998), I will refer to this approach as the mechanical design perspective. The key features of mechanical design that encompass many contemporary approaches to organizational interventions are the assumptions that organizations involve predictable sequences of causation analogous to the physical operation of machines and that organizations can be designed and operated somewhat like machines.

11. A *social intervention* is a design or process for reducing uncertainty in cause-effect relations and for producing intended effects on people. Social interventions work by transmitting information to or about people to change behavior (e.g., information provided by training or therapy) or to assist in making decisions about people (e.g., using test scores to make personnel selection decisions). For example, paper-and-pencil employment tests are social interventions for predicting the behavior of job applicants.

12. According to Hayek, who popularized the term, scientism is "a mechanical and uncritical application of habits of thought to fields different from those in which they have been formed" (1952, pp. 15–16). Hayek argues that scientism is in fact unscientific because it is "a very prejudiced approach which, before it has considered its subject, claims to know what is the most appropriate way of investigating it" (pp. 15–16). In a similar vein, Popper (1966) views scientism as the tendency in the social sciences to ape the natural sciences. By aping the natural sciences rather than through any fundamental understanding, it confers legitimacy on knowledge.

13. Fukuyama (1992) in *The End of History and the Last Man* argues that liberal democracies emerged not so much from social theory but were an indirect result of the development of the natural sciences. "The unfolding of modern natural science has had a uniform effect on all societies that have experienced it"—through technology it conferred military advantages and it allowed greater economic productivity, accumulation of wealth and the expansion of human desires (p. xiv).

14. This is similar to the role of research universities in the United States during the twentieth and twenty-first centuries.

15. The Yale School of Management eliminated its Ph.D. program in administrative science. In 1997, Yale University announced a reform to focus resources

on the strongest programs. The president of Yale stated that subjects like law and biomedical sciences were areas where the university would concentrate its resources. Other fields such as management, must remain small and seek excellence through specialization. Yale would not expand its faculty in these areas (Kotch, 1997).

REFERENCES

Abbagnano, N. (1967). Positivism. (Nino Languilli, Trans.). In Paul Edwards (Ed.), *The encyclopedia of philosophy* (Vol. 6, pp. 414–419). New York: Macmillan Publishing Co. & Free Press.

American Psychological Association. (2000). *Graduate study in psychology, 2000.* Washington, DC: American Psychological Association.

Argyris, C. (1990). *Overcoming organizational defenses.* Boston: Allyn & Bacon.

Argyris, C. (1976). Problems and new directions for industrial psychology. In M. D. Dunnette (Ed.), *Handbook of industrial and organizational psychology* (pp. 151–184). Chicago: Rand McNally.

Arvey, R. D., & Campion, J. E. (1982). The employment interview: A summary and review of recent research. *Personnel Psychology, 35,* 281–322.

Bartley, R. L. (1992). *The seven fat years: And how to do it again.* New York: Free Press.

Basalla, G. (1988). *The evolution of technology.* New York: Cambridge University Press.

Beer, M., Eisenstat, R. A., & Spector, B. (1990). *The critical path to corporate renewal.* Boston: Harvard Business School Press.

Beer, M., & Walton, E. (1990). Developing the competitive organization: Interventions and strategies. *American Psychologist, 45,* 154–161.

Belar, C. D., & Perry, N. W. (1992). The national conference on scientist-practitioner education and training for the professional practice of psychology. *American Psychologist, 47,* 71–75.

Bendix, R. (1956). *Work and authority in industry: Ideologies of management in the course of industrialization.* New York: John Wiley & Sons.

Bernstein, P. L. (1996). *Against the gods: The remarkable story of risk.* New York: John Wiley & Sons.

Boudreau, J. W. (1991). Utility analysis for decisions in human resource management. In M. D. Dunnette & L. M. Hough (Eds.), *Handbook of industrial and organizational psychology* (Vol. 2, pp. 621–745). Palo Alto, CA: Consulting Psychologists Press.

Boyd, R., & Richerson, P. J. (1985). *Culture and the evolutionary process.* Chicago: University of Chicago Press.

Brown, S. L., & Eisenhardt, K. M. (1998). *Competing on the edge: Strategy as structured chaos.* Boston: Harvard Business School Press.

Browne, K. R. (2002). *Biology at work: Rethinking sexual equality.* New Brunswick, NJ: Rutgers University Press.

Bureau of the Census. (1975/76). *County business patterns*. Washington, DC: Department of Commerce.

Bureau of Labor Statistics, Department of Labor. (2001, May 3). *News Release: Multifactor productivity trends, 1999*. Washington, DC: U.S. Department of Labor. Retrieved June 3, 2001, from the World Wide Web: *http://stats.bls.gov/news.release/prod3.nr0.htm*

Burt, B. A. (1978). Influence for change in the dental health status population: An historical perspective. *Journal of Public Health Dentistry, 38,* 272–288.

Campbell, D. T. (1975). On the conflicts between biological and social evolution and psychology and moral tradition. *American Psychologist, 30,* 1103–1126.

Campbell, J. P., McCloy, R. A., Oppler, S. H., & Sager, C. E. (1993). A theory of performance. In N. Schmitt & W. C. Borman (Eds.), *Personnel selection in organizations* (pp. 35–70). San Francisco: Jossey-Bass.

Cascio, W. F. (1998). *Applied psychology in human resource management* (5th ed.). Englewood Cliffs, NJ: Prentice Hall.

Center for Disease Control. (1999, October 22). Achievements in Public Health, 1900–1999: Fluoridation of drinking water to prevent dental caries. *Morbidity and Mortality Weekly Report, 48,* 933–940. Retrieved June 16, 2001, from World Wide Web: *http://www.cdc.gov/epo/mmwr/preview/mmwrhtml/mm4841a1.htm*

Chadderdon, L. (1998, September). Blurb buddies. *Fast Company, 20,* 54. Retrieved May 25, 2001, from the World Wide Web: *http//www.fastcompany.com/online/20/cdu.html*

Colarelli, S. M. (1998). Psychological interventions in organizations: A evolutionary perspective. *American Psychologist, 53,* 1044–1056.

Colarelli, S. M., & Boos, A. L. (1992). Sociometric and ability-based assignment to work groups: Some implications for personnel selection. *Journal of Organizational Behavior, 13,* 187–196.

Colarelli, S. M., & Stumpf, S. A. (1990). Compatibility and conflict among outcomes of organizational entry strategies: Mechanistic and social system perspective. *Behavioral Science, 35,* 1–10.

Coleman, J. S. (1974). *Power and the structure of society*. New York: W. W. Norton.

Collins, J. C., & Porras, J. I. (1994). *Built to last: Successful habits of visionary companies*. New York: Harper Business.

Commission on the Skills of the American Workforce. (1990). *America's choice: High skills or low wages!* Rochester, NY: National Center on Education and the Economy.

Comte, A. (1855/1974). *The positive philosophy*. (Harriet Martrineau, Trans.). New York: AMS Press.

Converse, P. E. (1986). Generalization and social psychology of "other worlds." In D. W. Fiske & R. A. Shweder (Eds.), *Metatheory in social science: Pluralisms and subjectivities* (pp. 42–60). Chicago: University of Chicago Press.

Crane, J. (Ed.). (1998). *Social programs that work*. New York: Russell Sage Foundation.

Cranston, M. (1967). Francis Bacon. In Paul Edwards (Ed.), *The encyclopedia of philosophy* (Vol. 1, pp. 235–240). New York: Macmillan Publishing Co., & Free Press.

Cronbach, L. J. (1986). Social inquiry by and for earthlings. In D. W. Fiske & R. A. Shweder (Eds.), *Metatheory in social science: Pluralisms and subjectivities* (pp. 83–107). Chicago: University of Chicago Press.

de Wolff, C. J. (1993). The prediction paradigm. In H. Schuler, J. Farr, & M. Smith (Eds.), *Personnel selection and assessment: Individual and organizational perspectives* (pp. 253–261). Hillsdale, NJ: Erlbaum Associates.

Diamond. J. (1999). *Guns, germs, and steel.* New York: W. W. Norton.

Dunnette, M. D. (1966). *Personnel selection and placement.* Belmont, CA: Wadsworth Publishing Co.

Dunnette, M. D. (Ed.) (1976). *Handbook of industrial and organizational psychology.* Chicago: Rand McNally.

Eastman, W. N., & Bailey, J. R. (1994). Examining the origins of management theory: Value divisions in the positivist program. *Journal of Applied Behavioral Science, 30,* 313–328.

Ferrill, A. (1986). *The fall of the Roman Empire: The military explanation.* New York: Thames & Hudson.

Fukuyama, F. (1992). *The end of history and the last man.* New York: Avon Books.

Gardner, H. (2002, February 22). Good work, well done: A psychological study. *The Chronicle of Higher Education,* pp. B7–B9.

Gharajedaghi, J., & Ackoff, R. L. (1984). Mechanisms, organisms and social systems. *Strategic Management Journal, 5,* 289–300.

Gillon, S. M. (2000). *That's not what we meant to do: Reform and its unintended consequences in twentieth-century America.* New York: W. W. Norton.

Guion, R. M. (1965). *Personnel testing.* New York: McGraw-Hill.

Hale, M., Jr. (1980). *Human science and social order: Hugo Münsterberg and the origins of applied psychology.* Philadelphia: Temple University Press.

Hartigan, J. A., & Wigdor, A. K. (Eds.) (1989). *Fairness in employment testing.* Washington, DC: National Academy Press.

Hawking, S. W. (1988). *A brief history of time.* New York: Bantam Books.

Hayek, F. A. (1952). *The counter-revolution of science.* Glencoe, IL: Free Press.

Herrnstein, R. J., & Murray, C. (1994). *The bell curve: Intelligence and class structure in American life.* New York: Free Press.

Hofstadter, R. (1972). *The Age of Reform: From Bryan to F.D.R.* New York: Alfred A. Knopf.

Hollenbeck, J. R., & Klein, H. J. (1987). Goal commitment and the goal-setting process: Problems, prospects, and proposals for future research. *Journal of Applied Psychology, 72,* 212–220.

Johns, G. (1993). Constraints on the adoption of psychology-based personnel practices: Lessons from organizational innovation. *Personnel Psychology, 46,* 569–592.

Kanigel, R. (1997). *The one best way: Frederick Winslow Taylor and the enigma of efficiency.* New York: Viking Press.

Kanter, R. M. (1983). *The change masters: Innovation for productivity in the American mode.* New York: Simon & Schuster.

Kotch, N. (1997, April 29). Yale focusing resources on strongest of programs. *New York Times,* p. B1.

Labor Letter. (1991, October 22). *Wall Street Journal,* p. A1.

Lagemann, E. C. (2000). *An elusive science: The troubling history of education research.* Chicago: University of Chicago Press.

Lemann, N. (2000). *The big test: The secret history of the American meritocracy.* New York: Farrar, Straus & Giroux.

Levy-Leboyer, C. (1994). Selection and assessment in Europe. In H. C. Triandis, M. D. Dunnette, & L. M. Hough (Eds.), *Handbook of industrial and organizational psychology* (Vol. 4, pp. 173–190). Palo Alto, CA: Consulting Psychologists Press.

Lewin, K. (1951). *Field theory in social science: Selected theoretical papers.* D. Cartwright (Ed.). New York: Harper.

Lijphart, A. (1999). *Patterns of democracy.* New Haven, CT: Yale University Press.

Likert, R. (1961). *New patterns of management.* New York: McGraw-Hill.

Lindblom, C. E., & Cohen, D. K. (1979). *Usable knowledge.* New Haven, CT: Yale University Press.

Locke, E. A., & Latham, G. P. (1990). *A theory of goal setting and task performance.* Upper Saddle River, NJ: Prentice Hall.

Loomis, C. J. (1995, May 15). Forty years of the 500. *Fortune, 131,* 182–188.

Manuel, F. E., & Manuel, F. P. (1979). *Utopian thought in the Western World.* Cambridge, MA: Belknap Press.

McGeary, T. (1995). *Society in prehistory: The origins of human culture.* New York: New York University Press.

McGregor, D. (1960). *The human side of Enterprise.* New York: McGraw-Hill.

McNeil, W. H. (1971). *A world history.* New York: Oxford University Press.

Meltzer, H., & Wickert, F. R. (1976*). Humanizing organizational behavior.* Springfield, IL: Thomas.

Moore, B. V. (1954). Educational facilities and financial assistance for graduate students in psychology: 1954–1955. *American Psychologist, 9,* 3–20.

Morgan, G. (1997). *Images of organization* (2nd ed.). Thousand Oaks, CA: Sage Publications.

Moynihan, D. P. (1996). *Miles to go.* Cambridge, MA: Harvard University Press.

Muchinsky, P. M. (2000). *Psychology applied to work: An introduction to industrial and organizational psychology* (6th ed.). Belmont, CA: Wadsworth/Thomson Learning.

Münsterberg, H. (1914). *Psychology: General and applied.* New York: Appleton.

National Center for Education Statistics, U.S. Department of Education. (1999). *Digest of Education Statistics, 1999.* Washington, DC: U.S. Government Printing Office.

National Science Foundation. (2000, February 17). *Summary of FY 2001, budget request to Congress: Summary of NSF accounts.* Arlington, VA:

National Science Foundation. Retrieved June 5, 2001, from World Wide Web: *http://www.nsf.gov/bfa/bud/ fy2001/summary.htm*

Nicholson, N. (2000). *Executive instinct: Managing the human animal in the information age.* New York: Crown Business.

Nisbett, R. E., Peng, K., Choi, I., & Norenzayan, A. (2001). Culture and systems of thought: Holistic vs. analytic cognition. *Psychological Review, 108,* 291–310.

Office of Technology Assessment. (1990). *Worker training: Competing in the new international economy* (OTA-ITE-457). Washington, DC: U.S. Government Printing Office.

Orton, D. J., & Weick, J. D. (1990). Loosely coupled systems: A reconceptualization. *Academy of Management Review, 15,* 203–223.

O'Sullivan, J. J., & Quevillon, R. P. (1992). Is the Boulder model still alive? *American Psychologist, 47,* 67–70.

Parsons, T. (1937). *The structure of social action.* New York: McGraw-Hill.

Passmore, J. A. (1970). *The perfectibility of man.* New York: Scribner Sons.

Peters, T. J., & Waterman, R. H. (1982). *In search of excellence: Lessons from America's best-run companies.* New York: Harper & Row.

Petroski, H. (1993). *The pencil: A history of design and circumstance.* New York: Alfred A. Knopf.

Pfeffer, J. (1994). *Competitive advantage through people: Unleashing the power of the work force.* Boston: Harvard Business School Press.

Phillips, J. M. (1998). Effects of realistic job previews on multiple organizational outcomes: A meta-analysis. *Academy of Management Journal, 41,* 673–690.

Plato. (1968). *The Republic of Plato.* (Allan Bloom, Trans.). New York: Basic Books.

Popper, K. R. (1966). *The open society and its enemies* (Vols. I and II). Princeton, NJ: Princeton University Press.

Porras, J. I., & Robertson, P. J. (1992). Organizational development: Theory, practice and research. In M. D. Dunnette, & L. M. Hough (Eds.), *Handbook of industrial and organizational psychology* (pp. 719–822). Palo Alto, CA: Consulting Psychologists Press.

Porter, L. W., & McKibbin, L. E. (1988). *Management education and development: Drift or thrust into the 21st century?* New York: McGraw-Hill.

Rabinbach, A. (1990). *The human motor: Energy, fatigue, and the origins of modernity.* New York: Basic Books.

Ravitch, D. (2000). *Left back: A century of failed school reforms.* New York: Simon & Schuster.

Ree, M. J., & Earles, G. A. (1992). Intelligence is the best predictor of job performance. *Current Directions in Psychological Science, 1,* 86–89.

Reich, R. B. (1991). *The work of nations: Preparing ourselves for 21st century capitalism.* New York: Alfred A. Knopf.

Roberts, K. H., Hulin, C. L., & Rosseau, D. M. (1978). *Developing an interdisciplinary science of organizations.* San Francisco: Jossey-Bass.

Rogers, E. M. (1983). *Diffusion of innovation*. New York: Free Press.

Ryle, G. (1967). *Plato's progress*. Cambridge: Cambridge University Press.

Saari, L. M., Johnson, T. R., McLaughlin, S. D., & Zimmerle, D. M. (1988). A survey of management training and education practices in U.S. companies. *Personnel Psychology, 41,* 731–743.

Savage, L. J. (1954). *The foundations of statistics*. New York: John Wiley & Sons.

Sackett, P. R. (1986). I/O psychology: The state of practice. *Professional Practice of Psychology, 7,* 15–26.

Schein, E. H. (1969). *Process consultation: Its role in organization development*. Reading, MA: Addison-Wesley.

Schmidt, F. L. (1993). Personnel psychology at the cutting edge. In N. Schmitt & W. C. Borman (Eds.), *Personnel selection in organizations* (pp. 497–515). San Francisco: Jossey-Bass.

Schmidt, F. L., & Hunter, J. E. (1983). Individual differences in productivity: An empirical test of estimates derived from studies of selection procedure utility. *Journal of Applied Psychology, 68,* 407–414.

Schmidt, F. L., Hunter, J. E., Mckenzie, R. C., & Muldrow, T. W. (1979). Impact of valid selection procedures on work-force productivity. *Journal of Applied Psychology, 64,* 609–626.

Schneer, C. J. (1960). *The search for order, the development of the major ideas in the physical sciences from the earlier time to the present*. New York: Harper.

Schneider, B. (1987). The people make the place. *Personnel Psychology, 40,* 437–453.

Schneider, B., & Schmitt, N. (1986). *Staffing organizations* (2nd ed.). Glenview, IL: Scott Foresman.

Scott, A. O. (2001, January 7). The smarty-pants king. *New York Times Magazine*, pp. 20–21.

Scott, W. R. (1998). *Organizations* (4th ed.). Upper Saddle River, NJ: Prentice Hall.

Sears, R. R. (1946). Graduate training facilities: I. General information, II. Clinical psychology. *The American Psychologist, 1,* 135–150.

Shanklin, W. L. (1986). Fortune 500 dropouts. *Planning Review, 14,* 12–17.

Shipper, F. (1999). A comparison of managerial skills of middle managers with MBAs, with other masters and undergraduate degrees ten years after the Porter and McKibbin report. *Journal of Managerial Psychology, 14,* 150–163.

Skinner, B. F. (1971). *Beyond freedom and dignity*. New York: Alfred A. Knopf.

Snyder, R. A., & Morris, J. H. (1984). Organizational communication and performance. *Journal of Applied Psychology, 69,* 461–465.

Society for Industrial and Organizational Psychology. (1987). *Principles for the validation and use of personnel selction procedures* (3rd ed.). College Park, MD: Author.

Sowell, T. (1995). *The vision of the anointed: Self-congratulation as a basis for social policy*. New York: Basic Books.

Taylor, F. W. (1967). *The principles of scientific management*. New York: W. W. Norton. (Original work published 1911.)

Taylor, F. W. (1911). *Shop management*. New York, London: Harper & Brothers.

Terpstra, D. E. & Rozell, J. (1997). Why some potentially effective staffing practices are seldom used? *Public Personnel Management, 26*, 483–495.

Thurow, L. C. (1992). *Head to head: the coming economic battle among Japan, Europe, and America*. New York: William Morrow.

Toulmin, S. (1990, June 28). A question of character. *New York Review of Books, 37*, 48–51.

Toulmin, S. (1977). From form to function: Philosophy and history of science in the 1950s and now. *Daedlalus, 106*, 143–162.

U.S. Census Bureau, Department of Commerce. (n.d.). *Statistics about business size (including small business)*. Washington, DC: U.S. Census Bureau. Retrieved June 4, 2001, from World Wide Web: *http://www.census.gov/ epcd/www/smallbus.html*

U.S. Department of Labor. (n.d). Occupational Safety and Health Administration. *Fatal workplace injuries*. Washington, DC: U.S. Department of Labor. Retrieved May 30, 2001, from the World Wide Web: *http:// www.osha.gov/oshstats/privtbl.html*

U.S. Department of Labor. (n.d). Occupational Safety and Health Administration. *Occupational injury and illness incidence rates per 100 full-time workers, 1973–1998*. Washington, DC: U.S. Department of Labor. Retrieved May 30, 2001, from the World Wide Web: *http//www.osha.gov/ oshstats/bltable.html*

U.S. News & World Report. (2001). 2001 Best graduate school: Top business schools. *U.S. News*. Retrieved June 5, 2001, from World Wide Web: *http://www.usnews.com/usnews/edu/beyond/gradrank/mba/mbatables/ gdmbas1.htm*

U.S. Small Business Administration, Office of Advocacy. (1999). *The State of Small Business: A Report of the President, 1998*. Washington, DC: Government Printing Office.

Wanous, J. P. (1973). Effects of job realistic preview on job acceptance, job attitude, and job survival. *Journal of Applied Psychology, 58*, 327–332.

Westfall, R. S. (1971). *The construction of modern science: Mechanisms and mechanics*. New York: John Wiley & Sons.

Williams, G. C. (1996). *Plan and purpose in nature*. London: Weidenfeld & Nicolson.

Wilson, E. O. (1998). *Consilience: The unity of knowledge*. New York: Alfred A. Knopf.

Zedeck, S., & Cascio, W. F. (1984). Psychological issues in personnel decisions. *Annual Review of Psychology, 35*, 461–518.

CHAPTER 2

Storms, Pilots, and Byzantium
The Evolutionary Perspective

All that man is,
All mere complexities,
The fury and the mire of human veins.
                    —William Butler Yeats (*Byzantium*, 1933/1962)

Man and rat are both incredibly stupid in an experimental room.
On the other hand, psychology has paid little attention to the things
they do in their normal habitats; man drives a car, plays complicated
games, and organizes society, and rat is troublesomely cunning in
the kitchen.
                    —Masanao Toda (1962, p. 165)

Probably the best illustration of a theory of complex phenomena
of great value though it describes merely a general pattern, whose
detail we can never fill in, is the Darwinian theory of evolution by
natural selection. It is significant that this theory has always been
something of a stumbling block for the dominant conception of
scientific method. It certainly does not fit the orthodox criteria of
"prediction and control" as the hallmarks of scientific method. Yet
it cannot be denied that it has become the successful foundation of
the whole of modern biology.
                    —Friedrich A. Hayek (1964, pp. 340–341)

THE MARVEL OF HUMAN ORGANIZATIONS

Organizations are messy, often unpleasant, places. However, like a wasp's nest or a bird's wings, human organizations are also marvels of evolved design. Despite their problems, when all is said and done, most organizations work, at least for a while and at least pretty well. Some work better than others and last longer. It is hard to make changes that improve them. Interventions may produce broad, general patterns, but it is foolishness to presume that they regularly produce specific, intended effects. These are some of the basic conclusions of the evolutionary perspective on organizations. Those with this perspective are *respectful tinkerers*. They marvel at human organizations, admiring their complexity and their ability to survive for a while and to achieve some objectives despite their inherent messiness. Useful changes come about more through tinkering and increments of trial and error than from grand design. In contrast to the constructive utopians—who, we will recall, regard organizations as malfunctioning, sputtering machines requiring expert mechanics before they can function adequately—respectful tinkerers regard organizations as repositories of functional wisdom, developed and honed over the years by evolutionary processes.

Consider the complexity involved in getting a simple meal, say a hamburger, in a restaurant in New York City. The food is grown in different parts of the country and world (vegetables in New Jersey, in season, perhaps in Florida in the winter; wheat for the bun from Kansas; beef from Montana or perhaps Argentina). The raw material is processed into semifinished or finished goods. These are then sent to distributors, who in turn sell them to restaurants in New York City and elsewhere. The restaurant is either in its own building or, more likely, located in a portion of a larger building. Someone had to design and build it, others manage it, rent offices and storefronts, and keep it working—cool in the summer, warm in the winter—and in good repair. The restaurant needs electricity, natural gas, and running water to produce its products and to serve customers. It needs streets and public transportation to ensure that people can get to the restaurant to buy a hamburger. Cooking hardware—stoves, pots, and pans—must be purchased and kept clean and in working order. The restaurant has an identity, a name and décor to differentiate it from all the other restaurants. It markets its products in media outlets. It hires and trains people to cook and sell the hamburgers. There must be a common language so that people working in the restaurant and customers can understand one another.[1] All this for a hamburger![2]

That we can buy a hamburger in New York City is not the result of a brilliant hamburger czar planning everything out to the smallest detail

and issuing commands. It is the result of hundreds of—often independent—details, decisions, and activities. Not only can people get a good
hamburger of any imaginable variety in New York City, but they can
get almost any imaginable type of meal. New York City is an epicure's
paradise. The city is full of marvelous restaurants and delicatessens ca-
tering to every taste. All of this occurs day in and day out, year after
year, without a grand plan. A simple hamburger involves a complex
matrix of human organization. More complex goods and services generate organizational processes that are all the more remarkable. Airlines
have their problems; yet it is also true that just about anyone with a
credit card and passport can buy a ticket and fly almost anywhere in
the world within 24 hours. What is perhaps more remarkable is that,
on most occasions, you will arrive within minutes of the scheduled
arrival time.

Complex organization is nothing new. The armies of Alexander the
Great and the ancient Roman Empire were marvels of complex organization, as were the construction bureaucracies of ancient Egypt and the
Middle Ages. People were able to develop and maintain highly sophisticated forms of social organization thousands of years before the advent of social science, applied psychology, industrial engineering, and
management consultants. Yet, complex organizations come and go. The
Roman Empire eventually fell into decline and disintegrated. Restaurants
eventually are sold, evolve into something else, or go out of business.
Although we cannot expect that *any particular* restaurant or army will
last indefinitely, the processes that create and maintain organizations are
regular and robust.

The Utilization Paradox

> One of the most commonly used and least valid of all predictors is
> the letter of recommendation. . . . Because of their limited validity,
> letters of recommendation should not be taken too seriously in
> making personnel decisions.
> —Paul M. Muchinsky (1999, pp. 123–124)

> Assistant and/or Associate Professor to teach in the areas of Entre-
> preneurial Management, Human Resource Management, Multina-
> tional Management, Strategic Management and Organizational
> Behavior Management. Candidates must have outstanding research
> potential as well as strong interest and competence in teaching.
> Salary is competitive. Indicate in your cover letter areas you wish
> to be considered for. Send application materials—cover letter, *three*

letters of recommendation, sample publications and abstracts—
. . . to: . . .
                    —University of Pennsylvania, The Wharton School
                                  (1999, p. 4; emphasis added)

Two paradoxes in modern human resource management are: (1) the continued and widespread use—even by social scientists themselves—of traditional practices that social science has pronounced invalid, and (2) the low rates of utilization among most private sector organizations of human resource practices that have been developed by social scientists. Letters of recommendation and employment interviews are widely used traditional hiring methods. Letters of recommendation are commonplace and have a significant impact on hiring decisions (Bureau of National Affairs, 1988; Friedman & Williams, 1982; Levy-Leboyer, 1994). Yet traditional letters of recommendation are notoriously unreliable; they are also poor predictors of job performance and are biased (Aamodt, Bryan, & Whitcomb, 1993; Muchinsky, 1979). The employment interview is also the most widely used selection method in the United States and Britain, and it has the strongest impact on the hiring decisions (Friedman & Williams, 1982). Yet the numerous reviews of the human resource literature on the subject have concluded that the employment interview is a poor predictor of job performance (Arvey & Campion, 1982; Harris, 1989; Wiesner & Cronshaw, 1988). On the other hand, few private sector organizations use mechanistic hiring methods—such as tests of cognitive ability, biographical questionnaires, and assessment centers—despite the considerable amount of research that has been conducted on them and the pronouncements by industrial psychologists that they are vastly superior to traditional methods (American Management Association, 1986; Friedman & Williams, 1982; Levy-Leboyer, 1994; Terpstra & Rozell, 1997). The same curious state of affairs exists with training methods, performance appraisal, leadership and supervision practices, and organizational design (Latham, 1988; Murphy & Cleveland, 1995).

Some cautious applied psychologists say that their advice is ignored because their field is young and has not had the time to mature; its methods and statistics are inadequate and more convincing research needs to be conducted. Other industrial psychologists believe that their pronouncements are correct: their interventions work (Cascio, 1998; Murphy, 1996; Schmidt, 1993). Ignoring their recommendations is a mistake, based on ignorance and prejudice.[3] These psychologists say that all that is needed is a better effort at educating the benighted about the value of professional applications of social science. Terpstra and Rozell

(1997) argue that there are not enough people with Ph.D.s in HRM in organizations. Many HR managers are not sufficiently knowledgeable to explain the latest scientific findings to operating managers. This problem would be alleviated if organizations hired more HR experts. Another approach that was popular for a time among industrial psychologists was utility analysis—a complex algebra attempting to estimate the economic value of HR interventions. The idea behind utility analysis was that mathematical demonstrations linking HR activities to economic payoffs would do the trick and convince managers that HR interventions were worthwhile. Although a virtual cottage industry developed around utility analysis among personnel psychologists from the 1970s through the early 1990s, enthusiasm for it faded by the mid-1990s. Utility analysis is emblematic of the problem associated with efforts to demonstrate that social science interventions "really" work. Continuing cycles like utility analysis come and go, suggesting that there are other, more fundamental reasons (such as the uncertainty inherent in social systems) why the claims of the constructive utopians are regularly ignored.

The perspective that psychologists use in thinking about interventions is the more probable reason for the utilization paradox. Applied psychology involves assumptions about human nature and about organizations—about systems, knowledge, and change. To the extent that a perspective is at odds with how people and organizations actually function, interventions based on that perspective are unlikely to meet expectations. The mechanical design perspective is, for the most part, at odds with how people and organizations function. The assumptions of the evolutionary perspective, on the other hand, are not.

EVOLUTION BY NATURAL SELECTION

The term *evolution* has had an important place in the history of biology, going back at least to the seventeenth century (Richards, 1992). The first biological meaning of their term apparently was *recapitulation*—the notion that an embryo of a higher organism would pass through the adult forms of lower forms of life as it developed. A later common historical meaning was change of species—the descent of a species from other species over time. The common meanings of the term now denote a process of formation or growth over time, or biological development over time through natural selection (Stein & Su, 1980). The first applies to nonbiological as well as biological evolution. Over the past 50 years we have witnessed the evolution of the computer from large machines using vacuum-tube technology taking up the space of a large room to small machines using microprocessors that can fit into a briefcase. The second meaning is based on Darwin's theory of evolution by natural selection. With these two meanings of the term as a starting point, we can discuss the evolutionary perspective. The evolutionary perspective, whether biological or sociocultural, can be characterized by seven key ideas: (1) natural selection through variation–selection–retention, (2) historical incrementalism, (3) exquisite but not perfect design, (4) conflict, (5) the interplay between biology and culture, (6) the "purpose" of evolution by natural selection, and (7) adaptations and functional wisdom. In broad strokes, the first idea defines evolution by natural selection, the second through the fifth ideas describe how it works, and the last two describe the products of the evolutionary process.

Natural selection through variation, selection, and retention follows from Darwin's three postulates, which I have modified slightly so that they are applicable to both biological and cultural evolution. The first postulate is that without constraints, populations can expand indefinitely; however, because resources are limited, the capacity of an environment to support any population is limited. The second is that the units of which a population is composed, such as organisms or social structures, vary; that is, they differ in slight ways from one another. These variations affect the ability of units to survive and replicate. The third postulate is that many, but not all, variations are transmitted from generation to generation. Variations that help a unit to survive become more numerous in subsequent generations, as long as the environment remains relatively unchanged.

Variation is of fundamental importance to evolution, for without variation, there can be no evolution. Variation is the production of differentiated elements in a system and its environment. Some variability has a positive influence on the fitness of a system. Reduced variation lowers adaptability, while sufficient variation helps to ensure that adaptive responses will be available as an organization's environment changes (Klingsporn, 1973). The idea that variation produces robust systems has a long history in evolutionary biology, and numerous studies have shown how important variability is to the viability of species and ecosystems (e. g., Grant, 1986).[4] Jared Diamond (1997) has developed a hypothesis about variability and early plant domestication in which he argues that variability was the major reason plant domestication first occurred in the Fertile Crescent rather than in other areas with similar climates and soil conditions. The Fertile Crescent, which extends eastward from what is now central Turkey through Jordan, Syria, and Iraq, and ends on the western border of the Zagros Mountains, "had the greatest climatic variation from season to season" (p. 138) among the Mediterranean zones. That climatic variation favored the evolution of a high percentage of annual plants (which are most suitable to domestication). The Fertile Crescent also had a variety of altitudes, which led to "staggered harvest seasons," (p. 140), thereby increasing the probability of domestication. A third advantage was that the Fertile Crescent contained considerable "biological diversity over small distance" (p. 141). This created a wealth of plants (and animals), increasing the probability of the existence of species that could be domesticated.

The principle of variation–selection–retention also operates in sexual selection, a special type of evolution by natural selection. The difference between natural and sexual selection is the reason for the evolution of a trait. With natural selection, traits evolve because they are directly related to survival and reproduction—the osprey's talons, the rabbit's running speed, the nurturing behavior of female mammals toward their young. With sexual selection, the criteria for the evolution of a trait are attractiveness to the opposite sex and besting other males in competition for females (Cronin, 1991). The classic example of sexual selection for attractiveness is the peacock's tail. The peacock's large, ornamental tail does not directly help the peacock survive and reproduce. In fact, it can be a hindrance because a large colorful tail makes a peacock more visible to predators and makes it more difficult to escape from them. However, the peacock's tail helps with reproduction: it is attractive to peahens. Peahens are more likely to mate with peacocks with large colorful tails than those with smaller, drab tails. The male deer's antlers are classic examples of sexual selection for competition. Antlers evolved through sexual selection as weapons to battle with other male deer in their annual competition for female deer. It is plausible that many human creative talents evolved through sexual selection (Miller, 2000).

Selection and retention mechanisms reject variations that are not adaptive and retain those that are adaptive. Evolution by natural selection operates by *consequences*, not intentions: systems with adaptive variations are more likely to survive and reproduce, while those with nonadaptive variations are less likely to survive and reproduce. Natural selection operates at individual levels and on the basis of individual self-interest, not at the group level and not on the basis of group interests. In biological evolution, natural selection operates at the level of genes, and it does so by retaining genetic variations that contribute to the propagation of the individual's genes (Williams, 1996). Nevertheless, the principle of variation–selection–retention, operating at the level of the individual, produces large complex adaptive systems. Thus, highly complex biological and social design emerges from a process of blind trial and error over time among individuals pursuing their genetic interests (Dawkins, 1986; Williams, 1996).

Evolution occurs through small incremental changes rather than through monumental leaps. Variation follows variation; small change follows small change. Dawkins (1986) gives three reasons why incrementalism (rather than large leaps) is a more probable explanation for the size of ongoing evolutionary changes. Although he gives them as three separate reasons, they are loosely related to a common thread: the ecology of interdependencies that is necessary for any system to survive. The first rather obvious reason why evolutionary change is more likely to occur incrementally than by leaps is that if a macro-mutation occurred in one member of a species, there would be no one to mate with. One might extend this logic to change in social systems as well. If a social practice were introduced in a social system that was dramatically different from other practices, there would be no connection between them. There would be few, if any, systems of support, institutional memory, few feedback mechanisms, and little basic know-how about how to make the intervention work. The same is usually true of large technological innovations. I recall from my days as a Peace Corps volunteer in Senegal how modern irrigation systems and American tractors would fall into disrepair and then disuse because there were few spare parts, few parts distribution systems, and few mechanics trained to repair American machinery.

Second, a system is more likely to move successfully from an existing condition to a different condition when the change is small. The explanation is simple. The probability that a major change will harm the system is greater than the probability that a small change will do harm (see Dawkins, 1986, pp. 231 ff., and Dennett, 1995, pp. 282 ff.). Dawkins borrows R. A. Fisher's microscope analogy to illustrate this point. If a very small object in a microscope is out of focus, a large adjustment to the microscope is much more likely to make matters worse than a small adjustment. Years earlier, Edmund Burke (1790/1964) made a similar argument about social change. A social system is a complex matrix of customs and relationships that often have been honed over hundreds, perhaps thousands, of years. Accordingly, a large change is more likely to disrupt customs and the complex institutional patterns than small changes.

The third reason is that evolution typically—though not inevitably—proceeds in the direction of greater complexity. Single-celled organisms tend to evolve into multicelled organisms; hunter-gatherer groups tend to evolve into complex societies. Some small businesses evolve into large, complex corporations. That being the case, large changes are problematic because leapfrogging from a simple system to a complex system requires that all the intervening parts and relationships be developed and set into motion simultaneously. This is one reason why Russia's change from a command economy to capitalism did not go like clockwork and is still sputtering, although it is progressing. It was too daunting a task to put everything into place when almost nothing existed in the first place—entrepreneurs, distribution systems, capital markets, and so on (Johnson, 2000).

The *pace* of evolution is a different matter from the size of evolutionary change, although the difference has been a source of some confusion due to strange interpretations and revisions of the theory of punctuated equilibrium. The gaps in the fossil evidence have been something of a problem for evolutionary theory, as Darwin himself noted. For some time it was assumed that evolution proceeded both incrementally and gradually. Gaps in the fossil record were difficult to explain and were used by some (and still are today) to discredit the theory of evolution by natural selection. Eldredge and Gould (1972) proposed a theory of punctuated equilibrium to explain the gaps solidly within the framework of neo-Darwinian logic. The initial theory made the simple and obvious point that evolution does not necessarily proceed gradually. Rather, there are long periods during which relatively little change takes place and other periods when it is rapid.[5] A problem arose when the theory began to be interpreted not as one about the pace of change but as a theory of the size of change. Pace and size became conflated—the theory came to be interpreted to mean that rapid changes were evidence of large, nonincremental changes. Dawkins (1986) and Dennett (1995) pointed out the foolishness of this interpretation, and they made it clear that punctuated equilibrium is no big deal. It is simply the notion—firmly within Darwinian theory—that evolution can proceed at different paces. However, regardless of the pace, the size of evolutionary change still tends to remain, on average, small and incremental.

Evolution is historical. Current organisms and social systems are products of a historical lineage; the features of an organism or social system are the result, in large measure, of adaptations to past environments. A large part of understanding why an organism or a social system is the way it is now requires understanding its history—the conditions under which it evolved and how it evolved. Changes build on existing structures that evolved under circumstances that may be quite different from the conditions under which new adaptations are emerging.

Evolved biological or cultural systems are rarely ideal. Evolved systems tend to be exquisite but far from perfect. They are satisfactory or "pretty good" in the sense that they work; they contribute to survival and reproduction. Adaptations perform useful functions. Indeed, biological and social systems and their parts are exquisite—the human eye, the hummingbird's wings, modern corporations, universities. However, evolved systems do not imply conflict-free, perfectly coordinated parts, operating in an optimal fashion. Exquisite as it is, the human eye has a blind spot where the optic nerve exits the eye. This is not the case for all eyes; the eyes of mollusks do not have a blind spot. Our blind spot is the result of a particular "cumulative historical burden" (Williams, 1996, p. 10).

Evolved systems also tend to be underengineered. That is, there are no precise instructions for performance under all circumstances. Although underengineered systems are less standardized and things are not necessarily done in the same way every time, they run pretty well most of the time. Underengineered systems also tend to be more flexible than highly engineered systems, and this allows for more variation and ongoing adjustment. But there is a price for such flexibility: variability and error. Underengineered systems are less rigid, so their outputs are not entirely consistent and they are likely to produce some mistakes. Nevertheless, variation and mistakes sometimes result in beneficial innovations (Alchian, 1950).

Variation is necessary for evolution to occur, and small mistakes and errors are an important source of variation, as Thomas (1974) brilliantly illustrates. The point also applies to sociocultural evolution.

> The capacity to blunder slightly is the real marvel of DNA. Without this special attribute, we would still be anaerobic bacteria and there would be no music. Viewed individually, one by one, each of the mutations that have brought us along represents a random, totally spontaneous accident, but it is no accident at all that mutations occur; the molecule of DNA was ordained from the beginning to make small mistakes.
>
> If we had been doing it, we would have found some way to correct this and evolution would have been stopped in its tracks. Imagine the consternation of human scientists, successfully engaged in the letter-perfect replication of prokaryotes, nonnucleated cells like bacteria, when nucleated cells suddenly turned up. Think of the agitated commissions assembled to explain the scandalous proliferation of trilobites all over the place, the mass firings, the withdrawal of tenure.
>
> To err is human, we say, but we don't like the idea much, and it is harder still to accept the fact that erring is biological as well. We prefer sticking to the point, and insuring ourselves against change. (Thomas, 1974, pp. 28–29)

Conflict is part and parcel of evolution by natural selection. It is inevitable in the evolutionary process because of competition for scarce resources in pursuit of self-interest. Competition over scarce resources is a major reason why natural selection occurs. If there were no competition, then no characteristics would have a survival advantage over others. Self-interest virtually assures that units in complex systems will be in conflict over differing interests (Alexander, 1987). What is in one individual's self-interest is not always in another individual's interest. As Alexander (1987, p. 77) wisely remarks, "it is difficult to exaggerate the significance of conflicts of interests." In biological evolution, there is conflict among phenotypes for the perpetuation of genes; in sociocultural evolution, there is competition among recipes for living and organizing.

Human cultural evolution is, to a significant degree, a result of human biology (Lumsden & Wilson, 1983; Tooby & Cosmides, 1992). As E. O. Wilson remarked, biology keeps culture on a leash. Human tool making is possible because of two primary biological facts: our opposable thumbs and our cerebral cortex. Our opposable thumbs allow us to manipulate and create artifacts, and our cortex allows us to imagine, design, and create. Most of our social and cultural activities evolved around and occur during the day because we cannot see well at night due to the limited number of cones in our eyes. Miller (2000) argues convincingly that much of the creative side of human culture—literature, music, drama, adornment, oratory, repartee, and so on—is due to sexual selection. Human females found creative, intelligent, and witty males more attractive, which in turn created selection pressure for those traits, and those traits helped to spawn much of human culture. Evolved sex differences in aggression influenced the nature of human warfare across cultures and time. As Buss points out, "The fact that men across cultures form coalitions whose purpose is to kill men in other coalitions is observed across cultures. . . . In no culture have women ever been observed forming coalitions designed to kill other human beings" (1999, p. 302).

Culture also affects biology. Increased mobility produces a greater frequency of racial intermarriage. Genetic outbreeding increases hybrid vigor. Nagoshi and Johnson (1986) found that the offspring of two parents who are genetically dissimilar couples (one parent of European ancestry, one of Japanese ancestry) tend to have higher IQs than the children from genetically similar couples (both parents of European or Japanese ancestry). Culture can affect the distribution and frequency of traits. Institutions where young people congregate and find marriage partners are increasingly segregated by IQ, and this in turn affects their offsprings' IQs (Herrnstein & Murray, 1994). Many high schools use cognitive ability tests to segregate students into curriculums that channel them toward or away from a university education; many types of occupations and organizations where young people find their first jobs are also segregated by IQ. The evolutionary perspective regards the old dichotomies of nature and nurture and culture and biology as less distinct and more interactive. Ultimately, they are false dichotomies and artificial.

Evolution is not goal directed in the sense of achieving any particular design. It does not involve a continuing progression to any sort of "higher" state of affairs or design. Rather, evolution operates by continually adjusting to the environment. Although evolution tends to proceed in the direction of greater complexity, this is not a purpose but a general tendency. Evolution is a process of consequences that systems experience—either changing or dying off—in response to changes in their environment. The prime governor of biological evolution is *inclusive fitness*—the propagation of the genes of individual organisms, either through reproduction or helping with the survival and reproduction of relatives (Williams, 1996). Sociocultural evolution is less well understood and probably more complex than biological evolution, but, as with biological evolution, consequences are what matter. It assumes that most behavioral norms, values, and social structures operate ultimately in the service of the biological survival and reproduction of individuals (Boyd & Richerson, 1985; Ridley, 1996; Tooby & Cosmides, 1992). Certainly, there is some degree of intention in the design of social systems. When an entrepreneur builds a business to make and sell chocolate bars, clearly two purposes of that organization are to make and sell chocolate bars. On the other hand, much of the design and purpose of social systems is *incidental* to the individual interests of their members. Beyond this, questions of purpose in sociocultural systems are largely ethereal.

Although evolution per se has no specific purpose, most *parts* of evolved systems have a specific function. They have been sculpted over time to perform specific functions that contribute to an organism's ability to survive and reproduce (Williams, 1966). The function of the eye is to enable an organism to see; the function of wings is to enable birds to fly; the function of the heart is to pump blood. Each part contributes to the ultimate goal of inclusive fitness—the successful transmission of one's genes into future generations by successful reproduction and by helping kin survive and reproduce. Parts that contribute to an organism's survival are called *adaptations*. An adaptation is "something functionally effective that arises from the long-continued action of natural selection" (Williams, 1996, p. 3; see also Buss, Haselton, Shackelford, Bleske, & Wakefield, 1998). An *adaptation* is any feature of an organism that has been important to increasing inclusive fitness, that is, the propagation of genes into future generations, either directly or by helping kin survive and reproduce (Williams, 1966, 1996). Adaptations serve a *function* reflected in "special design." The purpose of wings on most birds is flight; the purpose of the eye is to enable the organism to see; and so on. What distinguishes adaptations from other parts is *special design* (Williams, 1966). The features of special design are functionality, reliability, complexity, and good design. Psychological mechanisms are particularly important adaptations to human behavior and culture. They are neural processes that predispose people to behave or to make choices in particular ways in response to specific environmental stimuli. (Psychological mechanisms will be discussed at greater length later in this chapter in the section on evolutionary psychology.)

Of course, organisms have parts that are not adaptations. Buss (1999) classifies them as byproducts or noise (Buss, 1999). I would add a third category: leftovers. Byproducts are parts that do not solve adaptive problems but are coupled with adaptations. The belly button is not useful for survival and reproduction, but it is coupled with something that is, the umbilical cord. Noise is the random effects produced by natural selection that are neither functional nor carried along by adaptations. The shape of an individual's belly button is essentially random (Buss, 1999). Leftovers are remnants of adaptations that continue to be passed on reliably but no longer appear to serve a useful purpose. Leftovers in humans include nipples on males, muscles to move the outer ear, and the troublesome appendix.

Parts of social systems can also be thought of as adaptations—more precisely, as social adaptations. These are functionally effective social structures or processes that arise from the long-continued action of natural selection in sociocultural evolution. Social adaptations are the result of many years of trial-and-error learning, are passed on by learning from generation to generation, and help social systems survive. Therefore, it is quite likely that many traditional structures and processes have adaptive value (Campbell, 1975). However, it may not always be clear to human observers what purpose evolved adaptations served.

> Natural selection describes a process by which stupid, blind, unforesightful processes can produce adaptive wisdom. Just as human and octopus eyes have a functional wisdom that none of the participating cells or genes have ever had self-conscious awareness of, so in social evolution we can contemplate a process in which adaptive belief systems could be accumulated which none of the innovators, transmitters, or participants properly understood, a tradition wiser than any of the persons transmitting it. (Campbell, 1975, p. 1107)

Scholars and scientists with an evolutionary perspective regard evolved phenomena with scientific curiosity and respect. This attitude is generally absent among social scientists.

> When an evolutionary biologist encounters some ludicrous and puzzling form of animal life he approaches it with a kind of awe, certain that behind the bizarre form lies a functional wisdom that he has yet to understand. I believe the case for sociocultural evolution is strong enough so that psychologists and other social scientists, when considering an apparently bizarre, incomprehensible feature of their own social tradition, or that of another culture, should approach it with a similar awe, expecting that when eventually understood, when our theories have caught up with it, that seemingly bizarre superstition will turn out to make an adaptive sense. I find such an attitude totally missing in psychology... today. (Campbell, 1975, p. 1105)

This does not mean that a given adaptation is the best way something could be done. It means that applied social scientists should treat existing social structures and interventions with respect and curiosity; that they should approach them with a sense of curiosity about why they exist, what functions they serve, and what aspects of human nature predisposed people to develop and use them. That we may not know the adaptive significance of a traditional structure or practice does not mean that it is useless or harmful or that a newly designed structure will be an improvement. The economist and Nobel Laureate Friedrich A. Von Hayek makes this point:

> While the assumption of a sufficient knowledge of the concrete facts generally produces a sort of intellectual *hubris* which deludes itself that reason can judge all values, the insight into the impossibility of such full knowledge induces an attitude of humility and reverence toward the experience of mankind as a whole which has been precipitated in the values and institutions of existing society. (p. 348)

An Evolutionary Perspective

From an evolutionary perspective, it makes more sense to think of social systems as storms rather than clocks; to think of people as pilots rather than cave dwellers; and to think of the interventions as producing generally good but fallible outcomes (like the ancient city of Byzantium) rather than utopias. Although storms exhibit some regular characteristics—tornadoes have a funnel-like shape—their behavior is so complex as to be unpredictable. Although we might be able to gauge a storm's general direction, it is impossible to determine exactly what it will do or exactly where it will go. The evolutionary perspective is a stark contrast to mechanical design. Evolutionary theory views biological and social systems resulting from a slow process of small incremental change—adapting to their environments—rather than from *a priori* design. Evolutionary processes are too complex to fully predict their outcomes.

People are more like pilots than cave dwellers. Like pilots, they can operate very effectively in the world on the basis of practical, working knowledge. That they lack complete understanding of the world does not stop them from boldly exploring and acting effectively in it. Pilots master complex tasks (such as sailing a ship or flying an airplane). Through training and experience, with the application of intricate mental and physical abilities, people can learn to perform difficult and demanding activities. Although the pilot may not understand all of the scientific principles of flight, buoyancy, or navigation, he is still able to perform expertly and under variable, difficult, and novel conditions. It is possible to perform effectively even with limited knowledge.

Self-interest, conflicts of interest, changes in the environment, chance occurrences, incomplete knowledge, and limited control prevent the realization of utopian social systems. However, this is not to say that *reasonably* good social systems are impossible. It is possible to develop policies that enhance the probability that reasonably good systems will emerge. Some social systems that emerge realize more of the values of people than others. People live in greater safety, are free to pursue and express their creative instincts, and are more likely to find health and abundance. These might be likened to the civilization of Byzantium. Located at the crossroads of Europe and Asia, the Byzantine Empire lasted nearly 1,000 years (from the sixth century A.D. to 1453). Byzantine civilization was famous for achievements in arts, architecture, law, engineering, religion, and urban design. It was a crossroads where people and ideas from the East and West interacted and flourished. Byzantium was by no means a utopia, but by all accounts it was one of the great cities. It did not spring up fully formed from one grand design, but it evolved over time, within a historical context, and informed by certain values. Like all evolved systems, it eventually changed.

SOCIOCULTURAL EVOLUTION

Sociocultural evolution involves a Lamarckian type of evolution by natural selection whereby *acquired* characteristics—such as behaviors and values—are socially selected and retained (Boyd & Richerson, 1985;

Campbell, 1975). Some changes involve pure chance, but some social change is guided. Imitation, learning, and analysis play important roles in social evolution (Boyd & Richerson, 1985). As with biological evolution, the juice of sociocultural evolution is variation.

Variation–Selection–Retention

Two basic principles of natural selection also operate in social systems: (1) there is variation in forms, and (2) variation in forms relates to variation in survival and replication (Baum & Singh, 1994). Through mechanisms of cultural selection, organizations select some variations and typically retain those that are functional (Campbell, 1965; Weick, 1979).[6] However, the apparent utility of a human resource intervention does not ensure that organizations will select it or use it. Circumstances must favor its inclusion into a pool of variations available to organizations, selection mechanisms must capitalize on it, and conditions must favor its retention.

The production of social variation derives from economic needs, as well as from cultural and psychological forces. Social values, fantasy, and play contribute to variation, as well as scientific knowledge (cf. Basalla, 1988). Immigration, travel, the mix of cultures, and imperfect imitation also contribute. Selection in sociocultural evolution involves the choice of one variation from several. The selection systems in organizations include rational decision making, rules of thumb, imitation, and choice of leaders (Boyd & Richerson, 1985; Campbell, 1965; Endsley, 1997; Weick, 1979). The selection system traditionally favored by applied psychologists is meticulously calculating the likelihood that a decision will lead to a favored outcome (Johns, 1993). Variations of this approach are called "subjective expected utility" or "rational decision making." Yet, this method is not commonly used in organizational decision making or in many of the ordinary decisions that ordinary people make day in and day out during the course of their lives (Gigerenzer, Todd, & the ABC Research Group, 1999; Zsambok & Klein, 1997). It is too costly and complex. Managers typically make decisions using rules of thumb (Boyd & Richerson, 1985; March & Simon, 1958).

Boyd and Richerson (1985) illustrate the problems with rational decision making with a parable they call the Bayesian Horticulturalist (pp. 87 ff.). The parable describes a group of horticulturalists who move to a new area. Each man must decide how much land to cultivate in order to feed his family. However, there is one man whose plot may not yield enough produce to feed his family, so to hedge his bets, the Bayesian horticulturalist helps other men in their gardens. The custom is that a family must share some of its food with the person who helped them if the person runs short, but only if the person runs short. Yet it is also possible that the Bayesian horticulturalist may still run short, in which case he would have to borrow food from the headman, who charges exorbitant interest rates. "Being rational, the Bayesian horticulturist seeks to feed his family with the least amount of extra work" (p. 88). Boyd and Richerson describe the mathematical calculations that a horticulturalist would need to perform to rationally determine the amount of labor he must invest in helping his neighbors as a function of the probable yield of his field, his family's needs, and the cost of borrowing food from the headman. The calculations are formidable.

> To satisfy the canons of rationality, the Bayesian horticulturalist had to specify precisely an unrealistically large amount of information about the environment in the form of prior probability distribution and the likelihood function and then perform computations that are too difficult for anyone but mathematicians. As posed, the problem of the Bayesian horticulturist is an extremely simple problem—much, much simpler than any real decision facing a tropical horticulturalist. The difficulty and complexity of most real problems is so great as to preclude normatively rational choice. Even modern corporations that can afford to expend enormous resources . . . are unable to conform to the canons of Bayesian rationality. . . .
>
> Nonetheless, both humans and other animals seem to behave in an understandable, adaptive fashion. How do they achieve this semblance of rationality? It seems likely that the answer to this question is that both humans and other animals use simple "rules of thumb" to make decisions. It is plausible that simple rules of thumb may greatly reduce the cognitive complexity of decisions but still result in behavior that closely approximates normatively rational behavior. (1985, pp. 92–93)

A common rule of thumb is satisficing—choosing the first alternative that appears to be good enough after a brief search of possible alternatives. Imitation is also a common rule of thumb. Managers will at times select human resource interventions by imitating other organizations— the rule of thumb being if something works in another (similar) organization, it is a good bet that it will work in one's own organization (Nelson & Winter, 1982). Executives also selectively promote managers who share their values (Campbell, 1965). Here the rule of thumb is: if I prefer to do X and Sue is like me, then Sue will also prefer to do X. By hiring and promoting managers who share their values, decision makers help to ensure that particular types of human resource interventions will be selected.

Some interventions are selected, some are discarded, and others are retained. Selection and retention systems are part of a general system of organizational inheritance by which routines and other competencies are transmitted over time (Baum & Singh, 1994). Retention reflects organizational learning by capturing the lessons of history in routines (Levitt & March, 1988). Organizations tend to retain those routines that are functional (Levitt & March, 1988; Nelson & Winter, 1982). Routines include the structures, policies, and values that guide behavior. They are encoded into practices by formal and informal policies and taught to newcomers in such a way that the consequences of experience are accessible to people who have not experienced them. Once a human resource intervention becomes a routine, a tacit consensus emerges that this is the way things are done, and the routine operates more or less automatically (Lave & Wenger, 1991; Nelson & Winter, 1982).

Whether a human resource intervention produces consequences intended by its originators and whether it is functional are two different issues. A human resource intervention may produce intended effects but be dysfunctional. This occurs when it also produces *unintended* consequences which, taken as a whole, override the positive consequences of the intended effect and are dysfunctional to the system. On the other hand, a human resource intervention that does not produce intended effects may still be retained because it produces other consequences that are functional. Although managers use the employment interview because they believe that it identifies the best performers, it is probably retained because of other functions it serves, such as identifying applicants who are compatible with the interviewers (Adams, Elacqua, & Colarelli, 1994).

A sociocultural explanation for the paradox of utilization is that while decision makers select an intervention because of nominally stated goals, the intervention is retained because of the unstated functions it *actually* serves. A technology that is valid for one limited purpose may produce other consequences that are dysfunctional, and thus the organization will avoid that technology. Conversely, organizations may learn to use a technology that does not serve its originally stated purposes because it produces other, functional consequences. Managers often send their employees to training courses even though the employees may not learn the skills taught at the courses. The training courses continue because they serve other useful functions. They signal that the organization cares about its employees. They provide employees the opportunity to interact informally with colleagues, develop strong bonds with colleagues, and learn from people in other organizations. Retention systems perpetuate functional human resource interventions, even when their functional value is unknown or not explicitly described (Campbell, 1975). Retention systems are also attuned to the context, the *local* environment, in which a human resource intervention is used. To draw from evolutionary biology, it is evident that many biological adaptations arise from the local environment in which organisms typically live and evolve. Desert-dwelling animals evolve adaptations to stay cool in the heat, while arctic-dwelling creatures develop adaptations to stay warm in the cold. Similarly, local, contextual characteristics determine, in large measure, what practices will be functional within an organization.

Systems, Knowledge, and Change

Viewing organizations and organizational interventions from the perspective of sociocultural evolution implies evolutionary assumptions about systems, knowledge, and change.

Systems

Although the evolutionary perspective acknowledges the importance of identifying and understanding the parts of a system, it differs from the mechanical design perspective in how it describes the relation between parts and their combination into a whole (Baum & Singh, 1994). The evolutionary perspective suggests that parts are *loosely coupled* (Orton & Weick, 1990). That is, while an organization's parts are interdependent, the strength of relationships varies over time and the relationships are subject to spontaneous change. Relationships among parts are often indirect and weakly determined. Although it is reasonable to expect general trends in organizations, loose coupling suggests that—in most circumstances—it is unrealistic to expect accurate forecasts of organizational behavior, or that one could manipulate parts of a system to produce specific, intended effects (Connor, 1991; Hogarth & Makridakis, 1981; Lawshe, 1969).

The evolutionary perspective also suggests that parts combine in such a way that the whole is greater or different than the sum of its parts. The relationship between the parts and the whole is characterized by *emergence*. The combination of parts produces a whole that is greater than or different from the sum of the parts (Holland, 1995). An ant nest is made up of relatively simple creatures that engage in stereotyped, instinctual behavior, although the nest itself is a complex system that can adapt to a variety of environmental conditions (Holland, 1995). Emergence does not preclude reductionism. The evolutionary perspective is reductionistic, although in a different way than the mechanical design perspective. The mechanical design perspective seeks to explain the whole in terms of discrete parts with fixed relationships—for example, explaining the productivity or organizations or nations on the basis of the IQ scores of individual workers. The evolutionary perspective, on the other hand, employs what Dawkins (1986, p. 13) calls *hierarchical reductionism*, which used selectively, explains phenomena at adjacent levels in the hierarchy. Indeed, sciences are most likely to prosper when they discover the level of analysis most appropriate to their subject matter (Tooby & Cosmides, 1992).

Organizations have *deep structures* that influence how parts combine into and operate as a whole (Gersick, 1991). Although deep structures generate rules that govern choices, they allow for a variety of solutions (Gersick, 1991). In living organisms, deep structures include genetic codes that allow for morphological and physiological commonalities in a species, which also allow for variation among individuals (Tooby & Cosmides, 1990; Wake, Roth, & Wake, 1983). Deep structures in organizations include technology, power, and control. The interaction between the teacher and student is a fundamental part of the technology in schools and limits options for alternative methods of delivering schooling. The differences in governance between universities and business and military organizations are due in part to the differences in the deep structures of power. Power in military and business organizations has traditionally been based on the authority of position, whereas in universities power rests more on knowledge.

Organizations consist of multiple subsystems of *nested hierarchies*. A medical school in a university has a general hierarchy of management authority from the CEO on down. Nested within that general hierarchy are departments, such as surgery and psychiatry, and nested within each department are official and unofficial hierarchies. The official hierarchies are based on rank and position, with the department chairperson at the top, followed by full professors, associate professors, and so on. Unofficial hierarchies may be based on scholarly reputation or personality. These nested subsystems are interdependent, and their arrangement and interaction influence the structure of organizations. How they interact is complex. Often what is good at one level may not be good at another, and goals of different subsystems are often in conflict (Campbell, 1994; Colarelli & Stumpf, 1990; Kossek, 1989; March, 1991). Nested hierarchies permit the simultaneous occurrence of variety and standardization, typically at different levels because tightly controlled subsystems can operate inside or next to more complex and flexible ones. Some of the incompatibilities among subsystems are due to *design compromises*. Different units often have different goals and structures; therefore, it is impossible to obtain simultaneous efficiency and effectiveness throughout a system. Design compromises occur as organizations evolve, helping to ensure that the combination of parts contributes the greatest net benefit.

Organizations evolve historically and are therefore subject to *path dependencies*—branching processes that constrain the course of future events depending on which choice an organization made at a particular point. At any point in time, multiple choices exist, and choices at one point (particularly those early in a system's history) are likely to have lasting effects (March, 1994). This means, too, that the course of events that occur during the evolution of a system is unrepeatable because if the process was repeated, it is unlikely that similar paths would be used.

Knowledge

The principle that *everything is open to criticism* . . . leads to a simple solution of the problem of the sources of knowledge. . . . It is this: every "source"—tradition, reason, imagination, observation, or what not—is admissible and may be used, *but none has any authority*.
—Karl R. Popper (1966, Vol. 2, p. 378; emphases in original)

The evolutionary perspective suggests that useful knowledge originates from a variety of sources. Although social science, and science in general, are important sources of knowledge, they are not the only sources. Social science does not have a monopoly on useful social knowledge (Cronbach, 1986). Ordinary knowledge, social learning, and interaction are alternatives to what Lindblom and Cohen (1979) call "professional social inquiry." Ordinary knowledge is, essentially, common sense—casual empiricism and thoughtful speculation. Although fallible, ordinary knowledge is "the most basic knowledge we use in social problem solving" (p. 13). Ordinary knowledge, for example, tells us that children usually become angry when they don't get their way, that customers prefer friendly (rather than rude) service, or that a job applicant's past behavior is a good predictor of future behavior. Social learning involves experience, not the communication of analyses, facts, and procedures typical of social science. Social interaction can be a form of problem solving where people move toward a solution through interpersonal give-and-take. The efficient allocation of goods and services in market economies occurs not on the basis of a preplanned analysis but through numerous acts of buying and selling. Feedback from interaction leads to incremental adjustments, which are often more adaptive than analytically based predicted trajectories (Hogarth, 1981).

That ordinary knowledge, social learning, and social interaction are important sources of knowledge is compatible with an evolutionary perspective. They are historical, context-laden, and involve trial and error combined with feedback over time (Campbell, 1975; March, 1994). Moreover, they imply that evolved cognitive capacities, combined with mundane experience, allow people to build up useful reservoirs of information and judgment. Though fallible, these knowledge sources allow people to manage reasonably effectively in a complex reality (Einhorn & Hogarth, 1981; Gigerenzer et al., 1999).[7]

Applied Social Science

Applied social science can be a valuable supplement to ordinary knowledge. In the spirit of Bacon and Popper, standardized, self-correcting methods are necessary to enhance perception, minimize biases, and add to understanding of the true nature of phenomena. Human perceptual limitations are real. Social science methods are aids to perception that can help us accurately observe social phenomena. They are particularly helpful when evaluating the impact of social interventions where there are long time frames, where the change is subtle and difficult to perceive, and where the effects over large number of people need to be measured. Many social interventions produce results that are neither obvious nor immediate. Some activities of modern social science enable us to observe effects that would ordinarily go unobserved. Social science methods allow us to accumulate larger amounts of information about social phenomena than would otherwise be possible. It would be very difficult to make accurate estimates about the voting preferences or population demographics of Americans without the use of surveys administered by scientific sampling methods. Social science also aids in organizing and tabulating large quantities of data—quantities that could not be organized and tabulated by any individual without the aid of scientific equipment (e.g., computers, questionnaires).

Applied social science provides an additional feedback mechanism to evaluate claims of social knowledge. Unlike the traditional test of time, social science can generate information about social process fairly rapidly. The test of time is useful for evaluating structures and interventions that have been around for a while. Repeated failures over decades provide the most convincing evidence that communism and socialism are bankrupt political systems. However, when something new comes along or when it may be necessary to compare a new intervention with something that is tried and true, the test of time is not helpful to people who must make immediate decisions. Social science knowledge also can refine and validate ordinary knowledge by identifying the scientific bases that underlie common sense and wisdom (Gigerenzer et al., 1999; Root-Bernstein & Root-Bernstein, 1997). By the same token, ordinary knowledge can help in validating scientific knowledge. When ordinary knowledge conflicts with scientific knowledge, this often stimulates additional scientific research that advances understanding.

Variation and Knowledge

Variation, diversity, and novelty are critical to the emergence of technologies and interventions. Technological innovations emerge from a variety of sources. Innovations sometimes develop in response to specific needs. Many vaccines, such as the polio vaccine, have been developed in response to devastating diseases. On the other hand, factors beyond social or economic needs contribute to the development of innovations as well. These include personal or cultural values, fantasy, and play (Basalla, 1988). The personal computer, now a fixture of offices and homes throughout the world, was not developed due to any pressing need for it, but rather due to the personal interests of the inventors (Carlton, 1997). How much a culture values novelty and imitation and its beliefs about progress and the domination of nature have an effect on innovation. So do social and economic factors, including craft industries, market demand, labor scarcity, patents, and industrial research laboratories, as well as the transfer of technical knowledge through imperialism and immigration. Quality circles are recent HR interventions in the United States that were borrowed from other countries, and ability and personality tests developed in the United States have been adopted in other countries. Scientific knowledge is also an important source of variation. Science provides a font of ideas, some of which lead to practical innovations. When all of these sources interact, there can be exponentially increasing variation in knowledge.

Change

Much organizational change is largely uncontrolled and . . . the consequences of designed structural changes are difficult to anticipate. If this is so, organizations staffed by rational planners may behave essentially randomly with respect to adaptation.
—Michael T. Hannan and John Freeman (1989, p. 23)

> This extreme radicalism of the Platonic approach (and of the Marxian as well) is, I believe, connected with its aestheticism, i.e., with the desire to build a world which is not only a little better and more rational than ours, but which is free from all its ugliness: not a crazy quilt, an old garment badly patched, but an entirely new gown, a really beautiful new world .... Much as I may sympathize with the aesthetic impulse, I suggest that the artist might seek expression in another material.
>   —Karl R. Popper (1966, Vol. 1, pp. 164–165)

Any discussion of organizational or social change should address ideas about the purpose of change, how change occurs, and the extent to which change can be planned and manipulated so that people can bring about desired outcomes.

The Purpose of Change

The general purpose of programs of change that follow a mechanical design perspective is the realization of goals stemming from the values of those in authority. From the mechanical design perspective, the purpose of a change reflects organizational or social goals. Within the mechanical design perspective, an overarching goal—efficiency, market dominance, employee commitment, harmonious labor relations, or what have you—is the point of departure for an intervention. Change is presumed to occur through a hierarchy of interlocking subgoals and interventions, all of which are directed toward contributing to the overarching goal (Campbell et al., 1993; Simon, 1976).

Goals occupy a less lofty position in the evolutionary perspective. From this perspective, organizational goals are problematic. It makes little sense to think that goals define change. The very idea of *organizational goals* is a slippery one. Strictly speaking, organizations do not have goals. People have goals. And the goals of people are rarely identical and compatible; inevitably, some of their goals will be in conflict. To anyone who has worked more than a month in an organization, this is self-evident. To speak of organizational goals as though they were accepted and pursued by all members of an organization is unrealistic. Owners or upper management usually develop goals for an organization, but not everyone will see goals developed by executives to be in their own interests. If we ratchet the level of analysis down a degree, the same can be said for units within organizations, say, work groups or departments. The goals of the marketing department—to sell lots of product, even if it means extending credit to customers who are poor credit risks—are often in conflict with those of the accountants, who want a positive cash flow, even if it means refusing to sell products to customers who are poor credit risks.

The difficulty in communicating organizational goals also makes them slippery. To speak of organizational goals as though they were understood in the same manner by all members of an organization is unrealistic. Goals are replete with meaning. Perhaps a university president has established the goal of providing a "high-quality educational experience" for all undergraduates. Yet the professors and administrators will have differing definitions of a "high-quality educational experience." An organization's *official* goals ("high-quality education") are typically general and vague, which helps them accommodate to multiple interpretations (Perrow, 1961). Even with more precise and quantitative *operational* goals (students must read at least 5 classic books per course and 50 percent of their grade must be based on written assignments), there is always room for interpretation and controversy (what is a classic? what is a written assignment?).

Given the complex and loosely coupled nature of organizations, it is rare that organizational goals can be achieved as specified (Colarelli, 1998). Social systems are highly complex.[8] Large social systems (e.g., organizations, nations) have innumerable elements. And even if one could identify and keep track of all of the relevant elements, the number of *relationships* or potential relationships among elements is huge.[9] These relationships often produce *strong interactions* among elements, and this further compounds the problem of prediction. When there are strong interactions among parts, even if there are only a few parts, systems exhibit unpredictable behavior (Waldrop, 1992; see also Newman, 1988). Because of the complexity of social systems, it is exceedingly difficult, if not impossible, to precisely predict and control human behavior and achieve goals exactly as specified (Hayek, 1964; Ross & Nisbett, 1991). Long-range forecasts are notoriously inaccurate, and long-range plans rarely occur as originally conceived (Hogarth & Makridakis, 1981; Mintzberg, 1994). After studying the accuracy of a variety of long-range (two years or more) forecasts, Hogarth and Makridakis (1981, p. 122) concluded that they are "notoriously inaccurate."

Toward the end of the twentieth century, optimism about the prospects for planned social change began to fade, and scholars began to seriously examine the failures and unintended consequences of applied social science (Colarelli, 1998; Connor, 1991; Gillon, 2000; Johnson, 2000). Gillon (2000) examined some high-profile American domestic policies—welfare, community mental health, affirmative action, immigration, and campaign finance reform. All produced unintended consequences. He concluded that "awareness that our schemes for national betterment may have lurking within them results we do not like should produce humility" (p. 239).[10] One of the most visible examples of the failure of a system to change as planned is that of modern Russia. Johnson (2000) documented the "unexpectedly hapless outcomes" of the banking and economic reforms that Western experts sold Russia's post-Soviet government.[11]

The evolutionary perspective does not imply that all change is without purpose or goals. People do change their circumstances according to their goals. However, *the level of analysis* and the *scope of a goal* are critical to thinking about the purpose of change from an evolutionary perspective. The idea that change will proceed according to a plan becomes increasingly problematic as the system increases in size and complexity and as the goal of the change increases in scope. Parents of a teenager, if they are skilled (and lucky), may be able to increase her study habits from 30 minutes to 60 minutes a day. However, it is another matter to change the homework habits of all children in a school district or to change the structure of a nation's K–12 educational system. The owner of a small business may be able to implement an incentive system that increases her employees' productivity or attendance records. However, it is another matter to change the culture of a large organization.

A good deal of change is essentially random (Taleb, 2001). It is simply a result of perturbations that occur in any energetic system. At the level of the genotype (genes, as far as we know are not conscious), plants and animals change over time through natural selection, simply as a result of random mutations, genetic drift, and other processes (Dawkins, 1986; Dennett, 1995). Although they are composed of conscious beings, organizations per se are nonconscious systems. Despite images to the contrary, organizations are not "super-organisms" acting according to organizational intention. Much of the change that goes on in organizations is random. Although individuals may initiate change with the idea that it will serve a specific purpose, the effects become essentially random, due to the complex, loosely coupled, and political nature of organizations (Hannan & Freeman, 1989).

Even so, change often has beneficial effects. From an evolutionary perspective, one could argue that the *most important* effect of change in organizations is the cultivation of variation. Variation has a positive influence on the viability of a system. In contrast to the mechanical design perspective, which seeks to *reduce* variation so that an organization can move increasingly to the envisioned ideal, the evolutionary perspective suggests that *enhancing* variation is important. We cannot predict the future, but variation buys us insurance. Variation improves the probability that, within its broad repertoire, an organization will have resources to cope with uncertain futures. Human knowledge is limited and imperfect, and variation increases the likelihood that somebody will come up with something that works. Trying something a new way, or using something that was designed for one purpose for another purpose, or even making a mistake, have often led to important new discoveries (Eco, 1998; Roberts, 1989). Christopher Columbus discovered the New World while looking for a Western sea route to the Orient. Joseph Von Mering and Oscar Minkowski discovered insulin while studying the possible function of the pancreas in digestion.

Mechanical design approaches assume that managers can deal with the ever-changing environment by scanning the environment and planning for the changes that are likely to occur. It also assumes they will react quickly to unanticipated changes and rally the troops as quickly as needed. As appealing as this may sound in theory, it rarely works in practice. Mintzberg (1994) reviewed hundreds of studies on strategic and long-range planning and concluded that strategic planning has been a failure. Evidence from a host of studies using a host of methodologies suggests that firms cannot plan accurately for the future and that firms that engage in elaborate strategic planning fare no better (and often fare worse) than firms without elaborate plans and planning processes. After reviewing the empirical literature on it, Hogarth and Makridakis (1981, p. 122) state that "long-range forecasting (two years or longer) is notoriously inaccurate." Managers and human resource professionals cannot accurately forecast how the business environment will change future and what specific skills employees should learn to prepare them to perform effectively in future environments.

Organizations also cannot turn on a dime to adapt to change. In the 1960s and 1970s, many applied psychologists embraced "organizational development" (OD) to help organizations adapt and manage change. The field became popular, establishing its own professional organization. Some large corporations created departments of organizational development, and graduate programs in OD were created (Beer, 1980). However, as research on the impact of OD interventions accumulated, it began to look like OD rarely worked. In a comprehensive review of studies that evaluated the impact of OD interventions, Porras and Robertson (1992, p. 786) reported that "a lack of change . . . occurred more frequently than any change." Attempts to manage change are about as problematic as those that attempt to forecast change.

The evolutionary perspective does not rule out goals as a source of change. Using goals as a purpose for change is reasonable and compatible with an evolutionary perspective when the goals are small in scale, involve simple units of analysis, and address patchworks of small-scale problems in an *ad hoc* manner to alleviate suffering. Change can be purposeful. However, the evolutionary perspective suggests that we should limit our expectations about goals and change. Change to achieve a goal is likely to occur *when the goal is small in scale and occurs over a short period of time* (Basalla, 1988). It is reasonable to use HRM interventions to pursue goals that are limited in scope. The goal of a HRM intervention should be tied to a specific, short- to medium-term outcome (e.g., lower turnover within two years). In addition, these outcomes should be defined within restricted cultural and social boundaries (e.g., reducing turnover among computer programmers at a particular organization in a particular place). A HRM intervention should be evaluated within a restricted time period, using roughly parallel units of analysis and according to narrowly specified goals. As situations become more uncertain, specific goals are less appropriate, and goals should focus more on outcomes that are likely to improve adaptation (e.g., expanding the diversity of an organization's workforce). This follows from the nature of social systems and the nature of change. Social systems are complex, loosely coupled, and multilayered, and contain conflicting interests; they are therefore too fluid for large-scale change to remain on-course over a long time period. Small goals and shorter time frames are realistic because change, for the most part, occurs incrementally.

An argument against change in pursuit of grandiose ideals, utopia, progress, or human happiness and welfare does not mean that the evolutionary perspective is insensitive to human suffering. *Alleviating particular problems* is a workable alternative. As Popper suggests, the piecemeal social engineer

> will be aware that perfection, if at all attainable, is far distant, and that every generation of men . . . have a claim; perhaps not so much a claim to be made happy, for there are not institutional means of making a man happy, but a claim not to be made unhappy, where it can be avoided. They have a claim to be given all possible help, if they suffer. The piecemeal engineer will, accordingly adopt the method of searching for, and fighting against, the greatest and most urgent evils of society, rather than searching for, and fighting for, its greatest ultimate good. (1966, p. 158)

Change is more appropriately directed toward the alleviation of suffering and inefficiencies in particular situations than toward the attainment of an ideal. People typically initiate change when they are dissatisfied with the current state of affairs (Beer, 1980). Much of our psychology and physiology evolved to pursue activities that are pleasurable and avoid those that are painful.

Social scientists who subscribe to an evolutionary perspective are not guided by the desire to attain an ideal since they believe social programs are unlikely to provide aesthetic completeness and beauty (Berlin, 1991). Piecemeal social engineering views society and organizations as patchwork quilts (Popper, 1966), parts of the crooked timber of humanity (Berlin, 1991). Successful human resource interventions, then, shore up crooked timber but never make it completely straight; they repair the quilt by adding more patches.

HRM interventions should be disengaged from grandiose ideas—from utopian visions of organizational, economic, social, or cultural progress. Rather, in the spirit of Popper's piecemeal approach to social engineering, HRM interventions should focus on particular problems and be evaluated on those criteria. It is more appropriate to use a personnel selection method for the limited goal of identifying applicants who can perform reasonably well in training and in the early stages of the job than for the grandiose goals of identifying the "best person" for the job, of increasing organizational and national productivity, or of achieving social justice. Social and economic progress are unworkable criteria for evaluating human resource interventions (cf. Basalla, 1988; Harris, 1994; Hartigan & Wigdor, 1989). Evaluating human resource interventions in limited terms frees their developers from the tyranny of unrealistic expectations, and it allows them to focus on outcomes that are more within their control and are more perceptible to users.

How Change Occurs

Organizational change occurs on a continuum. At one end, change is chaotic and random, and things do not go as planned. At the other end, change is intelligently designed and orderly, and things go as planned. The mechanical design perspective views change as occurring primarily at the end points on the continuum—chaotic or planned. At one extreme is the unmanaged change presumed to occur when there are no qualified professionals to design change and no willing authorities to implement it. At the other extreme is the managed change that brings about intended consequences. This is presumed to occur when professionals and willing authorities are available to design and manipulate systems. Change occurs as soon as the parts have been rearranged or new parts have been added. I find it amusing to read the inevitable "to do" lists in management books—whether from the zippy best-sellers or the tomes penned by professors at business schools. These lists describe what managers must do to achieve particular outcomes. They reflect a premise of the mechanical design perspective that organizations can be designed and manipulated to achieve specific, intended outcomes.

The evolutionary perspective, on the other hand, questions the possibility that managers can orchestrate change to produce specific, intended outcomes. Plans for organizational change may look good on paper but rarely go as expected once managers try to implement them. The novelist Jim Harrison makes the point more poetically: "Maps made terrain so simple but four or five miles through the woods with no visible landmarks was a different matter" (1971, p. 47).

Change is usually neither chaotic nor orderly; it is most often slow and incremental. Change occurs via many small grafts onto or adjustments of existing systems. Variation is the driving force. Variations are continually introduced in organisms (e.g., through genetic mutations) or social systems (e.g., through imperfect imitations of existing practices). To the extent that the new variations are useful for survival and reproduction, those variations will gradually take hold. Most, however, disappear. Much of natural selection works to prevent change. As the evolutionary biologist George Williams points out: "What natural selection mainly does is to cull departures from the currently optimum (Williams, 1996, p. 32). Variations are more likely to be retained when the environment has changed and existing features of an organism or social system are no longer as adaptive as they once were.

Some organizational theorists who take an evolutionary perspective are strict selectionists. Hannan and Freeman (1989) suggest that organizations are usually unable to change because of internal and external pressures that maintain structural inertia. If they try to change, conflicting interests and uncertain means-ends connections mitigate against change going as planned. Adaptive change occurs among groups of organizations at the level of whole populations. Through a process of natural selection, those organizations that happen to have forms that fit with their environmental niches will probably survive. If their niches change, they will probably perish, and others (which happen to have more adaptive characteristics) will prosper. Nelson and Winter (1982) suggest that "highly flexible adaptation to change is not likely to characterize the behavior of individual firms" (p. 135). One reason is that organizational routines become tacit knowledge. Tacit knowledge is unconscious procedural knowledge about how to do something (like ride a bicycle). Because actions that flow from tacit knowledge are more or less automatic, they are difficult to change. Routines stemming from tacit knowledge are the "genes" of organizational structures.

Others argue that organizations can adapt to some extent (Bruderer & Singh, 1996; Levitt & March, 1988). Levitt and March (1988) suggest that organizations can adapt through organizational learning. Through trial and error, decision makers learn that a practice does or does not work and this knowledge is transmitted to other organizational members who act accordingly. Organizations learned that the Internet is an effective method for advertising job openings and recruiting job applicants, so they expanded their use of Internet recruiting. Many universities learned that courses offered on the Internet are not popular and that students do not learn particularly well from them, so they withdrew resources from Internet courses. Yet, organizational learning rarely proceeds smoothly. Competency traps people or groups into becoming so good at one thing that they do not notice the need for change and the need to acquire new skills. Selective and biased interpretations of experience and the political problems associated with defining organizational success compromise organizational learning. Bruderer and Singh (1996) view organizational learning from a different vantage point. They argue that learning and selection are interdependent processes. Because selection influences differential learning capabilities and learning capabilities influence selection, organizations with better capacities for learning are more likely to adapt and survive.

Change and Uncertainty

Organizational change involves uncertainty because of imperfect foresight, the limitations on our ability to solve complex problems, and the reactive and loosely coupled nature of social systems (Alchian, 1950).[12] Scholars in organizational design and HRM have suggested a number of methods for coping with uncertainty (Galbraith, 1977). Typically, these involve more control over the environment or increased information processing capacities. Considerably less theory and research, however, exist on how uncertainty influences the design, use, and effectiveness of other interventions. The evolutionary perspective suggests that a more effective way of dealing with change is to accept uncertainty. Managers can use uncertainty to their advantage by matching human resource interventions with system uncertainty and by using interventions to enhance variation.

Human resource interventions accommodate uncertainty when the specificity of expectations involves the uncertainty in the system. The greater the specificity of a technology's outcomes, the more compatible it is with high-certainty systems. Using a technology for one degree of certainty when a situation involves another degree of certainty will cause trouble (Einhorn, 1986). Under conditions of minimal uncertainty, a given action results in a specific effect most of the time. The results are fairly immediate and obvious, and the causes are clearly linked to their effects. Graphs and histograms are usually sufficient to demonstrate that a cause produced its intended effect. Human resource interventions based on operant conditioning are often congruent with conditions of high certainty. In manufacturing organizations where tasks, processes, and outcomes are clearly defined and structured, operant conditioning tends to produce intended effects (Stajkovic & Luthans, 1997). However, in situations where processes and outcomes are less well defined, where control over rewards is not straightforward, or where official goals are vague or in conflict with operational goals, operant conditioning fares poorly (Kerr, 1975; Stajkovic & Luthans, 1997).

Under conditions of moderate uncertainty, it is not possible to determine that a cause will have a specific effect in any particular instance, but there is a rational way to calculate the odds (Lieberson, 1991). Inferential statistics are useful because they acknowledge uncertainty. In personnel or student selection, the statistical approach is useful in estimating the proportion of applicants that will meet performance expectations. However, the accuracy of predictions in such situations is likely to remain modest due to our inability to understand and manipulate complex phenomena (Abelson, 1997).

Under conditions of high uncertainty, it is not possible to accurately estimate the likelihood that an intervention will be effectual. This is because some systems, despite their regularities, are so complex that it is beyond human capabilities to understand them; in others, there are no underlying regularities. Under such conditions, evolutionary algorithms are most appropriate for estimating how an intervention or cluster of interventions may influence organizational outcomes (Bruderer & Singh, 1996; Holland, 1995). Human resource interventions that focus on the processes by which change occurs rather than the changes or outcomes themselves are most useful (Hedberg, Nystrom, & Starbuck, 1976; Holland, 1995; Weick, 1979). Diversification or underengineering is likely to produce adaptive outcomes, although one cannot know in advance what the outcomes might be. Markowitz (1952), who won a Nobel Prize for his work, argued that a diverse portfolio of stocks is more likely to generate favorable returns than any one stock.

> The strategic role of diversification is Markowitz's key insight. As Poincare had pointed out, the behavior of a system that consists of only a few parts that interact strongly will be unpredictable. With such a system you can make a fortune or lose your shirt with one big bet. In a diversified portfolio, by contrast, some assets will be rising in price even when other as-

sets are falling in price; at the very least, the rates of return among the assets will differ. . . . Most investors choose the lower expected return on a diversified portfolio instead of betting the ranch. (Bernstein, 1996, pp. 252–253)

Similar logic can apply to organizational interventions. Using HR interventions to increase variation can help managers because variety often stimulates improvements. There is rarely "one best way" to accomplish a goal, particularly in complex and dynamic systems. Variation in the evolutionary perspective is a heuristic which, over time, provides effective ways to adapt, survive, and prosper in highly complex environments—despite the human inability, in most situations, to know the complete parameters of a situation and to obtain complete information on which to make optimal decisions.

Strategies that accept uncertainty and do not attempt perfect prediction make fewer errors in prediction than systems that deny uncertainty (Einhorn, 1986). This is the *paradox of uncertainty*. By acknowledging the inevitability of uncertainty in social systems and working within the limits of uncertainty, we can decrease uncertainty. The converse is also true. By attempting to precisely predict and control outcomes in inherently uncertain systems, we increase uncertainty. Applying human resource interventions that aim at prediction and control in uncertain systems will lead to unmet expectations (Mintzberg, 1994). Connor (1991) examines the failures of social scientists to predict the sweeping changes in the former Soviet Union and Eastern Europe (the fall of communism), China (the Tiananmen Square massacre and the resurgence of totalitarianism), and Iran (the fall of the Shah and the rise of Islamic fundamentalism). He argues that "the current world situation constitutes an indeterminate system" and hence predictions will not be accurate (1991, p. 183).

EVOLUTIONARY PSYCHOLOGY

Whereas sociocultural evolution deals with social systems, evolutionary psychology focuses on the human mind and behavior. Evolutionary psychology is a synthesis of modern psychology and evolutionary biology. Using the logic of natural selection to examine human mental processes and behavior, it is concerned with the functions of characteristically human behaviors and with how they are (or were) adaptive in responding to particular classes of stimuli. Two fundamental assumptions of evolutionary psychology are that the human mind is modular, consisting of numerous psychological mechanisms, and that these mechanisms evolved to solve particular adaptive problems that humans consistently faced over time.

Premises about the Mind

Most social scientists subscribe to what Tooby and Cosmides (1992) call the Standard Social Science Model (SSSM). The SSSM has been the dominant paradigm in the social sciences for the past century. The basis for the model stems from the observations that: (1) human infants the world over are remarkably similar, (2) yet adults are remarkably complex and different from one another, and (3) human cultures show a high degree of differentiation from one another. The SSSM posits that the transformation occurs due to *the influence of culture on the individual*. The SSSM assumes that the mind of the human infant contains only rudimentary equipment—a few basic instincts and the capacity to learn. The newborn mind is nearly the Lockean blank slate and grows complex through learning. It is through formal and informal learning over extended time—the process of socialization—that culture is transmitted to the individual.

The SSSM regards the mind as a general problem-solver. It has no specialized equipment for particular problems or classes of problems. The brain uses the same general machinery to solve the problem of finding a suitable mate as it does for programming a videotape player. In other words, the *content* of the problem is irrelevant (Pinker, 1997). Tooby and Cosmides use the analogy of a single-bladed hunting knife. Although it has just one large blade, a person who owns such a knife can use it for a host of different tasks. It can be used to skin an animal, cut bread, hack tree limbs, slice and spear pieces of roast beef, shave a beard, and so on—although it will not work equally well for all tasks. Humans are viewed as different from other animals. Instinct and limited capacities to learn limit the behavioral repertoire of other animals. Dogs behave pretty much like dogs, regardless of whether they are raised in Finland or Brazil. Humans, on the other hand, have a large capacity to absorb all sorts of responses to cultural stimuli.

This view of the mind gives learning, socialization, education, and training a central place in the SSSM.

> The belief that the human mind is content free is deeply embedded in the SSSM. The central concept in psychology is learning. The prerequisite that a psychological theory must meet to participate in the SSSM is that any evolved component, process, or mechanism must be equipotential, content-free, content-independent, general-purpose, domain-general, and so

on (the technical terms vary with movement and era). In short, these mechanisms must be constructed in such a way that they can absorb any kind of cultural message or environmental input equally well. . . . Consequently, the concepts of learning, socialization, general-purpose (or content-independent) cognitive mechanisms, and environmentalism have (under various names and permutations) dominated scientific psychology for at least the last 60 years. (Tooby & Cosmides, 1992, pp. 29–30)

The view of the mind as a blank slate, as a general problem solver, and as a vast sponge soaking up culture has been an article of faith in much of psychology and the social sciences for the past century. One particularly influential work in the early part of the twentieth century was Margaret Mead's *Coming of Age in Samoa* (1928). This book had "an extraordinary impact on the twentieth century, an impact centered in the social sciences but extending far beyond them" (Brown, 1999, p. 289). Mead reported on field work that she had carried out in American Samoa. Here, she described a culture, quite unlike our own, where there was no adolescent *Sturm und Drang*, no rape or war, no frigidity or sexual jealousy. According to Mead, the Samoan people were peaceful, sexually uninhibited, and happy because of a peaceful culture and a permissive style of child rearing. This was possible because people are profoundly shaped by culture. Human nature, according to Mead, "is almost unbelievably malleable, responding accurately . . . to . . . cultural conditions" (Mead, 1935, p. 279).[13] At about the same time, the psychologist John B. Watson was trumpeting the power of behaviorism to mold human behavior and character (1924). About 70 years later, psychologist Carole Beal, writing on the causes of sex differences, observed that with changes in socialization and training experiences, it is "just a matter of time" before men and women are fully interchangeable among virtually all roles in society, except perhaps bearing children—including military combat and coeducational football (1994, p. 287). The view of the mind as a blank slate and general problem solver has become so entrenched in modern psychology and social science that Pinker dubs it "psychological correctness" (1997, p. 44).

The Evolutionary Psychological Model

Evolutionary psychology's premises about the mind are different from those of the SSSM. Evolutionary psychologists maintain that the human mind is modular, composed of numerous psychological mechanisms that operate on specific adaptive problems. Psychological mechanisms are heritable neurological processes that influence decisions and behavior in response to specific stimuli (Buss, 1995). Psychological mechanisms were shaped over the course of 1.2 million years of the Pleistocene era—the Environment of Evolutionary Adaptation (EEA)—in response to recurrent adaptive problems. Table 2.1 provides a chronology of human evolution, beginning 65 million years ago, when it was estimated that the first primate evolved. The chronology shows that the modern circumstances we take for granted are only a blink of the eye in evolutionary terms. Even agriculture and writing are but a few thousand years old.

Most scientifically minded people accept the idea that the modern human skeleton and internal organs evolved from, and are not dramatically different from, the bodies of our early ancestors. They also accept the notion that the shape of the body and the functions of the organs evolved as they did because they were adaptive to human survival and reproduction. But many modern psychologists cannot accept the proposition that the human mind operates in the same way—that it produces characteristic behaviors, thoughts, and emotions when presented with those stimuli (such as the opposite sex, food, aggressors, and children) that have been part of human evolutionary history over millennia. The mind is not a general problem solver, but a rather federation of multiple problem-specific mechanisms. Just as the body contains many different organs that solve particular adaptive problems—the eyes to see, the heart to pump blood, the lungs to breathe, the liver to filter the blood—the mind contains mechanisms to solve adaptive problems in the realms of behavior, thought, and emotion. A Swiss Army knife is a useful analogy for the evolutionary psychological model of the mind. It contains different implements, each designed for a narrow range of functions or a specific function—a screwdriver, a corkscrew, an orange peeler, a nail file, tweezers, toothpick, and so on.

Psychological mechanisms are physically instantiated in the brain and are heritable; that is, they are transmitted genetically from one generation to the next. People who had these mental mechanisms would be more likely to survive and reproduce than those who did not. The human mind, as David Buss points out, is saturated with content. Psychological mechanisms are content specific. They do not respond to all classes of stimuli; rather, specific modules respond to specific types of stimuli and problems. Psychological mechanisms lead people to prefer ripe, rather than under-ripe or over-ripe, fruit; they motivate women to be nurturing toward their children, and so on. Most people respond to snakes and spiders differently than they do to attractive members of the opposite sex. Psychological mechanisms have developed over the course of human evolution as solutions to problems related to survival and reproduction. Consider, again, the attraction to comely members of the

Table 2.1
Time Table of Human Evolution

Years from Present	Human Ancestors	Social Structure	Technology and Culture
55 million years ago	First Primates	Family groups (?)	?
6 million	Common Ancestor	Family groups (?)	Gatherers (primarily vegetarians)
4.5 million	*Australopithecus ramidus*	Family groups (?)	Gatherers (primarily vegetarians)
3.5 million	*Australopithecus afarensis*	Family groups (?)	Gatherers (primarily vegetarians)
2.5 million	*Australopithecus africanus*	Troops/clans	Gatherers and scavengers
2 million	*Homo habilis*	Troops/clans	Stone tools (Oldowan), hunting, omnivores
1.8 million The Pleistocene	*Homo erectus*	Hunter/gatherer groups	Pear-shaped hand axes
300,000	Ancient *Homo sapiens* The Neanderthals	Hunter/gatherer groups	Carefully shaped flakes, (Lavallois method) big game hunting
100,000	Modern *Homo sapiens*	Hunter/gatherer groups	Ritual burial, bone tools
60,000–30,000			Beginning of "cultural explosion" Boat crossing to Australia Stone blades, tools from diverse materials (bone and ivory), dwelling, painting, carving, beads
10,000		Sedentary villages	Beginnings of agriculture
5,000			Writing
3,000		First civilizations and large organizations	Architecture

Sources: Megarry (1995) and Mithen (1996).

opposite sex and fear of snakes. Over human evolutionary history, mating with fecund partners and avoiding snakebites were important to survival and reproduction. Therefore, psychological mechanisms evolved which directed thought and behavior in ways that help solve these problems. Human males the world over regard healthy, shapely, young women as attractive and prefer them as mating partners (Buss, 1989). The evolutionary psychological explanation for these preferences is that they are largely instinctual. That men are sexually attracted to women who display high fertility cues makes obvious evolutionary sense. If they were attracted to postmenopausal or unhealthy young women, they would not leave any ancestors. Most people have an innate fear of snakes.[14] Yet relatively few humans in the industrialized world are exposed to poisonous spiders and snakes. However, snakes were a major threat during the EEA. Data on an indigenous tribe, the Yanomamö, living in conditions that are similar to humans in EEA, show that most people get bitten by a snake sometime in their lives and that bites from venomous snakes were a leading cause of death (Chagnon, 1997). If people learned to fear spiders and snakes only after repeated trial-and-error learning, few people would have survived to pass that knowledge along. By the time they learned that some spiders and snakes were deadly, it would be too late to apply that learning because they would already have been bitten and died. Research by Susan Mineka illustrates how the psychological mechanism for fearing snakes may work. Mineka and her colleagues (Mineka et al., 1984) placed snakes in front of monkeys who had been raised in captivity and who had not been exposed to snakes. They evidenced no fear when a snake was placed nearby. Later when these monkeys observed other monkeys, that had been raised in the wild and captured, react fearfully to snakes, they quickly became fearful of snakes. In a later study, Mineka and Cook (1993) showed zoo-bred monkeys films of monkeys reacting fearfully to a snake as well as to a flower and bunny. The monkeys quickly learned to fear the snake but evidenced no fear of flowers or bunnies. Monkeys appear to have an evolved mechanism that enables them to learn quickly to fear snakes by observing other monkeys react fearfully to snakes—or, rather, a mechanism that *awakens* the specific fear upon observing other monkeys reacting fearfully to a snake.

Table 2.2 lists some of the more common psychological mechanisms that have been identified by evolutionary psychologists. Recent research by neuroscientists is providing increasing physical evidence suggestive of content-specific mechanisms. One study found that pictures of attractive females activated a reward center, the nucleus accumbens, in the brains of heterosexual males to a greater degree than pictures of women

Table 2.2
Psychological Mechanisms

Psychological Mechanism	Functions	Author(s)
1. Fear of snakes	Avoid poison	Marks (1987)
2. Superior female spatial-location memory	Increase success at foraging/gathering	Silverman and Eals (1992)
3. Male sexual jealousy	Increase paternity certainty	Symons (1979)
4. Preference for foods rich in fats and sugar	Increase caloric intake	Rozin (1976)
5. Female mate preference for economic resources	Provisioning for children	Buss (1989)
6. Male mate preferences for youth, attractiveness, and waist-to-hip ratio	Select mates of high fertility	Buss (1989), Singh (1993)
7. Landscape preferences for savanna-like environments	Motivate individuals to select habitats that provide resources and offer protection	Kaplan (1992), Orians and Heerwagen (1992)
8. Natural language	Communication/manipulation	Pinker and Bloom (1990)
9. Cheater-detection procedure	Prevent being exploited in social contracts	Cosmides (1989)
10. Male desire for sexual variety	Motivate access to more sexual partners	Symons (1979)

Source: Buss (1995).

of average attractiveness (Aharon, Etcoff, Ariely, Chabris, O'Connor, & Breiter, 2001). Pictures of attractive males, on the other hand, suppressed reward circuitry. Another study found that eye contact with members of either sex activated reward centers in the brain, most likely responding to a stimulus that has over thousands of years typically signaled the promise of social rewards (Kampe, Frith, Dolan, & Frith, 2001).

The human mind, however, is not fully adapted to industrial and postindustrial society. Our mental hardwiring is the product of hundreds of thousands of years of evolution, when we lived in small hunter-gatherer bands on the African savanna. Changes in our mental mechanisms occur much more slowly than changes in culture. A cultural or technological change over decades or centuries is unlikely, therefore, to change human behavioral patterns that are deeply rooted in evolutionary adaptation. Although the birth control pill was heralded as bringing about a sexual revolution that would lead women to be as free with their sexuality as men, this has not happened. Men are still much more promiscuous, and women are still choosy.

Individual Differences

The evolutionary psychological perspective suggests that individual differences are relatively unimportant. Evolutionary psychology is more concerned with *what all humans have in common*, less with how they are different. It focuses on complex adaptations that are *common to the species*.

> When humans are described from the point of view of their complex adaptations, differences tend to disappear, and a universal architecture stands out in stark relief. This is both empirically the case (nearly everyone has two eyes, two hands, the same sets of organs, and so on) and theoretically expected to be the case if organisms are primarily collections of complex adaptations. (Tooby and Cosmides, 1992, p. 78)

If individual differences in, say, personality and mental ability (within the normal range) were important to survival and reproduction, then variation on those traits would have disappeared. We would all have pretty much the same personality and mental ability. Yet wide variation on those traits has persisted. Moreover, personality and mental ability are largely heritable—that is, our personality and mental ability are in some measure determined by the type of personality and mental ability of our parents. Parents who are anxious and bright tend to have children who are anxious and bright.

Yet traits that are adaptive for survival and reproduction show the *least* variability and *least* heritability (Vale, 1980). When traits contribute to survival and reproduction, they become common in a species. Almost everyone has them. Two eyes, two legs, two arms, two lungs, and ten fingers and toes are important for survival and reproduction, and almost all humans have them. Moreover, almost all humans will be born with them regardless of whether their parents have them. To the extent that a characteristic becomes an adaptation, it is no longer an individual difference that is *uniquely* passed on from parents; rather, it becomes a common characteristic of a species. The observance of that characteristic is not dependent on one's mother or father having it.

Many characteristics, however, are heritable or largely heritable—eye color, skin color, IQ, personality. The color of a person's eyes or skin, a person's intellectual capacity, or degree of extroversion are (in varying degrees) dependent on the existence of those traits in their parents and ancestors. Yet, from, an evolutionary perspective, these psychological characteristics tend to be superficial and unrelated to problems of survival and reproduction.[15] Tooby and Cosmides (1992) use the analogy of a car to illustrate the difference between adaptations and individual differences. All cars, if they are to work properly, must contain the basic adaptations of a motor, drive train, wheels, a steering mechanism, and an enclosure for passengers. Other aspects of cars—color, styling, stereo equipment, and so on—are superficial individual differences; they are irrelevant to whether the car functions as a car.

The SSSM, on the other hand, emphasizes the importance of individual differences. The doctrinaire version of the SSSM emphasizes the role of learning in producing individual differences. This affects categories of people as well as individuals. According to this view, most sex differences in social behavior are due to learning (Eagly & Wood, 1999). Men learn that it is more appropriate to engage in task behaviors and competition, whereas women learn that it is more appropriate to engage in socioemotional behaviors and cooperation. Similarly, the SSSM suggests that individuals learn abilities and dispositions that define their talents and personalities (e.g., Ericsson & Lehmann, 1996; Helson & Stewart, 1994). If a particular person is taught to be task-oriented, aggressive, and competitive, as well as a skilled tennis player and violinist, this is what that person will turn out to be.

Trait theory offers another perspective on the origin and importance of individual differences. It refers to a perspective in psychology that (1) focuses on individual differences in personality and ability, (2) assumes that individual differences in psychological traits are important, and (3) assumes that traits are generally stable (some are slow to change while others are virtually resistant to change). A trait is a *stable predisposition* to behave in a particular way (Eysenck, 1952). Trait theorists have examined differences among categories of individuals as well as differences among particular individuals.[16] Traits are internal to the person and influence a person's choices and responses to stimuli. I would include both theorists of cognitive ability such as Spearman, Thurstone, and Jensen and theorists of personality such as Allport, Murray, Cattell, McCrea, and Costa in the the general category of trait theorists. These scholars have differing versions of the origin of traits, but most include some degree of biological origin. Some suggest that learning plays a role and that traits can change over time, although the time frame tends to be long and traits are partially constrained by biological factors (Helson & Stewart, 1994). Others argue that traits are heavily influenced by biology and less by learning (Eysenck & Eysenck, 1985; Jensen, 1998; Tellegen et al., 1988).

The explanations of individual differences in the SSSM and in trait theory have remained virtually independent of one another. Yet they both acknowledge the importance of individual differences and often regard even small differences among individuals as important. However, discussions of the origins of individual differences have been anything but peaceful. Scholars from the learned-differences camp have been particularly critical of the inherited-differences view, particularly because of its supposed negative implications for egalitarian and activist social policies (Singer, 1999). Scholars from the camp favoring inherited-differences criticize advocates of the learning view for being naïve (Herrnstein & Murray, 1994). However, trait theory's view of *inherited differences is not incompatible with the major tenet of the SSSM that people are shaped by culture*. The inherited view still holds that culture has a large influence on a person's nature. The following passage from Arthur Jensen's *Bias in Mental Testing* (1980) illustrates this view. Jensen is an eminent scholar of individual differences and a proponent of inherited intellectual ability.

> As far as *abilities* are concerned, the "ideal" sex ratio for the vast majority of occupations in modern industrial societies is much closer to 1 than the actual sex ratios observed. . . . *The causes of the great disparities in sex ratios we see in most occupations . . . are much more a result of traditional sociocultural sex-role modeling and typecasting* of males and females for different vocational aspirations than a result of basic differences in cognitive abilities. (1980, pp. 632–633; first emphasis in original, the second added)

Jensen does not seem to consider whether sex differences deriving from evolved adaptations might account for the differences in occupational roles (see Browne, 2002). David Lykken (2000) also defers to the role of culture on behavioral patterns. Lykken has made significant contributions to behavioral genetics, providing evidence that many human psychological differences have at least a partly genetic basis (e.g., Bouchard et al., 1990). He, nevertheless, believes so strongly that parenting has a critical role in shaping the temperaments of children that he advocates licensing parents.

> We can try to ensure good rearing environments for . . . American children . . . [by] demanding the same minimal requirements for biological parenthood that we now require for adoptive parenthood—a mother and a father committed enough to be married to each other, who are mature and self-supporting, [and] neither criminal nor incapacitated by mental illness. . . . I believe that most of the 1.3 million Americans now languishing in prison might have become citizens, taxpayers, and welcome neighbors if the circumstances of the growing-up had included licensable parents. (Lykken, 2000, pp. 598–599)

An evolutionary perspective questions both the emphasis on the importance of individual differences and the belief that social engineers can manipulate complex environments to achieve specific outcomes.

CRITICISMS OF EVOLUTIONARY PERSPECTIVE

Critics attack the evolutionary perspective because it is alleged to unquestioningly accept the status quo, because it argues that features that evolved in past environments are relevant to the present, because its explanations of why characteristics evolved the way they did are allegedly little more than "just so" stories, and because an evolutionary perspective is of little relevance for designing interventions to ameliorate social problems. Other criticisms of evolutionary psychology allege that it implies genetic determinism, is a justification for Social Darwinism, and is a repackaging of instinct theory. On closer examination, these criticisms do not hold water.

A common complaint about an evolutionary perspective on social policy is that it justifies any status quo. The criticism goes as follows. Since practically all existing biological and social forms came into existence through evolution by natural selection and since evolution by natural selection is the most effective process known for eliminating dysfunctional forms, then everything that currently exists must be the best of all possibilities. Therefore, the status quo is as good as it gets, and change will make things worse. In Voltaire's *Candide*, Dr. Pangloss was wont to say, "Things cannot be other than they are. . . . Everything is made for the best purpose." There are, of course, several reasons why everything is not necessarily for the best and why an evolutionary perspective does not inherently justify the status quo. Panglossian optimism commits what G. E. Moore calls the *naturalistic fallacy*, an erroneous belief that whatever is found in nature is morally right. Obviously, not everything found in nature—which includes murder, cannibalism, incest, robbery, rape, and genocide—is morally right. The criticism that the evolutionary perspective implies the status quo is in error in another way: it does not take into account variation. Variation is the driving force in evolution; variation leads to change. If there were no variation, there would be no evolution. The different forms introduced through variation-creating mechanisms are essential for evolution. Yet we can rarely anticipate which variations will turn out to be adaptive. Therefore, by definition, the status quo is not, *in the long run*, for the best. Modifications from the way things currently are—through variation—are an essential part of evolution by natural selection.

A second criticism is that, because our current environment is different from the past environment in which we evolved, adaptations that evolved in past environments are no longer relevant. The criticism is valid to a point—there indeed are adaptations that are not nearly as relevant now as they were in the Pleistocene. Symons (1979; 1992) argues that the "roving eye" in human males evolved as a psychological mechanism because, in ancestral environments, men with roving eyes were likely to produce more offspring than men who were faithful to one woman. Yet in modern industrial societies, polygamy is illegal, adultery is grounds for divorce, and most women have effective contraception available to them. Therefore, the roving eye makes less reproductive sense in modern environments. Neither does our fear of snakes now that the bulk of humanity lives in urban settings. On the other hand, we face many of the same problems our ancestors faced. The most hostile force in nature that humans faced during the EEA and still face now is other humans (Alexander, 1987; Darwin, 1859/1958). Group life was one of the primary environmental pressures that stimulated the evolution of the large and complex human brain (Cummins, 1998). Developing friendships, coalitions, negotiating political battles, gaining status and power, identifying and dealing with enemies, as well as identifying a fertile mate and rearing children—these problems have remained with human group life at least since the upper Pleistocene (de Waal, 1982; Goodall, 1990; Megarry, 1995). Adaptations take a long time to develop, and this is why we have not yet developed adaptations to recurrent dangers in our present environment, such as automobiles, guns, and electrical outlets.

A third criticism of the evolutionary perspective is that its explanations are fictitious, "just so" stories. In Rudyard Kipling's *Just So* stories, the narrator makes up stories about why animals are the way they are (Kipling, 1996). The leopard got his spots because an Ethiopian touched the leopard with his fingers. The whale got his throat from a mariner who, after he was swallowed by a whale, fashioned a grating from parts of his boat in the whale's throat. The camel got his hump by saying "humph" too much when asked to work for man. Voltaire's Dr. Pangloss thought the human nose evolved to prop up eyeglasses. Critics of the evolutionary perspective argue that evolutionary scholars make up convenient explanations of evolved mechanisms. The claim that *post hoc* storytelling is the basis of evolutionary psychology has been used mainly by social scientists who have little understanding of evolutionary theory or biology. Serious evolutionary scientists do not make up stories to explain evolved mechanisms. Plausible explanations are developed from observation combined with current scientific research and theory. These are then refined into hypotheses and specific predictions (Alcock, 2001; Buss, 1995; Ketelaar & Ellis, 2000). The rub is that we normally cannot observe evolution occurring; nor is there usually detailed, cumulative evidence of each variation and modification leading to a current adaptation. Complete evidence is unattainable in any science. No theory can be completely proved (Popper, 1959). The best that scientists can do is to provide supporting or refuting evidence. The weight of the evidence will suggest whether the theory should be abandoned or whether it appears on the right track and should continue to be pursued (Lakatos, 1970; Newell, 1990).

Liz Von Muggenthaler's research on why cats purr and Alan Wilson's research on the functions of small leg muscles in horses illustrate the typical approach an evolutionary scientist takes to explain an adaptation (Fauna Communications Research Institute, n.d.; Gutterman, 2002). Muggenthaler developed a hypothesis that purring functions to repair bone and tissue damage. She formulated this hypothesis based on integrating the following facts and observations. Almost all known cats purr, and historical records going back at least 3,000 years indicate that cats purr. A number of studies have found that exposure to low sound waves in the range of 20 to 50 Hz increases bone density; exposure to frequencies in the 50 to 140 Hz range helps to relieve pain and heal injured muscles and tendons. Cats have a remarkable ability to recover from injuries involving broken bones and torn tissue. One study of "high-rise syndrome" found that 90 percent of 132 cats survived after falling from high-rise buildings, with an average height of 5.5 stories (Whitney &

Mehlhaff, 1987). Most species of cats purr when they are injured. Von Muggenthaler and other researchers are now in the process of conducting a series of controlled studies to test her hypothesis that the function of purring in cats is to speed recovery from injury by helping to heal bone and tissue damage through low sound frequencies. Alan Wilson was interested in the possible function of the small muscles (about one-tenth of an inch long) in horses' legs which connect the tendon to the humerus. He formulated the hypothesis that the muscles, which many zoologists thought were useless vestiges, functioned as shock absorbers to ease the stress on the horse's body from vibrations caused by the horse's legs pounding on the ground when it runs. Through a series of ingenious studies, Wilson and his colleagues were able to show that these tiny muscles do indeed function as shock absorbers in horses' legs (Wilson, McGuigan, Su, & van den Bogert, 2001).

A fourth general criticism is that an evolutionary perspective is of no practical value. It may explain the processes by which organisms and systems came to be and why adaptations function as they do, but it offers little in the way of pragmatic guidance for solving the problems of the here and now. The SSSM implies that training and education are cure-alls because it assumes that learning and acculturation are the primary influences on human thought and behavior. At the height of the Great Society in the 1960s, President Lyndon Johnson echoed this belief when he said: "The answer to all our national problems comes down to a single word: education" (Lyndon B. Johnson, cited in Tyack & Cuban, 1995, p. 2). The recurring crisis in education over the past 70 years and the failure of many Great Society programs do not bode well for the utility of the SSSM's assumptions about human nature and the usefulness of social programs based on those assumptions (Gillon, 2000; Ravitch, 2000).

An evolutionary perspective is more relevant to interventions than the SSSM because it is more realistic. By understanding *why* certain patterns of behavior occur, we are in a better position to respond to those we believe are morally wrong or ineffective. An evolutionary perspective takes a more complex and nuanced view of human behavior than the SSSM. Interventions based on an accurate model of human nature and systems are more likely to be successful. It informs us as to what behaviors are more or less amenable to change and how so. Behavioral propensities that are difficult to change are as real as those that can be changed. Keller and Marian Breland (1961) provide a number of amusing examples of failures of behaviorism in an article entitled "The Misbehavior of Organisms." The Brelands were students of Skinner, and they used his principles to train animals for zoos and advertisers. In one experiment, they tried to train a pig to pick up an oversized coin with its mouth and drop it in a piggy bank. The pig would not cooperate. The pig used its characteristic rooting behavior, pushing the coin with its snout, tossing it in the air, and pushing it again. The pig, like humans, had a particular evolved nature that circumscribed learning. Humans everywhere form status hierarchies. Yet, it is common for HR scholars or consultants to devise programs to reduce or eliminate hierarchies (e.g., Manz & Sims, 1993). Despite attempts from Karl Marx onward to eliminate them, dominance hierarchies persist and show no signs of withering away. Because any complex adaptation takes thousands of years to evolve, we are better off dealing with it realistically than wishing it away or assuming that we can simply change human behavior by changing cultural inputs. Understanding the original function of the adaptation and applying that knowledge to a new context is a more fruitful approach to designing HR interventions.

The belief that evolutionary psychology implies genetic determinism reflects a fundamental misunderstanding, perhaps because of the radical reductionism associated with the mechanical design perspective. The presumption is that the behavior of complex systems can be explained completely by basic elements. In this view, if behaviors have a genetic component, then nothing else matters. However, any serious student of evolution and genetics realizes that this is untrue and that there are few complex behaviors in humans that are inflexibly hardwired in the genes. The phenotype *is a function of an interaction between genes and environment.* Young female anoles (a small lizard found in the southeastern United States) develop ovaries more rapidly when regularly exposed to the courtship displays of territorially dominant male anoles than they do when exposed to castrated males or those not exposed to males at all (Alcock, 1993). Young female humans reach puberty later in homes where the father is present than in homes where the father is absent (Ellis, McFadyen-Ketchum, Dodge, Pettit, & Bates, 1999).[17]

An individual's genetic makeup typically places constraints on the phenotype. People who inherit genes that predispose them to be relatively tall (say, over six feet) will likely grow tall. However, even with a straightforward morphological trait like height, the environment makes a difference. A malnourished person is unlikely to grow as tall as a person with identical genes who is well fed. The evolutionary psychological perspective does not deny the effect of the environment, nor does it suggest that all behavior is "genetically programmed." To the contrary, the evolutionary perspective emphasizes the interaction between human nature and the environment. All normal humans acquire language. The regularities of language acquisition and the grammatical regularities across languages suggest that language arises from genetically coded mental capacities in humans. However, the content of language—whether a person speaks French or English—is a product of culture.

Critics of evolutionary psychology with a penchant for moral indignation argue that evolutionary psychology provides an intellectual basis for Social Darwinism (Degler, 1991; Richards, 1987). The original source for this criticism is probably a passage from Herbert Spencer's *Study of Sociology* (1873) in which he argued that legislation to aid the poor would be biologically unsound policy:

> The quality of a society is lowered morally and intellectually, by the artificial preservation of those who are least able to take care of themselves. . . . For if the unworthy are helped to increase, by shielding them from that mortality which their unworthiness would naturally entail, the effect is to produce, generation after generation, a greater unworthiness. (1873/1961, p. 313)

In this passage Spencer implies that the poor are in a wretched condition because of their biological makeup, that the well-off have prospered because of their biological makeup, and that all is for the best and that social conditions should be left well enough alone.

Modern evolutionary biologists and psychologists do not take Social Darwinism seriously because Spencer's assumptions and implications are in error. Spencer makes the erroneous argument that evolution proceeds toward goals—that the natural order of society is to evolve toward a progressively more advanced state (see Richards, 1987, pp. 300 ff.). Yet evolution by natural selection has no goal (other than survival and reproduction). Natural selection is a physical process of variation and selective retention (Dennett, 1995). Organisms that happen to have heritable characteristics that happen to be adapted to their environments are more likely to survive and reproduce than those without those characteristics, and those characteristics will become more numerous in future generations, as long as the environment remains the same. When the environment changes, the constellation of adaptive traits gradually changes. Social Darwinism's assumption about "worthiness" is biological Calvinism—the Elect are in their positions because of biological superiority and vice versa. However, from the standpoint of modern evolutionary biology, the only criterion of worthiness is *inclusive fitness*.[18] Happiness, wealth, or social position are not currencies of evolution by natural selection. As Betzig (1998, p. 271) aptly puts it, "in natural selection, babies are the only currency that count." From an evolutionary perspective, a wealthy, high-status couple without children is biologically unsuccessful, whereas a working-class, lower status couple who produced surviving offspring is biologically successful. Furthermore, when Spencer argues that all is for the best and should be left alone, he commits the naturalistic fallacy by suggesting that nothing should be attempted to rectify existing moral wrongs.

For Social Darwinism to have any empirical foundation in modern evolutionary biology, one would have to show, at a minimum, both (1) that people of high socioeconomic status (SES) have more children and (2) that specific characteristics, which are genetically transmitted, are reliably associated with high SES. Neither has strong support. In modern industrial societies, SES is *negatively* correlated with lifetime fitness (Borgerhoff, 1998).[19] It still remains unclear why this demographic transition has occurred, and scholars continue to argue over why it has occurred. Although IQ is positively correlated with SES to a moderate degree, a high IQ, at least in women, is negatively related to reproductive success (Herrnstein & Murray, 1994). There is little evidence that high SES is consistently associated with a specific constellation of inherited traits. In one of the most comprehensive studies on determinants of socioeconomic status in the United States, Jencks and his colleagues (1977) examined the effects of cognitive ability, personality, family background, and amount of schooling on economic success. All aspects of family background (including cognitive ability, personality, and education) predict about 48 percent of the variance in men's occupational status; 52 percent of factors that affect SES are independent of family background and thus independent of genetic factors. Of the 48 percent of the variance explained by family background, about one-third of that explains the resemblance in SES among brothers. Therefore, assuming that the resemblance among brothers is due to genetic factors, only about one-sixth of a male's SES could be explained by genetic factors. An additional piece of evidence that indicates that Social Darwinism is wrongheaded is research on economic mobility in the United States. If Social Darwinism were valid, then it would be reasonable to expect that the same people and their descendants would remain in the upper income brackets over time and, by the same token, that the same people and their descendants would remain in the lower income brackets over time. Studies that follow individuals over time show that people who constitute "the rich" and "the poor" change over time (Sowell, 1995). One study found that fewer than half of the families studied remained in the same income quintile between the years 1971 and 1978 (Duncan et al., 1984).

Finally, some critics argue that evolutionary psychology is old wine in a new bottle—the old instinct theory in a new package. Instinct theory in psychology had its heyday during the early twentieth century. It attempted to explain human behavior by instincts, inborn tendencies to behave in a particular manner. The problem with most of the early instinct theories was that they were descriptive without scientific foundation. Sex, aggression, cooperation, criminal behavior, and sloth were all due to instincts for those behaviors. The lists of instincts went on and on, with little theoretical or empirical justification for their existence. The idea that instincts existed by virtue of naming them as such is ludicrous (Plotkin, 1998). At the same time, several eminent psychologists, such as William McDougal, Sigmund Freud, and William James, advocated more sophisticated instinct theories and gave theoretical reasons for their existence. William James's view in particular was influenced by Darwin's theory of evolution by natural selection. James described numerous human instincts, but he believed that they were adaptations that evolved through natural selection (Buss, 1999). Nevertheless, the association of instinct theory with eugenics, the haphazard use of instinct theory, and the rise of behaviorism so weakened the effect of evolutionary ideas in psychology that they did not appear again in any major way until 50 years later (Plotkin, 1998).

In Summary

The evolutionary perspective approaches phenomena by first asking *why* questions. Why do cats purr? Why do organizations use the hiring practices that they do? Why do people prefer face-to-face contact with teachers? Even when something may be perceived as a problem or as undesirable, like workplace rudeness, the evolutionist's first inclination is to ask why it exists. If there is evidence that the phenomenon is an adaptation, then we would want to know its purpose—that is, what function it serves. An evolutionary perspective is also *historical and contextual*. The evolutionary history of an adaptation is important to understanding it. How long has it existed, where, and in what species are important questions to ask for understanding its evolution and function. Adaptations, whether biological or social, evolve in response to particular environmental conditions. To understand the development and function of an adaptation, it is important to consider the context in which it evolved.

The evolutionary perspective suggests that interventions in complex systems are inevitably problematic. Yet, nothing in the evolutionary perspective implies that moral wrongs or problems should be left alone because they are somehow in the natural order of things. A manager who finds that employees are rude should take steps to solve the problem. However, before making the usual knee-jerk attempts to address social problems with professionally designed social interventions, it is useful to look at traditional practices that are related to the problem at hand. Such practices evolved over years with the benefit of infinite trial-and-error adjustments in context. How might traditional practices be adapted to modern organizations? How might organizations be changed to be more compatible with human nature (Nicholson, 2000)? Any effort, whether resurrected traditional practices or those developed from scratch, should be compatible with human psychology. Understanding the functions of adaptations is an important first step to applying knowledge about biological and social systems.

NOTES

1. In New York City, a "regular" cup of coffee is with milk; in the Midwest, "regular" denotes black coffee.

2. Henry Petroski (1993) makes a similar argument for the evolution and manufacture of the common lead pencil.

3. Blaming public ignorance is not confined to industrial psychologists. The economist and Nobel Laureate George Stigler argued that the same is true of most economists: "Almost all economists subscribe [to the belief] that non-economists are slow and perverse in accepting the reasonably reliable findings of our science. Elsewise would not some of our relatively uncontroversial findings . . . long ago have been accepted?" (1976, p. 348). Yet Stigler asks, if public stupidity is behind the failure to use the ideas of social scientists, why then do physical scientists not appear to have this problem? The public eagerly swallows antibiotics, antidepressants, and contraceptives, and buys the latest electronic gadgets.

4. A newspaper opinion column on the outbreak of the "I love you" computer virus in the fall of 2000 applied ideas about variability and viability to computer systems (Quinlan, 2000). The columnist pointed out that he did not get the virus because he used Word Perfect made by Corel, and the virus was programmed to infect computers that used a Microsoft platform. Since the large majority of personal computers use the Microsoft Word, the virus was able to infect huge numbers of computers. However, if there had been more variation in the types of programs used, the virus would have infected a smaller number of computers and would have done less damage.

5. Dawkins (1986, pp. 237 ff.) offers a more cogent explanation for the gaps in the fossil record: the evolution of most species does not occur in one place.

6. A practice is *functional* to the extent that its "consequences . . . make for the adaptation or adjustment of a given system" (Merton, 1957, p. 51). *Adaptation* in this sense, as a verb, means aligning structures, processes, and outputs of a system with exigencies of its environment, thereby increasing the probability of its survival in that environment. However, current practices that have survived the test of time are adapted to past worlds. If an organization's environment has significantly changed, practices that were functional in the past may be dysfunctional in present environments.

7. Simple heuristics are also a type of knowledge that are based on some hardwiring. They are evolved mental mechanisms that operate as algorithms. They simplify decision making processes when people are presented with certain classes of stimuli (Gigerenzer et al., 1999).

8. Complexity is primarily a function of the number of elements in a system. Hayek (1964, p. 335) suggests that complexity is a function of "the minimum number of elements of which an instance of [a] pattern must consist in order to exhibit all the characteristic attributes of the class of patterns in question." That is, the degree of complexity reflects the "minimum number of distinct variables a formula or model must possess in order to reproduce the characteristic patterns of structures of different fields (or to exhibit the general laws which these structures obey)" (Hayek, 1964, pp. 335–336). In addition to number of distinct elements, I would add the degree of uncertainty in cause-and-effect relations among those elements. The greater the degree of uncertainty, the greater the complexity.

9. With just eight independent variables and six dependent variables, this requires defining 14 constructs and 48 relationships. Given the number of variables and relationships involved in human resource interventions, precise prediction is impossible.

10. Gillon's only recommendation for "what-do-we-do-now" is that American policymakers exercise more humility when proposing social programs. This uninspired recommendation illustrates the need for a new perspective for thinking about the nature of social interventions.

11. Even the changes to the human condition brought about by the supposed cure-all, technology, have had unexpected and unpleasant consequences (Tenner, 1996). For example, while better running shoes have allowed vastly more people to exercise and enjoy running almost anywhere, orthopedic injuries have also increased because these shoes increased the popularity of running and their comfort allowed people to do more running on hard surfaces.

12. "Uncertainty means unknown probabilities" (Bernstein, 1996, p. 133).

13. Half a century after Mead conducted her research in Samoa, Derek Freeman (1999) went to Samoa and interviewed Mead's original informants who were still alive. They informed Freeman that they had been hoaxing Mead—making up stories about life on Samoa. The Samoans, it turns out, are like the rest of us. They experience sexual jealousy and have conflicts over resources, and life as a teenager is stressful there too.

14. I taught for a semester at the University of Zambia as a Fulbright scholar. One of my colleagues, a visiting professor from England, was having trouble with thieves breaking into her apartment and stealing her possessions. She had tried all sorts of mechanical solutions to remedy the problem—bigger locks on the doors, bars on the windows—but none worked. The thieves outwitted her every time until she finally came across a solution that worked: rubber snakes. By chance she met someone who had gone on an expedition across Africa in a convoy of four-wheel drive vehicles, and he explained how they prevented theft from their vehicles (and of their vehicles) when they were camped at night. The outfitter who ran the expedition placed lifelike rubber snakes in a conspicuous

place on the dashboards. This had the effect of deterring thieves. My colleague put rubber snakes on her window sills and thereafter did not have a problem with thieves.

15. As Williams (1966, p. 14) points out: "I cannot readily accept the idea that advanced mental capabilities have ever been directly favored by [natural] selection. There is no reason for believing that a genius has ever been likely to leave more children than a man of somewhat below average intelligence."

16. Historically, psychologists within this tradition were strongly interested in looking for innate differences in classes of people. Galton was interested in proving that the English upper classes were innately mentally superior to the lower classes. In the early part of the twentieth century, Yerkes measured individual differences among new immigrants to the United States, and he attempted to show that those from southern and eastern Europe were innately inferior in a variety of ways to those from northern Europe and England.

17. Girls who reach pubertal maturation early have a higher risk for unhealthy weight gain, breast cancer in later life, teenage pregnancy, emotional problems such as anxiety and depression, problem behaviors such as sexual promiscuity, and alcohol consumption.

18. When an individual leaves no offspring, he or she is consigned to genetic oblivion. Inclusive fitness is the sum total of an individual's fitness—direct and indirect. Direct fitness is the individual's own reproductive success, production of viable offspring. Indirect fitness is reproduction by one's relatives. One can increase indirect fitness by helping nieces and nephews survive and reproduce.

19. Male SES is related to fitness in premodern societies (Betzig, 1986).

REFERENCES

Aamodt, M., Bryan, D., & Whitcomb, A. (1993). Predicting performance with letters of recommendation. *Public Personnel Management, 22,* 81–90.

Abelson, R. P. (1997). On the surprising longevity of flogged horses: Why there is a case for the significance test. *Psychological Science, 8,* 12–15.

Adams, G. A., Elacqua, T. C., & Colarelli, S. M. (1994). The employment interview as a sociometric selection technique. *Journal of Group Psychotherapy, Psychodrama & Sociometry, 47,* 99–113.

Aharon, I., Etcoff, N., Ariely, D., Chabris, C. F., O'Connor, E., & Breiter, H. C. (2001). Beautiful faces have variable reward value: fMRI and behavioral evidence. *Neuron, 32,* 537–551.

Alchian, A. A. (1950). Uncertainty, evolution, and economic theory. *Journal of Political Economy, 58,* 211–221.

Alcock, J. (1993). *Animal behavior: An evolutionary approach.* Sunderland, MA: Sinauer Associates.

Alcock, J. (2001). *The triumph of sociobiology.* New York: Oxford University Press.

Alexander, R. D. (1987). *The biology of moral systems.* Hawthorne, NY: Aldine DeGruyter.

American Management Association. (1986). *Hiring costs and strategies*. New York: AMACOM.

Arvey, R. D., & Campion, J. E. (1982) The employment interview: A summary and review of recent research. *Personnel Psychology, 35*, 281–322.

Basalla, G. (1988). *The evolution of technology*. New York: Cambridge University Press.

Baum, J.A.C., & Singh, J. V. (Ed.). (1994). *Evolutionary dynamics of organizations*. New York: Oxford University Press.

Beal, C. R. (1994). *Boys and girls: The development of gender roles*. New York: McGraw-Hill.

Beer, M. (1980). *Organization change and development: A systems view*. Santa Monica, CA: Goodyear.

Berlin, I. (1991). *The cooked timber of humanity: Chapters in the history of ideas*. (Henry Hardy, Ed.). New York: Alfred A. Knopf.

Bernstein, P. L. (1996). *Against the gods: The remarkable story of risk*. New York: John Wiley & Sons.

Betzig, L. (1986). *Despotism and differential reproduction: A Darwinian view of history*. New York: Aldine.

Betzig, L. (1998). Not whether to count babies, but which. In C. Crawford & D. L. Krebs (Eds.), *Handbook of evolutionary psychology: Ideas, issues, and applications* (pp. 265–273). Mahwah, NJ: Lawrence Erlbaum.

Borgerhoff, M. M. (1998). The demographic transition: Are we any closer to an evolutionary explanation? *Trends in Evolutionary Ecology, 13*, 266–270.

Bouchard, T. J., Lykken, D. T., McGue, M., Segal, N. L., & Tellegen, A. (1990). Sources of human psychological differences: The Minnesota study of twins reared apart. *Science, 250*, 223–228.

Boyd, R., & Richerson, P. J. (1985). *Culture and the evolutionary process*. Chicago: University of Chicago Press.

Breland, K., & Breland, M. (1961). The misbehavior of organisms. *American Psychologist, 16*, 681–684.

Brown, D. E. (1999). Review of the book, *The fateful hoaxing of Margaret Mead: A historical analysis of her Samoan research*. *Evolution and Human Behavior, 20*, 289–292.

Browne, K. R. (2002). *Biology at work: Rethinking sexual equality*. New Brunswick, NJ: Rutgers University Press.

Bruderer, E., & Singh, J. V. (1996). Organizational evolution, learning, and selection: A genetic-algorithm-based model. *Academy of Management Journal, 39*, 1322–1349.

Bureau of National Affairs. (1988). *Recruiting and selection procedures*. Personnel Policies Forum, Survey No. 146. Washington, DC: Author.

Burke, E. (1964). *Reflections of the revolution in France*. London: Dent. (Original work published 1790.)

Buss, D. M. (1999). *Evolutionary psychology: The new science of the mind*. Boston: Allyn & Bacon.

Buss, D. M. (1995). Evolutionary psychology: A new paradigm for psychological science. *Psychological Inquiry, 6*, 1–30.

Buss, D. M. (1989). Sex differences in human mate preferences: Evolutionary hypotheses tested in 37 cultures. *Behavioral and Brain Sciences, 12*, 1–49.

Buss, D. M., Haselton, M. G., Shackelford, T. K., Bleske, A. L., & Wakefield, J. C. (1998). Adaptations, exaptations, and spandrels. *American Psychologist, 53*, 533–548.

Campbell, D. T. (1994). How individual and face-to-face group selection undermine firm selection in organizational evolution. In J.A.C. Baum and J. V. Singh (Eds.), *Evolutionary dynamics of organizations* (pp. 23–38). New York: Oxford University Press.

Campbell, D. T. (1975). On the conflicts between biological and social evolution and between psychology and moral tradition. *American Psychologist, 30*, 1103–1126.

Campbell, D. T. (1965). Variation and selective retention in socio-cultural evolution. In H. R. Barringer, G. I. Blanksten, and R. W. Mack (Eds.), *Social change in developing areas* (pp. 19–49). Cambridge, MA: Schenkman.

Campbell, J. P., McCloy, R. A., Oppler, S. H., & Sager, C. E. (1993). A theory of performance. In N. Schmitt and W. C. Borman (Eds.), *Personnel selection in organizations* (pp. 35–70). San Francisco: Jossey-Bass.

Carlton, J. (1997). *Apple: The inside story of intrigue, egomania, and business blunders.* New York: Time Books.

Cascio, W. F. (1998). *Applied psychology in personnel management* (5th ed.). Englewood Cliffs, NJ: Prentice Hall.

Chagnon, N. A. (1997). *Yanomamö* (5th ed.). Fort Worth, TX: Harcourt College Publishers.

Colarelli, S. M. (1998). Psychological interventions in organizations: An evolutionary perspective. *American Psychologist, 53*, 1044–1056.

Colarelli, S. M., Alampay, M. R., & Canali, K. G. (2002). Letters of recommendation: An evolutionary perspective. *Human Relations, 55*, 315–344.

Colarelli, S. M., & Stumpf, S. A. (1990). Compatibility and conflict among outcomes of organizational entry strategies: Mechanistic and social systems perspectives. *Behavioral Science, 35*, 1–10.

Connor, W. R. (1991). Why were we surprised? *The American Scholar, 60*, 175–184.

Cosmides, L. (1989). The logic of social exchange: Has natural selection shaped how humans reason? *Cognition, 31*, 187–276.

Cronbach, L. J. (1986). Social inquiry by and for earthlings. In D. W. Fiske & R. Shweder (Eds.), *Metatheory in social science: Pluralisms and subjectivities* (pp. 83–107). Chicago: University of Chicago Press.

Cronin, H. (1991). *The ant and the peacock: Altruism and sexual selection from Darwin to today.* New York: Cambridge University Press.

Cummins, D. D. (1998). Social norms and other minds. The evolutionary roots of higher cognition. In D. D. Cummins and C. Allen (Eds.), *The evolution of mind* (pp. 30–50). New York: Oxford University Press.

Darwin, C. (1859/1958). *The origin of species by means of natural selection or the preservation of favoured races in the struggle for life.* New York: New American Library.

Dawkins, R. (1986). *The blind watchmaker: Why the evidence of evolution reveals a universe without design.* New York: W. W. Norton.

Degler, C. N. (1991). *In search of human nature: The decline and revival of Darwinism in American social thought.* New York: Oxford University Press.

Dennett, D. C. (1995). *Darwin's dangerous idea: Evolution and the meanings of life.* New York: Touchstone.

de Waal, F. (1982). *Chimpanzee politics: Sex and power among apes.* Baltimore, MD: Johns Hopkins University Press.

Diamond, J. (1997). *Guns, germs, and steel: The fates of human societies.* New York: W. W. Norton.

Duncan, G. J., Coe, R. D., Corcoran, M. S., Hill, M. S., Hoffman, S. D., & Morgan, J. N. (1984). *Years of poverty, years of plenty: The changing economic fortunes of American workers and families.* Ann Arbor: University of Michigan Press.

Eagly, A. H., & Wood., W. (1999). The origins of sex differences in human behavior: Evolved dispositions versus social roles. *American Psychologist, 54,* 408–423.

Eco, U. (1998). *Serendipities: Language & lunacy.* (William Weaver, Trans.). New York: Columbia University Press.

Einhorn, H. J. (1986). Accepting error to make less error. *Journal of Personality Assessment, 50,* 387–395.

Einhorn, H. J., & Hogarth, R. M. (1981). Behavioral decision theory: Processes of judgment and choice. *Annual Review of Psychology, 32,* 53–88.

Eldredge, N., & Gould, S. J. (1972). Punctuated equilibria: An alternative to phyletic gradualism. In T.J.M. Schopf (Ed.), *Models in paleobiology,* (pp. 82–115). San Francisco: Freeman, Cooper & Co.

Ellis, B. J., McFadyen-Ketchum, S., Dodge, K. A., Pettit, G. S., & Bates, J. E. (1999). Quality of early family relationships and individual differences in the timing of pubertal maturation in girls: A longitudinal test of an evolutionary model. *Journal of Personality and Social Psychology, 77,* 387–401.

Endsley M. R. (1997). The role of situation awareness in naturalistic decision making. In C. E. Zsambok and G. Klein (Eds.), *Naturalistic decision making* (pp. 269–283). Mahwah, NJ: Lawrence Erlbaum Associates.

Ericsson, K. A., & Lehmann, A. C. (1996). Expert and exceptional performance: Evidence of maximal adaptation to task constraints. *Annual Review of Psychology, 47,* 273–305.

Eysenck, H. J. (1952). *The scientific study of personality.* London: Routledge & Kegan Paul.

Eysenck, H. J., & Eysenck, M. W. (1985). *Personality and individual differences: A natural science approach.* New York: Plenum Press.

Fauna Communications Research Institute (n.d.). Healing and the cat's purr. *Fauna Communications Research Institute News.* Retrieved August 15, 2001 from World Wide Web: *http://www.animalvoice.com/news.htm.*

Freeman, D. (1999). *The fateful hoaxing of Margaret Mead: A historical analysis of her Samoan Research.* Boulder, CO: Westview Press.

Friedman, T., & Williams, E. B. (1982). Current use of tests for employment. In A. K. Wigdor & W. R. Garner (Eds.), *Ability testing: Uses, consequences and controversies* (pp. 99–169). Washington, DC: National Academy Press.

Galbraith, J. R. (1977). *Organization design.* Reading, MA: Addison-Wesley.

Gersick, C. J. (1991). Revolutionary change theories: A multilevel exploration of the punctuated equilibrium paradigm. *Academy of Management Review, 16,* 10–36.

Gigerenzer, G., Todd, P. M., & The ABC Research Group. (1999). *Simple heuristics that make us smart.* New York: Oxford University Press.

Gillon, S. M. (2000). *"That's not what we meant to do": Reform and its unintended consequences in twentieth-century America.* New York: London.

Goodall, J. (1990). *Through a window: My thirty years with the chimpanzees of Gombe.* Boston: Houghton Mifflin.

Grant, P. R. (1986). *The ecology and evolution of Darwin's finches.* Princeton, NJ: Princeton University Press.

Hamer, D., & Copeland, P. (1998). *Living with our genes: Why they matter more than you think.* New York: Doubleday.

Hannan, M. T., & Freeman, J. (1989). *Organizational ecology.* Cambridge, MA: Harvard University Press.

Harris, D. T. (Ed.) (1994). *Organizational linkages: Understanding the productivity paradox.* Washington, DC: National Academy Press.

Harris, M. M. (1989). Reconsidering the employment interview: A review of recent literature and suggestions for future research. *Personnel Psychology, 42,* 691–726.

Harrison, J. (1971/1989). *Wolf: A false memoir.* New York: Dell.

Hartigan, J. A., & Wigdor, A. K. (Eds.) (1989). *Fairness in employment testing.* Washington, DC: National Academy Press.

Hayek, F. A. (1964). The theory of complex phenomena (pp. 332–349). In M. Bunge (Ed.), *The critical approach to science and philosophy: In honor of Karl R. Popper.* New York: Free Press.

Hedberg, B., Nystrom, P. C., & Starbuck, W. H. (1976). Camping on seesaws: Prescriptions for a self-designing organization. *Administrative Science Quarterly, 21,* 41–65.

Helson, R., & Stewart, A. (1994). Personality change in adulthood. In T. F. Heatherton & J. L. Weinberger (Eds.), *Can personality change?* (pp. 201–225). Washington, DC: American Psychological Association.

Herrnstein, R. J., & Murray, C. (1994). *The bell curve: Intelligence and class structure in American life.* New York: Free Press.

Hogarth, R. M. (1981). Beyond discrete biases: Functional and dysfunctional aspects of judgmental heuristics. *Psychological Bulletin, 90*, 197–217.

Hogarth, R. M., & Makridakis, S. (1981). Forecasting and planning: An evaluation. *Management Science, 27*, 115–138.

Holland, J. H. (1995). *Hidden order*. Reading, MA: Helix.

Jencks, C., Bartlett, S., Corcoran, M., Crouse, J., Eaglesfield, D., Jackson, G., McClelland, K., Mueser, P., Olneck, M., Schwartz, J., Ward, S., & Williams, J. (1977). *Who gets ahead?* New York: Basic Books.

Jensen, A. R. (1980). *Bias in mental testing*. New York: Free Press.

Jensen, A. (1998). *The g factor: The science of mental ability*. Westport, CT: Praeger.

Johns, G. (1993). Constraints on the adoption of psychology-based personnel practices: Lessons from organizational innovation. *Personnel Psychology, 46*, 569–592.

Johnson, J. (2000). *A fistful of rubles: The rise and fall of the Russian banking system*. Ithaca, NY: Cornell University Press.

Kampe, K.K.W., Frith, C. D., Dolan, R. J., Frith, U. (2001). Reward value of attractiveness and gaze. *Nature, 413*, 589–590.

Kaplan, S. (1992). Environmental preference in a knowledge-seeking, knowledge-using organism. In J. Barkow, L. Cosmides, and J. Tooby (Eds.), *The adapted mind* (pp. 581–598). New York: Oxford University Press.

Kerr, S. (1975). On the folly of rewarding A while hoping for B. *Academy of Management Journal, 18*, 769–783.

Ketelaar, T., & Ellis, B. J. (2000). Are evolutionary explanations unfalsifiable?: Evolutionary psychology and the Lakatosian philosophy of science. *Psychological Inquiry, 11*, 1–21.

Kipling, R. (1996). *Just so stories* (B. Moser, illus.). New York: Books of Wonder, William Morrow and Co.

Klingsporn, M. J. (1973). The significance of variability. *Behavioral Science, 18*, 441–447.

Kossek, E. E. (1989). The acceptance of human resource innovation by multiple constituencies. *Personnel Psychology, 42*, 263–281.

Lakatos, I. (1970). Falsification and the methodology of scientific research programmes. In I. Lakatos and A. Musgrave (Eds.), *Criticism and the growth of knowledge* (pp. 91–195). Cambridge: Cambridge University Press.

Latham, G. P. (1988). Human resource training and development. *Annual Review of Psychology, 39*, 545–582.

Lave, J., & Wenger, E. (1991). Situated learning: Legitimate peripheral participation. New York: Cambridge University Press.

Lawshe, C. H. (1969). Statistical theory and practice in applied psychology. *Personnel Psychology, 22*, 117–123.

Levitt, B., & March, J. G. (1988). Organizational learning. *Annual Review of Sociology, 14*, 319–340.

Levy-Leboyer, C. (1994). Selection and assessment in Europe. In H. C. Triandis, M. D. Dunnette, & L. M. Hough (Eds.), *Handbook of industrial and organizational psychology* (Vol. 4, pp. 173–190). Palo Alto, CA: Consulting Psychologists Press.

Lieberson, S. (1991). Small N's and big conclusions: An examination of the reasoning in comparative studies based on a small number of cases. *Social Forces, 70,* 307–320.

Lindblom, C. E., & Cohen, D. K. (1979). *Usable knowledge.* New Haven, CT: Yale University Press.

Lumsden, C. J., & Wilson, E. O. (1983). *Promethean fire: Reflections on the origin of mind.* Cambridge, MA: Harvard University Press.

Lykken, D. T. (2000). The causes and costs of crime and a controversial cure. *Journal of Personality, 68,* 559–605.

Manz, C. C., & Sims, H. P., Jr. (1993). *Business without bosses.* New York: John Wiley & Sons.

March, J. G. (1994). The evolution of evolution. In J.A.C. Baum & J. V. Singh (Eds.), *Evolutionary dynamics of organizations* (pp. 34–49). New York: Oxford University Press.

March, J. G. (1991). Exploration and exploitation in organizational learning. *Organization Science, 2,* 71–87.

March, J. G., &, Simon H. A. (1958). *Organizations.* New York: John Wiley & Sons.

Markowitz, H. M. (1952). Portfolio selection. *Journal of Finance, 7,* 77–91.

Marks, I. M. (1987). *Fears, phobias, and rituals.* New York: Oxford University Press.

Mead, M. (1935). *Sex and temperament in three primitive societies.* New York: William Morrow.

Mead, M. (1928). *Coming of age in Samoa.* New York: Blue Ribbon Books.

Megarry, T. (1995). *Society in prehistory: The origins of human culture.* New York: New York University Press.

Merton, R. L. (1957). *Social theory and social structure* (rev. ed.). New York: Free Press.

Miller, G. F. (2000). *The mating mind: How sexual choice shaped the evolution of human nature.* New York: Doubleday.

Mineka, S., & Cook, M. (1993). Mechanisms involved in the observational conditioning of fear. *Journal of Experimental Psychology: General, 122,* 23–38.

Mineka, S., Davidson, M., Cook, M., & Keir, R. (1984). Observational conditioning of snake fear in rhesus monkeys. *Journal of Abnormal Psychology, 93,* 355–372.

Mintzberg, H. (1994). *The rise and fall of strategic planning.* New York: Free Press.

Mithen, S. (1996). *The prehistory of the mind.* London: Thames & Hudson.

Muchinsky, P. M. (1999). *Psychology applied to work: An introduction to industrial and organizational psychology* (6th ed.). Belmont, CA: Wadsworth/Thompson Learning.

Muchinsky, P. M. (1979). The use of reference reports in personnel selection: A review and evaluation. *Journal of Occupational Psychology, 52,* 287–297.

Murphy, K. R. (1996). Individual differences and behavior in organizations. In K. R. Murphy (Ed.), *Individual differences and behavior in organizations* (pp. 3–30). San Francisco: Jossey-Bass Publishers.

Murphy, K. R., & Cleveland, J. N. (1995). *Understanding performance appraisal*. Thousand Oaks, CA: Sage Publications.

Nagoshi, C. T., & Johnson, R. C. (1986). The ubiquity of g. *Personality and Individual Differences, 7,* 201–208.

Nelson, R. R., & Winter, S. G. (1982). *An evolutionary theory of economic change*. Cambridge, MA: Belknap.

Newell, A. (1990). *Unified theories of cognition*. Cambridge, MA: Harvard University Press.

Newman, J. R. (1988). *The world of mathematics: A small library of the literature of mathematics from A'h-mosé the Scribe to Albert Einstein*. Redomond, WA: Tempus Press.

Nicholson, N. (2000). *Executive instinct: Managing the human animal in the information age*. New York: Crown Business.

Orians, G. H., & Heerwagen, J. H. (1992). Evolved responses to landscapes. In J. Barkow, L. Cosmides, and J. Tooby (Eds.), *The adapted mind* (pp. 555–580). New York: Oxford University Press.

Orton, J. D., & Weick, K. E. (1990). Loosely coupled systems: A reconceptualization. *Academy of Management Review, 15,* 203–223.

Perrow, C. (1961). The analysis of goals in complex organizations. *American Sociological Review, 26,* 854–866.

Petroski, H. (1993). *The evolution of useful things*. New York: Alfred A. Knopf.

Pinker, S. (1997). *How the mind works*. New York: W. W. Norton.

Pinker, S., & Bloom, P. (1990). Natural language and natural selection. *Behavioral and Brain Sciences, 13,* 707–784.

Plotkin, H. (1998). *Evolution in mind: An introduction to evolutionary psychology*. Cambridge, MA: Harvard University Press.

Popper, K. R. (1959). *The logic of scientific discovery*. New York: Hutchison Education.

Popper, K. R. (1966). *The open society and its enemies* (Vols. I and II). Princeton, NJ: Princeton University Press.

Porras, J. I., & Robertson, P. J. (1992). Organizational development: Theory, practice, and research. In M. D. Dunnette and L. M. Hough (Eds.), *Handbook of industrial and organizational psychology* (2nd ed.) (Vol. II) (pp. 719–822). Palo Alto, CA: Consulting Psychologists Press.

Quillen, E. (n.d.). Biology might hold the explanation for cyber-epidemics. *Denver Post*. Retrieved August 15, 2001 from World Wide Web: *http://www.denverpost.com/opinion/quill0509.htm*

Ravitch, D. (2000). *Left back: A century of failed school reforms*. New York: Simon & Schuster.

Richards, R. J. (1987). *Darwin and the emergence of evolutionary theories of mind and behavior*. Chicago: University of Chicago Press.

Richards, R. J. (1992). *The meaning of evolution: The morphological construction and ideological reconstruction of Darwin's theory*. Chicago: University of Chicago Press.

Ridley, M. (1996). *The origins of virtue: Human instincts and the evolution of cooperation*. New York. Penguin Books.

Roberts, R. M. (1989). *Serendipity: Accidental discoveries in science*. New York: John Wiley & Sons.

Root-Bernstein, R. S., & Root Bernstein, M. R. (1997). *Honey, mud, maggots, and other medical marvels: The science behind folk remedies and old wives' tales*. Boston: Houghton Mifflin.

Ross, L., & Nisbett, R. E. (1991). *The person and the situation: Perspectives of social psychology*. New York: McGraw-Hill.

Rozin, P. (1976). Psychological and cultural determinants of food choice. In T. Silverstone (Ed.), Appetite and food intake (pp. 286–312). Berlin: Dahlem Konferezen.

Schmidt, F. L. (1993). Personnel psychology at the cutting edge. In N. Schmitt & W. C. Borman (Eds.), *Personnel selection in organizations* (pp. 497–515). San Francisco: Jossey-Bass.

Silverman, I., & Eals, M. (1992). Sex differences in spatial abilities: Evolutionary theory and data. In J. Barkow, L. Cosmides, and J. Tooby (Eds.), *The adapted mind* (pp. 533–549). New York: Oxford University Press.

Simon, H. A. (1976). *Administrative behavior* (3rd ed.). New York: Macmillan. (Originally published in 1945).

Singer, P. (1999). *A Darwinian left: Politics, evolution, and cooperation*. New Haven, CT: Yale University Press.

Singh, D. (1993). Adaptive significance of waist-to-hip ratio and female attractiveness. *Journal of Personality and Social Psychology, 65*, 293–307.

Sowell, T. (1995). *The vision of the anointed*. New York: Basic Books.

Spencer, H. (1987/1961). *Study of sociology*. Ann Arbor: University of Michigan Press.

Stajkovic, A. D., & Luthans, F. (1997). A meta-analysis of the effects of organizational behavior modification on task performance. *Academy of Management Journal, 40*, 1122–1149.

Stein, J., & Su, P. Y. (Eds.). (1980). *The Random House Dictionary*. New York: Ballantine Books.

Stigler, G. J. (1976). Do economists matter? *Southern Economic Journal, 42*, 347–354.

Symons, D. (1992). On the use and misuse of Darwinism in the study of human behavior. In J. Barkow, L. Cosmides, and J. Tooby (Eds.), *The adapted mind* (pp. 137–162). New York: Oxford University Press.

Symons, D. (1979). The evolution of human sexuality. New York: Oxford University Press.

Taleb, N. N. (2001). *Fooled by randomness: The hidden role of chance in the markets and in life*. New York: Texere.

Tellegen, A., Lykken, D. T., Bouchard, T. J., Wilcox, K. J., Segal, N., & Rich, S. (1988). Personality similarity in twins reared apart and together. *Journal of Personality and Social Psychology, 54,* 1031–1039.

Tenner, E. (1996). *Why things bite back: Technology and the revenge of unintended consequences.* New York: Alfred A. Knopf.

Terpstra, D. E., & Rozell, E. J. (1997). Why potentially effective staffing practices are seldom used. *Public Personnel Management, 26,* 483–495.

Thomas, L. (1974). *The medusa and the snail: More notes of a biology watcher.* New York: Viking Press.

Toda, M. (1962). The design of a fungus eater: A model of human behavior in an unsophisticated environment. *Behavioral Science, 7,* 164–183.

Tooby, J., & Cosmides, L. (1992). The psychological foundations of culture. In J. H. Barkow, L. Cosmides, and J. Tooby, *The adapted mind* (pp. 19–137). New York: Oxford University Press.

Tooby, J., & Cosmides, L. (1990). On the universality of human natures and the uniqueness of the individual: The role of genetics and adaptation. *Journal of Personality, 58,* 17–67.

Tyack, D., & Cuban, L. (1995). *Tinkering toward utopia: A century of public school reform.* Cambridge, MA: Harvard University Press.

University of Pennsylvania, The Wharton School. (1999, Spring). *Academy of Management Placement Roster* (p. 4). Academy of Management Placement Service, Division of Management and Marketing, The University of Texas at San Antonio.

Vale, J. R. (1980). *Genes, environment, and behavior: An interactionist approach.* Cambridge, MA: Harper & Row.

Wake, D. B., Roth, G., & Wake, H. M. (1983). On the problem of stasis in organismal evolution. *Journal of Theoretical Biology, 101,* 211–224.

Waldrop, M. M. (1992). *Complexity: The emerging science at the edge of order and chaos.* New York: Simon & Schuster.

Watson, J. B. (1924/1970). *Behaviorism.* New York: W. W. Norton.

Weick, K. E. (1979). *The social psychology of organizing.* Reading, MA: Addison-Wesley.

Whitney, W. O., & Mehlhaff, C. J. (1987). High-rise syndrome in cats. *Journal of the American Veterinary Medical Association, 191,* 1399–1403.

Wiesner, W., & Cronshaw, S. (1988). A meta-analytic investigation of the impact of the interview format and degree of structure on the validity of the employment interview. *Journal of Occupational Psychology, 61,* 275–290.

Williams, G. C. (1996). *Plan and purpose in nature.* London: Weidenfeld & Nicolson.

Williams, G. C. (1966). *Adaptation and natural selection: A critique of some current evolutionary thought.* Princeton, NJ: Princeton University Press.

Wilson, A. M., McGuigan, Su, A., & van den Bogert, A. J. (2001). Horses damp the spring in their step. *Nature, 414,* 895–899.

Yeats, W. B. (1962). *Selected poems and two plays of William Butler Yeats.* (M. L. Rosenthal, Ed., updated ed.). New York: Collier Books.

Zsambok, C. E., & Klein, G. (Ed.) (1997). *Naturalistic decision making.* Mahwah, NJ: Lawrence Erlbaum Associates.

CHAPTER 3

Splinters in the Mind
Methods of Hiring People

Employers want to hire the best workers; [cognitive ability] tests are one of the best and cheapest selection tools at their disposal.
—Richard J. Herrnstein and Charles Murray (1994, p. 479)

Paper-and-pencil [cognitive ability] tests do not fulfill their stated function. They do not reliably identify those applicants who will succeed in college or later in life, nor do they consistently predict those who are most likely to perform well in the jobs they will occupy.... Timed paper-and-pencil tests screen out applicants who could nevertheless do the job.
—Susan Sturm and Lani Guinier (1996, p. 969)

Criteria proposed by each group will be self-interested ones.... We should not look for heroes or villains but for parties with varying interests.... Although no criteria are disinterested—each benefits some groups more than others—all will be stated so as to appear universalistic and objective.
—W. Richard Scott (1998, p. 348)

Throughout human history, people have been making hiring decisions. In all human societies from prehistory to the present, people have been making decisions about who can join their groups and who can fulfill roles within the groups. Although the workplace is most often associated with hiring decisions, they regularly occur in other situations.

Parents select baby-sitters or nannies for their children. Colleges decide which high school graduates will be offered admission. Amateur sports teams choose new members, who will start, and who will sit on the bench. Women choose which male suitors will be their mating partners and husbands. In this chapter I give a historical overview of hiring practices, describe the components of the hiring process, point out differences between traditional and mechanistic hiring methods, and discuss limitations of both methods.

The literature on hiring methods is primarily of a legal and technical nature. Within the past 40 years, legal issues—equal employment opportunity, affirmative action, and employment discrimination—have become central concerns in the personnel selection literature (Sackett & Wilk, 1994); so, too, have narrow technical matters—such as validation strategies, test bias, generalizability, and utility (Guion, 1998). Very little has been written that takes a historical perspective on hiring methods. This is unfortunate. A historical perspective helps in understanding the development, change, and use of hiring practices over time. Without a historical perspective, it is all too easy to assume that hiring methods appeared out of cultural or scientific thin air or that the science behind modern tests renders them contextually inert. A historical perspective provides baselines for comparing traditional and modern hiring methods, and it provides a sharper lens for examining how cultural factors interact with psychological mechanisms to influence our responses to hiring methods.

A BRIEF HISTORY

Prior to the twentieth century, hiring decisions were made by what I will call *traditional hiring methods*. Toward the beginning of the twentieth century and thereafter, many hiring decisions included what I will call *mechanistic hiring methods*. Traditional hiring methods are informal and intuitive; they are based on common sense and are accessible to ordinary people. Typically, the same people who make the hiring decisions will also be working or interacting with the people they hire. Most parents use traditional approaches to hiring decisions about baby-sitters. Parents meet with prospective baby-sitters, talk with them, possibly talk to references, size them up, and make a decision. Mechanistic approaches, on the other hand, are formal and explicit; they use formal rules and algorithms that are comprehensible only to experts. The people making hiring decisions rarely work or interact with the people they select. Most large universities make admissions decisions with mechanistic practices. Applicants' high school grades and SAT scores are entered into an equation that ranks applicants. The mechanistic approach is relatively new, yet it has had a profound impact on admissions in universities and on hiring policies in government organizations. Even so, traditional selection practices persist and, in many organizations, remain more widely used than mechanistic practices (Colarelli, 1996).

Before the Twentieth Century

> Because humans are such a highly social species, social skills are required to harvest many of those resources we get from others. But one of the most important of those social skills is the ability to size up other people as potential cooperators or competitors: members of the opposite sex as potential partners; newcomers to a group for their potential as leaders, workers, or troublemakers. What can this new person do for me, for good or ill?
> —Gaulin & McBurney (2001, p. 182)

Humans are social creatures. From the earliest humans onward, living in groups provided protection from predators and enhanced humans' capacity to obtain resources necessary for survival and reproduction. Other people are critical resources, but they are also threats.

> Humans have become their own principal "hostile force of nature." . . . No other sexual organisms compete in groups as extensively, fluidly, and complexly as humans do. No other organisms at all play competitively group-against-group. Most importantly, so far as we know, in no other species do social groups have as their main jeopardy other social groups of the same species. (Alexander, 1987, pp. 79–80)

The ability to accurately assess other people is a critically important part of our evolved psychology. Because the problems of group living are so central to human existence, natural selection favored humans who had the capacity to accurately assess attributes of other people (Buss, 1995). Perhaps most critical is the capacity to gauge the fertility of members of the opposite sex. People who erred in this regard would not be successful in passing on their genes into the future. There is ample evidence that male and female preferences for mates follow this evolutionary logic. People are attuned to and are attracted to specific physical and psychological features that are related to fertility, health, parenting, and partnership. Both males and females are more attracted to members of the opposite sex with symmetrical features, even at the most subtle levels, because bodily and facial symmetry are indices of health and fertility (Thornhill & Møller, 1997). Females are attuned to indicators of male

ambition and kindness—signs that a male will be a good provider and
parent (Buss, 1994). Males are particularly sensitive to female age, com-
plexion, and body shape—signs of fertility (Buss, 1994; Singh, 1993).

Dominance hierarchies are ubiquitous in human groups, particularly
all-male and mixed sex groups. Studies of chimpanzees and contemporary hunter-gatherers suggest that dominance hierarchies have been part
of the primate social structure for hundreds of thousands of years
(Boehm, 1999; Omark, Strayer, & Freeman, 1980). The ubiquity of
hierarchies suggests that people evolved psychological mechanisms for
assessing their own and others' abilities (Buss, 1999). Numerous studies show that people are very sensitive to rank and inevitably sort themselves according to rank. Children as young as three years old can
accurately identify rank in dominance hierarchies; indeed, they are able
to reason about transitive relations in dominance hierarchies earlier than
they are able to reason about transitive relations with other stimuli
(Cummins, 1998). Adults (and children) placed in new groups quickly
assess their own and others' abilities. They establish stable hierarchies
within a matter of minutes. In a study of 59 three-member groups of
people who had previously not known one another, clear dominance
hierarchies emerged in 50 percent of the groups in one minute. Dominance hierarchies emerged in the other 50 percent within five minutes
(Fisek & Ofshe, 1970). The ubiquity of such hierarchies suggests that
assessing one's own and others' abilities has long been a capacity of the
human mind.

People find it necessary to assess the intentions of others in all sorts
of everyday interactions, from potential sexual encounters to bartering
over food. Assessments of emotion, primarily through facial expressions
and other nonverbal behaviors, are remarkable. People can make accurate judgments of others' emotional states within a few seconds. This
also makes evolutionary sense. Nonverbal behaviors are interpreted rapidly and often subconsciously; this is particularly true of nonverbal behaviors that are hardwired to the emotional system (DePaulo, 1992).
These probabilistic judgments of others are remarkably accurate, probably because they were (and are) adaptive for survival and reproduction (Ambady & Rosenthal, 1992).

Hunter-gatherers did not select people into their groups in the way
that modern organizations select new employees. For most of human
history, people were born into their groups and roles and remained
within them for their entire lives. Most of the roles in ancient and modern hunter-gatherer societies are partitioned by sex. Women were involved in food gathering and preparation and child care, and the men
participated in hunting, warfare, and tribal politics (Tooby & DeVore,

1987). Selection undoubtedly took place within groups when competence was critical to a group's success or was associated with elevated status, as would be the case with warfare and hunting. According to recent studies, males from extant hunter-gatherer groups could make accurate and reliable distinctions about which of them were the best warriors and hunters (Chagnon, 1997; Patton, 1997).

The agricultural revolution that began about 10,000 years ago created surpluses of food sufficient to allow civilizations to develop; with civilizations came greater degrees of occupational specialization (Diamond, 1997; McNeill, 1971). Occupational specialization in the ancient and medieval civilizations occurred primarily in government, religion, the military, skilled crafts, and the arts, where there was a need to regularly recruit, select, train, and evaluate personnel. Unfortunately, there is little information about personnel selection practices in premodern civilizations. Few records were kept, and scholars did not write much about it. That this was the case is itself interesting. Like all administrative procedures, selection methods are not tangible artifacts; they exist primarily in peoples' minds and to a lesser degree in fragile written documents that quickly deteriorate. As a result, knowledge of them can be quickly lost. Some information has probably been lost because selection procedures have not been a major topic among historians, who have not regarded hiring procedures as interesting or significant in the course of human events. Nevertheless, some historical sources provide a glimpse of how selection was carried out in some ancient and medieval civilizations. Although the historical record is thin, it indicates that membership in most groups was ascriptive; people were chosen for membership in groups according to characteristics unrelated to performance. In many societies, only people of certain castes or classes are eligible to hold particular positions, regardless of their ability. At the opposite pole is selection based on achievement, where people are selected according to characteristics related to performance, as would be the case when orchestras conduct auditions and select musicians on the quality of their playing.

As was the case in hunter-gatherer groups, roles in ancient and medieval civilizations were divided primarily by age and sex, and most people followed in their parents' footsteps (McNeill, 1971; Young, 1959). Group and occupational memberships in ancient and medieval civilizations were, for most people, determined primarily at birth via nepotism or by caste. Inheritance was the principal means by which positions of leadership were assumed, war and conquest notwithstanding. Among the ruling elites, sons typically inherited land and titles from their fathers (McNeill, 1971). In agricultural-feudal civilizations, most people's roles in life were tied to the land. The ruling elites owned or controlled land, and inheritance helped to ensure that this valuable resource remained in the family. This in turn helped to ensure the survival of offspring for generations. Because occupational opportunity was also primarily tied to the land, inherited land perpetuated nepotism and ascription as the means of determining group membership. Passing on land, titles, and occupational skills helped to ensure that resources remained in the family, and, hence, increased the chances of survival and offspring. It also increased the chances that the offspring would in turn reproduce and that their offspring would survive and reproduce.[1]

Yet farmers and estate owners must have made choices about which people would be best suited for particular tasks. Like hunter-gatherers, they undoubtedly made distinctions on the basis of obvious characteristics and demonstrated skill. Obvious physical characteristics such as size and strength were important, as were signs of health and resilience. The following passage from Westermann describing how ancient Romans selected slaves is illustrative:

> It was the custom of dealers . . . to exhibit [slaves] upon a raised platform. . . . [T]he slave might be compelled to leap about in order to display his agility. . . . The inspection of prospective purchases by the buyers also became more rigid, and an attempt was made to obtain in the slave the type of physical equipment needed for a particular kind of work. . . . Roman law . . . contained a section . . . which required that the placard placed about the slave's neck should state any serious sickness from which the slave was suffering and whether he was a runaway or had a tendency to wander away. (1955, pp. 98–99)

Governments in ancient, medieval, and Renaissance civilizations had large administrative bureaucracies, which needed to be staffed with functionaries. Ruling elites needed semiliterate and literate people to run the machinery of administration. It appears that selection for administrative positions occurred through connections and patronage. Literate men could gain access to positions through patrons. One may surmise that nobles sized up potential applicants for competence, loyalty, and personality. Competent bureaucrats would also come to the attention of the ruling elites, who would attempt to enlist them in their service, just as contemporary executives attempt to lure talented employees from competitors. Niccolo Machiavelli's career progressed in this manner when his diplomatic ability came to the attention of Gonfalonier Piero Soderini, the head of the Florentine government. Soderini hired Machiavelli as his confidant.

Imperial China's system for selecting bureaucrats stands out as an anomaly in the premodern world. Its selection system appears to have been unique in that it involved a standardized, competitive examination system. Ichisada Miyazaki (1976) traces the beginnings of the system to the Sui emperors (589–618), who used it to override the influence of old aristocratic families. It provided the emperors with a means for selecting administrators on the basis of ability rather than aristocratic lineage and privilege. Over time, China's hereditary aristocracy came to be replaced by literati-administrators who staffed government bureaucracies from the Sung dynasty (960–1279) to the early twentieth century. The examinations were open to virtually all males regardless of social background, and by and large they were administered fairly. The main materials for the tests were the Confucian classics. The Chinese examination system has been criticized for creating a government of mandarins and for stifling creativity and responsiveness to changing circumstances. The intense competition and the psychological toll the examinations took have also been points of criticism, as they are today of standardized admissions and employment tests.[2] That the examination system lasted 1,300 years suggests that it had merits. The Chinese civil service examinations were a well-thought-out and generally accurate test of job knowledge. Confucianism, the basis of the tests, contains a clear set of ethical proscriptions for personal behavior, as well as guidelines for good government.

> The examination gave practical value to education while defining what was to be studied and how the student was to approach his texts. The core of the curriculum was the classics of Confucianism, which, as the state orthodoxy, supplied the moral rationale for the elite and provided all men with a set of personal values while justifying the political structure. (Miyazaki, 1976, pp. 7–8)

These tests also provided an incentive for students to be literate, and literacy was important for many tasks in addition to government administration.

Personnel selection and training were of obvious importance to military organizations in ancient and modern civilizations. The recruitment, selection, and training of enlisted soldiers and officers were important personnel activities that emerged in the early civilizations. An organized, capable military was essential to a civilization's ability to survive (Diamond, 1997; McNeill, 1971). From ancient civilizations to the present, maintaining a sufficient number of competent soldiers was a primary goal of military recruiting. The earliest records of military selection indicate that applicants were selected on the basis of characteristics that were easily observable and had a common-sense relevance to soldiering. The Greek historian Polybius provides a description of selection procedures and criteria used by the army of the Roman Republic in the second century B.C. (from Keppie, 1984). The primary characteristics were age and wealth. Every year, all men of military age, between 17 and 46, were required to go to Rome or other large cities for the selection process, called the *dilectus*. It involved choosing the best candidates who presented themselves. For many years during the Republic, only property owners were eligible for service. Among those who presented themselves, physical attributes seem to have been critical selection criteria. The Roman historian Vegetius provides another description of Roman recruiting.

> The main qualifications were sound health and a good physique. Vegetius informs us . . . that in ancient times, the minimum height of six Roman feet, which is equivalent to 5 ft 10 in. (1.78m), was another qualification. There was a strict medical examination—the young recruit should have a clear eye, carry his head high, have a broad chest, his shoulders muscular, his arms long, his waist small, his legs and feet wiry and not too fleshy. (Webster, 1985, p. 120)

Those selected were grouped by age and wealth. Wealth was an important characteristic because men had to provide their own arms, and wealthier men could obviously afford more expensive armaments. The youngest and poorest were assigned to the ranks of the *velites*, the most expendable and lightly armed soldiers. The richest and oldest men were *equites*, who typically served in the cavalry.

In the army of the great eighteenth century Prussian king Frederick the Great, soldiers were selected simply because they were "big men." Apparently, army officers believed that larger men would make better soldiers than smaller men (Asprey, 1986).

> Sickness and age dictated an annual attrition rate [in the Prussian army] of about 20 percent, which meant that each year a regiment had to recruit some three hundred sound specimens. . . . Commanders vied with each other in recruiting at home and abroad. If commanders were to gain royal favor, at least some of the recruits had to be "big men," bought abroad or kidnapped with considerable difficulty and risk. . . . [Frederick] wrote to the king that he had learned of a shepherd in Mecklenburg who was at least six feet, four inches tall, and asked permission to kidnap him, which the king readily granted. The attempt failed and the shepherd was shot to death, but Frederick gained credit for trying. (Asprey, 1986, p. 94)

Others were not as picky. When Napoleon and Wellington were recruiting soldiers for their continental armies, they took almost any able-bodied male of military age. It was a common practice to send officers to working-class sections of cities, forcibly extract men from bars and brothels, and send them to induction centers (Keegan, 1987).

By and large, it was unnecessary to select soldiers on the basis of characteristics that are difficult to observe.[3] Soldiering was physical work, and obvious physical characteristics are good indicators of strength and the capacity to do physical work. Fine-tuned selection was also unimportant because new soldiers acquired most of their military skills through training and experience. Sound military organizations from Alexander the Great on spent considerable effort training new recruits. Recruits were not expected to hit the ground running. Considerable time was spent on training. These armies also used an unyielding system of discipline to keep soldiers in line and on task (Asprey, 1986; Keppie, 1884; Webster, 1985).

Artisans typically learned their trade through some type of apprentice system. While young people had to be selected into an apprenticeship, the core of the system relied on training and discipline. The selection process was basic and general, and skill development was predicated on years of working with and instruction from a master craftsman. In the Middle Ages, apprenticeships typically ranged in length from 6 to 12 years (Renard, 1918). Typically, parents found a master craftsperson who would take their son on as an apprentice. Since youngsters had no experience in the craft, masters had to size up their potential to learn the craft and to work productively and dependably.

> The apprentice was a child whom his parents or guardians wished to be taught a trade as soon as he was ten or twelve years of age, although there was no fixed age limit. A master was found who would take him. Every instructor must be a master; he must also be of good life and character, endowed with patience, and approved of by the officers of the guild. If he were recognized as capable of carrying out his duties, the two parties bound themselves by a contract, often verbal, often also made before a notary. (Renard, 1918, p. 10)

Since we do not have surveys of or interviews with medieval craftsmen about their hiring practices, there is no way of knowing how they assessed apprentices. However, since the parents would bring the child to a master, we can surmise that the master observed and interviewed the child and the child's parents. If the craft required strength and stamina, masters probably looked for indicators of those traits—body size, musculature, vigor, and so on. Because an apprentice would work closely with a master for at least six years and often more, a master probably tried to get a sense of the applicant's health, personal compatibility with the master, motivation to work, personal integrity, and reliability. Renard (1918) notes that probationary periods, usually of about two weeks, were common, and that either party could cancel the agreement during that period.

When an apprentice became a journeyman, he might continue to work for the same master, work for a new master, or set up his own shop. It was common among journeymen in the building trades to travel to areas where work was available and to seek jobs. Here there appears to have been a fairly systematized selection process. It involved certificates of qualification, letters of reference from former employers that spoke to character and quality of work, and other indicators of responsible behavior, such as freedom from debts.

> [Journeymen] were hired in certain places where the unemployed of all trades assembled. They were required to give proof that they were free of all other engagements, and to present certificates, not only of capability, but of good conduct signed by their last master. Thieves, murderers, and outlaws, and even "dreamers" and slackers, stood no chance of being engaged, while those who, though unmarried, took a woman about with them or who had contracted debts at the inns, were avoided. . . . The master, when he was satisfied with the references given, and when he had assured himself that he was not defrauding another master who had more need of hands than himself, could engage the workman. (Renard, 1918, p. 14)

Work samples were also used in the premodern era to assess skills. Auditions are one such work sample, and numerous references to them appear in the music history literature. In the baroque, classical, and romantic periods, the church and the aristocracy employed most musicians and composers. Composers and musicians would audition before church authorities and nobility. J. S. Bach probably got his first job in the music profession by passing an audition.

> Not wishing to proceed to university or lacking the funds to do so, [Bach] began to look for job openings in the profession of music. The first to come along seems to have been at the Jacobikirche in Sangerhausan, near Halle, where a successor was needed to Gottfried Christoph Graffenhayen, who had died early in July 1702. Bach submitted to the customary Probe (examination), which normally included the performance of a piece of concert music by the applicant, and despite his youth and lack of experience he was immediately offered the post. (Boyd, 2000, p. 15)

It was not uncommon for intellectuals to gain employment or to be admitted to scientific and intellectual societies on the basis of demonstrated competence. Condorcet was admitted to the French Academy because of the quality of his early mathematical writings; Newton's work in mathematics and physics earned him an invitation to the Royal Society. Winning a prize from the Academy of Dijon for his *Discours sur les sciences et les arts* in 1750 helped to launch Rousseau's literary career, and Voltaire's literary and philosophical writings gained him admission to the French Academy in 1746.

This brief survey of hiring methods in pre-industrial eras suggests that people used practices that, for the most part, made functional sense. People tended to use methods that provided immediate and obvious information about job candidates, such as physical stature and demonstrations of performance. They used methods that involved minimal inferences about the relationship between performance on a test and performance on a job. When Johann Sebastian Bach applied for his first job as a musician, he was not given a musical ability test; rather, he was asked to perform music. Although employers were obviously concerned about estimating how well applicants would perform on the job, they were also concerned about avoiding harm. Employers would often look for cues (reputation, marital status, and signs of disease) that could provide information about whether an applicant would cause harm.

The Testing Revolution in the Twentieth Century

In the early twentieth century, a revolution occurred in methods for assessing and selecting people into organizations. Modern, mechanistic assessment and hiring methods arose from developments in science, from the intellectual currents of positivism, from the industrial revolution, and from the rise of the democratic and individualistic ethos. The Baconian view of science—which emphasized method, empiricism, and the social utility of science—was firmly established. Positivism—which advocated application of the scientific method to problems in organizations and society—provided an intellectual foundation for applied psychology (Eastman & Bailey, 1994). Many scientists and intellectuals were swept up in the belief that by using applications of social science they could design organizations to meet specific social and managerial goals. At about the same time, psychologists had begun to systematically study individual differences and develop tests to measure them. With positivism a dominating philosophy among scientists and intellectuals, it was a small step to view the new psychological tests as a tool with which to improve organizations and society.

The industrial revolution changed much work from small-scale, primarily home and craft-based jobs to large industrial enterprises. It bought about a high degree of specialization and division of labor. People who worked in the growing factory system tended machines. This required minimal training and skill. Occupational demographics changed, with employment in agriculture and home-based industry and crafts decreasing. Large numbers of people migrated from these sectors to the industrial sector. Employment tests were viewed as a means to help "rationalize a chaotic labor market" (Hale, 1982, p. 3). They also fit with the rising belief that individual merit rather than privilege should be the basis for opportunity and advancement. The use of tests reflected "a general movement in the twentieth century toward 'democratizing' American society" (Hale, 1982, p. 4).

Early use of standardized tests in the United States occurred in the nineteenth century in the federal bureaucracy, motivated by a desire to root out corruption and to base personnel decisions on objective assessments of talent. The Civil Service Act of 1883 authorized the use of tests for hiring certain federal employees as a necessary remedy of the spoils system that had crippled the civil service with favoritism and incompetence. In partial imitation of the British civil service examination system, positions were filled on the basis of competitive examinations; however, fearful of creating a mandarinate, Congress required that the tests be of a practical nature, unlike the academically based tests used in the British and Chinese civil service systems (Hale, 1982). By the early twentieth century, approximately 60 percent of federal civil service jobs were filled through testing; personnel testing was also becoming common in state governments. The use of tests for jobs in industry emerged in the early twentieth century, spurred on in no small measure by the high turnover rates, industrial accidents, and strikes associated with radical changes occurring in the new industrial workplace.

> To many employers . . . waste and inefficiency in the workplace pointed directly to poor selection procedures. A systematic science of selection, they argued, would go far toward eliminating the disorders of scale . . . that beset modern industry. Indeed, it soon became a central tenet of the new profession of personnel management that all labor problems would be eliminated "when a scheme has been devised which will make it possible to select the *right man for the right place*" (Link, 1919, p. 23). (Hale, 1982, p. 8, emphasis in original)

During World War I, standardized testing emerged on a mass scale. Intelligence tests were used to evaluate recruits when the United States entered the wars. These tests were again widely used in World War II. The labor exigencies of the two world wars and the federal government's intervention into labor relations during the wars had a major impact on the subsequent bureaucratization of employment in large organizations throughout the United States (Baron, Dobbin, & Jennings, 1986).

Other major social influences on employment and educational testing were the legislation and court decisions on civil rights from the 1960s through the 1980s. These legislative and legal decisions wrestled with a problem: tests used in employee hiring and university admissions had the effect of excluding some minority groups who scored lower than whites. Therefore, the courts and government agencies, such as the Equal Employment Opportunity Commission (EEOC), became increasingly influential in the debate over the technical standards and fairness of tests. The *Uniform Guidelines on Employee Selection Procedures* (1978) specify technical procedures that employers must follow to demonstrate that their tests are job related when there is evidence that tests adversely impacted the hiring rates of minorities.

Educational testing followed a similar course. There was a strong belief that individual differences in students have a major impact on student performance, and democratic culture has deep-rooted beliefs about merit, efficiency, and accountability (Resnick, 1982). The advent of mass education, which brought large numbers of students from a great variety of backgrounds into public schools contributed to the widespread use of standardized testing. Standardized educational testing came to "enjoy the support of not only the organized groups which have fostered its development—psychologists, school administrators, and publishers alike—but of public agencies, state and federal, and of taxpayers, whose contributions help to support our desire to keep our schools accountable for their costs and their educational quality" (Resnick, 1982, p. 174). Testing addressed the demographic and structural problems that education faced, and at the same time there were supporting scientific, technical, cultural, and intellectual forces. Educational and business institutions valued individualism, merit, and efficiency (Callahan, 1962; Kanigel, 1997). The computer was a major technological influence on testing by the 1960s. Computers allowed large numbers of tests to be scored quickly and efficiently.

Even so, by the end of the twentieth century, debates about the advantages of mechanistic selection methods over the traditional methods were far from resolved. Traditional hiring methods are still widely used in the private sector; the employment interview and letters of recommendation remain the most widely used selection devices. Although psychological tests are widely used in education, the civil service, and the military, they remain controversial and have engendered considerable political, legal, and academic debate (Lemann, 1999; Ravitch, 2000; Rothstein, 2000; Sturm & Guinier, 1996). It is also unclear how often people responsible for hiring decisions actually use formal testing procedures. Procedures are often circumvented so that the informal methods can be used (Holmen & Docter, 1972; Samelson, 1979). For example, although the Army Alpha test that was administered to 1,750,000 soldiers during World War I has assumed a mythic stature among testers, it "is now clear that the program contributed little to the war effort. Test scores were never used consistently in the assignment or rating of recruits" (Reed, 1987, p. 84). "[T]here was a vast difference between the actual operation of the [Army Alpha testing] system and the neat tables and correlation coefficients of test results presented in the psychologists' publications" (Samelson, 1979, p. 145).

The industrial revolution and the cultural, social, and technological changes that accompanied it occurred with astonishing speed. Many of the newly developed selection methods were attempts to adapt to those changes. Yet human nature changes considerably more slowly than culture and technology. Hence, it is not surprising that people still prefer hiring methods—face-to-face interaction, observation, and narrative—that rely on primary psychological mechanisms. Similarly, the inevitable politics and conflicts of interest endemic to organizations worked against the ideal that tests and test scores would be used impartially and by the book. The introduction of mechanistic hiring methods resulted in a mismatch between these new methods and human nature. Humans had evolved to survive in hunter-gatherer groups during the Pleistocene, and their fundamental psychological makeup had not changed with the advent of modernity, which sprang up within an evolutionary blink of an eye.

THE COMPONENTS OF HIRING METHODS

One way to get a better handle on the effects of hiring methods and people's reactions to them is to analyze their components. Mechanistic hiring methods involve components that go beyond immediate and obvious perception and traditional social interpretation. They can produce effects that contradict common sense or custom (Dunbar, 1995). Hiring procedures involve at least five components: (1) purposes, (2) information, (3) method of information gathering, (4) analysis, and (5) decision making.[4] (See Table 3.1.)

Table 3.1
Hiring Process Components

Components	Hiring Method	
	Traditional	Mechanistic
Purpose	Usually implicit	Usually explicit
Beneficiaries	People who gather information and make decisions on applicants	Testing experts, test makers, people who score high on tests, and people who value what tests attempt to predict
Type of information	Intimate, diffuse, immediate, obvious, concrete, and particular Qualitative	Distant, specific, delayed, opaque, abstract, and universal Quantitative
Amount of information	Large	Small
Method of information gathering	Face-to-face narrative	Standardized tests
Who gathers information	People with a stake in new employees	Professionals in test administration
How decisions are made	Intuition, personal judgment	Algorithms
Who is involved in making decisions	People with a stake in new employees	People in authority and consultants

Purpose

At first glance, the purpose of any hiring practice seems obvious: to enable an organization to hire the best person for the job.[5] Yet, the purpose of hiring practices is rarely this straightforward. The purposes of hiring practices are more nuanced. Some are explicit; some are implicit. Explicit purposes are often written out, and organizational members have a shared understanding of them. Implicit purposes are beneath the surface; a practice may serve a purpose without any or all parties being aware of it. Or, although people are aware of an implicit purpose, they may avoid discussion of it for social or political reasons. Still another way to think about the purpose of a hiring practice is to ask whether its primary function is selection or rejection—that is, whether it attempts to predict how a job applicant will perform in the future or to reject unsuitable applicants who are likely to cause harm.

The justification for using modern mechanistic hiring methods in work organizations is that they enabled organizations to hire the "best person for the job." People differ in their abilities, skills, motivations, and personalities; different jobs require particular abilities, skills, motivations, and personalities; and one person in the applicant pool is likely to have more of the requisite characteristics than others. That individual is the best person for the job. The idea of the best person for the job goes back at least as far as Plato, who wrote that that there are ideal types of people for roles in the ideal state, Callipolis, that he envisioned in *The Republic*. The guardian, or gold, class would be the rulers. Educated in philosophy, they are the wisest and most intelligent—and are the best persons for the job of ruling society. The auxiliary, or bronze, class is reasonably fit, intelligent, and willing to take orders. They are best suited to be police, soldiers, artisans, and farmers. The rest, the least intelligent, would be the menial laborers.

In the early twentieth century, Frank Parsons, a founding father of vocational psychology, and Hugo Münsterberg, a founding father of industrial psychology, championed the use of testing procedures developed by professional psychologists to match workers to jobs and thereby increase efficiency and industrial harmony. Parsons argued that "men work best when they are doing what Nature has especially fitted them for. . . . A sensible industrial system will seek . . . to put men, as well as timber, stone, and iron in the places for which their natures fit them" (cited in Hale, 1980, pp. 121–122). Münsterberg believed that organizations were like large organisms. They functioned best when the right people were in the right jobs. These ideas of Parsons and Münsterberg are intellectual descendants of Plato, and they remain the cornerstones of modern vocational and industrial psychology. If a date and author were not listed after the following quote, it could easily be mistaken as a passage from Parsons or Münsterberg.

> Our goal [is] . . . to assess each individual's aptitudes, abilities, personality, and interests, to profile these characteristics, and then to place all individuals in jobs perfectly suited to them and to society. Each individual would make the best and wisest possible use of his or her talents, while in the aggregate, society would be making maximal use of its most precious resource. (Cascio, 1998, pp. 2–3)

Beginning in the 1980s, a new view of what made someone "the best" person for a job emerged, primarily from management scholars. The sustained viability of an organization requires more than people just doing their jobs well. It requires that organizations have an effective, competitive business strategy. Therefore, the "best" person not only has the ability to do the job well but also has the values, beliefs, and background that fit with the organization's strategy. In the 1990s, Snow and Snell (1993) devised a third approach, which they called "staffing as strategy implementation." This approach assumes that the business environment is too complex for managers to develop effective overall strategies. The most effective strategies are likely to emerge from the bottom up, from the employees themselves. For this to occur, organizations need to hire "high-caliber" individuals and accumulate a workforce with a broad base of skills.

Snow and Snell (1993) classify staffing models into three categories (see Table 3.2). What they call Model 1 involved matching people to jobs; Model 2 matched people to strategy; and Model 3 involved staffing as strategy formation. All three models are based on the notion of "fit." Modern, mechanistic personnel selection in organizations is essentially like a jigsaw puzzle. Specific pieces go in specific places, and when the pieces are all in the right place, the organization will function optimally (Dunnette, 1976). With Model 1, the best person is the one whose characteristics fit best with the job tasks; with Model 2, the best person is the one whose characteristics fit best with the organization's strategy; and with Model 3, the best person is the one with the most intelligence and the greatest array of useful skills. Furthermore, they assume that each model is suited for different types of organizations. Model 1 is best suited for stable organizations, Model 2 for organizations with clear strategies, and Model 3 for organizations that must change strategies often and quickly.

Snow and Snell's analysis is limited because it is unrealistic to assume that there are three distinct organizational types. *All* organizations have

Table 3.2
Three Models of the Staffing Process

	Staffing Process		
	Model 1: Staffing as Person-Job Match	Model 2: Staffing as Strategy Implementation	Model 3: Staffing as Strategy Formation
Characteristics	Staffing based on job analysis Many candidates available per job Tests to measure individual differences Validation studies Closed-system perspective	Staffing based on competitive strategy (part of implementation) Role descriptions Interdepartmental team synergies Open-system perspective	Staffing based on strategy formation Broad skill base Rapid deployment of resources Open-system Perspective
Assumptions	Organizations and jobs can be separated into individual components People and jobs are stable Job performance can be measured validly and reliably	Deductive logic Reactive staffing Tight fit between strategy and staffing	Inductive logic Proactive staffing Loose fit between strategy and staffing (slack)

Applications	Organizations with stable, definable jobs	Organizations with clear strategies and known competencies	Organizations that need the ability to develop or change strategy quickly
Recruitment	Expand pool of job applicants	Attract targeted individuals to enhance core competencies	Build relationships with potentially useful human resources
Selection	Achieve person-job fit by rejecting less desirable applicants	Develop a configuration of individuals that meets synergistic needs of strategy	Enhance strategic capability by choosing individuals who bring new skills to the company
Appraisal	Based on job performance	Based on strategy implementation	Based on strategy formation
Promotion	Reward is upward movement within a hierarchy	Reward is increased centrality to current strategy	Reward is greater inclusion in strategy-formation process

Source: Snell and Snow (1993).

to fit people to jobs, have to implement strategy, and have to develop strategy. Organizations have to fit people to jobs as well as to strategies.

Traditional hiring methods typically involve more than an explicit purpose; many purposes are implicit and informal. People rarely decide to use traditional methods based on a careful analysis of means and ends. Rather, people use traditional methods on the basis of custom and habit (Nelson & Winter, 1982). They interview employees or request letters of recommendation because "we have always done it that way." People sometimes have no shared explicit understanding of why a traditional method is being used, what the rules applied to it are, and what outcomes it is intended to predict. Most organizations use the employment interview or letters of recommendation; yet the procedures and decision rules for using these methods are rarely explicit (Adams et al., 1994; Arvey & Campion, 1982; Muchinsky, 1979). In traditional methods, implicit purposes operate at two levels: (1) the group and organizational levels and (2) the individual level. At the group and organizational levels, traditional methods, over time, have "worked" to serve some purpose or purposes that are valuable to organizational survival. Traditional hiring practices have been selected and retained by a general system of organizational inheritance (see Chapter 2). At the individual level, practices tend to be used because individuals benefit from them.

Beneficiaries

The principal beneficiaries of traditional hiring methods are the people who gather information and make decisions on applicants. Traditional hiring methods advance the interests of people involved in the hiring process. Because traditional hiring practices often do not have standardized procedures, formal decision rules, or evaluative criteria, it is easy for people to use them to advance their own personal goals and interests. People are likely to use the interview to determine whether job applicants will be compatible with them, helpful to them, and advance their interests and goals (Adams et al., 1994). This is one reason why they are so widely used and why their use is persistent: people are generally unwilling to change practices from which they derive personal benefit. Claims that people use hiring methods to advance *organizational interests* are not complete. Individuals are interested in and pursue their self-interests.

Adam Smith's notion of the invisible hand may be relevant to the relation between individual interests and organizational functioning. A hypothesis worth looking into is this: the good of the organization is maximized as an incidental result of organizational members pursuing their self-interests. Traditional hiring methods are compatible with people's evolved ability to assess potential harm from other people; this is one reason why these methods have persisted and remain widely used. Over the course of human evolution, people have evolved preferences for face-to-face and narrative methods for obtaining information about people. Such encounters provide rich and detailed information, which is compatible with evolved psychological mechanisms related to the detection of cheaters, the assessment of risk, and the avoidance of harm.[6] People prefer interviews and letters of recommendation to paper-and-pencil tests because they provide information that will be more personally useful. Traditional methods are concerned with evaluating risk and potential harm as much as they are with predicting performance. This makes good evolutionary sense. A person is more likely to survive and reproduce by erring on the side of caution, rejecting any people who appear to be potential threats. One mistake, one acceptance of a person or situation that is in fact harmful, could prove fatal. People are also more emotionally responsive to negative than positive information (Taylor, 1991). People's propensity to react more strongly to negative than positive information is an evolved adaptation: over evolutionary history, it has been more difficult for people to reverse the consequences of a severe assault than of a missed opportunity (Cacioppo & Berntson, 1999). Therefore, people prefer methods of gathering information about people that allow them to assess the risk of loss or harm.

Traditional methods typically benefit the people who are gathering information on candidates, since the information they gather via interview and narrative can be interpreted with respect to their interests. How will this applicant possibly benefit or harm me? Is this person friendly or hostile to me? Will this person be an ally or a competitor? Here, then, are two other reasons for the utilization paradox introduced in Chapter 2. Ordinary people prefer to use hiring methods that do not meet the approval of professional testers because they perceive that traditional methods are in their self-interest, and traditional methods provide information in a way that is more compatible with evolved preferences for information about other people. Conversely, ordinary people are less likely to use methods that do not meet the professional testers' approval because they do not believe that it is in their self-interest to use mechanistic methods, and mechanistic methods provide information that is difficult for them to comprehend.

If one accepts the premise, as most testers do, that mechanistic hiring methods identify people who contribute positively to organizational goals and that individual contributions have an additive effect on organizations and society, then one is also likely to accept, as most testers do, the corollary that organizations and society benefit from the use of mechanistic hiring practices. However, the goals that managers are attempting to achieve are based on *their own* interests; so managers, and the psychologists who work for them, often use other values to justify using tests to select people with particular characteristics. The specific behavior that a test predicts is rarely sufficient justification by itself. The values invoked to justify use of the Scholastic Aptitude Test (SAT) over the years are illustrative. Soon after the development of the test in the early 1930s, James Bryant Conant, then president of Harvard University, and an assistant dean at Harvard, Henry Chauncey, were searching for a way to admit people into college based on "natural ability." At the time, whether a student's parents could afford the tuition was the primary basis for admission. This was creating a self-perpetuating upper class in the United States of rich, middlebrow, white, Protestant males. Conant wanted to dethrone this "artificial aristocracy," return the United States to its democratic nature, and replace it with a ruling class based on brains. Conant and other educators at the time shared Thomas Jefferson's desire that "the best geniuses be raked from the rubbish annually and be instructed, at the public expense." However, Conant needed a technology that would identify Jefferson's "natural aristocracy" and make education the wellspring of American greatness. With the SAT he found such a technology. "Science, which Conant believed in no less whole-heartedly than Jefferson, now offered in mental testing a way of selecting the country's deserving new leaders. The SAT, in other words, would finally make possible the creation of a natural aristocracy" (Lemann, 1999, p. 43). Chauncey envisioned an even broader purpose for ability tests. He hoped to conduct a census of abilities to identify splinters in the mind.

> To Chauncey's way of thinking . . . testing and ETS [the Educational Testing Service, which Chauncey became president of after leaving Harvard] were going to move beyond aptitude into a new era when testing would achieve a broad, nuanced understanding of the whole spectrum of human abilities. . . . Just as the Manhattan Project had split the atom, the Educational Testing Service . . . would decode the mind. Many more people than just aspiring college and graduate students would be tested. . . . This new knowledge would help human affairs to take on a new conformation: rational understanding would replace prejudice, hatred, emotion, and superstition. Human nature itself would be reformed. (Lemann, 1999, p. 68)

Society and organizations do not benefit from mechanistic hiring methods as much as testers claim because most of the ostensible benefits are based on a panoply of unrealistic assumptions. They presuppose that organizations and societies have a coherent set of goals, that mechanistic hiring methods perform only one primary function, and that function is congruent with organizational and social goals. Moreover, it is in part misleading to say that *organizations* and *society* at large benefit from a particular hiring method because b*enefits accrue to individuals*. Individuals who benefit from mechanistic hiring methods include the people who develop and sell tests, the testing consultants who help managers use tests, people who score high on tests, and the personnel administrators who have the responsibility for screening large numbers of applicants. People who may be reprimanded or fired if they visibly base hiring decisions on private values and interests can also benefit from tests because they can cloak their personal interests in a shroud of legitimacy provided by objective test scores. The people who do not benefit are (1) those who do not score highly on tests and (2) individuals whose authority to make hiring decisions is usurped by mechanistic testing methods. From the standpoint of an individual who is involved in making a hiring decision about a potential colleague, it's hard to say whether an applicant will be a competitor or an ally based on an SAT or IQ score. Hiring decisions affect the lives of people doing the hiring, at times for the worse; therefore, people are likely to prefer hiring methods that provide information that is personally useful.

Information

Hiring methods differ in the type and amount of information they provide, and they can be described along a number of dimensions related to information. I will focus on information related to evolved psychological mechanisms for perceiving and processing information about people—intimacy, diffuseness, immediacy, obviousness, concreteness, and particularity. Figure 3.1 provides a typology of the types of information associated with traditional and mechanistic hiring methods. Hiring methods can range from intimate to distant. The intimacy of information is based on the number of the senses involved in processing information about a person. Information that is highly intimate involves most or all of the senses—sight, hearing, smell, and touch—whereas information that is more distant involves fewer senses. An employment interview allows a person to gather information on a more intimate level than a paper-and-pencil test because the interview involves at least three senses (sight, hearing, and smell), whereas a test score involves one sense (sight). The interview necessarily involves direct contact between the applicant and employer. A paper-and-pencil test typically

Figure 3.1
A Typology of Characteristics of Information and Hiring Methods

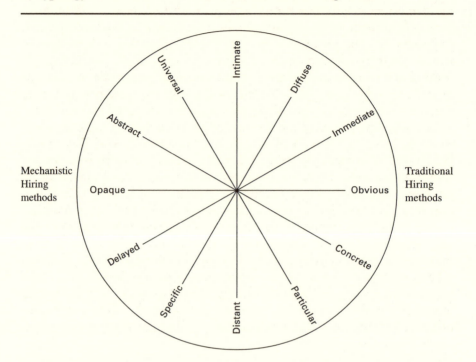

requires no contact—the employer views a piece of paper with the applicant's score printed on it. Hiring methods differ in the degree to which the information they provide about a person is diffuse or specific. A diffuse method provides information on a wide variety of attributes of an individual, whereas a specific method provides information about one or a small number of attributes. Interviews are diffuse, providing an employer with information about an applicant's physical characteristics, sex, age, speech patterns, style of dress and grooming, racial origin, style of interaction, communication skills, and possibly information on goals, values, and job skills. IQ tests, on the other hand, provide one piece of specific information: a number that indicates the applicant's level of intelligence.

Information provided by hiring methods differs in the degree to which it is immediate and obvious. Immediate information is available quickly. When information is obvious, its meaning is readily apparent. If I want to know what sex or what age a person is, the information is usually obvious and can be obtained immediately by looking at the person. For many jobs, a variety of immediate and obvious attributes signal whether or not a person can perform a job. If a job requires that a person speak in public or play baseball, observing a person speak in public or play baseball would provide immediate and obvious evidence that the person could do the job. If one cannot actually see the applicant behave in a way that indicates the capacity to perform the job, a second-best preference would be one or several narrative accounts describing the person's behavior. At the opposite pole is delayed and opaque information. Whether a person is kind, hard-working, honest, works well under pressure—these are neither noticeable right away nor plainly obvious.

The degree to which information is concrete or abstract is important. Concrete information is a sample of the thing itself. A work sample test provides concrete information about how well a person can perform a specific task. It is not a sign of something else. If applicants for a mechanic's job at an auto repair shop are asked to assemble a transmission that has been taken apart, this provides concrete information about how well they can assemble a transmission. Abstract information is a sign of something other than itself. An IQ test score is a number that is a *sign* of something, a person's intelligence. Particular information applies to one or a few situations, whereas universal information is typically abstract and applies to many situations. Information from a work sample test provides particular information related to one or a few jobs, whereas a personality test for conscientiousness provides universal information that is relevant to a wide variety of jobs.

Traditional hiring methods are, by and large, intimate, diffuse, immediate, obvious, concrete, and particular. Mechanistic methods, on the other hand, tend to be distant, specific, delayed, opaque, abstract, and universal. The preference for the type of information found in traditional hiring practices has been shaped by thousands of years of human evolution. Face-to-face interaction and narrative were the only sources of information about other people for most of our evolutionary past, and our neurocognitive system developed to utilize information about people gathered from everyday language and gesture (Baron-Cohen, 1997; Sugiyama, 2001). Natural selection shaped human preferences for information about people from face-to-face interaction and narrative. Consider how much of social life and reproduction involves this type of information. A large component of human moral systems is based on direct and indirect reciprocity (Alexander, 1987). To reciprocate, people must identify the individuals who did (or did not) do them good turns. Specific identification requires face-to-face interaction or its narrative equivalent. In addition, the biological imperative for helping people who are genetically related to one's self—altruism based on inclusive fitness (Hamilton, 1964)—requires a means of identifying kin. Human kin recognition systems are largely visual. People must see, interact with, and listen to descriptions of others to determine their degree of physical similarity and the probability of relatedness. In addition, information from narratives and face-to-face interaction was and is adaptive for surviving in dominance hierarchies. Dominance hierarchies require following a set of complex social norms and obligations, engaging in deceptions, jockeying for power, attempting to outwit dominant individuals, and detecting instances of cheating (Cummins, 1998). However, the detection of rule violations and the communication of rule violations to others require face-to-face interaction or its narrative equivalent.

Face-to-face interaction is rich and redundant, and humans have evolved a sophisticated capacity to accurately process a considerable amount of information about other people. On the basis of brief encounters, people can accurately assess each other's emotional states. This assessment is made primarily from nonverbal facial cues and is typically processed without conscious awareness. People can make remarkably accurate assessments of others' personalities and how much they like each other in encounters as short as 10 seconds (Ambady & Rosenthal, 1992, 1993). Similarly, humans are able to assess fertility cues from brief face-to-face encounters with the opposite sex. These cues are processed quickly (and largely unconsciously). Many of the characteristics that people respond to seem to be adaptations that were beneficial to survival and reproduction. Men's judgments about the attractiveness of females are based on cues related to a female's probable degree of fertility and probability of bearing healthy offspring (Buss, 1998). These features include age, skin luster, waist-to-hip ratio, and body and facial symmetry. Similarly, women make judgments about male attractiveness from obvious cues that relate to the probability of fathering healthy offspring and providing resources to support offspring (Buss, 1998). These cues include age, symbols of economic and social status, position in dominance hierarchies, friendliness, facial symmetry, and degree of masculinity in facial features (e.g., squareness or roundness of the jaw). When women are in the ovulating phase of their monthly cycle, they are most sexually attracted to men with masculine features, suggesting an appraisal based on "good genes" (Penton-Voak, et al., 1999). Women also use the obvious cue of male height in their mating decisions. Taller men have greater reproductive success than shorter men, even after controlling for education and status. The use of height as a cue to male health and gene quality is not entirely due to acculturation. Taller men are, on average, healthier than shorter men (Pawlowski, Dunbar, & Lipowicz, 2000).

That almost all people can make such remarkably accurate assessments and do so in such brief periods of time and largely at a non-conscious level strongly suggests that these are evolved adaptations. People often need to quickly identify potential friends or foes, allies and enemies, and sexual partners. People who could make such assessments accurately and quickly had a better chance of survival and reproduction than those who could not. Face-to-face interaction is suited to assessing risk and potential harm because of the rich array of cues it provides about a person's emotional state. Therefore, it is understandable that people have a strong preference for gathering information about other people this way.[7]

Traditional hiring methods provide immediate and obvious information about people. During most of human evolution, humans did not have the benefit of scientific technology to probe beneath surface phenomena. Relevant information about a person could be gathered immediately (this person is a frail old man) and what it meant was obvious (he probably cannot personally harm me physically). People were able to know about other people only from obvious and immediate characteristics (e.g., age, sex, health and fertility cues, size, dominance, obvious skills). Therefore, people developed psychological mechanisms to allow them to respond to and make decisions about other people on the basis of immediate and obvious features.

A high school basketball coach, at the beginning of every season, must make decisions about which of the students who tried out for the basketball team should be selected. Observing how well each student played basketball during a team tryout would certainly be more useful than each student's cognitive ability test score. The manager of a large public swimming pool, at the beginning of each summer, must hire lifeguards and swimming instructors. Asking job applicants to demonstrate their skills in mock rescue and swimming instruction situations is a better predictor of how well they would perform as instructors and lifeguards than their scores on a personality test. Many prestigious universities normally do not tenure younger faculty based on promise. They wait to grant tenure only to professors who have a track record of scholarly achievements—which is why the average age of Harvard's tenured arts-and-sciences professors is 55 (Golden, 2002). The danger of a policy that grants tenure to younger people who show early promise is that a university's faculty will fill up with tenured mistakes. An entrepreneur who is starting a software design company and needs to hire computer programmers is better off making hiring decisions by evaluating samples of work than by looking only at test scores. A partner in a prestigious law firm gets applications from hundreds of graduates from top law schools every year. Virtually all people who gained admission to a top law school had to meet selective entrance requirements, although there is certain to be some variability in LSAT scores. How should the law firm make hiring decisions? Choose applicants with the highest IQ scores? Interview them and choose applicants with whom the interviewers are comfortable and believe would to fit into the firm? Or institute a summer internship program where the firm's partners hire second-year students during the summers and evaluate their work and potential as future employees? The latter is a common practice among many law firms—with good reason.

The type of information used by mechanistic hiring methods is very different from that used by traditional hiring methods. The mechanistic method of hiring people imitates modern science—using methods that go beyond immediate and obvious perception, using concepts and analyses that are understood primarily by specialists, and producing results that may contradict common sense or custom. The goal of modern science is to understand how nature works, and to do so often requires that scientists go beyond ordinary perceptual capabilities. Learning about the galaxies and the life cycles of stars required sophisticated radio telescopes and spectrometers; charting the human genome required not only an adequate theoretical understanding of genetics, but also a vast array of technology to enable scientists to sequence genes. Similarly, without modern social science methods, it would not be possible to gather and interpret information on the characteristics of large groups of people or to understand subtle regularities in behavior across populations or cultures. Ordinary perceptual processes are not capable of sampling and summarizing the political attitudes and demographic characteristics of millions of citizens.

Modern mechanistic hiring practices use the methods of social science to describe characteristics of people, to measure and quantify those characteristics, to estimate the relationship of those characteristics to desired outcomes, and to aid in formulating decision rules (AERA, 1985). The information used in mechanistic hiring practices has three primary features. It involves a numerical test score that is a sign of where a person ranks on a characteristic measured by a test. Second, the number associated with a test score cannot be interpreted by itself; ancillary technical information is needed to interpret the meaning and accuracy of the test score. A large amount of esoteric statistical and psychological knowledge is required to understand the meaning of the test score and inferences that can be made from it. Thus, only people with a high degree of specialized knowledge can develop psychological tests and interpret test scores. A third feature of the information related to mechanistic hiring methods is that terms reflect psychological theory rather than ordinary meanings. Psychologists use both common and esoteric terms to describe the characteristics of people—dominant, intelligent, neurotic, Machiavellian, conscientious, and so on. The terms are defined precisely and often go beyond common meaning. Professionally developed tests are assumed to provide better and more useful information for decision making than alternatives, such as the information ordinary people glean through observation, interaction, or narratives. According to the American Educational Research Association (AERA), "Available evidence supports the judgment of the Committee on Ability Testing of the National Research Council that the proper use of well-constructed and validated tests provides a better basis for making some important decisions about individuals and programs than would otherwise be available" (1985, p. 1).

Method of Information Gathering and Who Gathers It

Traditional methods gather information about job applicants from interaction, observation, and narration. Most employers talk to applicants themselves and to others who know the applicants, and read narrative descriptions written about applicants, written by applicants, or written by people who know the applicants; employers may also watch them perform at job tryouts or during probationary periods (Bureau of National Affairs, 1988). In addition, *several* people typically gather information. In the course of most hiring procedures, job applicants are interviewed by several people, and several people may also read their application as well as the letters of recommendation (Colarelli, 1996; Friedman & Williams, 1982). The people who gather information on job applicants are likely to be ordinary employees who will end up working with the new employee and thus have a stake in how the new employee performs (cf. Brown, 1979). Hiring in domestic settings works the same way. When hiring a baby-sitter for their children, parents gather information using interviews and referrals. Interviews, referrals, and observation provide diffuse information about many characteristics of an applicant. Face-to-face interaction and observation also permit employers to get a sense of their level of personal comfort and safety with an applicant. That traditional systems involve multiple people making an assessment about an applicant increases the reliability of the final judgment about an applicant. Von Neumann's *principle of redundancy* states that reliable *systems* can be developed from multiple components, even though each component itself is somewhat unreliable (Hogarth, 1981).

With mechanistic hiring methods, psychologists or personnel specialists gather the information about job applicants. The mechanistic perspective assumes that information gathered by ordinary people is superficial, that their judgments are often biased and flawed, and that improvements in reasoning and prediction will occur when information is gathered by specialists and mechanistic methods (AERA, 1985; Swets, Dawes, & Monahan, 2000). The mechanistic approach maintains that specialists are necessary for effective hiring decisions. As Shrauger and Osberg point out, "[Most psychologists assume that] the [professional] assessor, by virtue of his or her knowledge of psychological principles . . . and of attributes of the person being judged, is in the best position to make evaluations and predictions about that individual" (1981, p. 322).

Personnel psychologists have been partly successful in arguing that ordinary people's judgments are flawed and biased. Decision makers in educational and government organizations seem to readily accept such claims and grant psychologists control of information or hiring. As early as Münsterberg and Taylor, professional psychologists belived that the organization of work, including hiring procedures, belonged in the hands of experts. According to Münsterberg, "Everything which is usually left to tradition [and] to caprice [should be replaced with] entirely new means and tools, where nothing [is] left to arbitrariness" (cited in Hale, 1980, pp. 150–151). Almost a century later, Robert Guion (1998) echoed a similar sentiment.[8] If managers and human resource professionals applied scientific principles of personnel selection, "fewer personnel decisions would be based on whim and prejudice" (p. ix). Conspicuously absent are discussions of the effects of their own prejudices on the expertise they are peddling.

Ordinary people are also assumed not to truly understand their own and others' mental processes, personalities, and capabilities (Nisbett & Wilson, 1977). This precludes ordinary individuals from making informed and objective hiring decisions. People applying for jobs, or for admission to universities, are generally not sufficiently aware of their capacities to determine whether they will be successful in a given situation. Similarly, they are not sufficiently aware of their biases and cognitive limitations to make effective decisions about others. At the turn of the twentieth century, Frank Parsons asserted that people needed expert assistance to determine the line of work that best suited them. Münsterberg extended Parsons' ideas about vocational guidance: "The ordinary individual knows very little of his own mental functions. . . . Half an hour's experiment in the laboratory may tell us more about a man's attention than half a year's living with him (Münsterberg, 1913, cited in Hale, 1980, p. 123).[9]

The realities of large, modern organizations—in conjunction with the individual's limited capacities for processing large amounts of complex information and—have no doubt increased the need for tests and specialists to make hiring decisions. Humans cannot efficiently deal with large numbers. For most of human evolution, it is likely that humans used only simple counting systems involving small numbers (Geary, 1995; Moore, 1996). Even today, some primitive people have very simple numerical systems. The Yanomamö of the Amazon have only three numbers in their vocabulary: one, two, and more than two (Chagnon, 1997). Similarly, humans are not intuitive statisticians and have difficulty dealing with statistics and probability. Statistics and probability theory are recent inventions, emerging only after the Renaissance. The advent of modern society in the nineteenth century brought large organizations, large nations, and mass education to much of the world. These new institutional forms required new methods for dealing with and making decisions about large numbers of people. These were methods that did not come intuitively to people but had to be learned through years of specialized study (Geary, 1995). Thus, few people are likely to have a working facility with statistics, while almost all understand the evidence that the human mind evolved to use regularly (frequencies, counting, face-to-face interaction).

Decision Making

Decision making involves choosing one alternative from several, and choices require information and analysis. In making hiring decisions, information is gathered on job applicants; it is analyzed; and a choice is made about whom to hire and whom to reject. The procedure may or may not be evaluated to assess how well it worked. This general framework can apply to both traditional and mechanistic hiring methods, but the nature of each component in the framework differs in the two methods.

Probability theory combined with some version of expected utility theory or Bayesian modeling is the usual framework for mechanistic hiring methods. With mechanistic hiring methods, numerical information is entered into an algorithm that uses statistical prediction rules (SPRs). To establish the SPRs, studies are conducted to evaluate the strength of the relationship between the sources of information, which are typically test scores, and desired outcomes, which are usually some

criteria of performance. Decision makers establish a cutoff point for selection and rejection. The cutoff score is established by estimating a level
on the predictor that is associated with a minimally acceptable outcome.
After the procedure is used for some time, it may be evaluated to determine whether it produces reasonably accurate predictions. With the
"strong" version of this approach, hiring decisions are made only on
the basis of the information that goes into the algorithm, the results of
the SPR, and quantitative decision-rules for making the hiring or admissions decision (Dawes, Faust, & Meehl, 1989). A "moderate" version
uses the results of the SPRs and the cutoff rule as the primary bases for
hiring, but decision makers will also include other information that is
harder to quantify. The "weak" version simply provides the decision
makers with the results of the SPRs, which they are free to use or not
to use as they please (e.g., Brown, 1979).

Interestingly, personnel researchers have conducted few studies that
examine *actual* personnel decisions that use mechanistic hiring methods.
Textbooks typically describe how hiring decisions *should* be made, but
we know little about how they are actually made.[10] University admissions appear to be something of an exception. Because of increasing legal scrutiny of admissions in colleges and universities, their admission
processes have become more widely studied and publicized. Swets et al.
(2000) describe the procedure for admitting students to the University
of Virginia Law School, which is a textbook example of a strong-to-
moderate version of decision making using mechanistic methods.

> At the University of Virginia Law School . . . a new and expanded Admis-
> sions Index is being used. . . . This index includes [the applicant's under-
> graduate grade point average (GPA) and Law School Admission Test
> (LSAT) score and] two additional variables: the mean LSAT score achieved
> by all students from the applicant's college who took the LSAT (a proxy
> for the quality of the undergraduate institution) and the mean GPA
> achieved by students from the applicant's college who applied to law
> school (a proxy for the extent of grade inflation . . .). This new four-
> variable SPR predicts first-year law school grades (correlation $r = .48$)
> significantly better than the old two-variable [GPA and LSAT] SPR (cor-
> relation $r = .41$). . . . [The procedure shifts from a strong to moderate
> version when] the results of this expanded SPR are still adjusted by the
> admission committee to take into account, harder-to-quantify variables,
> such as unusual burdens borne or achievements experienced during col-
> lege, to produce the final decision to admit or reject. (2000, p. 18)

The final rank of applicants is based on the scores of applicants as determined by the algorithm and admission committee's judgments about

hard-to-quantify variables. Exactly how much impact the "harder-to-quantify variables" have, what they are, and how the admissions committee deals with them remain a mystery. As much as Swets et al. admire this algorithmically driven process for selecting law students, they probably could not convince the law school faculty to hire law faculty this way.[11]

Decision making occurs quite differently with traditional hiring methods. They do not use massive amounts of numerical information gathered over a large time period. They do not use an explicit, formal calculus for estimating the utility of a hiring method. They do not use formal algorithms for combining numerical information or explicit decision-rules designed to use that information. Traditional methods involve fast and frugal heuristics at the individual level of decision making and coalitional politics at the group and organizational levels. Gigerenzer et al. (1999) coined the term *fast and frugal heuristics* to describe decision-rules that involve few parameters, are computationally simple, and are ecologically and socially rational. Such rules reflect features of the environment or social world that enhance people's capacity to survive and reproduce. Most interviewers will quickly reject an applicant who exhibits threatening or hostile nonverbal behavior during an employment interview, even if the applicant's job skills are impressive (Bolster & Springbett, 1961). Some of these decisions involve an emotional response. People may not be aware of the components of their decision-making rules and how much weight they give to each component. They may use mental shortcuts to help them cope with the many possibilities. People respond positively to people who are similar to themselves (Wexley, Alexander, Greenawalt, & Couch, 1980); they reject applicants when they receive negative information about them. The goals of traditional hiring methods have little (if anything) to do with organizational goals. People typically judge others using fast and frugal heuristics based on *self-interest*. They are interested in whether the applicant will help advance their personal goals (Adams et al., 1994).

Traditional methods presuppose that people making hiring decisions will have, or believe they will have, frequent personal contact with an applicant after he is hired. People involved in hiring are likely to assume that their lives will be affected by who is hired; therefore, it is important to them that they are able to size up the applicants. This belief is generally correct. In 1998, about 37 percent of working adults in the United States were employed in organizations of under 100 people where they were likely to have personal contact with many of the people who worked in their organizations (U.S Census Bureau, n.d.). Even in large organizations, hiring decisions frequently involve some degree of decentralization so that people in a work group have the opportunity to interview or otherwise assess at least the finalists for job openings in their group.

Many hiring decisions are made by a group of people rather than by one individual or by an algorithm (Colarelli, 1996; Klitgaard, 1985; Topor, 2000). Therefore, the ranking and choice of candidates involves political maneuvering. Individuals first form their own preferences based on the information they have and their reactions to it. Since not everyone shares their preference, they engage in political activity to build coalitions to support their preferences (Cyert & March, 1963). The political maneuvering may then alter each individual's personal rank order, as people reconcile conflicts among their self-interest, their preferred candidate, and their survival and status within the group. People in authority often have significant influence in determining who is hired, and the preferences of those in authority have a significant impact on decision-making politics. The final rank order is usually the result of a group decision that has been affected by individual preferences and political processes.

Another factor influencing decision making in traditional hiring practices is the organizational habits that Nelson and Winter (1982) call "routines." They are the tacit, implied, often nonconscious organizational procedures that are the ways that things are typically done, day after day, year after year. Routines are passed on from one generation of employees to the next. People do not have to be aware of how the routines originated and what their actual functions are. Routines are extremely difficult to change because of social inertia.

PROBLEMS WITH HIRING METHODS

Both traditional and mechanistic hiring methods have their problems. The problems are generally different, and the severity and implications of the problems depend on the situation. Traditional methods suffer from a lack of standardization. Because they differ from place to place, it can be difficult to interpret the meaning of judgments based on a traditional method. School grades are a classic problem. Different teachers and different schools have different standards for assigning grades. Other judgments are also based on subtle and subjective characteristics. The results of traditional methods often vary from person to person. When college professors write letters of recommendation, there is virtually no consistency among letters from different professors for the same student (Colarelli, Alampay, & Canali, 2002). Traditional methods can be time-consuming and inefficient. Another problem involves mismatches between evolved adaptations, on which many traditional methods are based, and the modern world. People evolved in small groups and still respond strongly to symbols of group membership. Accordingly, people using traditional hiring methods are likely to evaluate candidates on the basis of in-group and out-group characteristics, such as race or ethnicity. People are likely to evaluate more favorably those who are similar to themselves than people who are different (Wexley, Alexander, Greenawalt, & Couch, 1980). These proclivities can be inimical to standards of fairness or effectiveness in modern organizations and societies (Campbell, 1994; Moore, 1996). Because traditional hiring methods are grounded in evolved propensities, it is difficult to change them (Moore, 1996).

Although mechanistic hiring methods have the advantages of quantification, standardization, objectivity, and efficiency, they have major problems. They do not work much better than traditional methods. Other means can be used to achieve the same results. They contain unrealistic assumptions about organizational goals and about the relationships among individual characteristics and outcomes. In addition, organizational realities inevitably make proper implementation of mechanistic hiring practices problematic. These problems have been ignored or glossed over by many of the researchers and technicians who work with mechanistic hiring methods.

Mechanistic Methods Are Not That Much Better Than Traditional Methods

The *raison d'etre* of mechanistic methods is that they are presumed to work better than traditional methods (AERA, 1985). Most personnel psychologists define "working better" as more accurately predicting behavior (Sackett, Schmitt, Ellingson, & Kabin, 2001; Swets, Dawes, & Monahan, 2000). Mechanistic hiring methods, it is argued, predict intended outcomes with greater accuracy than traditional methods.[12]

> Extensive research has demonstrated that well-developed tests . . . are valid for their intended purpose. They are useful, albeit imperfect, descriptors of the current level of knowledge, skill, ability, or achievement. Thus, they are meaningful contributors to credentialing decisions and useful *predictors of future performance in employment and academic settings.* (Sackett, et al., 2001, p. 302; emphasis added)

However, a close look at the literature suggests that this is not universally the case. The SAT is one of the most widely used tests of cognitive ability, administered annually to about 1.5 million high school students in the United States. One reason that SAT scores are used is because they can predict freshman-year grades with some accuracy. Colleges, in wanting to select good students, need some indicator of how well they will perform in college. Although the level of prediction is fairly low (about $r = .25$), it is reliable, and some level of prediction is better than none. However, prior to the widespread use of the SAT, college admissions officers typically relied on high school grades, their own examinations, and other obvious indicators of academic skill to predict how well a student might do in college (Crouse & Trusheim, 1988). The simple and obvious method of estimating college performance by high school grades turns out to be about as effective as using SAT scores. SAT scores add very little incremental validity over and above high school grades. Colleges gain only a minuscule level of prediction of freshman grades of students selected by the SAT plus high school grades over those selected by high school grades alone. Correlations between predicted freshman grades based on high school grades alone and predictions based on high school grades plus the SAT range between .88 and .92, depending on the data set (Crouse & Trusheim, 1988). The gain ranges from between .02 and .03 in freshman GPA on a four-point scale (Crouse & Trusheim, 1988). High school GPA has some similarities with the tests used by mechanistic methods: it is a number, an abstraction. It requires only one sense to comprehend, and it is one specific piece of information about a person. However, high school GPA has much in common with traditional methods. It is essentially a composite score from a work sample test. GPA is a summary of actual academic performance, not an indicator of an abstract characteristic.

Assessment centers are another mechanistic method touted as a particularly effective tool for hiring for jobs, particularly for jobs that involve interpersonal and administrative skills (Bray, Campbell, & Grant, 1974). Assessment centers involve group exercises where multiple, trained assessors judge multiple applicants. They also include exercises simulating administrative tasks (e.g., prioritizing items in an in-basket) and paper-and-pencil tests. The assessment center procedure takes several hours to several days, requires a trained staff of assessors, and is one of the most costly mechanistic hiring methods. Proponents of assessment centers argue that despite their high costs, they are good investments (Cascio & Ramos, 1986). This claim was refuted when the effectiveness of assessment centers was compared with that of a commonly used traditional method—managers reviewing a candidate's personnel files. The assessment center was no better. Hinrichs (1978) compared predictions of performance from assessment centers and those made from managers evaluating job candidates' personnel files. For management level at both Year 1 (the year when the study was conducted) and Year 8 (eight years after the assessment ratings were collected), the evaluations by managers were better predictors of career progress than the assessment center. The validity coefficients for the managers' predictions at Year 1 and Year 8 were .32 and .58, respectively, and the respective validity coefficients for the assessment center ratings were .26 and .46. Here again, an appropriate traditional method of assessment performed as well or better than a mechanistic method. As Hinrichs points out:

> Users of the assessment center method should clarify just what it is that their center is designed to accomplish. If the center focuses solely on predicting advancement, they should question whether simpler and less expensive techniques are available. . . . It makes little sense to use a sledgehammer to swat a fly! (1978, p. 600)

The whole range of mechanistic hiring methods does not hold an overall edge over traditional methods. Schmidt and Hunter (1998) conducted a meta-analysis of 19 hiring methods that combined and summarized the results of 85 years of research on the validity of hiring methods for predicting training and job performance. Table 3.3 classifies 17 of the hiring methods as traditional or mechanistic and lists their validity coefficients.[13] I also calculated the average coefficient of validity for the traditional and mechanistic methods. I classified methods as traditional if most people without specialized training could and typically do develop and use such methods and feel confident making judgments based on the results of those tests. The traditional methods are work sample tests, peer ratings, job knowledge tests, job tryouts, unstructured employment interviews, reference checks, job experience, and years of education. I classified methods as mechanistic if the development of a test or the interpretation of a test score typically would require a personnel or psychological specialist. People without specialized knowledge and training would be unable to develop such a test or interpret the meaning of the scores it produced. The mechanistic methods are general mental ability tests (GMA), structured interviews, the training and education (T & E) behavioral consistency method, tests of integrity, assessment center, biographical data measures, tests of conscientiousness, the T & E point method, and interest inventories.

The average validity for the traditional methods, .36, is slightly higher than that of the mechanistic methods, .35. Work sample tests, a traditional method, has the highest validity of all methods, .54. GMA and structured interviews have the highest validities of mechanistic methods; both are .51. Hiring methods that involve face-to-face interaction have

Table 3.3
Predictive Validity of Traditional and Mechanistic Hiring Methods

Category	Hiring Method	Validity
Traditional	Work sample test	.54
	Peer ratings	.49
	Job knowledge tests	.48
	Job tryout procedure	.44
	Employment interview (unstructured)	.38
	Reference checks	.26
	Job experience	.18
	Years of education	.10
	Average of Traditional Methods	*.36*
Mechanistic	GMA Test	.51
	Employment interview (structured)	.51
	T & E behavioral consistency method	.45
	Integrity tests	.41
	Assessment center	.37
	Biographical data measures	.35
	Conscientiousness tests	.31
	T & E point method	.11
	Interests	.10
	Average of Mechanistic Methods	*.35*

a higher average validity than those that do not. Four of the traditional methods (work sample tests, peer ratings, job tryouts, and unstructured interviews) and two of the mechanistic methods (structured interviews, assessment centers) involve face-to-face interaction. The average validity of these six methods is .46. The other methods do not involve face-to-face interaction. Their average validity is .30.

Two criticisms of commonly used traditional methods have been made: they either require that applicants have previous job experience, or the methods are expensive and time-consuming. The four most effective traditional methods—work sample tests, job knowledge tests, peer ratings, and job tryouts—require that applicants have previous experience. Job tryouts differ somewhat from the others in that they can also be used for applicants without job experience who are applying for entry-level jobs that are simple enough for a person to do without previous experience. Job tryout periods have the disadvantage of being time consuming and expensive; they can only be done in certain situations. Thus, advocates for mechanistic methods argue that GMA tests are particularly valuable because they assess candidates with no previous job experience in a relatively reliable way. In addition, they are less time consuming and less expensive than job tryouts or other commonly used traditional methods.

A hallmark of the modern mechanistic approach is that experts are necessary to accurately assess an individual's psychological characteristics. However, people can assess themselves on many characteristics as well as experts. After reviewing numerous studies that compared self-assessments with procedures commonly used in professional psychological evaluations, Shrauger and Osberg (1981) concluded that "self-assessments are at least as predictive . . . as other assessment methods against which they have been pitted" (p. 322). They found that self-assessments are "comparable to aptitude" tests in predicting academic performance (p. 329), are "perhaps superior to interest inventories in predicting occupational choice" (p. 332), and tend to be comparable or better predictors of peer ratings than psychometrically sophisticated tests. The results of Shrauger and Osberg's review indicate that Münsterberg was wrong when he wrote that "the ordinary individual knows very little of his own mental functions." In a review comparing self, peer, and supervisor ratings of job performance, Harris and Schaubroek (1988) found that self-ratings correlated significantly with ratings by supervisors and with peers.

The Same Results by Other Means

A fundamental tenet of mechanistic methods is that the relationship between scores on an employment test and predicted job performance is stable over time. The mechanistic method assumes that essential characteristics of an individual are related to job outcomes in a predictable way. These relationships last a long time; they occur in a wide variety of situations, and, therefore, effective selection will have a lasting impact on important organizational outcomes, such as productivity and morale. To hire only people with higher scores becomes a defensible proposition. However, if people with lower test scores can be trained to perform as well as people with higher test scores, then it is difficult to justify the use of test scores by assuming that people with lower test scores will not make the grade. A number of studies have shown that there is not an inalterable relationship between the characteristic that a test measures and the outcome(s) it is supposed to predict. That is, people with significantly different scores can attain similar levels of performance, depending on a variety of situational factors.

Brown (1979) did one of these studies. His work suggests that the relationship between scores on valid employment tests and job performance is not as stable as testers would like to believe. Brown studied
the validity of a biographical information blank, known as the AIB, that
had been used for years by life insurance companies to select life insurance sales agents. According to Brown, "over the past 40 years, the
validity of the AIB has been well documented" (p. 461). The initial purpose of Brown's research was to look at the effects of a newly implemented pass/fail cutoff procedure (the previous cutoff procedure had
been top-down). In looking at the data, Brown noticed that some of the
applicants who did not pass were, nevertheless, subsequently hired (5.1
percent of the total hires in this study). The test scores of applicants were
made available to agency managers, but agency managers had the final
say in who was hired, and they hired some people who had scores below the cutoff. Brown also noticed that *the success rates were higher
among those who had the lowest scores than those who had passing
scores.* The overall success rate of those who received failing scores and
were subsequently hired was 20 percent, while the success rate of applicants who received passing scores was 16 percent. To find out why
this occurred, Brown spoke with company representatives. Apparently,
he discovered, when managers went out on a limb and selected an applicant with a failing test score, they gave that applicant particularly careful training and supervision.

The effects of expectations on educational and job performance have
been demonstrated in hundreds of studies of the Pygmalion effect.
Pygmalion, a play by George Bernard Shaw, dramatizes a fictional response to expectations. Professor Higgens believed that Elisa Doolittle,
a young working-class woman with a cockney accent and rough manners, had the capacity to speak and behave like an aristocrat. Higgens
expected that Elisa could be transformed, proceeded on that assumption, and succeeded in training her to pass for a patrician. The Pygmalion
effect in organizations operates when supervisors *believe* that their subordinates have high abilities, even though the subordinates are average.
The supervisors' high expectations affect their behavior. They set higher
goals, accept fewer excuses for subpar performance, and so on. As a
result, the Pygmalion subordinates produce above-average results. Studies in educational, military, and industrial settings have demonstrated
the Pygmalion effect (Dusek, Hall, & Meyer, 1985; Eden, 1990).

The dynamics in groups, the way groups are structured, and their reward systems can sometimes override individual differences in ability.
Amy Boos and I conducted a study of college students who participated
in semester-long group projects (Colarelli & Boos, 1992). Students were

assigned to 3-person groups and worked on a group project over the course of a semester. We collected students' ACT scores and college GPAs; we also asked students to fill out questionnaires on the quality of communication and collaboration in their groups, and we collected data on performance of the groups. We found that variation in group dynamics had a stronger impact on group performance than did variation in the group members' ability. The effects of group characteristics worked both ways. If the group dynamics were good, they raised the performance of groups whose members had mediocre abilities; if the group dynamics were poor, groups with highly able members did worse than expected. One group was particularly memorable. The group consisted of two young women and one young man. Their project was of poor quality, yet the group's average ability level was reasonably high. In investigating the matter more closely, I found that the two young women had high ability, while the young man had modest abilities (the scores of the two women gave the group a relatively high average). The young man was also dominating and aggressive. It appeared that the dull but pushy young man imposed his ideas on the two women, and the group ended up doing the project that he wanted and in the way he wanted. The women's ideas and talents were ignored. Therefore, a group with a majority of able members can still be ineffective when a stupid bully ends up making decisions for the group (see Fiedler & Garcia, 1987).

The larger work environment has a considerable effect on productivity and can override the impact of individual employees, as illustrated in a study of university scientists by Allison and Long (1990). They examined the productivity rates of scientists who moved from top-tier to middle-tier universities and vice versa. They found that the productivity of scientists decreased when they moved from top-tier to middle-tier universities, whereas the productivity of scientists increased when they moved from middle-tier to top-tier universities. They attribute the change not to the differences in the abilities of the scientists but to differences in the universities. Top-tier universities have better facilities and more resources, greater intellectual stimulation, lower teaching loads (which free up more time for research and writing), and reward systems that motivate research productivity.[14] They did not measure situational characteristics directly but inferred them from typical differences between top-tier and middle-tier universities. They also did not measure the abilities of the scientists directly but inferred that the differences in cognitive ability among the scientists were relatively small. This is a reasonable inference because the range in intellectual ability does indeed narrow progressively up the occupational ladder (Lancaster, Colarelli, King, & Beehr, 1994).[15] In a study that Roger Dean, Connie Konstans, and I conducted with accountants, we had actual measures of the work environment and employees' cognitive ability (Colarelli, Dean, & Konstans, 1987). We found that differences in the characteristics of work environments had a significant impact on job performance. Accountants who worked in environments with more autonomy and more feedback about their work performed better than accountants in environments with less autonomy and feedback. Differences in IQ scores had no effect on accountants' performance. All of the accountants in our sample were from large, prestigious accounting firms. Although all were bright, there was some difference in their IQ scores. Thus, the lack of effect of IQ scores on productivity was probably not due to a lack of variation in IQ scores. We did find one individual difference that affected productivity: personal goals. Accountants who had specific career goals performed better than those without goals.

Situational factors can override the effects of individual differences in ability in educational settings. Although much has been made about the importance of SAT scores and college performance, Allison (1977) found that the effects of individual differences in academic ability, as measured by the SAT, could be overcome by differences in teaching. In a study with Harvard undergraduates, Allison found that good teaching could overcome a 200-point SAT score deficit. Students with SAT scores 200 points lower than others attained the same degree of academic achievement in an introductory economics course when the low SAT students were given the best teachers and the high SAT students were given the worst teachers.

The effects of cultural factors seem to have an impact on test scores and academic performance as well. A classic study by Stevenson and his colleagues found that study habits played an important role in the remarkable academic success of new Asian (primarily Vietnamese) immigrants to the United States (Stevenson, Chen, & Lee, 1993). Although their parents could speak little English and held low-level jobs, these students regularly scored among the highest on school achievement tests. Stevenson suggests that valuing educational success and daily participation in study groups, primarily composed of siblings and other kin, were key influences on the impressive performance of the Vietnamese immigrant children. McWhorter (2000) argues that values and study habits have played a significant role in the underachievement of African American students. He suggests that African American students have low expectations and negative attitudes toward academics and academic achievement because of an African American subculture that devalues academic achievement. As a result, many African American students direct only minimal effort to academics.

It has been known for quite some time that standardized tests over-predict grades for African Americans. *That is, African Americans earn lower grades than their test scores predict.* Bowen and Bok (1999) present data from Caucasian and African American students at highly selective schools that vividly portray this phenomenon. African Americans with combined SAT scores of 1,300 or higher held class ranks about equal to Caucasian students whose combined SAT scores were 1,000 or less. Something besides individual differences in ability causes African Americans to do less well than expected.

As the studies that I have reviewed here demonstrate, differences in initial ability do not necessarily result in differences in individual or organizational outcomes. Despite the evidence of such studies, advocates of mechanistic hiring methods seem unable to recognize that situational factors can override the effects of individual differences, and they continue to argue that tests of individual differences are essential to maintaining high levels of productivity (Sackett et al., 2001). This continuing rigidity reflects the self-interest of testers. They gain in status and wealth with the use of mechanistic hiring tests. The use of tests creates the demand for their services in organizations and elevates the profession (cf. Cohen & Pfeffer, 1986). In addition to selling expert services, many have a hand in developing and selling tests, which can be quite lucrative financially (Lemann, 1999). As early as the 1920s, Walter Lippmann observed that if intelligence testing caught on, the testing experts would occupy "a position of power which no intellectual has held since the collapse of theocracy" (in Lemann, 1999, p. 69).

Testers have fervent beliefs in the importance of tests of individual differences. Henry Chauncey, the long-time president of ETS and the man who was primarily responsible for the widespread use of the SAT, saw the use of tests in a quasireligious fashion. In his early days at ETS, he wrote in his diary: "What I hope to see established is the moral equivalent of religion but based on reason and science rather than on sentiments and tradition" (quoted in Lemann,1999, p. 69). Many advocates of mechanistic hiring methods have turned Chauncey's effort to escape blind faith into a new kind of blind faith.

Unrealistic Assumptions about Organizational Goals

> It is difficult to exaggerate the significance of conflicts of interest.
> —Alexander (1987, p. 77)

The primary goal of mechanistic selection practices is to identify the person who is best suited for the job. The statement, "the best person for the job," presupposes that the job involves an identifiable and stable set of tasks and that agreement exists among stakeholders about what those tasks are. It presupposes a tightly interlocking hierarchy of tasks and goals in which tasks and goals at lower levels are directly linked to tasks and goals of larger units, ultimately contributing to organizational goals (Campbell et al., 1993). This, in turn, presupposes that organizational goals and unit subgoals are compatible with one another. If goals are not compatible, the idea of the best person for the job is problematic because a person that is best for one goal may be inappropriate for another goal. Belief in a best person also presupposes that organizational and unit subgoals are transparent—that is, organizations have clearly identified goals and employees know what those goals are. Finally, the belief presupposes that employees agree with the organization's goals and support them.

The idea that organizations have a synchronous hierarchy of goals is implicit in many of the mechanistic approaches to hiring and other interventions. Campbell et al. (1993) state that individual job performance "includes only those actions or behaviors that are relevant to the organization's goals and that can be scaled (measured) in terms of each individual's proficiency (that is, level of contribution [to the organization's goals])" (p. 40). The work on the economic utility of personnel selection programs also generally makes explicit mathematical connections between individual attributes, job performance, and organizational performance (Schmidt, Hunter, McKenzie, & Muldrow, 1979). Individual ability determines how well jobs are done and thus whether job-level goals are met; the attainment of goals at the job level contributes in a direct, additive fashion to the attainment of goals at the organizational level; increases in organizational performance are therefore an additive function of increases in individual ability (see Figure 3.2). The whole equals the sum of the parts.

As appealing as this may sound, the relationship between individual and organizational goals is rarely, if ever, so straightforward. At least two reasons suggest why there are few, if any, tightly synchronous relationships among goals. First, organizations are loosely coupled systems (Orton & Weick, 1990), and the strength of relationships among organizational components varies over time and is subject to spontaneous change. Relationships among parts are often indirect and weak. Although it is reasonable to expect general trends in organizations, loose coupling suggests that, in most circumstances, it is unrealistic to expect accurate forecasts of organizational behavior or to expect that one could manipulate parts of a system to produce specific, intended effects (Connor, 1991; Hogarth & Makridakis, 1981; Lawshe, 1969). Second,

Figure 3.2
Synchronous Hierarchy of Goals

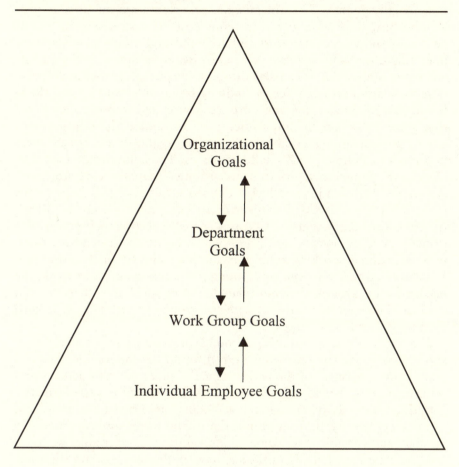

organizations are emergent systems. That is, the combination of parts produces a whole that is greater than or different from the sum of the parts (Holland, 1995). Thus, the assumption that goals at one level are tightly linked to goals at another level is highly questionable. As Hannan and Freeman (1989) point out:

> Much organizational change is largely uncontrolled and . . . the consequences of designed structural changes are difficult to anticipate. If this is so, organizations staffed by rational planners may behave essentially randomly with respect to adaptation. In other words, *organizational outcomes are often decoupled from individual intentions.* (1989, p. 23; emphasis added)

Organizations have multiple goals. Official, publicly stated goals are often quite different from operative goals, the goals that an organization actually pursues. The official goals of a restaurant might be to provide healthy, tasty food at a reasonable cost. Its operative goals might be to underprice its competitors and drive them out of business, decrease operating costs, and increase owner profits. Some sets of official goals can be incompatible, as can sets of operative goals. Official and operational goals can also conflict. A study by Friedlander and Pickle (1968) found that organizational goals are weakly related to one another and that some goals are incompatible. They examined the relationships among internal and external components of organizational effectiveness in a random sample of 97 small businesses. The components included: owners, the community, government, customers, suppliers, creditors, and employees. Friedlander and Pickle defined effectiveness as "the degree to which the needs of [organizational] components were fulfilled" (p. 294). The components had various needs (reflecting their goals). The primary need of owners was presumed to be profit; the needs of employees included working conditions and pay, and so on. The study results revealed that relationships among the components were weak; the needs of some groups were not related, and the needs of others were in conflict. These conflicts are difficult for groups to reconcile. It is hard to cut costs and raise wages.

In a study of the relationships among job performance criteria, Seashore, Indik, and Georgopoulos (1960) found similar results. They examined five measures of the performance of pizza delivery persons and pizza stations at the individual and unit levels: effectiveness (performance ratings), productivity, chargeable accidents, unexcused absences, and errors (nondeliveries). They found the relationships among criteria to be small and variable, with some relationships being in conflict with one another. The fact that organizations have multiple goals and that they are often in conflict has implications for hiring and for the notion that there is a best person to do a job. If many goals are moderately related or unrelated to one another, then one cannot assume that a person who has the abilities or skills to perform one task well will necessarily perform another well.

The members of an organization cannot be aware of an *organization's* goals because, strictly speaking, organizations do not have goals; only individuals do. What are called organizational goals are usually the goals of the dominant coalition of owners or top managers (Cyert & March, 1963). Some goals are not clearly articulated or well communicated. Other goals are ambiguous because managers may disagree about which goals the organization should pursue or because managers may espouse goals that are quite different from the goals they privately pursue. Even in the rare instances when goals are well communicated and clear, they will not receive equal support by all organizational members. Consider the "goals" of a middle-tier university. The goals of the university's administrators and faculty normally vary. With some administrators wanting cost efficiency, happy students, and satisfied trustees, and some faculty wanting lighter teaching loads, smaller classes, more teaching assistants, and more resources for writing and research. When it comes to hiring faculty, what is "the best" from administrators' point of view is likely to be out of synch with what some of the faculty want. Some administrators view "the best" faculty as those who are excellent teachers and mentors or those who are willing to work for modest salaries and take on heavy teaching loads. Some faculty may view "the best" faculty as committed researchers who can attract graduate students and who produce a large quantity of publications.

Unrealistic Assumptions about the Relationships between Individual Characteristics and Goals and among Individual Characteristics

The mechanistic approach posits that the relationship between the characteristics measured by a test and the outcome it predicts is stable over time. The notion of hiring the best person presumes that people have stable characteristics that have stable relationships with the outcomes that an employer wants. The idea of a best person is less tenable when the relationship between a person's traits and the outcomes desired by an employer is not stable over time. As it turns out, the relationships between many traits and outcomes decrease over time (Hulin, Henry, & Noon, 1990). Ability tests show modest correlations with performance measures that are assessed shortly after applicants take the test but much smaller correlations when performance is assessed at longer and longer intervals of time after the test was given (see Figure 3.3)

Hulin et al. (1990) reviewed 41 articles, yielding 71 independent validity sequences—that is, correlations between test scores and performance measured at increasing intervals of time after the test was taken. Here is an illustration of how one study might look: a group of high school students took the SAT in September 1989; their college grades were measured in June 1991, 1992, 1993, and 1994; correlations were calculated measuring the relationship between the students' SAT scores in September 1989 and their college grades in the four subsequent years. Hulin et al. found that in 82 percent of the studies of prediction validities

Figure 3.3
Typical Correlations between Ability Test Scores and Performance over Time

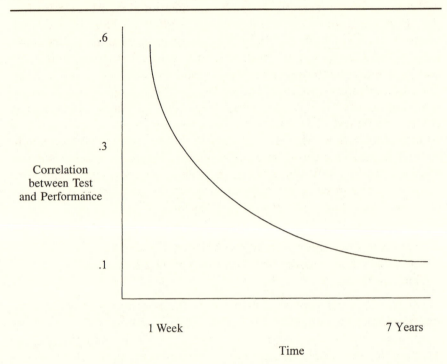

decreased over time. Their estimates' decrements of validity ranged from −.15 to −.60. Moreover, they found "a great deal of consistency in the relationship between temporal position of performance and the predictive validity of tests across a variety of tasks, populations, and situations" (p. 332). Back to our example, the correlations between the SAT taken in September 1989 and college grades in 1991 might be something like .4; the correlation between the same SAT and college grades in 1992 might be .28; in 1993, it might be .2; and by 1994 it might be only .11. The practical implications of their findings are that the validity and utility of tests of ability are limited mainly to early performance. How well people will do over the long haul is influenced by many factors besides those measured by the test (e.g., time on task, deliberate practice, personal goals, supervisory and work-group expectations, task-related resources, and systems of motivation).

Apologists for mechanistic hiring methods fall into two utopian camps. In one camp are advocates of jigsaw puzzle utopias; in the other are advocates of spray paint utopias. The jigsaw puzzle utopians presume that jobs contain a specific number of concrete tasks that require corresponding individual characteristics, such as aptitudes and personality characteristics (Dunnette, 1966, 1976; Guion, 1998; Hough, 1998; Murphy, 1996).[16] The trick is to fit all the pieces (tasks and individual characteristics) of the puzzle together so that optimal job performance occurs.[17] The goal is to piece together all the pieces of a complete taxonomy. This will then enable personnel specialists to tightly fit people to jobs. If, say, a job involved programming a computer, working alone, performing fine-grained finger movements, and attention to detail, the best fit might be a person with high scores on a test measuring the following traits: mathematical ability, introversion, hand-eye coordination, and detail perception. Theoretically, all of these traits should relate positively to one another and the outcomes, which should also relate positively to one another. Advocates of spray paint utopias, on the other hand, argue that jigsaw puzzles are too complex, too time consuming, and not necessary. What is needed is a one-color-fits-all paint, or set of a few paints, that can be sprayed on any job to assure good performance. This would be a master trait, such as intelligence or conscientiousness. Many industrial psychologists regard tests of general intelligence and tests of conscientiousness as universally appropriate for virtually all jobs (e.g., Barrick & Mount, 1991; Schmidt & Hunter, 1981). Underlying the conviction that general intelligence and conscientiousness are useful and universal predictors of job performance is the implicit assumption that they are *unrelated* to undesirable traits.

A core assumption in both camps is that traits that correlate positively with one valued organizational outcome also correlate positively, or at least neutrally, with other valued outcomes and negatively with undesirable outcomes. Most research on mechanistic hiring methods has focused on the relationship between *one* trait and *one* outcome, and the outcome that most validation studies use is job performance. Therefore, a trait is considered useful if it correlates positively with a measure of job performance—typically a supervisor's ratings of an employee's job performance. Yet, many outcomes are useful to organizations—good citizenship, organizational commitment, job satisfaction, and retention. It is not inevitable that the relationship between a given trait, X, and one outcome, Y, will be the same as the relationship between X and *another* outcome, Z. Several studies have found that in some jobs IQ is negatively associated with job satisfaction. Ganzach (1998) reported that intelligence is negatively related to job satisfaction when job complexity is held constant. The relationship is strongest when jobs are simple. When high-IQ individuals work in simple jobs, they tend to be dissatisfied.

In a study of bank tellers, I also found a negative relationship between IQ scores and job satisfaction and a positive relationship between IQ and higher turnover (Colarelli & Stumpf, 1990). In another study my colleagues and I found that IQ was negatively related to internal work motivation and to organizational commitment among accountants (Colarelli, Dean, & Constans, 1987). Steers (1977) found a negative relationship between educational level (which is related to IQ) and organizational commitment. These studies indicate that hiring people with high IQ scores can produce negative effects on valued organizational outcomes (see Figure 3.4).

Some employers probably realize that hiring people with high IQ scores for some jobs is problematic. The New London, Connecticut, Police Department rejects applicants for police officer jobs with high IQ scores, assuming that high-IQ applicants would be more likely to quit after they were hired. One of these rejected applicants sued the Department for this practice. In *Robert Jordan vs. City of New London* (1999 US District Court for the District of Connecticut, Civil No. 3:97CV1012 PCD), the plaintiff charged that his civil rights were violated when he was rejected by the New London Police Department because his IQ score was too high. However, the court accepted the Police Department's argument that it had a reasonable concern with retention and that high-IQ trainees were more likely to quit than those with lower IQ scores. Some middle-tier colleges reject or wait-list applicants who have high SAT scores because they are more likely to enroll at prestigious colleges and often use middle-tier schools as "safety schools" (i.e., fallback schools in case their first choices reject them). A college enhances its selectivity, and hence its ranking on some reports of college quality, by rejecting top applicants before

Figure 3.4
Inconsistent Relations with Multiple Outcomes

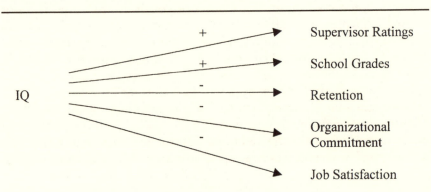

they turn them down. It does so without compromising the quality of its student body because many of the top-scoring students it rejects would not have enrolled anyway (Golden, 2001).

The same arguments can be made with respect to personality traits. One trait that has received a good deal of attention from personnel psychologists is conscientiousness. Conscientiousness correlates positively with job performance in a variety of jobs and generalizes about as much with job performance as does IQ (Barrick & Mount, 1991; Tett, Jackson, & Rothstein, 1991). Conscientiousness, broadly speaking, refers to the propensity to work hard, follow the rules, and obey authority figures. Conscientiousness people are dutiful, self-disciplined, and deliberate. Barrick and Mount (p. 22) state that it is "difficult to conceive of a job in which the traits associated with the Conscientiousness dimension would not contribute to job success." A moment's reflection should illuminate the absurdity of this statement. It is unlikely that conscientiousness relates positively to *all* organizational outcomes. People who strictly adhere to the rules and obey authorities would be a liability in some jobs. In some situations, there is benefit from people who do not always follow the rules, who step out of bounds and do things differently. Conscientiousness is negatively correlated with creativity (Barron, 1965). Groups composed of only conscientious members have difficulty solving open-ended problems; that is, groups without a member who scores low on conscientiousness do not perform as well solving open-ended problems as those with at least one member who scores low on conscientiousness (Morrison, 1993). In her classic analysis of Nazi bureaucrats, *Eichmann in Jerusalem*, Hannah Arendt (1965) coined the phrase, "the banality of evil," to describe the behavior of Nazi bureaucrats like Adolf Eichmann. These were *conscientious* employees who followed the rules, obeyed authority, and worked hard. Arendt argued that many of the horrors of the Nazi regime were due to bureaucrats following the rules and obeying authority—in other words, behaving like conscientious employees. Eichmann himself expressed an overwhelming desire to please his superiors: "[Eichmann] did his *duty*, as he told the police and the court over and over again; he not only obeyed *orders*, he also obeyed the *law*" (Arendt, 1965, p. 135; emphases in the original). Perhaps if some Nazi bureaucrats had been less conscientious, had been less deferent to authority, fewer atrocities would have occurred.

In a study of personality and the performance of salespersons, McDaniel (1997) showed that valued traits do not always relate positively to valued outcomes. She found that, among sales personnel, "adjustment" related negatively with sales volume; "ambition" related positively to turnover; and "sociability" related negatively to work completed. "Prudence" related negatively to *six* measures of sales performance. Traits that are deemed valuable because they relate to some valued behaviors (a prudent person is more likely to consider options carefully before making a decision) can also relate to undesirable behaviors (a prudent person may be hesitant to act and to take decisive action).

A general personality disposition called *affective orientation* has been found to relate to a number of valued outcomes; therefore, some behavioral scientists have argued that it is an important characteristic to use in personnel selection (George, 1996). Affective orientation is the extent to which a person tends to be happy (or unhappy), satisfied or unsatisfied, or optimistic or pessimistic.[18] People who score high on positive affectivity scales "tend to have an overall sense of well-being and to be positively engaged in the world around them, in terms of both achievement and interpersonal relations" (George, 1996, p. 146). Individuals who score low "do not think and behave in ways that will promote positive moods and emotions and do not have a strong sense of overall well-being" (p. 147). Happy people receive higher performance ratings, show less evidence of work-related strain, and are more satisfied at work. Positive mood is also associated with helping behavior, the protection of organizational interests, constructive suggestions, lower absenteeism and turnover, and greater leadership effectiveness. Like intelligence and conscientiousness, positive affectivity is presumed to be a valuable trait to look for in job applicants. Yet even a happy disposition relates negatively to some valuable outcomes. In situations where accurate social judgments are required, misanthropes are useful. Negative dispositions and low moods improve judgments and heighten creativity. People with negative dispositions make more accurate social judgments than people with positive dispositions. Unpleasant affective states elicit effortful, systematic, and detailed information processing, whereas positive emotional states elicit simple, global processing strategies (Clore, Schwarz, & Conway, 1994). Scientific eminence is also associated with negative affectivity. Cattell (1965) studied the personality profiles of a group of eminent scientists, and they were, on average, unsociable, brooding, undependable, and sensitive. Sociability and agreeableness are negatively related to creativity (Hough, 1998), while bipolar disorder (depression alternating with mania) is positively associated with creativity, particularly with extraordinarily creative talent (Jamison, 1995).[19] If organizations were to hire only happy people, conflict and dissatisfaction would be less likely to occur, but conflict at reasonable levels of intensity is important for creativity and change. Similarly, dissatisfaction is an important precursor to change. To change and improve, people normally need to experience dissatisfaction with the current state of affairs (Beer, 1980).[20]

People are a mix of traits. A single individual can be intelligent, creative, introverted, disorganized, and hostile toward authority, while another can be intelligent, conventional, extroverted, organized, and compliant. Unfortunately, we know relatively little about the relationships among different psychological traits. Few scholarly books about intelligence contain any references to personality, and vice versa. In two influential and widely cited books on intelligence (Herrnstein & Murray, 1996; Jensen, 1980), the term *personality* is not even listed in the indexes. In a later book on intelligence, Jensen (1999) reviews several studies on the relationship between intelligence and personality and concludes that there is little, if any, relationship between g (general intelligence) and personality. The evidence that does exist on the relationships among traits suggests that some traits go together, others don't, and for some the relationships are inconsistent. Ackerman and Heggestad (1997) found weak, general patterns among some cognitive abilities, personality traits, and vocational interests (see Figure 3.5).

However, they also found inconsistencies. Traits related to extraversion correlated positively, albeit slightly, with cognitive abilities. Yet enterprising vocational interests, which are correlated with extraversion, correlated negatively with cognitive ability. Neuroticism correlates slightly negatively with cognitive abilities. Yet artistic vocational interests, which often correlate positively with neuroticism, correlate positively with verbal ability, which is positively related to general intelligence. Ackerman and Heggestad did not find clear patterns between conscientiousness and cognitive abilities; Hunter and his colleagues found a trivially small correlation ($r = .07$) between cognitive ability and conscientiousness (Hunter, Schmidt, Rauschenberger, & Jayne, 2001). Interestingly, Ackerman and Heggestad found that conventional vocational interests, which correlate positively with conscientiousness, correlated negatively with several cognitive abilities.

When one looks at the relationships among personality traits themselves, the same pattern of tradeoffs and contradictions occurs. McDaniel (1997) found that the Big Five has a dark side.[21] She looked at the correlations between the Hogan Personality Inventory (HPI—a personality inventory that measures common traits, similar to those in the Big Five) and the Hogan Development Survey (HDS—an inventory that measures dysfunctional dispositions). Her study included three large samples of employed adults—a heterogeneous sample of occupations, a sample of executives, and a sample of sales personnel. As one would expect, the executives had higher scores on ambition than the sales or

Figure 3.5
Relations among Intelligence, Personality, and Vocational Interests

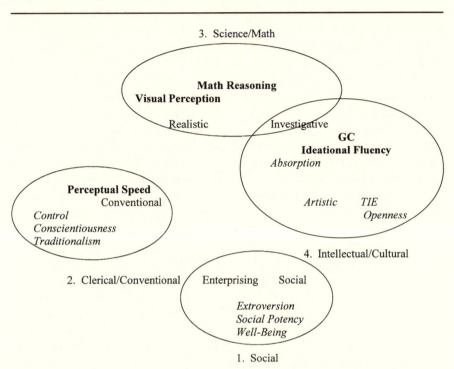

3. Science/Math

Math Reasoning
Visual Perception

Realistic   Investigative

GC
Ideational Fluency
Absorption

Perceptual Speed
Conventional

Control   *Artistic*   *TIE*
Conscientiousness   *Openness*
Traditionalism

4. Intellectual/Cultural

2. Clerical/Conventional   Enterprising   Social

Extroversion
Social Potency
Well-Being

1. Social

Trait complexes, including abilities (bold type), interests (regular), and personality (italic) traits, showing positive commonalities. Number categories are trait complexes. GC = Crystallized Intelligence; TIE = typical intellectual engagement.

Source: Ackerman and Heggestad (1997, p. 239).

general samples. So far, so good. Ambition is a characteristic that an executive recruiter would look for in applicants for executive positions. But McDaniel found that ambition also related with traits that we ordinarily think of as bad. A person high on the trait of ambition also tends "to be overly self-confident and have feelings of grandiosity and entitlement (Arrogant), tends to be deceitful (Mischievous), and needs to be the center of attention (Melodramatic)" (pp. 11–12). Executives who scored high on Prudence also scored high on the HDI Perfectionist scale. So although these executives were reliable and thoughtful, they were also micromanaging and critical. Correlations from the sales sample were also mixes of good and bad. To get the full flavor of the results, here are McDaniel's original words:

For the sales sample, high scores on the HPI Ambition and Intellectance scales are positively associated with high scores on the HDS Arrogant, Mischievous, Melodramatic, and Eccentric scales. This is a profile of a person who is driven and persistent (Ambition), creative and inquisitive (Intellectance) and when under pressure seems self-promoting and demanding (Arrogant), impulsive (Mischievous), self-centered (Melodramatic), and at times seems to come from "out of left field" when expressing ideas. High scores on the HPI Sociability scale are associated with high scores on the Mistrustful, Passive Aggressive, Arrogance, Mischievous, Melodramatic, and Eccentric scales. This is the profile of a person who is outgoing and talkative (Sociability) and when under stress seems argumentative (Mistrustful), resentful and preoccupied with his/her own goals (Passive Aggressive), overbearing and aggressive (Arrogant), boisterous and unfocused (Melodramatic), and somewhat unusual or odd. In addition, this is a profile of a person who does not learn from past mistakes (Mischievous). (1997, p. 13)

Organizational Realities Make Implementation Problematic

Even if organizational goals could be identified and a consensus could be reached about them, even if those goals could be linked to performance criteria for specific jobs, even if relationships between traits and outcomes held over time, and even if the traits related positively to many valued organizational outcomes—it is still unlikely that the best person for a job would be hired. Hiring methods, like other organizational interventions, are rarely, if ever, *implemented* as planned. Notwithstanding the problems already mentioned, for mechanistic hiring methods to work, they need to be implemented properly. This rarely occurs (Holmen & Docter, 1972). Hiring occurs within social systems, which are often chaotic. Hiring takes place at the boundaries of organizations, where organizations do not have control over applicants. And hiring is political. These facts militate against hiring methods being implemented as testing specialists recommend. A huge gap exists between the ideal mechanistic hiring model and hiring practices in the trenches.

A fundamental premise of mechanistic hiring methods is *top-down selection*—that applicants can be ranked in order of qualification, from best to worst. The applicant with the highest test score, or combination of scores, should be the first to receive a job offer. If that applicant refuses, the offer goes to others in descending order. According to advocates of the mechanistic hiring method, this is the only sensible and proper way to proceed (Schmidt, 1995; Swets et al., 2000). In reality, the selection process in organizations is more like a blindfolded person picking marbles out of an urn: applicants who are reasonably qualified are akin to the marbles in the urn. Usually, all of the candidates receiving serious consideration have the knowledge and skills for the job. Beyond that, the complexities associated with organizational chaos, boundary spanning, and politics foul up carefully laid plans for top-down selection.

Administration is not clockwork; mistakes, errors, and mishaps muddle procedures. Clerical errors are bound to occur when clerks compile information on applicants and organize dossiers. Errors occur when tests are scored and reported. Decision makers sometimes overlook critical information on an applicant, misplace a file, or make addition errors. All of these add up to a high probability that simple administrative errors regularly affect the selection process. Although administrators are not inclined to announce their mistakes to the public, nevertheless they are occasionally discovered and reported in the press. *The New York Times* recently reported a massive foul-up based on clerical errors with test scores. A total of 8,600 students in New York City were wrongly assigned to summer school for remedial education because of a miscalculation by a standardized test publisher (Hartocollis, 1999).

The complications of timing and competition from other organizations also make it unlikely that selection will proceed in a strict top-down fashion. An orderly top-down process assumes that there is a stopping point when all applications can be collected and ranked.[22, 23] However, many organizations may not have this luxury and may have a rolling selection process. In addition, the timing of job offers may be slowed down when managers must get approval from their supervisors or wait until further critical information about a candidate has arrived. Compounding timing problems is competition from other organizations for good candidates. Top applicants are likely to have offers from other organizations. If an organization makes a job offer a day later than a competing organization, it may lose its top choice. Top applicants will often stall on responding to an offer while negotiating for a better offer from another organization. If an applicant has a spouse who is also looking for a job at the same time, this can increase complications exponentially. In most organizations and universities, typically half of applicants who receive offers do not accept them (*Journal of Career Planning & Employment*, 1995).

Political factors also militate against a top-down selection strategy because self-interested human beings implement hiring practices. Many university administrators make exceptions to top-down selection for athletes, for children of alumni, for wealthy donors, and for influential politicians. The interests of individuals will not always be identical with the ideals of hiring programs. Individuals doing the hiring in organizations favor applicants who can advance their interests and oppose those whom they view as potential adversaries. Of course, expressions of self-interest are couched in terms of organizational interests (Adams et al., 1994; Scott, 1998). All of these reasons suggest that the mechanistic-hiring method's ideal of top-down selection is (at best) an approximation in practice. It is more likely that *some* applicant from the *pool of acceptable and available applicants* will be hired. Organizations may eventually end up hiring some people on their shortlist. But the process is more likely to resemble random selection from the shortlist than a top-down selection.

MECHANISTIC HIRING PRACTICES— WHERE ARE THEY NOW?

On balance, mechanistic hiring practices do not work any better than traditional practices. Although there have been expectations that they would greatly improve efficiency and harmony in organizations and society, the promise of psychological tests for personnel selection has not been fulfilled. Within a decade following World War I, Clark Hull (1928) concluded, after an extensive review of the literature on aptitude tests, that the capacity of psychological tests to predict job performance was limited and that their forecasting efficiency would probably always remain quite limited. Almost 70 years later, Robert Abelson (1997) remarked that "for correlational studies . . . of relationships between widely used selection tests and specific job or school performance, the strongest effect sizes may still only be moderate. . . . [Such moderate effect sizes are probably a] 'glass ceiling' on our understanding of complex psychological phenomena" (p. 14). After nearly a century, the correlations between test scores and job performance remain, on average, between about .2 and .3 (Hartigan & Widgor, 1989). Psychologists have not been able to improve the predictive accuracy of mechanistic tests, despite decades of work. Nevertheless, improving prediction of selection methods has been nothing less than the Holy Grail of personnel psychology. The following quote by Roberts, Hulin, and Rosseau summarizes this pursuit nicely:

> Organizational scientists engaged in personnel-selection research are responsive to both low levels of predictability of behavior by means of psychological tests and our lack of progress over the span of sixty years. Numerous suggestions are offered as panaceas. . . . Most of these approaches are little more than minor tinkerings with the elements of the basic selection paradigm. . . . Every few years our attention moves from one new approach to a different new approach. . . . Whatever approach

is in vogue, it is normally fitted out with more elaborate statistical procedures than those preceding it, and results are produced that initially
appear to justify the use of the new methods. Unfortunately, the next wave
of research frequently indicates that the clothing of the new emperor is
just as transparent as that of the previous one. (1978, p. 118)

The research on personnel selection methods has had little effect on
the hiring practices of the private sector. Traditional methods remain
widely used (American Management Association, 1986; Friedman &
Williams, 1982; Levy-Leboyer, 1994).[24] Terpstra and Rozell (1997)
found that only 20 percent of organizations they surveyed used cognitive ability tests and 24 percent conducted any studies evaluating the effects of their selection procedures. In a study I conducted on the use of
hiring practices, the interview was the most widely used hiring practice
(Colarelli, 1996). In my sample of 62 organizations, every one used it,
and job candidates went through an average of 1.4 interviews per job.
The second most widely used selection device was the probationary
period. Probationary periods were required for 39 percent of the jobs.
Standardized tests, on the other hand, were required for only 24 percent of the jobs. Similar patterns have been found in other studies conducted in the United States and abroad (Ahlburg, 1992; Dakin &
Armstrong, 1989; Shackleton & Newell, 1991).

The testing industry has always had trouble selling standardized tests
to private industry. The reasons are that tests do not produce immediate and obvious results. They require a class of experts to control personnel information. They are used in the public sector because the
quantitative nature of standardized tests is amenable to the illusions of
social control and crafting societies. They lend themselves to social engineering. Private sector organizations, on the other hand, are more interested in immediate and obvious results, common sense, and the
authority of managers rather than experts.

At the end of the twentieth century, government organizations—at all
levels in the United States—used employment tests extensively, with the
military being the largest user (Friedman & Williams, 1982). Standardized tests are also widely used in university admissions (Lemann, 1999).
However, it is unclear how much of an effect test scores have in selection decisions. Different federal agencies place different emphases on test
scores, and passing a competitive exam does not ensure that an applicant will be hired (Sadacca & Brackett, 1971). The use of alternative
methods and pathways for selection in the federal government makes it
even more difficult to determine how tests are really used (Friedman &
Williams, 1982). With universities, it is also unclear what impact tests

have on admissions decisions. Although some universities use rigid algorithms that give test scores a fixed weight in admission decisions, others use test scores as one of many sources of information available to admissions officers (Hargadon, 1981). A growing number of universities are abandoning the SAT and returning to more traditional means of assessment, such as high school class rank and more specific content-oriented achievement tests (Gose & Selingo, 2001).

The Response of Advocates of Mechanistic Hiring Methods

One response to the issues I have raised has been to ignore the problem. The chapter on personnel selection in the *Handbook of Industrial and Organizational Psychology* cites no studies on the use of hiring practices (Guion, 1991).[25] In fact, I have been unable to find surveys on the use of hiring practices in any major U. S. industrial and organizational psychology journal. Despite 80 years of research on personnel selection, very little scholarly work has been done on examining *why* organizations use the hiring practices they do (for exceptions, see Adams et al., 1994; Colarelli, 1996; Colarelli et al., 2002). Another lame response has been to blame the legal climate. Tenopyr (1981) blames Title VII of the Civil Rights Act of 1964 and the Equal Employment Opportunity Commission. She complained that the Civil Rights Act created a litigious climate surrounding testing, causing companies to stop using tests rather than increase their exposure to lawsuits. Guion (1998) also lays blame on the Civil Rights Act. Interestingly, neither Tenopyr nor Guion provides a shred of evidence that companies abandoned testing for that reason. Lawsuits or the threat of them do not inevitably stop profit-making organizations from producing or using a product, service, or policy that significantly enhances productivity or profitability. The tobacco industry continues to produce millions of cigarettes despite an avalanche of lawsuits. The liquor industry and the automobile industry have not been significantly sidetracked by lawsuits. If lawsuits threaten a practice or product that enhance profitability, organizations engage lawyers to defend their practices and hire lobbyists to convince lawmakers to change the laws in their favor. They do not roll over and play dead when profits are at stake. The simple fact is that most organizations in the private sector probably do not regard personnel tests as critical to increased profits. If the threat of lawsuits caused organizations to stop using employment tests, then one would expect to find a more uniform lack of use. Yet most government organizations continue to use employment tests, while few private organizations do so (Friedman & Williams,

1982). Lawsuits also do not explain why tests are used predominantly for lower level jobs (Colarelli, 1996).

Guion (1998) also blames organizational psychologists for employment testing's poor image and its lack of popularity among many employers. Organizational psychologists have dismissed the importance of traits as factors in job and organizational performance. Yet, all scientific enterprises involve debates, and psychology is no exception. If the testers believe that traits and test scores are so important, then it is up to them to provide the evidence. But the correlations between traits and performance still remain at .2 and .3 after all of these years. Some personnel psychologists have indeed responded by attempting to show that tests have a positive impact on productivity. They have provided more elaborate statistical arguments purporting to demonstrate that mechanistic selection tests actually do make a difference. A considerable amount of research was done in the late 1980s on the economic utility of selection tests and other psychological interventions. After initial enthusiasm and the development of elaborate statistical models, the emperor turned out to have no clothes (e.g., Latham & Whyte, 1994). As the Committee on the General Aptitude Test Battery states:

> There is no well-developed body of evidence from which to estimate the aggregate effects of better personnel selection. A number of theoretical models have been developed that imply various estimates of productivity gains from improved selection and placement. But we have seen no empirical evidence that any of them provides an adequate basis for estimating . . . aggregate economic effects. . . . Given the state of scientific knowledge, we do not believe that realistic dollar estimates of aggregate gains from improved selection are even possible. *They lend a spurious certainty . . . that can only mislead* policy makers, employers, and those who administer [employee testing programs]. (Hartigan & Wigdor, 1989, pp. 247–248; emphasis added)

The use of sophisticated statistical models in many of these instances is a vainglorious effort to pony the prestige of mathematics into an area not amenable to precise mathematical modeling.[26] Interestingly, psychologists who have argued that mechanistic hiring methods are such a boon to productivity have failed to mention a particularly ironic fact: mechanistic hiring methods are *most widely used* by those organizations that are not subject to the competitive pressures of the marketplace, that have vague goals, and that are notoriously inefficient—government organizations. They are least used by private sector organizations—those that must make a profit to survive, are subject to competitive pressures of the marketplace, and of necessity are concerned with efficiency.

Others have responded by suggesting that human resource managers are just not getting the message. Terpstra and Rozell (1997) argue that mechanistic methods work and that the evidence in their favor is clear. The problem is that managers have not gotten the message. They recommend more education—facilitating "the transfer of more information from the academic literature to HRM practitioners" (p. 492). This is a curious recommendation since over 50 percent of the people who responded to their survey about testing practices had college degrees in HRM. They sent out surveys about test use to the heads of the human resource departments in a random sample of 1,000 U.S. private sector firms. The most frequently cited reason for not using mechanistic staffing practices was that they did not believe that they were useful. The second and third most frequent reasons were a lack of time to implement them and a lack of familiarity with the practices, respectively. Legal concerns were the seventh most frequently cited reason.

Although I have been somewhat critical of mechanistic hiring methods, I am not, nor is an evolutionary perspective, inherently opposed to them. My concern is more with the chauvinism of their proponents: their blind adherence to the notion that mechanistic methods are superior to traditional methods and that traditional methods are foolish practices with no useful functions. Mechanistic hiring methods are part of the mix of social practices that humans create, and as such they are subject to the evolutionary crucible.

NOTES

1. Even in modern America, family businesses are widespread. Approximately 90 percent of U.S. businesses are family owned or controlled. About one-third of the firms on *Fortune* magazine's list of the 500 largest companies are family owned or controlled (Bizoffice, 1997). Nearly 30 percent of family-owned businesses pass control from the founding generation to the second generation (Apex Business Consulting, nd/2001).

2. Taking examinations and failing them were as anxiety producing then as now. Miyazaki (1976, pp. 57–58) quotes a satire that P'u Sung-ling (1640–1715) wrote about the seven transformations of a candidate. He was a literary man who failed the provincial examination many times.

> When he first enters the examination compound and walks along, panting under his heavy load of luggage, he is just like a beggar. Next, while undergoing the personal body search and being scolded by the clerks and shouted by the soldiers, he is just like a prisoner. When he finally enters his cell, along with the other candidates, stretches his neck to peer out, he is just like the larva of a bee. When the examination is finished at last and he leaves, his mind is a haze and his legs tottering,

he is just a sick bird that has been relieved from a cage. While he is wondering when the results will be announced and waiting to learn whether he passed or failed, so nervous that he is startled even by the rustling of the trees and the grass and is unable to sit or stand still, his restlessness is like that of a monkey on a leash.

When at last the results are announced and he has definitely failed, he loses his vitality like one dead, rolls over on his side, and lies there without moving, like a poisoned fly. Then, when he pulls himself together and stands up, he is provoked by every sight and sound, gradually flings away everything within his reach, and complains of the illiteracy of the examiners. When he calms down at last, he finds everything in the room broken. At this time he is like a pigeon smashing its own precious eggs. These are the seven transformations of a candidate.

3. However, the Romans did use at least one less obvious characteristic in the selection of some soldiers: the area where a soldier was born and grew up. The leaders of the Roman army did not want local individuals as members of Praetorians Guards, the emperor's bodyguards, for fear that they would easily be corrupted and would be hesitant to carry out their duties because of close ties to local people. The generals believed that non-Romans would be more loyal to their commanding officers (Webster, 1985).

4. Several scholars have developed typologies of the components of selection methods, broadly conceived. Meehl (1954) made the distinction between statistical and clinical methods of predicting how people will behave. Statistical methods combine data "mechanically" in an equation of statistical prediction. Clinical methods are based on the educated, albeit intuitive, judgment of an individual, without the aid of statistical algorithms. Sawyer (1966) expanded Meehl's typology to include mechanical and clinical *assessment* methods in addition to mechanical and clinical *prediction* methods. "Data collection is mechanical if rule can be pre-specified so that no clinical judgment need be involved in the procedure" (Sawyer, 1966, p. 181). Clinical data collection involves individual, and presumably idiosyncratic, judgments about what data to collect. Hunter and Hunter (1984) presented a typology that included the *method* of measurement (observation of behavior versus judgments about a trait) and the *content* of assessment (e.g., skill, ability, personality). Meehl and Sawyer were motivated primarily by the long-standing concern (particularly in clinical psychology but also in educational and industrial psychology) as to whether clinical or statistical methods best predict behavior. Hunter and Hunter's typology was primarily a heuristic device to categorize employment tests.

5. Let me clarify how I am using the term *purpose* here compared with my earlier use of the term in Chapter 2. There I said that evolution by natural selection has no purpose. By that I meant that evolution is not a sentient process consciously striving toward a particular end—such as less aggressive or more intelligent humans. Humans, however, are sentient beings, and they have goals.

Therefore, many human activities, including hiring practices, involve people's goals. I am also using purpose in a second sense here to mean *function*. Just as we can say that the purpose, or function, of the heart is to pump blood, we can say that the purpose, or function, of a hiring practice is to select people with requisite skills to perform a job.

6. They are also essential for kin recognition and the process of reciprocity, which of course are related to well-being and harm avoidance.

7. A colleague recounted to me a particularly amusing story about the preference for gathering information about people from face-to-face interaction. This colleague had taught for a number of years at the University of Washington in Seattle. Because of the large number of computer and Internet companies in that area, he became acquainted with many people who worked in those fields. One of his colleagues from the University of Washington gave a talk about the personal networking that goes on among Internet company managers, venture capitalists, and Internet entrepreneurs. He described a weekly luncheon where people in the business regularly gather. Apparently, many business deals had their genesis at this luncheon where prospective partners and investors meet *face-to-face* and size one another up. It is amusing and ironic that the high-tech Seattle Internet crowd, which is so fond of selling the Internet as a means of replacing face-to-face contact, uses the same method of sizing people up for potential alliances that indigenous tribes in the Amazon use: conversation over a meal (Chagnon, 1997).

8. There is also a long tradition in cognitive psychology that argues that people's decision making and judgment processes are frequently biased (Simon, 1956; Tversky & Kahneman, 1974). These arguments about human decision-making biases have garnered considerable support among social and behavioral scientists over the years. Herbert Simon and Daniel Kahneman won Nobel Prizes for their work on human fallibility in judgment.

9. Another pioneer in applied psychology, Edward Thorndike, echoed similar sentiments:

> There is excellent reason to believe that it is literally true that the result of two hours' tests properly chosen from those already tested gives a better diagnosis of an educated adult's general intellectual ability than the result of the judgments of two teachers or friends who have observed him in the ordinary course of life each for a thousand hours. (Thorndike, 1913, cited in Hale, 1980, p. 217)

10. On the other hand, a considerable amount of work under the rubric of "utility analysis" (mainly theoretical and simulation studies) has been done to demonstrate the (presumed) advantage of making hiring decisions according to the normative mechanistic method (Boudreau, 1991).

11. One could argue that the sheer volume of applicants to schools demands an efficient algorithmic approach. Yet if it is inherently superior, the algorithmic approach should also be applied to faculty hiring.

12. A prediction is a statement that a particular event will occur at some time in the future. One type of prediction does not involve a decision. It is simply a

statement that something will occur at some time in the future (e.g., the sun will rise tomorrow morning in the east at 5:30 A.M.). Other types of predictions involve decisions, and they are more complex. With this type of prediction, one might state that if alternative X is chosen from two or more alternatives and acted upon, then a particular event will be more likely to occur than if X had not been chosen.

13. The two methods from the original 19 that I did not include were age and graphology. Except for occasional legal restrictions, age is rarely used as a hiring method. Graphology (handwriting analysis) is rarely used in the United States, although it is used more widely in France and Germany. These two predictors do not fit well within the categories of traditional or modern methods. Their average correlations with job performance are .02 for graphology and −.01 for age.

14. There is an interesting story—perhaps an urban legend—about an admissions error that occurred at one of the top graduate programs in psychology in the United States. One year a secretary accidentally reversed the order on the list of applicants that the faculty evaluated. Acceptance letters were sent to applicants who had been rejected, and denial letters went to those who had been accepted. Faced with a potentially embarrassing situation of telling the students who received acceptance letters that they had actually been rejected, the department went ahead and admitted the students who erroneously received the acceptance letters. Several years later, when the progress of those students could be assessed, it turned out that their performance was no different from that of students who had been normally admitted.

15. Assuming that most people can reasonably accurately assess their abilities and are motivated to succeed rather than fail, they are likely to apply only for jobs where they have a realistic chance of success. Moreover, the educational systems in the United States, and most other advanced industrial countries, begin tracking and funneling students into educational and training curriculums from an early age. Therefore, by the time people finish, say, a professional degree program, the range of ability has been significantly narrowed through successive waves of testing and admissions from high school to college to graduate school.

16. Guion looks forward to the day when "the ideal of an empirically developed matrix . . . of predictors and criteria can be finally achieved" (1998, p. 155).

17. This is an absurd notion. It presumes the following, all of which are questionable. First, within any current generation of employees, there exists a stable, uniform set of ability and personality traits. Second, these characteristics continue to exist in humans from one generation to the next. Third, there is a stable, uniform set of work-related tasks and behaviors that are consistent across time, jobs, and organizations. And fourth, a nontrivial proportion of these characteristics is related to performance on these tasks. These assumptions presume that there exists a coherent and stable taxonomy of human individual differences in abilities, skills, and personality characteristics. Yet, it is likely that most

individual differences are products of random genetic noise and that only few are likely to be adaptations (Tooby & Cosmides, 1990). Therefore, the notion of a stable, relatively enduring, functional universe of individual differences is probably false. The idea of a fixed set of tasks and behaviors relevant to work across time and place is also unrealistic. Many of the tasks at work and in school are arbitrary or social constructions and are not stable across time and place (cf. Geary, 1995). The idea that individual differences should be consistently and functionally related to work tasks is unrealistic because it presumes that those individual differences must have originated for the purpose of solving those specific work tasks. Yet individual differences that are functional adaptations evolved over hundreds of thousands of years. They evolved in response to problems that individuals faced during the EEA, not in response to a matrix of work-related tasks in the current environment. Therefore, any relationships between individual differences and current job tasks cannot in any sense be fundamental and enduring. They are, rather, probably the result of the coincidence of particular individual differences matching up with particular job tasks at a point in time when they are readily available.

18. There is some evidence that affective orientation is influenced by genetics and brain dopamine levels (Depue, Luciana, Arbisi, Collins, & Leon, 1994).

19. Just as the physical experience of pain is functional, the psychological experience of low mood can also be functional (Nesse, 1990). Studies of people who are incapable of feeling physical pain show that these individuals are more likely to die earlier and suffer more severe injuries than people who experience pain normally. The reason is obvious: the function of pain is to serve as a warning and learning mechanism to prevent people from engaging in behaviors that cause them harm. Similarly, people who are consistently in a good mood may lack the benefits that bad moods and sadness produce. The capacity for both high and low moods may have evolved as a mechanism to allocate the body's resources in a way that is propitious to current opportunities. Evolutionary psychologists have asked whether the behaviors characteristic of sadness and mild depression help a person bounce back from a loss. Nesse and Williams (1995) argue that the inactivity that accompanies sadness and mild depression motivates people to stop doing what they were doing. This is likely to be helpful if their previous behavior was causing personal losses. Low moods also lower activity levels and diminish interests; this keeps people from making precipitous decisions, which they might regret later. By taking off rose-colored glasses, a mild depression may make people more realistic and help them objectively reassess their goals and strategies. Finally, self-absorption can help people focus on possible causes of current problems and develop alternative strategies and goals. Therapists have known for some time that depression often subsides when a person changes goals and refocuses energies.

20. Dissatisfaction over airport security and intelligence-gathering increased (to put it mildly) after terrorists hijacked commercial jetliners on September 11, 2001, and crashed them into the World Trade Center Towers and the Pentagon. The U.S. Congress and the Federal Aviation Administration instituted dramatic

changes in airport security. Prior to the attacks, passengers were allowed to carry pocketknives up to 4 inches in length. Now, penknives and fingernail clippers are prohibited. Prior to the attacks, there was little dissatisfaction with the system and changes occurred slowly. After the attacks, dissatisfaction was widespread and changes occurred rapidly.

21. Although there are literally hundreds of personality traits, words that describe personality traits tend to cluster into five dimensions (McCrae & Costa, 1987). Commonly known as the "Big Five," these dimensions are extroversion, agreeableness, conscientiousness, neuroticism, and openness to experience (i.e., an inquiring intellect, interest in culture).

22. Universities and government organizations typically have set time parameters for collecting applications, ranking them, and making selection decisions. Organizations with less predictable routines are less able to do this and often make hiring decisions as soon as a good applicant appears.

23. Consortiums of organizations in some industries make gentlemen's agreements to synchronize hiring offers and acceptance dates so that timing does not play a factor. This occurs, for example, in college and professional sports and in admissions to many university graduate and professional programs.

24. That there is relatively little research on test usage is an interesting commentary on the role and importance of hiring practices in organizations. People measure things that are important to them. The more important something is, the more extensively and systematically it is measured. That little information exists on the use of hiring practices indicates that test use has not been important to researchers, industry, or government.

25. European psychologists apparently have more interest than American psychologists in the hiring practices that organizations use. In Levy-Leboyer's (1994) chapter on personnel selection in Europe in the *Handbook of Industrial and Organizational Psychology*, she cites 13 surveys conducted by European and British psychologists on the use of hiring practices. However, these were studies primarily documenting the frequency with which various types of selection practices were used. They offer little in the way of theory or testing theories about why different types of hiring practices are used.

26. Complex phenomena are difficult to model mathematically. Dickinson (2001) describes research on the dynamics of insect flight where scientists could not develop equations to model the flight of bees and flies. They were forced to use simulations of insect flight (working mechanical models of bees in wind tunnels) rather than mathematical models to describe and understand the dynamics of insect flight. If insect flight defies precise mathematical models, then it is not unreasonable to assume that it will still be a while before the complexities of human behavior in organizations (and predicting human behavior in organizations) can be precisely described by formal mathematical models.

REFERENCES

Abelson, R. P. (1997). On the surprising longevity of flogged horses: Why there is a case for the significance test. *Psychological Science, 8,* 12–15.

Ackerman, P. L., & Heggestad, E. D. (1997). Intelligence, personality, and interests: Evidence for overlapping traits. *Psychological Bulletin, 121,* 219–245.

Adams, G. A., Elacqua, T. C., & Colarelli, S. M. (1994). The employment interview as a sociometric selection technique. *Journal of Group Psychotherapy, Psychodrama, & Sociometry, 47,* 99–113.

Ahlburg, D. A. (1992). Predicting the job performance of managers: What do the experts know? *International Journal of Forecasting, 7,* 467–472.

Alexander, R. D. (1987). *The biology of moral systems.* New York: Aldine de Gruyter.

Allison, E. (1977). *Educational production function for an introductory economics course,* (Discussion Paper No. 545). Cambridge, MA: Harvard University, Harvard Institute of Economic Research.

Allison, P. D., & Long, J. S. (1990). Departmental effects on scientific productivity. *American Sociological Review, 55,* 469–478.

Ambady, N., & Rosenthal, R. (1993). Half a minute: Predicting teacher evaluations from thin slices of nonverbal behavior and physical attractiveness. *Journal of Personality & Social Psychology, 64,* 431–441.

Ambady, N., & Rosenthal, R. (1992). Thin slices of expressive behavior as predictors of interpersonal consequences: A meta-analysis. *Psychological Bulletin, 111,* 256–274.

American Educational Research Association (AERA), American Psychological Association, and National Council on Measurement in Education. (1985). *Standards for educational and psychological testing.* Washington, DC: American Psychological Association.

American Management Association. (1986). *Hiring costs and strategies.* New York: AMACOM American Management Association.

Apex Business Consulting. (n.d./2001). Planning for the succession of the family-owned business. Retrieved August 15, 2001, from World Wide Web: *http://www.apexbc.com/web_new/articles/faimilyowned_article/htm*

Arendt, H. (1965). *Eichmann in Jerusalem: A report on the banality of evil* (rev. ed.). New York: Viking Press.

Arvey, R. D., & Campion, J. E. (1982). The employment interview: A summary and review of recent research. *Personnel Psychology, 35,* 281–322.

Asprey, R. B. (1986). *Frederick the Great: The magnificent enigma.* New York: Ticknor & Fields.

Baron, J. N., Dobbin, F., & Jennings, P. D. (1986). War and peace: The evolution of modern personnel administration in U.S. industry. *American Journal of Sociology, 92,* 350–383.

Baron-Cohen, S. (1997). How to build a baby that can read minds: Cognitive mechanisms in mindreading. In S. Baron-Cohen (Ed.), *The maladapted mind: Classic readings in evolutionary psychopathology* (pp. 207–239). East Sussex, UK: Psychology Press.

Barrick, M. R., & Mount, M. K. (1991). The Big Five personality dimensions and job performance: A meta-analysis. *Personnel Psychology, 44,* 1–26.

Barron, F. X. (1965). The psychology of creativity. In D. Cartwright (Ed.), *New directions in psychology* (Vol. 2, pp. 1–134). Troy, MO: Holt, Rinehart, & Winston.

Beer, M. (1980). *Organization change and development: A systems view*. Santa Monica, CA: Goodyear.

Bizoffice. (1997, September 24). Transferring management in the family-owned business. Retrieved August 15, 2001, from World Wide Web: *http://www.bizoffice.com/library/files/trans.txt*

Boehm, C. (1999). *Hierarchy in the forest: The evolution of egalitarian behavior*. Cambridge, MA: Harvard University Press.

Bolster, B. I., & Springbett, B. M. (1961). The reaction of interviews to favorable and unfavorable information. *Journal of Applied Psychology, 45*, 97–103.

Boudreau, J. W. (1991). Utility analysis for decisions in human resource management. In M. D. Dunnette & L. M. Hough (Eds.), *Handbook of industrial and organizational psychology* (Vol. 2, pp. 621–745). Palo Alto, CA: Consulting Psychologists Press.

Bowen, W. G., & Bok, D. (1998). *The shape of the river: Long-term consequences of considering race in college and university admissions*. Princeton, NJ: Princeton University Press.

Boyd, M. (2000). *Bach*. New York: Oxford University Press.

Bray, D. W., Campbell, R. J., & Grant, D. L. (1974). *Formative years in business: A long-term AT&T study of managerial lives*. New York: John Wiley & Sons.

Brown, S. H. (1979). Validity distortions associated with a test in use. *Journal of Applied Psychology, 64*, 460–462.

Bureau of National Affairs. (1988). *Recruiting and selection procedures*. Personnel Policies Forum, Survey No. 146. Washington, DC: Author.

Buss, D. M. (1999). *Evolutionary psychology: The new science of the mind*. Needham Heights, MA: Allyn & Bacon.

Buss, D. M. (1998). The psychology of human mate selection: Exploring the complexity of the strategic repertoire. In C. Crawford & D. L Krebs (Eds.), *Handbook of evolutionary psychology: Issues, ideas, and applications* (pp. 405–429). Mahwah, NJ: Lawrence Erlbaum Associates.

Buss, D. M. (1995). Evolutionary psychology: A new paradigm for psychological science. *Psychological Inquiry, 6*, 1–30.

Buss, D. M. (1994). The strategies of human mating. *American Scientist, 82*, 238–249.

Cacioppo, J. T., & Berntson, G. T. (1999). The affect system: Architecture and operating characteristics. *Current Directions in Psychological Science, 8*, 133–136

Callahan, R. (1962). *Education and the cult of efficiency*. Chicago: University of Chicago Press.

Campbell, D. T. (1994). How individual and face-to-face group selection undermine firm selection in organizational evolution. In J.A.C. Baum & J. V. Singh (Eds.), *Evolutionary dynamics of organizations* (pp. 23–38). New York: Oxford University Press.

Campbell, J. P., McCloy, R. A., Oppler, S. H., & Sager, C. E. (1993). A theory of performance. In N. Schmidt & W. C. Borman (Eds.), *Personnel selection in organizations* (pp. 35–70). San Francisco: Jossey-Bass.

Cascio, W. F. (1998). *Applied psychology in personnel management* (5th ed.). Englewood Cliffs, NJ: Prentice Hall.

Cascio, W. F., & Ramos, R. A. (1986). Development and application of a new method for assessing job performance in behavioral/economic terms. *Journal of Applied Psychology, 71,* 20–28.

Cattell, R. B. (1965). *The scientific analysis of personality.* Baltimore, MD: Penguin.

Chagnon, N. A. (1997). *Yanomamö* (5th ed.) Fort Worth, TX: Harcourt Brace College Publishers.

Clore, G. L., Schwarz, N., & Conway, M. (1994). Affective causes and consequences of social information processing. In R. S. Wyer, Jr., & T. K. Srull (Eds.), *Handbook of social cognition, Vol. 1: Basic processes; Vol. 2: Applications* (2nd ed.) (pp. 323–417). Hillsdale, NJ: Lawrence Erlbaum Associates.

Cohen, Y., & Pfeffer, J. (1986). Organizational hiring standards. *Administrative Science Quarterly, 31,* 1–24.

Colarelli, S. M. (1996). Establishment and job context influences on the use of hiring practices. *Applied Psychology: An International Review, 45,* 153–176.

Colarelli, S. M., Alampay, M. R., & Canali, K. G. (2002). Letters of recommendation: An evolutionary perspective. *Human Relations, 55,* 315–344.

Colarelli, S. M., & Boos, A. L. (1992). Sociometric and ability-based assignment to work groups: Some implications for personnel selection. *Journal of Organizational Behavior, 13,* 187–196.

Colarelli, S. M., Dean, R. A., & Konstans, C. (1987). Comparative effects of personal and situational influences on job outcomes of new professionals. *Journal of Applied Psychology, 72,* 558–566.

Colarelli, S. M., & Stumpf, S. A. (1990). Compatibility and conflict among outcomes of organizational entry strategies: Mechanistic and social systems perspectives. *Behavioral Science, 35,* 1–10.

Connor, P. E. (1991). Developing managers: A case study in laying the groundwork. *Journal of Management Development, 10,* 64–76.

Crouse, J., & Trusheim, D. (1988). *The case against the SAT.* Chicago: University of Chicago Press.

Cummins, D. D. (1998). Social norms and other minds: The evolutionary roots of higher cognition. In D. D. Cummins (Ed.), *The evolution of mind* (pp. 30–50). New York: Oxford University Press.

Cyert, R. M., & March, J. G. (1963). *A behavioral theory of the firm.* Englewood Cliffs, NJ: Prentice Hall.

Dakin, S., & Armstrong, J. S. (1989). Predicting job performance: A comparison of expert opinion and research findings. *International Journal of Forecasting, 5,* 187–194.

Dawes, R. M., Faust, D., & Meehl, P. E. (1989). Clinical versus actuarial judgment. *Science, 243,* 1668–1674.

DePaulo, B. M. (1992). Nonverbal behavior and self-presentation. *Psychological Bulletin, 111,* 203–243.

Depue, R. A., Luciana, M., Arbisi, P., Collins, P., & Leon, A. (1994). Dopamine and the structure of personality: Relation of agonistic–induced dopamine activity to positive emotionality. *Journal of Personality and Social Psychology, 67,* 485–498.

Diamond, J. (1997). *Guns, germs, and steel: The fates of human societies.* New York: W. W. Norton.

Dickinson, M. (2001, June). Solving the mystery of insect flight. *Scientific American, 284,* 48–57.

Dunbar, R.I.M. (1995). *The trouble with science.* London: Faber & Faber.

Dunnette, M. D. (1966). *Personnel selection and placement.* Belmont, CA: Wadsworth Publishing Co.

Dunnette, M. D. (1976). Aptitudes, abilities, and skill. In M. D. Dunnette (Ed.), *Handbook of industrial and organizational psychology* (pp. 473–520). Chicago: Rand McNally.

Dusek, J. B., Hall, V. C., & Meyer, W. J. (Eds.). (1985). *Teacher expectations.* Hillsdale, NJ: Lawrence Erlbaum Associates.

Eastman, W. N., & Bailey, J. R. (1994). Examining the origins of management theory: Value divisions in the positivist program. *Journal of Applied Behavioral Science, 30,* 313–328.

Eden, D. (1990). *Pygmalion in management: Productivity as a self-fulfilling prophecy.* Lexington, MA: Lexington Books.

Fiedler, F. E., & Garcia, J. E. (1987). *New approaches to effective leadership: Cognitive resources and organizational performance.* New York: John Wiley & Sons.

Fisek, M. H., & Ofshe, R. (1970). The process of status evolution. *Sociometry, 33,* 327–346.

Friedlander F., & Pickle, H. (1968). Components of effectiveness in small organizations. *Administrative Science Quarterly, 13,* 289–304.

Friedman, T., & Williams, E. B. (1982). Current use of tests for employment. In A. K. Wigdor & W. R. Garner (Eds.), *Ability testing: Uses, consequences, and controversies* (Part II, pp. 99–169). Washington, DC: National Academy Press.

Ganzach, Y. (1998). Intelligence and job satisfaction. *Academy of Management Journal, 41,* 526–539.

Gaulin, S.J.C., & McBurney, D. H. (2001). *Psychology: An evolutionary approach.* Upper Saddle River, NJ: Prentice Hall.

Geary, D. C. (1995). Reflections of evolution and culture in children's cognition: implications for development and instruction. *American Psychologist, 50,* 24–37.

George, J. M. (1996). Trait and state affect. In K. R. Murphy (Ed.), *Individual differences and behavior in organizations* (pp. 145–171). San Francisco: Jossey-Bass.

Gigerenzer, G., Todd, P. M., & The ABC Research Group. (1999). *Simple heuristics that make us smart*. New York: Oxford University Press.

Golden, D. (2002, January 11). Roiling his faculty, new Harvard president reroutes tenure track. *Wall Street Journal*, pp. A1–A2.

Golden, D. (2001, May 29). How colleges reject the top applicants—and boost their status. *Wall Street Journal*, pp. A1, A6.

Gose, B., & Selingo, J. (2001, October 26). The SAT's greatest test: Social, legal, and demographic forces threaten to dethrone the most widely used college-entrance exam. *The Chronicle of Higher Education*, pp. A10–A15.

Guion, R. M. (1998). *Assessment, measurement, and prediction for personnel decisions*. Mahwah, NJ: Lawrence Erlbaum Associates.

Guion, R. M. (1991). Personnel assessment, selection, and placement. In M. D. Dunnette and L. M. Hough (Eds.), *Handbook of industrial and organizational psychology* (Vol. 2, pp. 327–397). Palo Alto, CA: Consulting Psychologists Press.

Hale, M. (1982). History of employment testing. In A. K. Wigdor & W. R. Garner (Eds.), *Ability testing: Uses, consequences, and controversies* (Part II, pp. 3–38). Washington, DC: National Academy Press.

Hale, M. (1980). *Human science and social order: Hugo Münsterberg and the origins of applied psychology*. Philadelphia: Temple University Press.

Hamilton, W. D. (1964). The general evolution of social behavior. I and II. *Journal of Theoretical Biology, 7*, 1–52.

Hannan, M. T., & Freeman, J. H. (1989). *Organizational ecology*. Cambridge, MA: Harvard University Press.

Hargadon, F. (1981). Tests and college admissions. *American Psychologist, 36*, 1112–1119.

Harris, M., & Schaubroek, J. (1988). A meta-analysis of self-supervisor, self-peer, and peer-supervisor ratings. *Personnel Psychology, 41*, 43–62.

Hartigan, J. A., & Widgor, A. K. (Eds.). (1989). *Fairness in employment testing: Validity generalization, minority issues, and the General Aptitude Test Battery*. Washington, DC: National Academy Press.

Hartocollis, A. (1999, September 17). Miscalculation on scores shows a weakness of tests. *New York Times*, p. A23.

Herrnstein, R. J., & Murray, C. (1994). *The bell curve: Intelligence and class structure in American life*. New York: Free Press.

Hinrichs, J. R. (1978). An eight-year follow-up of a management assessment center. *Journal of Applied Psychology, 63*, 596–601.

Hogarth, R. M. (1981). Beyond discrete biases: Functional and dysfunctional aspects of judgmental heuristics. *Psychological Bulletin, 90*, 197–217.

Hogarth, R. M., & Makridakis, S. (1981). Forecasting and planning: An evaluation. *Management Science, 27*, 115–138.

Holland, J. H. (1995). *Hidden order*. Reading, MA: Helix.

Holmen, M. G., & Docter, R. F. (1972). *Educational and psychological testing: A study of the industry and its practices*. New York: Russell Sage Foundation.

Hough, L. (1998). Personality at work: Issues and evidence. In *Beyond multiple choice: Evaluating alternatives to traditional testing for selection* (pp. 131–159). Hillsdale, NJ: Lawrence Erlbaum Associates.

Hulin, C. L., Henry, R. A., & Noon, S. L. (1990). Adding a dimension: Time as a factor in the generalizability of predictive relationships. *Psychological Bulletin, 107,* 328–340.

Hull, C. L. (1928). *Aptitude testing.* Yonkers-on-Hudson, NY and Chicago: World Book Co.

Hunter, J. E., & Hunter, R. F. (1984). Validity and utility of alternative predictors of job performance. *Psychological Bulletin, 96,* 72–98.

Hunter, J. E., Schmidt, F. L., Rauschenberger, J. M., & Jayne, M.E.A. (2001). Intelligence, motivation, and job performance. In C. L. Cooper & E. A. Locke (Eds.), *Industrial and organizational psychology: Linking theory with practice* (pp. 278–303). Oxford: Basil Blackwell.

Jamison, K. R. (1995, February). Manic-depression illness and creativity. *Scientific American,* 62–67.

Jensen, A. R. (1998). *The g factor: The science of mental ability.* Westport, CT: Praeger.

Jensen, A. R. (1980). *Bias in mental testing.* New York: Free Press.

Journal of Career Planning & Employment. (1995, Spring). Author, pp. 37–49.

Kanigel, R. (1997). *The one best way: Frederick Winslow Taylor and the enigma of efficiency.* New York: Viking Press.

Keegan, J. (1987). *The mask of command.* New York: Viking Press.

Keppie, L. (1984). *The making of the Roman army: From Republic to Empire.* Totowa, NJ: Barnes & Noble Books.

Klitgaard, R. E. (1985). *Choosing elites.* New York: Basic Books.

Lancaster, S. L., Colarelli, S. M., King, D. W., & Beehr, T. A. (1994). Job applicant similarity on cognitive ability, vocational interests, and personality characteristics: Do similar persons choose similar jobs? *Educational and Psychological Measurement, 54,* 299–316.

Latham, G. P., & Whyte, G. (1994). The futility of utility analysis. *Personnel Psychology, 47,* 31–46.

Lawshe, C. H. (1969). Statistical theory and practice in applied psychology. *Personnel Psychology, 22,* 117–123.

Lemann, N. (1999). *The big test: The secret history of American meritocracy.* New York: Farrar, Straus & Giroux.

Levy-Leboyer, C. (1994). Selection and assessment in Europe. In H. C. Triandis, M. D. Dunnette, & L. M. Hough (Eds.). *Handbook of industrial and organizational psychology* (2nd ed.) (Vol. 4, pp. 173–190). Palo Alto, CA: Consulting Psychologists.

Link, H. C. (1919). *Employment psychology: The application of scientific methods to the selection, training and grading of employees.* New York: Macmillan Co.

McCrae, R. R., & Costa, P. T. (1987). Validation of the Five-Factor Model across instruments and observers. *Journal of Personality and Social Psychology, 52,* 81–90.

McDaniel, S. L. (1997). *The dark side of the Big Five: New perspectives for personnel selection*. Paper presented at the 14th Annual conference for the Society of Industrial and Organizational Psychology.

McNeill, W. H. (1971). *A world history* (2nd ed.). New York: Oxford University Press.

McWhorter, J. H. (2000). *Losing the race: Self-sabotage in Black America*. New York: Free Press.

Meehl, P. E. (1954). *Clinical vs. statistical prediction: A theoretical analysis and a review of the evidence*. Minneapolis: University of Minnesota Press.

Miyazaki, I. (1976). *China's examination hell: The civil service examinations of Imperial China*. (C. Schirokauer, Trans.). New York: Weatherhill.

Moore, R. F. (1996). Caring for identified versus statistical lives: An evolutionary view of medical distributive justice. *Ethology & Sociobiology, 17,* 379–401.

Morrison, J. D. (1993). Group composition and creative performance. Unpublished doctoral dissertation, University of Tulsa. Abstracted in *Dissertation Abstracts International* (1993), *54 (2B),* 1136.

Muchinsky, P. M. (1979). The use of reference reports in personnel selection: A review and evaluation. *Journal of Occupational Psychology, 52,* 287–297.

Münsterberg, H. (1913). *Psychology and industrial efficiency*. Boston: Houghton Mifflin.

Murphy, K. R. (1996). Individual differences and behavior in organizations: Much more than g. In K. R. Murphy (Ed.), *Individual differences and behavior in organizations* (pp. 3–30). San Francisco: Jossey-Bass.

Nelson, R. R., & Winter, S. G. (1982). *An evolutionary theory of economic change*. Cambridge, MA: Belknap.

Nesse, R. M. (1990). Evolutionary explanations of emotions. *Human Nature, 1,* 261–289.

Nesse, R. M., & Williams, G. C. (1995). *Why we get sick*. New York: Vintage.

Nisbett, R. E., & Wilson, T. D. (1977). Telling more than we can know: Verbal reports on mental processes. *Psychological Review, 84,* 231–259.

Omark, D. R., Strayer, F. F., & Freeman, D. G. (Eds.). (1980). *Dominance relations: An ethological view of human conflict and social interaction*. New York: Garland Press.

Orton, J. D., & Weick, K. E. (1990). Loosely coupled systems: A reconceptualization. *Academy of Management Review, 15,* 203–223.

Patton, J. Q. (1997, June). *Are warriors altruistic? Reciprocal altruism and war in the Ecuadorian Amazon*. Paper presented at the Human Behavior and Evolution Society Meetings, University of Arizona, Tucson, AZ.

Pawlowski, B., Dunbar, R.I.M., & Lipowicz, A. (2000). Tall men have more reproductive success. *Nature, 403,* 156.

Penton-Voak, I. S., Perrett, D. I., Castles, D. L., Kobayashi, T., Burt, D. M., Murray, L. K., & Minamisawa, R. (1999). Menstrual cycle alters face preference. *Nature, 399,* 741–742.

Ravitch, D. (2000). *Left back: A century of failed school reforms*. New York: Simon & Schuster.

Reed, J. M. (1987). Robert M. Yerkes and the mental testing movement. In M. M. Sokal (Ed.), *Psychological testing and American society: 1890–1930* (pp. 75–94). New Brunswick, NJ: Rutgers University Press.

Renard, G. (1918). *Guilds in the middle ages*. (D. Terry, Trans.). London: G. Bell & Sons.

Resnick, D. (1982). History of educational testing. In A. K. Wigdor & W. R. Garner (Eds.), *Ability testing: Uses, consequences, and controversies* (Part II, pp. 173–194). Washington, DC: National Academy Press.

Roberts, K. H., Hulin, C. L., & Rosseau, D. M. (1978). *Developing an interdisciplinary science of organizations*. San Francisco: Jossey-Bass.

Rothstein, R. (2000, November 15). Education policymaking requires more than polls. *New York Times*, p. A–25.

Sackett, P. R., Schmitt, N, Ellingson, J. E., & Kabin, M. B. (2001). High-stakes testing in employment, credentialing, and higher education: Prospects in a post-affirmative-action world. *American Psychologist, 56*, 302–318.

Sackett, P. R., & Wilk, S. L. (1994). Within-group norming and other forms of score adjustment in preemployment testing. *American Psychologist, 49*, 929–954.

Sadacca, R., & Brackett, J. (1971). *The validity and discriminatory impact of the Federal Service Entrance Examination*. Washington, DC: Urban Institute.

Samelson, F. (1979). Putting psychology on the map: Ideology and intelligence testing. In A. R. Buss (Ed.), *Psychology in social context* (pp. 103–168). New York: Irvington Publishers.

Sawyer, J. (1966). Measurement and prediction, clinical and statistical. *Psychological Bulletin, 66*, 178–200.

Schmidt, F. L. (1995). Why all banding procedures in personnel selection are logically flawed. *Human Performance, 8*, 165–177.

Schmidt, F. L., & Hunter, J. E. (1998). The validity and utility of selection methods in personnel psychology: Practical and theoretical implications of 85 years of research findings. *Psychological Bulletin, 124*, 262–274.

Schmidt, F. L., & Hunter, J. E. (1981). Employment testing: Old theories and new research findings. *American Psychologist, 36*, 1128–1137.

Schmidt, F. L., Hunter, J. E., McKenzie, R. C., & Muldrow, T. W. (1979). Impact of valid selection procedures on work-force productivity. *Journal of Applied Psychology, 64*, 609–626.

Scott, W. R. (1998). *Organizations: Rational, natural, and open systems* (4th ed.). Englewood Cliffs, NJ: Prentice Hall.

Seashore, S. E., Indik, B. P., & Georgopoluous, B. S. (1960). Relationships among criteria of performance. *Journal of Applied Psychology, 44*, 195–202.

Shackleton, V., & Newell, S. (1991). Management selection: A comparative survey of methods used in top British and French companies. *Journal of Occupational Psychology, 64*, 23–36.

Shrauger, W. H., & Osberg, T. M. (1981). The relative accuracy of self-predictions and judgments by others in psychological assessment. *Psychological Bulletin, 90,* 322–351.

Simon, H. A. (1956). Rational choice and the structure of environments. *Psychological Review, 63,* 129–138.

Singh, D. (1993). Adaptive significance of female physical attractiveness: Role of waist-to-hip ratio. *Journal of Personality & Social Psychology, 65,* 293–307.

Snow, C. C., & Snell, S. A. (1993). Staffing as strategy. In N. Schmitt & W. Borman (Eds.), *Personnel selection in organizations* (pp. 448–478). San Francisco: Jossey-Bass.

Steers, R. M. (1977). Antecedents and outcomes of organizational commitment. *Administrative Science Quarterly, 22,* 46–56.

Stevenson, H. W., Chen, C., & Lee, S. Y. (1993). Mathematics achievement of Chinese, Japanese, and American children: Ten years later. *Science, 259,* 53–58.

Sturm, S., & Guinier, L. (1996). The future of affirmative action: Reclaiming the innovative ideal. *California Law Review, 84,* 953–1036

Sugiyama, M. S. (2001). Food, foragers, and folklore: The role of narrative in human subsistence. *Evolution and Human Behavior, 22,* 221–240.

Swets, J. A., Dawes, R. M., & Monahan, J. (2000). Psychological science can improve diagnostic decisions. *Psychological Science, 11,* 1–26.

Taylor, S. E. (1991). Asymmetrical effects of positive and negative events: The mobilization-minimization hypothesis. *Psychological Bulletin, 110,* 67–85.

Tenopyr, M. L. (1981). The realities of employment testing. *American Psychologist, 36,* 1120–1127.

Terpstra, D. E., & Rozell, E. J. (1997). Why some potentially effective staffing practices are seldom used. *Public Personnel Management, 26,* 483–495.

Tett, R. P., Jackson, D. N., & Rothstein, M. (1991). Personality measures as predictors of job performance: A meta-analytic review. *Personnel Psychology, 44,* 703–742.

Thorndike, E. L. (1913). Educational diagnosis, *Science, 37,* 139.

Thornhill, R., Møller, A. P. (1997). Developmental stability, disease and medicine. *Biological Reviews, 72,* 497–548.

Tooby, J., & Cosmides, L. (1990). On the universality of human nature and the uniqueness of the individual: The role of genetics and adaptation. *Journal of Personality, 58,* 17–67.

Tooby, J., & DeVore, I. (1987). The reconstruction of hominid behavioral evolution through strategic modeling. In W. G. Kinsey (Ed.), *The evolution of human behavior: Primate models* (pp. 183–237). Albany, NY: SUNY Press.

Topor, D. J. (2000). An examination of personnel selection decision-making: What influence do constructs and assessment methods have upon human resource practitioners' evaluations of job applicants? Unpublished doctoral dissertation, Central Michigan University.

Tversky, A., & Kahneman, D. (1974). Judgment under uncertainty: Heuristics and biases. *Science, 185*, 1124–1131.

Uniform Guidelines on employee selection procedures (1978). *Federal Register, 43*, 38290–38315.

U.S. Census Bureau. (n.d.). *Statistics about business size (including small business) from the U.S. Census Bureau.* Retrieved August 26, 2001, from World Wide Web: *http://www.census.gov/epcd/www/smallbus.html*

Webster, G. (1985). *The Roman imperial army: Of the first and second centuries A.D.* (3rd ed.). Totowa, NJ: Barnes & Noble Books.

Westermann, W. L. (1955). *The Slave systems of Greek and Roman antiquity.* Philadelphia: American Philosophical Society.

Wexley, K. N., Alexander, R. A., Greenawalt, J. P., & Couch, M. A. (1980). Attitudinal congruence and similarity as related to interpersonal evaluations in manager-subordinate dyads. *Academy of Management Journal, 23*, 320–330.

Young, M. (1959). *The rise of meritocracy.* New York: Random House.

Zedeck, S., & Cascio, W. F. (1984). Psychological issues in personnel decisions. *Annual Review of Psychology, 35*, 461–518.

CHAPTER 4

Alternatives to Jigsaw Puzzle and Spray Paint Utopias
Evolutionary Approaches to Hiring People

[Traditional] recipes for living have [been] tested and winnowed through hundreds of generations of human social history. On purely scientific grounds, [they] might be regarded as better tested than the best of psychology's and psychiatry's speculations on how lives should be lived.

—Donald T. Campbell (1975, p. 1103)

Probability entered mathematics with gambling theory, and stayed there as a mere computational device. Recently, an entire industry of "risk measurers" emerged, specializing in the application of these probability methods to assess risks in the social sciences. Clearly, the odds in games where the rules are clearly and explicitly defined are computable and the risks consequently measured. But not in the real world. . . . The game is not a deck of cards. . . . No matter how sophisticated our choices, how good we are at dominating the odds, randomness will have the last word.

—Nassim Nicholas Taleb (2001, pp. 188, 192)

By now, it should be clear that there are fundamental problems with mechanistic approaches to hiring people. Mechanistic methods are not necessarily better than traditional methods; traditional methods can achieve the same results as mechanistic methods. Mechanistic hiring methods make unrealistic assumptions about organizational goals and about the relationships between individual characteristics and goals, as well as about the relationships among different individual characteristics. Orderly, normative prescriptions for hiring decisions do not take into account the chaotic political realities of the hiring process in most organizations. An evolutionary approach to hiring decisions is based on assumptions that are more compatible with these realities, and therefore offers a different starting point for thinking about what makes a good hiring practice. The evolutionary principles described in Chapter 2 suggest at least five assumptions for an evolutionary approach to hiring practices. First, hiring practices exist in social systems: complexity, uncertainty, and conflict characterize social systems and therefore the operation of hiring practices. Second, people are driven by self-interest, and they will prefer to use hiring methods and make hiring decisions that are based on self-interest, rather than in the (mythical) best interests of the organization. Third, hiring practices exist in a nexus of interests, so hiring practices inevitably involve multiple and conflicting interests and goals. Conflict between hiring goals, criteria, and decisions is inevitable. Fourth, the environments of social systems continually change and variation is the primary means by which biological and social systems adapt to uncertain futures: variability plays an important role in hiring practices. Fifth, hiring practices that have withstood the test of time have probably done so because they embodied functional wisdom; they were adaptive. Through sociocultural evolution and by being compatible with evolved psychological mechanisms, some hiring practices have proven more adaptive to people and social systems than others. Social systems tend to retain those practices that have proven functional, and people are likely to favor practices that tap into evolved psychological mechanisms related to gathering information and making decisions.

This chapter begins with a general discussion of the effectiveness of hiring practices and argues that this is a difficult problem. Attempts to nail down a set of criteria for effectiveness are beset with problems of levels of analysis, aggregation, and complexity. I then describe some traditional hiring practices from an evolutionary perspective, examine their possible functions, point out why they may be useful, and suggest that a number of traditional practices are worth keeping while others should be modified to fit better with modern environments. In the last section I make the case that hiring practices should enhance variation. I describe some existing practices, such as affirmative action and diversity programs, which people view as enhancing variation. I argue that, from an evolutionary perspective, they are flawed in a number of respects and I describe alternative approaches based on theory and research from evolutionary psychology and on evolutionary approaches to understanding organizations. These approaches deal more realistically with the technical and political difficulties of hiring people.

THE EFFECTIVENESS OF HIRING PRACTICES

Characteristics, Functions, and Levels

We can think of the effectiveness of hiring practices with respect to characteristics, functions, and levels. *Characteristics* are attributes of individuals that are presumed to relate to job behavior; *function* is the purpose of job behavior, its contribution to the unit where the behavior occurs; and *level* is the unit of aggregation where the behavior occurs (see Figure 4.1).

Hiring practices typically involve some combination of individual differences, functions, and levels. The effectiveness of a hiring practice can be assessed by relating the characteristic or characteristics used in the hiring process to functional criteria at a particular level.

The characteristics commonly used in hiring include skills and knowldege, cognitive abilities, personality, background and values, and demographics. Two features of characteristics affect hiring practices: their sheer number and their degree of malleability. The sheer number of individual difference characteristics is remarkable; there are literally hundreds of personality traits, mental abilities, values, interests, and skills. This raises the questions of what characteristics should be used in hiring decisions and how these characteristics are related to different functions at different levels. A second feature of human individual differences is malleability. Some characteristics are more easily changed than others. This raises questions about whether a characteristic can be changed and, if so, how long the change will take and how much it will cost. Intelligence and personality are difficult to change and generally cannot be changed much. Knowledge and skills, on the other hand, can be changed often and substantially—although the more complex the knowledge or skill, the longer it takes. Most physical characteristics cannot be changed. The issue of malleability is important because most hiring methods make assumptions about the permanence of characteristics and about the permanence of the relationship between characteristics and outcomes.

The primary functions that people perform in organizations are task, interpersonal, and innovation (Bales & Slater, 1955; March, 1991). Tasks are activities related directly to outputs. Interpersonal functions

Figure 4.1
Hiring Practice Effectiveness

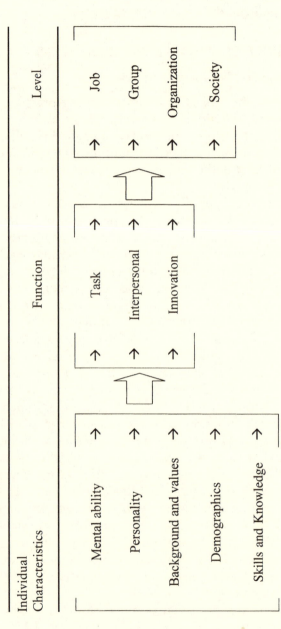

involve the support and encouragement of others and the generation of good-will and harmony. Innovation involves the development of—or the encouragement of others to develop—new goals, new approaches to solving problems, and new ways of performing tasks. The effectiveness of a hiring practice can also be assessed at four levels—the job, group, organization, and society. The task, interpersonal, and innovation functions operate at each level. At the level of the *job*, we can evaluate a hiring practice by how well it predicts job performance, cooperation with co-workers, or new ways of doing the work. At the level of the *group*, we can evaluate a hiring practice by how it relates to group performance, cooperation and collaboration among group members, and innovations produced by the group. At the *organization* level, a hiring practice could be evaluated by its effects on the organization's primary tasks of production and profitability, its effects on conflict and civility, and the rate of new innovations in products and services. Even at the level of a society, one can examine the contributions of hiring practices to overall economic or intellectual performance, social conflict and integration, and the rate of change and innovation.

Most evaluations of the effectiveness of a hiring practice focus on the job and on the task—that is, how well a test score correlates with job performance (Schmidt & Hunter, 1983).[1] A smaller number of researchers have also evaluated tests with respect to innovation and interpersonal functions—such as how individual characteristics predict creativity and being a good organizational citizen (e.g., George, 1996; MacKinnon & Hall, 1972). Considerably less research has been conducted on how attributes used in making hiring decisions contribute to group, organizational, and societal functions. The effects of individuals on larger units become complicated because it is unclear how to aggregate individuals who compose the whole (Klein, Dansereau, & Hall, 1994). Combining individual differences with different functions and levels gives rise to the problems of aggregation and complexity.

The Problem of Aggregation

Whenever an administrator wants to estimate the impact of a trait used in selecting applicants, she needs first to clarify the basis for relating the trait in the individual to the aggregation of traits in the group. There are at least three bases for doing so: adding up each individual's standing on a trait; calculating the proportion of individuals with the trait; or identifying a proper mix of traits.

Aggregating Individuals

One approach is to aggregate the effects that a hiring practice produces on individual employees. When a selection test relates positively to job performance, increments in test scores can be used to estimate increments in the job performance of each employee. Estimating productivity gains to a larger unit, such as an organization, becomes an exercise in addition: adding up the estimated productivity gains per individual over the number of individuals hired using the new selection device at a given cutting score (Schmidt, Hunter, McKenzie, & Muldrow 1979). Schmidt et al. (1979) used this logic to estimate the effects of using the Programmer Aptitude Test (PAT) in hiring decisions for an organization and for the nation as a whole. They estimated that the federal government could increase productivity from $5.6 to $97.2 million if PAT was used to hire computer programmers. The range in their estimate is due to the impact of differing assumptions about the validity of previous selection procedures and the ratio of applicants to job openings. Using the same algorithm, they estimated that the gain in productivity to the nation as a whole would range from $93 million to $1.6 billion if all organizations that hired computer programmers used the PAT. The premise of this approach is that the whole is equal to the sum of the parts, an assumption that few organizational scholars find tenable (Scott, 1998).

The effects of educational admissions practices on society have been widely debated for decades (Lemann, 1999; Ravitch, 2000). Most of these debates implicitly assume an additive model. That is, the effects of admissions practices on individual students add up to produce effects on society at large. One practice that has received considerable attention is the use of cognitive ability tests. By the middle of the twentieth century, testing proponents were advocating ability testing (primarily the SAT) for all college applicants (Lemann, 1999). Their argument went as follows. Gaining a place in a university should be determined by academic merit rather than by social class, wealth, or connections. Proponents of the SAT believed that by using the test for making college admissions decisions, *the country as a whole* would become more productive. Future leaders would be selected based on ability, and the nation's higher education resources would be used wisely and efficiently. By the end of the century, the idea that society would benefit by channeling the brightest students into college preparatory courses and colleges came under attack. On one flank, the system was criticized for creating a cognitive class structure in America (Herrnstein & Murray, 1994; Reich, 1991). Those with high SAT scores who had been channeled into college came to dominate the country's political, economic, and technological institutions. On the other flank, some have attacked cognitive ability tests from the perspective of educational equality and employment opportunity. Using cognitive ability tests to make selection decisions produces broad negative social consequences, such as excluding some racial minorities from higher education and gainful employment, perpetuating a legacy of oppression and discrimination (Sturm & Guinier, 1996).[2]

The Proportion of Types of Individuals

Another approach to aggregation looks at the proportion of individuals of a particular type in a social unit. This approach estimates the effects of individual characteristics on larger units by relating the proportion of individuals who have a specific characteristic with organizational outcomes (Schneider, 1996). This approach assumes that a critical mass of employees of a certain type will create a climate that in turn will affect organizational or social outcomes. Schneider (1996) believes that organizations with a critical mass of people with prosocial characteristics—such as conscientiousness and agreeableness—will lead to climates conducive to good customer service, which in turn will lead to greater customer satisfaction and profitability. At the level of societies, Nisbett and Cohen's (1996) research on the culture of violence suggests that a critical mass of particular types of people has important effects. Societies or regions of countries are more violent when a critical mass of individuals believe that violence is the most appropriate way to solve conflicts or deal with personal affronts. Nisbett and Cohen argued that the southern states in the United States have high rates of violence because many of the original immigrants to the South were herders from Scotland. Herders and other nomadic people are prone to violence because they do not have the physical protection afforded by permanent buildings and police forces available to sedentary peoples. This critical mass of herders enabled a culture of violence to be established in the South, which has been passed on for generations.

Mix of Types

A variant of this view focuses on the mix of types. This view suggests that individuals should be aggregated on the basis of the degree to which a social unit has a homogeneous or heterogeneous composition. It is the *mix* of types of individuals in a group, organization, or society rather than the proportion of any one type that influences important outcomes. One approach is to assess how similar group members are to one another. Groups that are more heterogeneous generate more creative solutions to problems, but they also have more disagreements and conflict.

Too much heterogeneity often produces conflict to the point where the group cannot function. Groups that are more homogeneous are more productive and harmonious. Too much homogeneity, however, results in the uncritical acceptance of ideas, even when they are poor ideas, and in a reluctance to entertain new ideas. Much research has defined heterogeneity on the basis of personality characteristics (Hoffman, 1959; Hoffman & Maier, 1961). However, cultural background and sex have also been used to define heterogeneity (Bettenhausen & Murnighan, 1985; Wood, 1987). In the current zeitgeist, race, ethnicity, sex, and sexual orientation are characteristics that commonly define group heterogeneity (Cox, 1993).

Selective universities have grappled with the proper mix for entering classes of students. When a university has more applicants than available slots for new students, university administrators can tinker with the mix of students for their entering classes. Some believe that they can engineer mixes to achieve specific social and educational goals. Although some selective universities could fill all of the freshman class with honors students, administrators may believe that the educational experience of the student body will be enhanced with a mix of top students, athletes, and others who have distinguished themselves in areas such as social service, leadership, and the creative arts. The diversity of the entering class is a major objective of admissions officers at Harvard College. Robert Klitgaard, a former special assistant to the president of Harvard University, writes:

> The most celebrated of Harvard College's justifications concerns "diversity" in the student body. Admitting some students with less academic talent actually enhances, rather than dilutes, the overall educational experience. The less qualified students, through their "diversity" in non-academic dimensions, actually improve the learning environment for the more qualified, and possibly vice versa. (1985, p. 25)

Although grades and LSAT scores are the major factors in admission to Harvard Law School, "diversity matters: among the considerations that affect decisions are race, geography . . . economic disadvantage, unusual work experience, and sex" (Klitgaard, 1985, p. 37). At the Graduate School of Arts and Sciences, "few departments worry about 'diversity' or 'balance' in an entering class, with two exceptions: academic subfield and race" (p. 33). Administrators from the University of Michigan Law School argued that a racially heterogeneous student body enhances the quality of legal education by bringing different perspectives to class discussions (Schmidt, 2001). William Bowen and Derek Bok, former presidents of Princeton and Harvard universities, respectively, argue that university administrators can and should intelligently craft the composition of the student body to achieve educational and social goals (Bowen & Bok, 1998).

The idea that administrators or personnel experts can craft an optimal mix of characteristics is problematic. Rigorously defining, operationalizing, and justifying the appropriate type and level of heterogeneity for a social unit is inordinately complex. One must determine which characteristics, out of a myriad of human characteristics, define diversity. One must then measure and assign weights to these characteristics. The optimal composition of a student body or workforce must be estimated. To justify this procedure, it is necessary to correlate various characteristics and compositions (which are theoretically infinite) with desired outcomes. Klitgaard concludes that "these complications probably preclude an analytical solution to the problem of the optimal composition of the student body" (p. 74). Lee J. Cronbach echoes a similar view: "an attempt to reason rigorously about diversity is doomed to failure" (cited in Klitgaard, 1985, pp. 74–75). Another problem is political. The selection of characteristics on which to craft an ideal mixture of types inevitably involves political judgments. The diversities of opinions about optimal characteristics and optimal mixes of characteristics lead inexorably to conflicts of interests. People can also manipulate diversity characteristics for ulterior motives. One can use a seemingly innocuous characteristic, such as "geographical diversity," as a ruse to exclude people for reasons other than geography. In describing the freshman admissions process at Princeton University, David Samuels points out that:

> Applicants from sparsely populated states like Nevada, Montana, and Wyoming . . . received preference over students from competitive high schools in cities like New York. This system dated to the end of the First World War, a time when officials at Harvard, Princeton, and Yale were working hard to find an answer to what they called the "Jewish question." They arrived at a formula for "geographical distribution" (now styled "geographical diversity") that would increase the number of "white" students on their campuses while radically decreasing the numbers of Jews. These rules of the game were not exactly those described in the admissions brochures. (2001, p. 74)

Even if an ideal mix could be identified, selection procedures involve personal interests as well as ordinary human frailties. Given conflicts of interest among those who participate in admissions decisions, it is unlikely that an ideal mix of applicants could be selected dispassionately. In reality, the selection process will be messy, with different individuals and coalitions jockeying for influence so that their values will be realized.

The Problem of Complexity

Hiring procedures potentially involve a multiplicity of individual differences, multiple functions, and multiple levels. This creates complexity. Hiring occurs in the context of a social system where a large number of variables are potentially in play, and these variables are not normally independent of one another. It is not possible to isolate a few traits used in a hiring procedure from other traits; nor is it possible to isolate their effects. Therefore, it becomes difficult to predict the *effects* of a trait or a small number of traits on *a system or parts of it*. Hiring procedures present at least five problems associated with complexity: (1) combinations, (2) emphases, (3) contradictions, (4) moderators, and (5) levels.

The problem of *combinations* involves determining what combination of characteristics will produce satisfactory outcomes. For example, if we assume six individual characteristics, three functions, and four levels, this results in 72 possible combinations. The problem becomes more severe when other factors are introduced, such as additional characteristics or sublevels. The problem of *emphasis* involves determining which characteristic or characteristics should be stressed in hiring decisions. Mechanistic hiring methods view this primarily as a technical problem that can be solved by a dispassionate analysis of the job. However, the problem of emphasis is often complex. People are constellations of many characteristics, and a high score on one characteristic does not necessarily imply a high score on another characteristic. Therefore, it is unlikely that an organization can hire only individuals who scored high on *all* desired characteristics. Such individuals are rarities. So, decision makers must develop priorities about which characteristics are important and which characteristics are irrelevant. A coach recruiting players for a fifth grade girls' basketball team might have the following emphases: anyone can join the team who is female and in the fifth grade; they must want to play basketball and be capable of playing basketball; they must not be violent toward other team members; their race, ethnicity, social class, IQ score, and height are irrelevant. Different traits may be valuable at different levels of analysis. The priorities of top managers might be cost control and meeting affirmative action goals; thus, they might emphasize inexperience (since the inexperienced are more willing to accept low wages), race, and gender in hiring. Department managers may be interested in prestige and job performance; accordingly, they would want to emphasize the accomplishments and skills of the applicant. Members of a work group might be interested in values and collegiality, so they would emphasize traits that reflect those qualities. These can be viewed as legitimate conflicts of interest.

Another type of conflict occurs when characteristics relate in a contradictory manner to valued outcomes or other characteristics. This is the problem of *contradictions*. This would be the case when a trait that relates positively to one outcome relates negatively to another. As discussed in Chapter 3, conscientiousness relates positively to task performance but negatively to creativity, and cognitive ability relates positively to task performance but negatively to job satisfaction and retention for some jobs. These contradictions, combined with the problem of combinations, make it exceedingly difficult to sort out the net effect of several characteristics. *Moderators* are a fourth source of complexity because the relationship between a characteristic and an outcome can change depending on the context. Time and job complexity are powerful moderators of the relationship between mental ability and job performance. The relationship between an ability and task performance changes over time. Initially, the relationship is moderate—that is, people with higher ability levels tend to perform somewhat better on the job. However, after about five years initial ability is essentially unrelated to current performance (Hulin, Henry, & Noon, 1990). Job complexity also affects the relationship between mental ability and performance. Mental ability has a stronger relationship with job performance on complex jobs than simple jobs (Hunter, Schmidt, & Judiesch, 1990). Numerous other moderators of trait-performance relationships have been identified. Stress moderates the relationship between intelligence and leadership so that intelligence is unrelated to leadership in high-stress situations (Fiedler & Garcia, 1987). Career stage moderates the relationship between conscientiousness and job performance (Steward, 1999); supervisor coaching appears to moderate the relationship between a subordinate's background characteristics and job performance (Brown, 1979).

The problem of *levels* arises because the effects of characteristics may vary across levels. The whole is not equal to the sum of the parts, and the parts affect the whole differently depending on how one defines the whole. There are at least two facets to this problem: (1) proportions and (2) within-versus-between variation. The proportion necessary for a social unit to function effectively can change depending on the level of analysis. Differences in proportions of skilled members vary in importance according to the size of a social unit. For a small group such as a basketball team, it is necessary that a high proportion of the group members have an adequate level of skill for the team to function effectively. However, a small group can also perform exceptionally well with only a small proportion of exceptionally talented members, assuming the other members are at least adequately capable. An exceptionally skilled basketball player is likely to have a considerable impact on the effectiveness of a team composed of otherwise average players. However, larger social units may require different proportions. A larger unit can function with a smaller proportion of skilled people because it has more resources to take up the slack caused by underperformers (Galbraith, 1973). A large university can still operate efficiently even if some administrators are incompetent because so many other parts of the system can cover for them. On the other hand, a small proportion of exceptionally talented people is unlikely to have much of an effect on a large social unit because their efforts are more readily dissipated by a large system. Another complication is how proportions should be allocated among different characteristics. Suppose that conscientiousness and cognitive ability are important attributes to an employer. How many employees with high levels on one or both characteristics are necessary for the organization to create the type of climate it desires? We know little about the problems of proportions, and it is unclear that the problem can be solved in any exact way, given the multitude of traits, the differing sizes of social units, and the many ways traits can be allocated.

Levels also influence the question of whether it is best for variability to occur *within or between* units. Given that some variability in people and characteristics is advantageous, at what level should variability be emphasized? Is it preferable to increase variability among individuals within a unit or to minimize variability within units but increase it between units? This is a problem that school and university systems face when determining how educational objectives should be partitioned. One approach is to maximize variability within units. This approach is characteristic of large state universities. State university systems have a small number of large universities, each of which contains a wide variety of students, educational programs, and value orientations. Most of the variability occurs within each school. Another approach is to maximize variability between units. This is more evident among private colleges and universities in the United States. These colleges usually have more homogeneous values, curricula, and students. Most of the variability occurs between schools. A human resource department might face this problem when determining how to place new employees in the organization based on personality test scores. Assume the organization has three departments, A, B, and C, and that each department employs 15 people. For the sake of simplicity, assume that people come in only one of three personality types: creative, conscientious, and agreeable. Assume further that the organization seeks a mix of personality types among its employees. Is it better that the same types of personalities be hired within each department so that variation occurs between departments? In this case, Department A would have, say, only conscientious employees, Department B only creative employees, and Department C only agreeable employees. Or would it be better for variability to occur within departments? If so, then each department would get some creative, conscientious, and agreeable employees.

Assessing the effectiveness of a hiring practice is not a simple matter. The notion that organizations can engineer hiring practices that precisely fit round pegs into round holes is hopelessly naïve. People are not one-dimensional pegs; they consist of many characteristics. Jobs do not involve only the task function; jobs also involve interpersonal and innovation functions. The old saw that a hiring practice is effective if it predicts job performance is simplistic. "Job performance" means different things depending on the function and on the level of analysis. Moreover, different levels of analysis lead to problems of aggregation—determining the proper level, proportions, and mix of types—for which there is no easy solution. The problem of complexity also makes it difficult to formulate precise models of hiring method effectiveness. Different combinations of characteristics, internal contradictions, moderators that change the relationship between characteristics and outcomes, and different levels of analysis are not quantifiable in accurate ways.

AN EVOLUTIONARY PERSPECTIVE ON THE USE OF TRADITIONAL HIRING METHODS

An evolutionary approach suggests that we take a hard, respectful look at traditional hiring practices. They have withstood the test of time, probably because they were adaptive (Campbell, 1975). We should devote more effort to understanding why traditional practices are used and what functions they may serve. Modifying traditional practices, where appropriate, is also compatible with an evolutionary perspective, but modifications should be based on understanding their functions and the context in which they operate.

Respect Tradition

An evolutionary approach requires respect for traditional hiring practices, although it does not require uncritical reverence. Traditional hiring methods should not be dismissed out of hand as worthless or inferior to mechanistic methods, just because they were not developed and validated by academic psychologists. This is true, even though some widely used traditional hiring practices do not work as well as some mechanistic practices in predicting specific outcomes. The employment interview and letters of recommendation have fared worse than ability tests in predicting job performance (Friedman & Williams, 1982). Yet the interview and letters of recommendation are much more widely used than cognitive ability tests, and interviews have a stronger influence on hiring decisions than any other method. These facts suggest that a respectful effort to explain these traditions is in order. Psychologists need to look at traditional practices with more respect. Rarely does one come across a research study that looks at the possible functions of the interview or letters of recommendation. One rarely finds a study that examines why interviews or letters of recommendation continue to be so widely used.

An exception is an analysis and review by Adams, Elacqua, and Colarelli (1994), who argued that the employment interview serves a number of useful functions. They argue that the interview is, in fact, a sociometric method of selection. Sociometric selection is a traditional selection method in which "the selection of individuals into a group is based on group members' affective responses toward the applicants" (Adams et al., 1994, p. 100). Sociometric methods involve open-ended and unstructured information gathering. They are directed toward selecting groups members who are compatible, who "fit in." The selection judgments in interviews are based primarily on implicit criteria related to each interviewer's self-interest. Because it relies on face-to-face interaction, the employment interview allows group members to identify candidates who share their values and with whom they feel compatible (Colarelli, 1996). By functioning to select individuals who are compatible with other members, interviews enhance communication, cooperation, and satisfaction. These, in turn, are likely to affect group productivity, although they may be unrelated to individual productivity (Colarelli & Boos, 1992; Van Zelst, 1951, 1952). The interview may also function to improve performance by enhancing the employees' commitment to helping the new-hire succeed. Work-group members frequently interview applicants, at least in the later stages of selection (Colarelli, 1996). Having expended some effort in interviewing and decision making, employees are more likely to be committed to new-hires (Klitgaard, 1985).

Like interviews, letters of recommendation are widely used hiring methods that have a strong impact on hiring decisions (Bureau of

National Affairs, 1988; Friedman & Williams, 1982). Yet, letters of recommendation have been severely criticized for years as unreliable, as
poor predictors of job performance, and as biased (Aamodt, Bryan, &
Whitcomb, 1993; Muchinsky, 1979, 1999). Most of the research on
letters of recommendation has focused on how to improve their capacity to predict job performance, rather than look at the potential functions they might already be serving. Because letters of recommendation
are so widely used and have such a strong impact on hiring decisions,
they likely serve useful functions (Colarelli, Alampay, & Canali, 2002).
One possible function of letters of recommendation is to identify people
who are likely to cause harm. That is, letters of recommendation may
be good indicators of whether a person is likely to cause harm. Research
by Anstey (1966) supports this view. In a study of British Foreign Service officers, Anstey found that, of eight officers who received negative
letters of recommendation but were subsequently hired, six received poor
performance ratings and four received the lowest possible ratings. Employers typically regard negative comments in recommendations as
grounds for rejecting an applicant (Knouse, 1983; Muchinsky, 1979;
Sheehan, McDevitt, & Ross, 1998).

Keep Traditional Methods That Work

If a traditional method works, researchers and practitioners should
think long and hard about the wisdom of discarding it for a mechanistic
method just because a mechanistic method may be more effective for
some purposes.[3] Some traditional practices work as well as mechanistic methods in terms of predicting performance. High school grades
predict freshman college grades about as well as the SAT (Crouse &
Trusheim, 1986). Colleges and universities gain minimal predictive
power by using the SAT. Similarly, using a cognitive ability test to make
hiring decisions makes little sense when traditional job sample tests or
job tryout periods are being used. Job sample tests are the most accurate predictors of job performance (Schmidt & Hunter, 1998). Abandoning a traditional hiring method that does not produce one desired
outcome is not a wise course of action. The traditional method may
produce *other* valued outcomes, or it may indeed produce desired outcomes that existing research methods cannot detect. This is the case with
the employment interview. From the 1950s to the early 1980s, industrial psychologists argued that the employment interview was ineffective because it did not predict job performance. That employers used
the interview at all when researchers had found so little evidence that it
predicted performance was deemed the "black hole" of personnel

research. However, later reviews indicated that the interview worked if one defined "worked" in other ways, such as predicting communication skill (Harris, 1989). Recently, a review that used larger samples and different statistical techniques reported that structured interviews actually predict performance as well as many standardized tests (McDaniel, Whetzel, Schmidt, & Mauer, 1994). It turns out that interviews worked after all. Ironically, ordinary people may have been right and experts wrong for all of those years.

Modify Traditional Practices to Be More Compatible with Modern Environments

Traditional hiring practices also present problems. In some instances, there is a mismatch between humans' evolved preferences for acquiring information on people and the realities of modern organizations. The appeal and consumption of junk food is a good illustration of the problem of mismatch (Colarelli & Dettmann, in press). Junk food is an aspect of the modern environment that is a mismatch with our evolved food preferences. Junk food is appealing because it coöpts humans' evolved preferences for sweets, fat, and salt, yet its high concentrations of fat, sugar, and salt pose significant health risks when they are part of a regular diet (Boyd & Silk, 1997).[4] During the approximately 1.9 million years that humans lived as hunter-gatherers, people evolved a preference for foods with a high nutritional value (Buss, 1995). Foods high in fat were the most efficient form of calories. Foods that were sweet, such as ripe fruits, generally indicated high levels of nutrients, especially carbohydrates. A salty flavor indicated high mineral content. People who preferred those tastes would be more likely to survive and reproduce than people who, say, had preferences for bitter and putrid foods. However, fat, ripe fruit, and salt were not easy to come by for hunter-gatherers. People's preferences would motivate them to seek out such foods, but their relative scarcity and difficulty of acquiring meant that people did not overdo their intake of such foods. In the modern era, such foods are easily available. This aspect of the modern environment renders humans' evolved appetite for fat, salt, and sugar problematic. The appeal of these foods, combined with the modern novelty of junk food, often produces adverse health consequences—obesity, heart disease, and high blood pressure. Our bodies were not designed for such high concentrations of sweets, fats, and salt. There is a mismatch between, on the one hand, our evolved food preferences and metabolism and, on the other hand, the availability of junk food with high concentrations of salt, fats, and sugar. Yet by understanding the nature of the mismatch, it becomes possible to modify the modern environment to ameliorate the problem. We can educate people about the benefits of eating less junk food, require food manufacturers to list the fat, sodium, and sugar content of their foods, use fat and sugar substitutes, restrict children's access to junk food, and so on.

Part of the appeal of the employment interview and letters of recommendation in modern organizations likely reflects a mismatch. These practices have coöpted our evolved preferences for information about people, and thus our ancient preferences are probably a large part of the reason for the widespread use of the employment interview and letters of recommendation. Since these preferences did not evolve in the context of large organizations, they do not match with some exigencies of modern organizations. Yet by understanding the appeal and functions of traditional hiring methods, we are in a better position to modify features contributing to mismatches and preserve features that contribute to effective hiring decisions (Moore, 1996).

People respond to interviews and letters of recommendation in part out of ancient, evolved responses to face-to-face and narrative information about other people.[5] Much of the appeal of these traditional methods lies in the way that they convey information about people. The interview uses face-to-face interaction, and letters of recommendation use written narrative. People prefer these sources of information about other people (Dunbar, 1996; Rook, 1987). Face-to-face interaction and narratives were the only sources of information about other people for most of our evolutionary past, and our neurocognitive system evolved to utilize information about people in the rich form of everyday language and gesture (Baron-Cohen, 1997; Sugiyama, 2001). As discussed in Chapter 3, natural selection shaped the human mind to prefer information about people from face-to-face interaction and narrative rather than from statistical analyses—or what Moore (1996) refers to as "identified" versus "statistical" lives. Because human cognitive architecture evolved to solve many of the problems of social life through face-to-face interaction, people are more likely to believe, make decisions on, and act upon face-to-face and narrative information about people (Moore, 1996). They are likely to be unresponsive, and even antagonistic, to abstract information about people—such as the information provided by IQ tests, numerical performance appraisals, and employee attitude surveys.

The appeal of interviews and letters of recommendation also relates to the human response to risk and mechanisms for avoiding harm. People are more comfortable taking a risk to avoid a loss than to pursue a gain (Kahneman & Tversky, 1981). Moore (1996) argues that the preference for risk when loss is possible evolved because losses in sub-sistence economies—the conditions under which humans evolved—had a high probability of severely impairing reproductive potential. People are also more emotionally responsive to negative than positive informa-tion (Taylor, 1991). Cacioppo and Berntson (1999) argue that our pro-pensity to react more strongly to negative than to positive information is an evolved adaptation. Over evolutionary history, it has been more difficult for people to reverse the consequences of severe assault than of missed opportunity. People therefore prefer modes of information about others that allow them to assess the risk of loss and to describe negative attributes. When people use information from interviews and letters of recommendation in making hiring decisions, it is likely that they are responding to cues related to threats, harm, and self-interest. They are more likely to attend to information that psychological mecha-nisms were designed to monitor rather than to information that person-nel experts say should be attended to for the good of "organizational goals." These are evolutionary explanations for why the employment interview and letters of recommendation are appealing and why face-to-face interaction and narrative information have been functional in past environments. *The widespread use of interviews and letters of rec-ommendation, particularly among professionals who ostensibly know about their shortcomings, makes a strong case that evolved psychological mechanisms influence the use of letters of recommendation.*

Hunter-gatherers did not interview and select new members of their hunting groups. The routine selection of people into groups is evolu-tionarily novel. Humans evolved preferences for face-to-face and narrative information about people because they are useful to the *individual's* interests. If we are going to work with someone or engage in another relationship, we want to assess whether this person will be useful, helpful, and safe. Most people are probably not concerned with whether candidates will be useful to some "organizational interest." Because self-interest drives perceptions and hiring decisions, interviews and letters of recommendation are largely responsible for hiring people who are similar to the decision makers conducting the interviews and reading letters of recommendation. And here is a potential for mis-match. For organizations to remain innovative and flexible and to maintain the capacity to adapt to changing environments, they need variation among their employees. Groups and organizations also re-quire a certain degree of similarity among members to maintain effec-tive communication and coordination and to keep conflict to a manageable and productive level. But excessive similarity and too little variation will limit an organization's ability to adapt to a changing environment. Using interviews and letters of recommendation can produce too much similarity.

People who interview applicants and read letters of recommendation often have full or partial power to reject an applicant. Interviews and letters of recommendation restrict variability by providing people the opportunity to reject applicants. By relying on interviews and letters, organizations end up selecting "right types"—that is, people who "fit in" and are similar to existing employees, particularly those making hiring decisions (Argyris, 1957; Schneider, 1987). The research on the dynamics of interviews and letters of recommendation demonstrates that people are, at least in part, pursuing self-interested strategies and reacting to information about people through evolved mechanisms designed to enhance their own survival and reproduction. Interviewers typically make judgments about whether to hire an applicant within the first four minutes of the interview (Webster, 1964); they are primarily engaged in a search for negative information about applicants. Once an interviewer forms just one negative impression, this is followed by a rejection of the applicant 90 percent of the time (Bolster & Springbett, 1961). In addition, interviewers form stereotypes about ideal applicants, and they normally reject applicants who deviate from their stereotype (Rowe, 1963; Webster, 1964). These findings suggest that the employment interview is most likely tapping into mechanisms that evolved for making quick judgments about a person's intentions to help or harm and the likelihood of being an ally or enemy.[6] A similar process seems to occur with letters of recommendation. People probably use letters of recommendation to evaluate the risk of harm and to reject applicants deemed likely to cause harm. Most employers take negative comments in letters of recommendation seriously and usually regard them as grounds for rejecting an applicant (Knouse, 1983; Muchinsky, 1979; Sheehan, McDevitt, & Ross, 1998).

Another potential mismatch with letters of recommendation has to do with the motivation of people who write them. People normally write letters of recommendation as a favor to the applicant, not to help the organization requesting the letter. The recommender's primary interest is not with the organization requesting the letter but with the applicant. The history of social exchange between an applicant and a recommender influences the tone of letters of recommendation; the applicant's qualifications for a particular job or compatibility with an organization's goals are tangentially irrelevant to the person writing a letter of recommendation. The recommender is writing it as a favor to the applicant and is most likely to write a positive letter when he likes the applicant—that is, perceives that the applicant has helped or will continue to advance his interests (not the organization's). In a study I conducted with Gina Alampay and Kris Canali (Colarelli et al., 2002), we found that applicants' objective qualifications for a job were unrelated to the tone of letters of recommendations, whereas the amount of collaboration between the recommender and applicant was.

Modifications to the Employment Interview

An evolutionary perspective suggests that modifications should be made to the interview so that it does not result in hiring just applicants who are similar to the interviewers. This calls for structural changes in the administration of interviews. These include changing how often and how many interviews are conducted, who does the interviewing, and how closely the interviewer is tied to hiring decisions. One modification is to limit the use of interviews. A small group of new-hires, say, about 20 percent, could be hired on the basis of paper qualifications only. This would increase the probability that a greater number of new-hires would have different values and backgrounds from those of the organization's culture. However, because 80 percent of applicants are interviewed, the organization would still have many employees who fit in with the culture and facilitate smooth communication and cooperation. The people hired without the filter of the interview would offer useful variation. That some organizations that do not use interviews at all function quite successfully suggests that such an approach is feasible. Most universities, for example, do not base admissions decisions for entering undergraduates, graduate students, or students to professional schools on the interview (Toor, 2001).

Another modification would separate decision making authority from those who conduct interviews—interviewers who have decision making authority will be disposed to hire applicants who are similar to them. Information could be channeled from interviewers to an independent committee composed of people without a personal stake in the hiring decision. Separating decision authority from those conducting interviews makes self-interest less of a factor in the final decision. Certainly, interviewers' own biases and interests will affect how they perceive and describe candidates. However, the use of multiple interviewers compensates for individual bias. Also, interviews should typically be only one of many sources of information that committee members use. This will further attenuate the perceptual biases of individual interviewers.

Breaking up monopolies on the interview process is a third modification that can increase variability. This involves structuring an organization's hiring practices so that no individual or group has sole responsibility for interviewing candidates and making decisions on them.

When no one individual or group has a monopoly on interviewing and decision making for large numbers of people, there is less chance that an idiosyncratic bias will dominate hiring decisions. The process as a whole becomes more reliable (Hogarth, 1981). A monopoly on interviewing and hiring decisions is problematic in situations where large numbers of people are hired on a relatively routine basis. Here the collective nature of the people hired has the potential to influence the character of an entire organization or unit within an organization. Demonopolizing the interview process involves first taking a look at who does the interviewing and at who makes the hiring decisions for a class of jobs to determine whether a monopoly problem exists. If an individual or a small group has a monopoly on interviewing and hiring decisions or if the people who do the interviewing and hiring are inbred, then there is likely to be a problem. The remedy is to distribute interviewing and hiring authority more widely, by including people with divergent interests and outlooks.

Suppose an organization that designs and manufactures automobiles has a policy where only the people from the automotive design department are involved with hiring new people into that unit. This is likely to produce inbreeding, keeping the automotive design group homogeneous. Most of the automotive designers might be younger males who are car enthusiasts with automotive design backgrounds. When job openings occur, they tend to hire other younger males just like themselves. This might present a problem when the market demographics change and women with children become a large segment of car buyers. These buyers will be interested in different features than 30-year-old male car enthusiasts. The female buyers will probably be more interested in safety features, child seats, ease of entry and exit for children, dogs, and child equipment, and amusements to keep children occupied on long trips. But if the design department does not hire people with this sort of background, they may be less likely to include those features in the car, with a possible loss in market share. Therefore, the hiring practice should be restructured so that, say, people from marketing and customer relations are included among those who interview and make decisions on who is hired into the automotive design unit. On the other hand, hiring monopolies do not pose much of a problem to variability in situations involving small numbers and when the hiring is spread out across many employees. The monopoly managers have over hiring their assistants or secretaries is unlikely to have much of an impact on the variability of human resources throughout the organization.

Modifications to Letters of Recommendation

The evolutionary perspective also provides suggestions for improving the usefulness of letters of recommendation. Most suggestions for improving letters of recommendations view them as flawed but salvageable methods for predicting performance. As such, they are improved by adjustments that enhance their reliability and validity (e.g., recommender confidentiality, more structured formats, trained recommenders, and statistical techniques that remove "bias" from letters). For example, Judge and Higgins (1998) found that the affective disposition of recommenders biased the favorability of letters. Accordingly, they suggested that organizations apply a scaling factor when interpreting letters. "If the positivity vs. negativity of the letter writer is known, the employer may . . . discount letters by positive people" (p. 218). This is an interesting suggestion, but hardly realistic—it is rare that employers who receive letters know the recommenders, much less their "positivity" relative to one another.

An evolutionary perspective suggests that improvements to letters of recommendation be based on their actual functions, their relationship to psychological mechanisms, and the social context in which they are used. Because a primary, albeit latent, function of letters of recommendation is to identify threats, the information in letters of recommendation is more useful for rejecting unsuitable applicants than for predicting performance. Proper use of letters of recommendation gives less emphasis to their potential for predicting performance and recognizes that they are a rough screening device for identifying potentially harmful applicants. A second modification is for organizations, rather than applicants, to choose recommenders. This recognizes the element of social exchange in letters of recommendation. Because asking for and writing a letter of recommendation involve doing and returning favors, psychological mechanisms related to self-interest and social exchange are activated when an applicant asks an individual to write a letter of recommendation. The tone of most letters of recommendation is positive because they are basically the result of a friend doing a favor for a friend. When applicants choose their own recommenders, these are typically acquaintances with whom applicants have positive, cooperative relationships. Recognizing this, organizations, rather than applicants, should solicit recommendations. Organizations could request recommendations from a sample of an applicant's colleagues. Such a procedure would provide more diverse information about an applicant. It would not eliminate bias from letters—people who do not like the applicant would write more negatively toned letters. However, it would provide a broader array of information about an applicant, which, in the aggregate, would provide a more realistic picture of an applicant.

Since most recommenders have little, if any, relationship with the organizations requesting letters, they have little motivation to write an accurate letter. Therefore, another modification would be for organizations to compensate recommenders for writing letters of recommendation. Organizations routinely pay consultants, testing specialists, and test producers; therefore, why not pay recommenders? This would create an exchange relationship and provide greater motivation for recommenders to write more accurate letters. To minimize the expense of paying large numbers of recommenders, organizations could solicit recommendations from only the most promising applicants. Depending on the legal climates in different countries, it may be necessary to try various approaches to soliciting letters of recommendation and to paying recommenders. If people are concerned about the potential legal liability for including negative information in a letter, organizations could require applicants to sign waivers.

These modifications to interviews and letters of recommendation acknowledge that self-interest, biases, and conflicting interests are inherent parts of the hiring process. Modifications that leverage self-interest and innate psychological mechanisms enhance the value of hiring practices to organizations. The value of variability is also a common theme underlying many of the modifications suggested here. Traditional practices become problematic when they result in too much similarity and decrease variation, so modifications should work to maintain a healthy level of variability. In the next section, I expand on the role of variability in hiring and suggest new approaches to hiring that help maintain variability.

ENHANCING VARIATION

Variation is the spark of evolution; without it, there is no evolution. Therefore, enhancing variation can help organizations maintain a range of mental and behavioral repertoires sufficient to cope with uncertain futures. Psychological monocultures are unhealthy because they limit response repertoires, and this in turn limits an organization's capacity to adapt to changing conditions.[7] Yet this is an effect of mechanistic selection methods, which emphasize consistency. By identifying a few traits that relate to job performance and then by hiring only people with high levels of those traits, mechanistic hiring methods reduce variability. Moreover, if the traits that an organization uses in hiring correlate with other traits, values, or background characteristics, variation is reduced further. This emphasis on consistency has two negative effects. It creates psychological monocultures, and it limits the attention that researchers give to the role of variation in human resources and in human resource practices.

Klimoski and Strickland (1977) argued that assessment centers operate to select "right types." That is, they select managers who fit into an organization's culture rather than truly effective managers.[8] They argue that assessors base their ratings on the similarity of candidates to existing managers. Organizations that use this procedure are less likely to hire managers who think or act differently than current managers do, which in turn perpetuates inertia and reduces innovation. Herrnstein and Murray (1994) and Robert Reich (1991) argued that the increasing use of cognitive ability tests to channel bright students into universities and graduate schools is creating two psychological monocultures in the United States: a cognitive elite and a cognitive underclass. Prior to the 1960s, people of high intelligence were intermixed in a wide range of communities and vocations, whereas over the past 40 years they have become increasingly channeled into professional and geographical enclaves. The cognitive elite has become segregated into the professions, business, and affluent communities, whereas the cognitive underclass has increasingly been segregated into the lower rungs of the socioeconomic ladder. Interestingly, both Reich (a political liberal) and Herrnstein and Murray (political conservatives) argue that these monocultures produce significant problems. There will be a greater concentration of affluence and cognitive ability, "an unprecedented coalition of the smart and the rich" taking advantage of the legal system and government for their own advantage (Herrnstein & Murray, 1994, p. 519). Herrnstein and Murray envision a growing underclass and a custodial state in which the cognitive elite engineer programs and services to take care of a growing and cognitively homogeneous underclass.

The evolutionary perspective suggests that hiring practices and other human resource interventions can serve a useful function by *enhancing* variation (Klingsporn, 1973). Thus far, significant attention has been paid to variation in hiring practices only in the context of affirmative action and diversity. The idea that variability in hiring is more broadly useful to organizations is absent from the personnel selection literature. In this section I describe and critique approaches to variation that have their genesis in the politics of affirmation action and diversity programs. Although they do enhance variability in some respects, I will argue that they are unsatisfactory in others. I argue that an evolutionary perspective provides a better theoretical framework for thinking about variation in hiring, and I describe an approach to enhancing variation in hiring—random selection above a threshold—based on this perspective.

Affirmative Action and Diversity Programs

Affirmative action originated in response to civil rights protests against the inequality of economic and educational opportunity in the United States. The earliest uses of the term *affirmative action* appeared in Executive Order 10925, signed in 1961, decreeing equal opportunity employment by the federal government, and in Title VII of the Civil Rights Act of 1964. Its initial meaning was that employers should actively seek out qualified minority job applicants. Over the ensuing years, its meaning expanded to include activities used to redress current discrimination, to provide role models for women and minorities, and to promote workplace diversity (Campbell, 1996). However, it is the activities themselves that came to provide the *operational* definitions with which most people are familiar (Holzer & Neumark, 2000). These include: (1) conducting training programs to change management attitudes toward women and minorities, (2) actively recruiting underrepresented groups to apply for jobs, (3) favoring a minority candidate in a hiring decision when all candidates are roughly equal in qualifications, and (4) establishing hiring quotas for underrepresented groups.

About 30 years after affirmative action appeared in the lexicon, the terms *diversity* and *managing diversity* appeared in the organizational literature (Cox, 1993; Henderson, 1994). As the term is commonly used, diversity is associated with a type of moral pluralism associated with minorities and women. Diversity implies that efforts to include women and racial and ethnic minorities in an organization are morally and economically important. Managing diversity means that valuing differences, rather than encouraging assimilation, is the proper approach to managing a workforce. Unlike affirmative action, which has historically been based on redressing wrongs, the diversity movement emphasizes the positive value of a diverse workforce. However, both the diversity movement and affirmative action are mechanisms for legitimizing the recruiting and hiring of women and minorities, and as such both have increased variation in the workforce.

Problems with the Affirmative Action and Diversity Programs

From an evolutionary perspective, affirmative action and diversity programs have three shortcomings: (1) they have a limited impact on variation, (2) their structure creates intractable perceptions of unfairness, and (3) they are difficult to implement.

A goal of diversity programs is to increase variation. Yet what is being enhanced is a narrow range of variation, what I call "designer diversity." Designer diversity requires someone to decide what groups receive protected status and become eligible for special treatment, and what mix of groups is appropriate. University administrators, politicians, and business executives typically end up as the designers of diversity programs, programs that end up as reflections of their values. The rules about which groups should be protected often change, and there are often no hard and fast rules about the criteria for determining who is a member of a protected group. A key assumption of the diversity movement is that people from different sexual, racial, and ethnic groups, *by definition*, bring with them different psychological characteristics, and these different characteristics combine in ways that allow an organization to solve problems and work more effectively (Henderson, 1994). However, advocates of diversity rarely articulate the particular psychological characteristics that people from different racial and ethnic and sexual groups are supposed to bring to the table. It turns out that people from preferred groups do not differ much at all on many characteristics measured by standard psychological tests. About the best one can say for diversity and affirmative action programs is that they have increased variability by sex and by a few narrow racial and ethnic categories.

Humans vary on a wide range of attributes, and organizations do not gain much psychological diversity by restricting diversity categories to sex, race, and ethnicity. Men and women differ moderately or not at all on most personality characteristics. In an analysis of sex differences in personality traits, Hyde and Plant (1995) reported that 25 percent of psychological characteristics produced sex differences with effect sizes close to zero and 35 percent produced small effects. Only 13 percent produced large or very large effects. Feingold (1994) found similar results, as did Hough (1998). Hough examined sex differences on nine commonly used personality scales. Using data from test manuals, with sample sizes ranging from about 1,500 to over 66,000, she found small differences on five characteristics, moderate differences on three, and a large difference on only one ("rugged individualism"). The large differences in these studies appeared in traits related to aggression and nurturance, with men being more aggressive and women more nurturing. Hough also examined differences in personality among racial and ethnic groups. She found that, on average, racial and ethnic groups show no large differences in personality characteristics and only a few small differences; on most of the characteristics she examined, there were no differences. Sheppard (1997) looked at differences in personality characteristics between men and women and between Caucasians and African Americans down to the level of differences in responses to individual test items. On many items there were no differences.

Programs based on racial and sexual diversity probably do little to increase diversity in values and beliefs.

> "Diversity" . . . often stands for a quite narrow social agenda, as if those who reiterate the word "diversity" endlessly had no idea that diversity is itself diverse and has many dimensions besides the one with which they are preoccupied. Advocates of diversity in a race or gender sense are often quite hostile to ideological diversity. (Sowell, 1995, p. 95)

From a genetic standpoint, the argument is even stronger that these programs do little to increase variation. Eighty-five percent of the genetic differences among individuals occurs *within* racial and ethnic groups (Hoffman, 1994; Vines, 1995).

Affirmative action and diversity programs create problems of fairness, owing to the ambiguities associated with placing people into distinct racial or ethnic categories and owing to the complex reasoning used in awarding protected status to some groups and not to others. An objective of these programs is to identify individuals who belong to protected groups so that they can receive preferential treatment. Yet the criteria for inclusion into a protected racial and ethnic groups are fuzzy. The phrase "having origins in" seems to be the operative criterion according to the Executive Office of the President's Office of Management and Budget (2000). For example, a person is classified as an African American who has "origins in any of the black racial groups of Africa" (p. 6). Where does one draw the line? Apparently, it is up to each individual to decide. According to the definition of "having origins in," both a person with just one distant ancestor (say, a great, great grandparent) and a person with many close relatives from a black racial group of Africa could legitimately consider themselves African American.[9] Grouping people into racial categories depends on the choice of classification scheme (Boyd & Silk, 1997; Wolpoff & Caspari, 1996).

Race is far from a distinctive biological phenomenon. It is not a characteristic that nature carved at the joints, and classifying a person into one group or another is often quite arbitrary. One of the least examined and most widely held assumptions in affirmative action and diversity programs is that race is categorical. When politicians and experts earmark groups for affirmative action, they assume that individuals are *either* one race *or* another—say, African American *or* Asian *or* Native

American *or* Caucasian. Although affirmative action presumes that group memberships based on race and ethnicity are inviolate, objective, and meaningful entities, the hard evidence is not convincing. Racial differences evolved because of geographical separations between people and adaptations resulting from those particular geographic environments (Wolpoff & Caspari, 1997). Darker skin color evolved in sunny climates because people with darker skin were less likely to sunburn and get melanoma. However, with the advent of modernity, human habitation and mating were no longer constrained by geographic separation. There is considerable mixing of races in the United States and in other modern societies where people from different races live in close proximity. Most of the people in the United States who consider themselves African American trace their ancestry to West Africa, but about 20 to 30 percent of African Americans' genetic heritage is European or American Indian (Shreve, 1994). From a genetic standpoint, racial differences are trivial. The sequence of the genetic code of any two randomly selected humans is, on average, 99.8 percent alike. Of the two-tenths of a percent that is different, only 6 percent of *that* is related to race (Hoffman, 1994; Vines, 1995).

The race a person considers himself is partially a product of identity construction. Two people may have a similar racial genetic makeup—say, 25 percent Native American and 75 percent Caucasian—yet one individual may identify himself as one race (Native American) and the other may consider herself a different race (Caucasian). One study found that 34 percent of people who completed a census survey two years in a row actually changed the racial groups they claimed to be members of from one year to the next (cited in Shreve, 1994).[10] When one considers possible mixes of races, the problems of identity construction and categorization are more apparent. What racial category box on college affirmative action cards should a young woman check whose father is 50 percent Caucasian and 50 percent Native American and whose mother is 100 percent Japanese? Suppose that she graduates from college and marries a young man whose mother is Caucasian and whose father is African American. They have a child, and 18 years later the child applies to college. What race box should their child check?[11] Substituting *degree* for *category* is unlikely to add much precision. Such an approach might ask people to attribute a percentage to their racial makeup. Although this might be more realistic than exclusive one-race categories, it is still unsatisfactory. The number of possible racial combinations in modern societies is, theoretically, infinite. Any list will inevitably exclude some combinations. Moreover, as long as race is established primarily by self-report, accuracy will be a problem.[12]

If about 30 percent of people were changing their racial classification from one year to the next when they could only classify themselves as one race or another, how much confusion would arise when people could describe gradations of racial backgrounds? There is also the problem of categorization and self-interest. When a person is of mixed race and it is to that person's advantage to classify herself as one race rather than another, the incentive exists to classify herself as a member of a protected group, even when her circumstances or self-image do not warrant being classified in that group.

Ultimately, whenever *group* membership is used for preferences in hiring or university admissions, people from nonpreferred groups are those whose ox gets gored. There will be endless debates about which group classifications are fair. Affirmative action and diversity programs inevitably exclude ethnic groups that are not favored by the designers. The Association of American Medical Colleges does not consider students of Central American ancestry as underrepresented minorities; hence they are ineligible for certain types of medical school scholarships. However, it does consider students with Mexican and Puerto Rican ancestry as members of underrepresented minorities, and these students are eligible for scholarships (Mangan, 2000). Once certain groups have been given protected status, it then becomes in their interest to maintain that classification and keep other groups from receiving it. This leads to diversity gerrymandering that—through political pressure, bureaucratic rules, and the legal system—has the effect of keeping diversity defined in terms of a small number of favored groups (Mangan, 2000).

Affirmative action programs are also perceived as unfair because they are difficult to understand. Two approaches have been used to justify the fairness of affirmative action: statistical and historical. Both involve complex reasoning and complex causal inferences. As a result, arguments about fairness are not intuitive. The statistical approach addresses fairness based on the prediction of performance, with discussions of fairness revolving around complex statistical models.[13] Although a variety of statistical models were proposed during the 1960s and 1970s, they all viewed test fairness in terms of the degree to which test scores *predict* job performance in the same manner for members of majority and minority groups. The regression model of fairness has evolved as the standard, and it focuses on the meaning of scores from individuals of different groups. It asks the following question: does a given score predict job performance with the same level of accuracy across groups? Other models, such as the Thorndike model, focus on success rates. The Thorndike model asks, does the job success rate of individuals from different groups match their success rate on the selection test? These models use a narrow and specific set of factors to assess fairness, and they involve complex statistical reasoning. They require that individuals be categorized into majority and minority groups and that a test score and a criterion score be available for each individual. Top-down selection is regarded as the default procedure. Deviations from top-down selection are justified only when the predictive accuracy of a test differs between majority and minority group members. In such cases, score adjustment can be justified. Score adjustment is a deviation from top-down selection—such as adding bonus points—that favors a particular group. Because most cognitive ability tests seem to predict about equally well for majority and minority groups—or are biased in some minority groups' favor—many advocates of the statistical approach regard top-down selection based on objective test scores as fair.[14]

The historical approach views the fairness of affirmative action from the perspective of past and present opportunity structure, distribution of rewards, and patterns of exclusion that are related to class, sex, and race. It argues that because of the long legacy of racism, minorities have been excluded from the same quality of education as Caucasians. Lower quality education in turn leads to lower test scores. The historical approach maintains that it is unfair to base selection decisions solely on test scores when minority groups have not had the opportunity to gain the experiences that would enhance their test scores. Similar arguments have been made with respect to socioeconomic status and test scores (Sturm & Guinier, 1996). The historical approach to fairness downplays the statistical evidence that objective tests can, to some degree, predict job performance. Historical proponents argue that tests explain a limited amount of variance and that they can predict only short-term outcomes (e.g., first-year college grades). Given the opportunity to perform, most individuals from minority groups would perform higher than their test scores predict. Moreover, because humans have many traits and capacities, because many factors affect job and educational performance, and because performance can be defined by a variety of criteria, it is unfair to equate merit with the score on one test. The historical model uses many factors to assess fairness, and the relation of these factors to fairness involves long and complex chains of causality. However, like the statistical model, the historical model also requires that individuals be categorized into groups.

At their cores, both approaches seek fairness. A person should be hired or admitted because she deserves to be. According to the statistical perspective, as long as the test is unbiased, people with the highest scores are the most deserving because they are most likely to perform the best. According to the historical perspective, minorities who are basically qualified but may not have the highest test scores, are most deserving because the legacy of discrimination has denied them opportunity. These notions of fairness are based on the fundamental human psychological mechanism of reciprocity: one gets as one gives. However, given the complexities associated with testing, with statistical and sociological models of fairness, and with changing legal interpretations, it is naïve to suppose that such approaches to fairness can be convincingly demonstrated, widely understood, or broadly accepted.

That affirmative action debates have continued at the same high pitch for over 30 years without any hint of resolution is perhaps the best evidence of the problem. Given the complexity of these models of fairness, how can ordinary individuals—those applying for jobs and those doing the hiring, those applying for admission to universities and those making decisions, as well as those who are friends and relatives of applicants—determine who is operating fairly? The complexity of current approaches to selection suggests that the present strategies will remain ambiguous, divisive, and difficult to apply consistently. From an evolutionary perspective, both approaches to fairness are problematic. Despite their different emphases, both the statistical and historical approaches to fairness are overly complex. Although the statistical approach has a more narrow focus and range of variables, it involves complex statistical arguments that are difficult for non-statisticians to comprehend. The historical approach is also complex because of the sheer number of variables brought to bear on fairness and the many possible interpretations of those variables. For example, while advocates of the historical approach argue that poor economic status causes lower ability, an opposite argument is also reasonable: poor economic status is, at least in part, a result of low cognitive ability (Jensen, 1998, see especially pp. 568–569).

There is substantial evidence that humans possess psychological mechanisms for detecting cheaters—cheaters being defined as people who take benefits in group life without paying the costs (Cosmides & Tooby, 1992). A mechanism for detecting cheaters became hardwired into the human psychological makeup because humans evolved as group-living animals, and social exchange is one of the processes that have allowed humans to cooperate and live in groups successfully. Detecting cheaters had and continues to have important benefits to survival and reproduction. However, the cheater-detection mechanism evolved when humans lived in relatively small, racially and ethnically homogeneous hunter-gatherer bands of anywhere from about 12 to 150 people. Individuals knew one another, interacted with most other people in the group, and were aware of others' behavior and reputations (Chagnon,

1997; Klein, 1989; Megarry, 1995). Our abilities to detect cheaters, therefore, operate most effectively in situations where people interact with one another and where fairness is assessed in terms of fairly straightforward social exchanges (Cosmides & Tooby, 1992). Current affirmative action programs are problematic because they involve high stakes (such as getting a job or getting into college), are justified in terms of fairness, and yet the arguments justifying their fairness are not intuitively obvious to most people who are affected by them.

From an evolutionary perspective, we can regard debates about models of fairness in hiring and admissions as, to some degree, problems of self-interest (Alexander, 1987). People see particular models of fairness as more or less fair depending on how those models affect their self-interest. Therefore, the *process* of dealing with perceived unfairness is often more important than any particular instance of unfairness. Arguing the merits of different models and providing opportunities for different models to *compete* do more to ensure fairness in the long run than the merit of any particular model. As the philosopher Stuart Hampshire (2000) appropriately argues, justice *is* conflict.

Another problem with affirmative action and diversity programs is that they are difficult to implement. Their ability to produce intended outcomes is problematic. Affirmative action rests on the same assumption about social engineering as mechanistic hiring methods: properly designed social programs can produce specific, intended outcomes. However, the results of affirmative action programs belie this assumption. As Gillon concludes:

> The strange history of affirmative action provides a striking example of the unpredictability of public policy. The greatest strength of the American political system occasionally can be its greatest weakness: Power is so diffuse and decentralized that it is difficult, if not impossible, for one branch of government to control the outcome of its actions. (2000, pp. 161–162)

Improving the economic status of women and minorities has been a long-standing goal of affirmative action programs. However, over the past 30 years, the average income of African Americans has *declined* and unemployment rates have *grown* (Heilman, 1996). Women continue to earn less than men. In the United States in 1998, women earned from about 75 to 85 percent of what men earned (Browne, 2002).[15] Women's influence at management and policy levels has not grown proportionally with women's increased participation in the workforce (Valian, 1997). Women hold less than 3 percent of the top management positions in Fortune 500 corporations (Spaid, 1993). Although women fill

50 percent of the entry-level positions in public accounting firms, they comprise only 13 percent of the accounting partners (Coolidge, 1994). Even the apparent integration of females into the U.S. workforce is deceptive. Instances where females have made inroads into male occupations sometimes mark a trend toward resegregation (Maccoby, 1998). When substantial numbers of women enter formerly male-dominated occupations, males often leave the profession and it becomes a predominant female profession (Reskin & Roos, 1990). Affirmative action programs have also had negative psychological effects. They have increased the stigmatization of women and minorities when they are perceived to be hired on the basis of affirmative action. Diversity programs have increased self-doubts among those hired under the aegis of such programs (Heilman, 1996). McWhorter (2000) and Carter (1992) have suggested that affirmative action programs have also lowered expectations for educational excellence for members of some minority groups.

Bowen and Bok (1998) are proponents of affirmative action, arguing that affirmative action has worked in elite universities. They base their claim on a study of graduates of the nation's most elite colleges and universities. They found that minorities who were admitted under affirmative action guidelines succeeded by a number of criteria: they graduated from college at rates about equal to nonminorities; many went on to graduate school, earned high salaries, and became leaders in their communities, business, and the professions. They believe this is due to affirmative action. Yet they also admit that

> Many of these students would have done well no matter where they went to school, and we cannot know in any precise way how their careers would have been affected as a result. But we do know that there is a statistically significant association, on an "other things equal" basis, between attendance at the most selective schools . . . and a variety of accomplishments during college and in later life. Generally speaking, the more selective the school, the more the student achieved subsequently. (1998, p. 281)

Rather than providing evidence that affirmative action per se works, their study shows that students who score a few points lower on the SAT than students who are regularly admitted to elite universities still do well in college and in life. This is more of an argument against the predictive power of the SAT and against setting rigid cutoff scores. Their data suggest that, as long as one is capable, a student of *any* race or ethnic group is likely to do well if he attends a prestigious university. Of the graduates from their 1976 entering cohort, those earning the highest annual salaries were white men with the *lowest* SAT scores. They were men who graduated from the most selective colleges and who had combined SAT scores below 1,000 (p. 143). Bowen and Bok's study could be seen as nothing more than a thinly disguised advertisement for prestigious universities: look how well students who attend our universities do in later life (even students who were admitted with test scores that were lower than our usual high standards).[16]

The political nature of organizations makes implementation of affirmative action and diversity programs problematic. Regardless of the initial intentions of policies and programs, there is considerable wiggle room between policy goals and implementation. Self-interest comes into play whenever there is wiggle room in organizational administration. *Individuals* implement human resource policies, and individuals are more inclined to pursue their own interests than to pursue an organizational policy that an administrator or expert thinks is a good idea. A human resource program may have a grand narrative, claiming to increase ethnic diversity or make up for past discrimination, but the actual operation of a program involves individuals making streams of small decisions related to their self-interest (see, e.g., Boyer, 2001).

The environment of an organization is another factor that intercedes between intentions and the effect of a policy. The environment is a changing context of opportunities, constraints, resources, and threats, many of which affect affirmative action and diversity programs. These include the numbers and location of protected or desired racial and ethnic groups available to an organization, competition with other organizations, and the cultural milieu in which an organization is located. In a situation where there are fewer qualified minority applicants than there are available positions and where there is pressure to hire minorities, a fierce competition ensues for qualified minority applicants, which favors prestigious and wealthy organizations. To illustrate, assume that there are 100 organizations, ranked from 1 (low) to 100 (high) in wealth and prestige, and that there are two job openings per organization. Furthermore, assume that there are 6 exceptionally qualified minorities on the job market, 10 qualified minorities, and 16 marginally qualified minorities. After all the applicants have been hired, it is unlikely the minorities will be distributed across evenly among the top 50 organizations. The wealthiest and most prestigious organizations will be able to make the most attractive offers. Therefore, it is likely that the 6 exceptionally qualified minority applicants will probably end up in the top three or four organizations; the 10 qualified minority applicants will probably take jobs in the next most prestigious five or so organizations. This leaves all of the remaining organizations competing for 16 marginally qualified minorities. Assuming that there are some qualified majority job applicants, the quotidian organizations are forced to choose between hiring qualified majority or marginally qualified minority applicants to meet affirmative action goals because the elite organizations scooped up most of the qualified minorities.

An organization's cultural milieu can also influence affirmative action and diversity programs. Most people like to live and work in environments where they are with people who are similar to them. Therefore, broad national policies that encourage diversity and affirmative action disadvantage organizations located in areas without a sizable minority population. Universities located in small Midwestern farming communities where most of the population is of, say, German or Scandinavian ancestry are likely to find it more difficult to attract African American or Hispanic faculty than universities located in, say, New York City or Houston. People generally prefer to live in areas that are culturally congruent with their own backgrounds.

Score Adjustment

The original intent of affirmative action was simply to seek out qualified minorities and encourage them to apply for positions and then choose applicants on a color-blind basis.

> What does affirmative action mean? In the context of civil rights the phrase had appeared for the first time in Executive Order 10925, signed by President Kennedy in March 1961. The phrase "affirmative action" lay buried in the forty-five-hundred-word decree calling for "equal opportunity in employment by the government or its contractors." This original definition of affirmative action required employers only to search aggressively for qualified minority applicants. Once found, minority applicants would go into the same pool with everybody else, and the final selection would be made on a color-blind basis. (Gillon, 2000, p. 125)

This implied a color-blind *top-down* strategy. However, this did not have the desired effect of sufficiently increasing minority representation. Some minorities, primarily African Americans and Hispanics, remained underrepresented in universities and in professional and managerial occupations. One reason is that people generally prefer to associate with others who are similar to themselves (Tajfel, 1982). Despite the strong moral value of color-blind policies in American culture (Skrentny, 1996), people have evolved psychological mechanisms that predispose them to make in-group and out-group distinctions (Kurzban, Cosmides, & Tooby, 1998). Similarity can have a powerful effect on how people evaluate and rate applicants (Webster, 1964; Wexley, Alexander, & Greenawalt,

1980). Test score differences were another reason affirmative action programs did not work as planned. African Americans and Hispanics score, on average, lower than Caucasians on cognitive ability tests.[17] When applicants are selected on the basis of cognitive ability scores using a top-down strategy, minorities are excluded from admission to selective colleges, and graduate schools, and from jobs where selection is based on cognitive ability test scores.

The pre- and post-affirmative action composition of the student body at the University of California provides a good illustration of the effects of score adjustments. In 1995, the university banned the use of race and sex in admissions decisions, and California voters approved Proposition 209 in 1996, which prohibited using race and sex in state government contracting, hiring, and university admissions. In 1998, the first year that the ban on race and sex in admission decisions went into effect, the number of African Americans in the freshman class decreased by more than half and the percentage of Hispanics decreased by 43 percent (Arenson, 2000). Because cognitive ability test scores have a disparate impact on African Americans and Hispanics, some civil rights advocates and social scientists argue that basing selection decisions on cognitive ability tests *and* using a top-down strategy is unfair and thwarts the goals of equal employment opportunity. One argument against a top-down strategy is based on the fact that cognitive ability tests are imperfect predictors of future performance. Differences in cognitive test scores do not have a one-to-one correspondence with differences in job or school performance (Hartigan & Wigdor, 1989).

An alternative is to use some form of *score adjustment* whereby the test scores of minority applicants will be raised so that they can achieve educational and occupational parity with majority group applicants. Consequently, score adjustment has become part of affirmative action and diversity programs throughout the United States. A variety of methods of adjustment have been proposed over the years in attempts to meet the goals of affirmative action, diversity, and productivity. These include bonus points, race-norming, banding, and the search for alternative predictors with less adverse impact (Sackett & Wilk, 1994).[18] With bonus points, points are added to an applicant's total score above and beyond the points awarded on the basis of criteria that apply universally to all applicants. Bonus points apply to individuals from favored groups. Veterans typically get bonus points when applying for jobs with the federal government. Many colleges and universities award bonus points to athletes and children of alumni. Some universities appear to add points to applications to increase racial and ethnic diversity (Cohn, 1997). Race norming involves converting raw scores to standard scores, such as percentiles, for separate groups and then basing selection decisions on percentiles within groups rather than on raw scores. This has the effect of creating standard score parity between groups and reducing adverse impact. Banding involves establishing a range of test scores that can be considered equivalent. It is based on the statistical premise that any test score includes a certain amount of error; thus, it is technically inaccurate to say that one applicant has more of whatever quality is being measured than another applicant if the two applicants' scores fall within the range of measurement error. Applicants whose scores are within a band are considered equivalent on the characteristic measured by the test. Preferences based on race, ethnicity, or any other group difference are applied within a band. The purpose of this procedure is to maximize diversity while minimizing any negative effects on performance.

Score adjustment methods are overengineered attempts at designer diversity. They are based on the untenable assumption that highly engineered social interventions can produce specific, intended results in complex social systems. Many score adjustment programs make categorical distinctions based on race and ethnicity, which, as discussed previously, are fraught with problems. And score adjustment methods do perpetuate perceptions of unfairness. When scores are adjusted, some people are favored on the basis of group membership and others are not.

X Percent Plans

X percent plans are a response to the political problems created by affirmative action, particularly the highly charged problems associated with score adjustments that favor some groups over others in college admissions. The purpose of these plans is to increase ethnic and racial diversity in a race-neutral manner (Bush, 2000). One such program is Florida's Talented 20 Percent plan. All high school students who are in the top 20 percent of their high school class are guaranteed a place in one of the state's universities. A similar plan exists in Texas, and California. In Texas, high school seniors in the top 10 percent of their high school classes can attend any of the public universities in the state. Most in the top 10 percent choose to attend the flagship university, the University of Texas at Austin; the lower-tier universities in Texas admit virtually all students who apply. California has two X percent plans: a long-standing plan to admit the top 12.5 percent of high school students throughout the state, regardless of high school, and a plan to admit the top 4 percent of students from each high school in the state (Arenson, 2000).

X percent plans address the three major problems associated with affirmative action and diversity programs—designer diversity, categorical distinctions based on race and ethnicity, and perceptions of fairness. Unlike affirmative action or diversity programs, X percent plans make no attempt to engineer diversity in order to produce specific results. The primary objective of these plans is more modest: to increase or maintain racial and ethnic diversity in a way that is perceived as fair. X percent plans do not carve nature at the joints by making categorical distinctions on the basis of race or ethnicity. They also convey a sense of fairness by admitting everyone above a given cutoff score. The top X percent is a straightforward concept that is easy to understand. It minimizes political maneuvering because there is little wiggle room that interest groups can maneuver in to promote their interests.

As appealing as they may appear, X percent plans are problematic. They can be too restrictive, minimizing variation, when the top X percent is a small percent. Restrictive X percent plans, such as California's top 4 percent plan or possibly Texas' top 10 percent plan, are similar to top-down selection in that they make an assumption about a gold standard for the best person for the job. It is difficult to justify a highly restrictive top X percent (e.g., the top 4 percent) by expected performance benefits. Moderate differences in the cutoff point will not make much difference in student outcomes (Bowen & Bok, 1998). Students within, say, the top 10 percent are unlikely to perform, on average, better than students in, say, the top 15 percent over four years and beyond (Bowen & Bok, 1998; Hulin et al., 1990). Conversely, *some* students in, say, the top 25 percent are likely to perform as well as those in the top 4 percent.[19]

Fixing the top X percent plans at a given number—Texas admits the top 10 percent, Florida the top 20, and California the top 4 percent—can result in administrative difficulties. This can place financial and administrative strains on a university system when the population of high school students increases. The problem of limited capacity and surplus students can be solved by tightening the admissions standard—say from the top 10 to the top 5 percent—but this has the undesirable effect of rejecting many capable students. Conversely, when student numbers decrease, a fixed percentage system may provide too few students. Another problem with X percent plans occurs when allocating students to multiple universities in a state system. If there is more than one university in a state system, some selection criteria need to be established to determine which students in the top X percent go to which universities. The Florida and California plans admit students into the university system, so choices need to be made—and criteria need to be established on which to make those choices—to determine *which students are placed in which universities*. Florida's criteria for placing students into particular universities include "socioeconomic background, geographic diversity, and whether the student comes from a low-performing public school or is a first-generation college student" (Bush, 2000, p. A–31). This shifts the problems of preferential treatment and fairness from admission to a university to placement within the university system (C. W. Blackwell, personal communication, May 3, 2002). Under the Texas plan, the top 10 percent are guaranteed admission to the public university of their choice, but beyond the top 10 percent, universities can apply a variety of criteria in selecting other students. In the fall of 2000, top-10-percent students comprised less than 50 percent of the incoming freshman class at the University of Texas (D. Keith, personal communication, May 6, 2002). These types of situations increase the wiggle-room factor, leaving the door open for score adjustment and its attendant problems.

When selection is made according to an X percent plan, the top X percent needs to be defined according to a specified unit of analysis. In university admissions, the unit can be defined by the top X percent of seniors from each high school in a state, by the top X percent of all high school seniors in the state, or by some other arbitrary unit. Texas and Florida use the top X percent from each high school. The University of California system, on the other hand, has used all high schools in the state as its unit of analysis since the 1960s. It admits 12.5 percent of all high school seniors in the state based on high school grades and test scores. However, California's more recent top 4 percent plan uses each high school as its unit (Arenson, 2000). In theory, the unit could be high school districts, counties, or whatever unit politicians and administrators choose. Political maneuvering will inevitably accompany the specification of units because the nature of the unit is likely to favor some groups and not others. For example, selecting the top X percent from each high school often helps to attain the goal of greater ethnic and racial diversity because high schools tend to be ethnically and racially homogeneous (Arenson, 2000). The unit and cutoff point recently became sources of political maneuvering in Texas. The top 10 percent plan in Texas is in effect limited to the University of Texas at Austin and Texas A & M University because the other public universities in the state practice essentially open admission policies (Berry, 2000). Because the Texas plan allows students to choose which university they will attend, universities must compete to attract the top 10 percent of high school seniors. Universities are under even greater pressure to attract minority students in the top 10 percent due to the prominence of diversity programs. The prestigious University of Texas at Austin has not experienced a reduction in the number of minority students due to the top 10 percent plan. But the plan has reduced the number of minorities attending the less prestigious Texas A & M—apparently more are going to the University of Texas (Berry, 2000; Selingo, 2002). One way to improve admission numbers is to change the admission criteria. The Board of Regents at Texas A & M approved a top 20 percent plan, but it is a 20 percent proposal with a twist. Only students from 250 "low-performing" high schools can be admitted under the 20 percent rule; students from all other high schools must still be admitted under the top 10 percent rule. Apparently, the rationale for the gerrymandered 20 percent plan was to increase the number of minority students (Selingo, 2002).

Another problem with X percent plans is that they tend to be limited in their application to state universities. X percent plans require coordination and consensus between the unit doing the admitting and the units from which the top percent are chosen. This is feasible for state university admissions because high schools and state university systems are part of one political entity (a state), because there is a history of coordination between high schools and universities, and because much of the business of high schools involves preparing students for a university education. However, X percent programs do not work well for admitting nonresident students. Nonresident applicants to a state system are excluded from X percent programs because their high schools are not part of the unit that defines the top X percent. A student from Nevada who applies to a university in California could not be included in a X percent plan that, by definition, is calibrated on students from Californian high schools. The same complication affects students within a state who did not graduate from a traditional high school—home schoolers or students who earned a high school degree by passing an equivalency test. X percent plans are particularly problematic for the elite, nationally ranked private colleges and universities. These schools draw students from throughout the country and world. The use of any unit (country, state, high school, or whatever) to define the top X percent would be problematic. The criteria for selecting a unit from which to take a top X percent would be subject to endless debate. Also, the variability within a unit when the range is so broad (e.g., all high schools in the world) would be so great that it would be difficult to assign meaning to a top X percent. These are the same difficulties that many graduate and professional programs would encounter if they used a X percent plan, since they draw students from a wide intellectual and geographic universe. These difficulties are compounded when applying X percent plans to work organizations. Colleges are essentially "hiring" high school seniors for one type of job—college student. Work organizations, on the other hand, hire people for many different types of jobs. As such, it would be difficult to standardize admission criteria and units of admission.

There is a need for a better approach to admissions and hiring that introduces variation, eliminates illegal discrimination, and maximizes fairness. A feasible alternative would have the following characteristics: It would be workable in many types of organizations; it would enhance diversity; it would be responsive to moral and legal injunctions against discrimination based on sex, race, and ethnicity; and it would maintain standards of quality. Random selection above a threshold has these characteristics.

Random Selection above a Threshold

The objectives of random selection above a threshold are to enhance diversity in hiring, to be responsive to moral and legal injunctions against discrimination based on sex, race, and ethnicity, to maximize fairness, to allow implementation to occur in a straightforward way by minimizing the opportunity for political manipulation and administrative slippage, and to maintain standards in the selection of employees and students. Random selection above a threshold works by randomly selecting applicants from *a pool of qualified applicants*. In a random selection, *every applicant within the pool has an equal probability of being selected*. If there are 100 applicants in the pool and 10 openings, *each* applicant has a 10 percent chance of being selected. Selection from the applicant pool is the easy part. Determining how people are included in the applicant pool is more difficult; it involves establishing criteria for selection, identifying a means for assessing a person's standing, and developing assessment standards for the threshold of the pool of applicants.

The objectives of random selection above a threshold are most likely to be met when organizations use *core competencies* as selection criteria. Core competencies are those skills and abilities necessary for successful performance on the job.[20] The first step is to identify the most important dimensions of a job—the major tasks required by the job. These are obvious to people with experience in the job.[21] For example, the critical dimensions of the job of ski instructor include teaching people to ski and to improve their skiing, monitoring and enforcing safety standards, and maintaining people's interest and enthusiasm for the skiing lessons and the sport. The next step is to identify the core competencies associated with the job dimensions. Again, these are generally obvious to people who have experience with the job. The core competencies for a ski instructor would include: (1) good skiing skills, (2) skills in teaching people at different levels how to ski and to improve their skiing, (3) capacity to keep people interested and satisfied with skiing lessons, and (4) knowledge of safety standards and capacity to maintain a safe environment during skiing lessons. Core competencies are best assessed by *samples* of behavior that are necessary for successful performance on the job. Samples of behavior are more strongly associated with job performance than signs (see Chapter 3). Performing a mechanical activity—such as making a bird house from scratch—is a sample of mechanical skills, whereas a score on a mechanical aptitude test is a sign of mechanical ability or skill. Organizations need people who can perform skillfully in their designated roles, and by keeping the selection criteria focused on samples of core competencies, individuals selected into the applicant pool will have a high probability of performing successfully on the job.

If selection criteria are esoteric and difficult to understand, they are more likely to lose acceptability. People have more confidence that hiring decisions are sound and fair when the decisions are based on tests that involve samples rather than signs (Steiner & Gilliland, 1996). There should also be no expectation that core competencies will predict job performance beyond the short to medium term—that is, beyond six months to a few years. The correlations between test scores and performance typically decline to trivial levels after five years (Hulin et al., 1990); the criteria for success can change over time (Ghiselli, 1956), and random events are increasingly likely to affect an individual's performance record with the increasing passage of time (Taleb, 2001). In setting the cutoff standard for the threshold, it is best to define "qualified" people as those who have a reasonable probability of succeeding over the short to medium term. Long-term prediction is problematic, at best. What constitutes qualified is fairly straightforward for most situations, particularly at the extremes. Universities can be reasonably certain that if they admit high school seniors with B+ to A grade point averages, most of them will do reasonably well during their freshman year in college. Similarly, they can be reasonably certain that, if they admit high school seniors with D+ to F grade point averages, most of them will do poorly during their freshman year. There is less certainty in the middle. However, regardless of where one sets the standard, there is no ideal level. Any level involves some degree of arbitrariness. One could always argue that people who score just a point or two below the threshold have about the same probability of succeeding as those who score at or just above the threshold. They are right. However, for practical purposes, a line must be drawn. This is the case with any selection system.

It is true that there can be important distinctions in the quality of applicants who are above the threshold. However, random selection above a threshold assumes that, above a level where people have the skills to perform acceptably, making fine-tuned distinctions is not essential. Multiple criteria often define successful performance and different core competencies associated with those criteria. Although a person may be generally competent, the constellation of competencies within any individual is always nuanced. A person with a high level of one competency will not necessarily have as high a level of another competency. A ski resort manager, a supervisor of a ski school, and a senior ski instructor probably would not rank qualified job applicants in the same order. One applicant might be a fantastic skier with a stellar reputation that would be helpful in promoting the resort and increasing its visibility, but might also be arrogant and less popular with students. Another might be a less able skier but have a pleasing personality that would keep students happy and returning for lessons. Moreover, any of the qualified applicants could be more or less valuable under different conditions—and future conditions cannot be predicted with certainty. The mix of students at the ski school might change from season to season, and attempting to make a precise match of an applicant and the type of students the resort attracts would be an exercise in futility.

Random selection above a threshold offers at least four advantages over top-down selection, score adjustment, and X percent plans. First, it deals effectively with both enhancing diversity and acquiring talent; second, it avoids the inherent complications associated with making racial and ethnic categorizations; third, it is easy to understand and likely to be perceived as fair; fourth, it is compatible with the organizational realities of complexity, self-interest, and politics. Random selection above a threshold maximizes diversity in the true sense of the word. Other than meeting the threshold requirement, no distinctions are made about who is included in the threshold pool. Similarly, because selection is *random*, no distinctions are made about who is selected. Members of any group, however defined, who are within the pool have a chance of being selected in proportion to their percentage within the threshold group. With random selection above a threshold, diversity ceases to be a code word for whatever groups happen to be politically favored. Rather, diversity denotes people with a wide mix of characteristics who are not preselected on any characteristics except those core competencies related to inclusion in the threshold pool. Random selection above a threshold does not make rigid, categorical distinctions by race or ethnicity. It avoids all of the attendant problems of classifying people into one group or another, of classifying someone as one race or another, of mixed racial heritage, of biased self-report, of the effects of cultural norms on racial classifications, and of changing views of racial and ethnic identities. Diversity across the largest number of characteristics has the best chance of being maximized when the smallest number of characteristics are used in making selection decisions.

Random selection above a threshold is easy to understand and is more likely to be perceived as fair than programs that single out individuals from particular groups for preferential treatment. From an evolutionary perspective, the more straightforward the approach to admissions and hiring, the better. Human psychological mechanisms for understanding fairness are *unlikely* to respond well to complex models of fairness that involve statistical reasoning and long causal chains. Random selection above a threshold is more compatible with human information processing mechanisms. While controversies over affirmative action, diversity, and top-down selection based on cognitive ability test scores are a staple in the news, controversies about the fairness of lotteries—picking winners at random—are virtually nonexistent. Because selection is random and no *a priori* distinctions are made over group membership among people in the threshold pool, random selection above a threshold avoids the political land mines of specifying groups and determining which groups will be favored. Random selection above a threshold virtually assures that the representation of groups among those hired will be proportional to the representation of groups in the threshold pool. With group membership eliminated as a criterion for selection, this also eliminates the problem of stigmatization stemming from preferential treatment. No longer would people from formerly protected minority groups have to wonder whether they were selected because of their race, sex, or ethnicity. People would be less likely to stereotype those who are different from themselves as "affirmative action hires," since everyone who is in the threshold pool was qualified and had an equal chance of being selected.

Random selection above a threshold is unlikely to significantly compromise performance. Given uncertain futures, multiple goals, ambiguity, and conflict in the links between individual attributes and organizational goals, reasonably qualified people have reasonably equivalent chances of performing successfully after they are selected. The characteristics of the applicant pool have considerably more impact on an organization's productivity than the characteristics of selection systems (Murphy, Osten, & Myors, 1995). Small differences on a trait used in hiring decisions are unlikely to lead to noticeable differences in performance because small differences on test scores are usually due to measurement error and differences in outcome scores are typically smaller than differences on predictor scores (Cascio, Alexander, & Barrett, 1988; Hartigan & Wigdor, 1989). Moreover, even when differences on ability among applicants are larger, the effects of these differences on performance typically diminish over time to the point where they are trivial (Hulin et al., 1990). The problem of correlation among traits and outcomes (see Chapter 3) also suggests that moderate differences among people on traits will not make all that much difference in performance: some beneficial traits may correlate with some detrimental traits and vice versa. It is unlikely that any trait will correlate positively with all possible important outcomes to an organization.

Random selection above a threshold has a better chance of being implemented faithfully than other programs because there is less room for self-interest and personal values to intrude. Self-interest, politics, and judgment affect only one variable in random selection above a threshold: the threshold score. Even here, there is less wiggle room than with other methods because the primary criteria for the threshold are core competencies. After the threshold is established, individual decision making does not factor into selection decisions. With score adjustment programs, banding, and X percent programs (when placement decisions must be made about people in the top X percent), there are numerous decision points throughout the selection process, and individuals, with their attendant interests and values, make these decisions. With these programs, a decision must be made for each individual about racial or ethnic group membership, about whether the individual is qualified, and about whether the score should be adjusted and by how much. Even when algorithms are used, such as automatically assigning points for various qualities, judgments determine the parameters of the algorithms. Individual judgments also influence whether an applicant is assigned to a preferred group.[22] Random selection above a threshold avoids these problems.

Yet random selection above a threshold is an administrative procedure, and any administrative procedure involves judgments and conflicting interests. It is beyond the scope of this chapter to list the contingencies and possible problems and then develop a blueprint. However, two of the key issues should be mentioned, the unit of analysis and the threshold. A critical issue in random selection above a threshold is the unit of analysis where the system applies—across all units or within each unit. Officials of a state university system would have to decide whether the procedure operates at the statewide level or at the level of each university. I would argue that it is most effective when it operates at the smallest reasonable unit so that threshold scores can be tied to the needs of particular institutions. Using large units, such as a statewide approach, would gloss over important differences among the smaller units that compose the larger system. Setting the threshold will obviously involve conflict among differing values and interests. Determination will have to be made for selection criteria and the cutoff point.[23] Although core competencies are the primary selection criteria, other criteria may come into play, such as whether a person is a state resident. These secondary criteria will need to be factored in, and this will not occur without a clash of interests. Similarly, setting the cutoff point will involve political wrangling.

Objections

Random selection above a threshold is likely to generate objections from people who are uncomfortable with the notion of *randomly* selecting applicants, believing that they can design a system to more precisely identify meritorious applicants and to achieve specific effects. They will object that random selection above a threshold plays dice with critical skills and abilities and will lower productivity by not deliberately selecting the "best" person for the job. In their book supporting affirmative action and designer diversity, Bowen and Bok state that random selection is "too crude" (1998, p. 276). Interestingly, they do not say *why* it is too crude. Nor do they provide any evidence showing that random selection from among a group of qualified applicants would provide outcomes any different from the score adjustment methods used in affirmative action hiring or top-down selection as it occurs in the real world. They assume that college administrators and politicians can determine precisely which admissions would be best and would achieve the best social and academic outcomes. This is nonsense. Indeed, a strategy that randomly enhances diversification is more likely to result in increased productivity than attempting to "pick winners." Randomness within parameters is hardly crude. In sexually reproducing organisms, chromosomes segregate randomly during reproduction (Williams, 1996). The most consistently effective method of investing in the stock market is to buy a diverse portfolio of stocks rather than to attempt to predict the behavior of a single stock or a select group of stocks (Malkiel, 1985).

One might also object that random selection above a threshold has a detrimental effect on the motivation of applicants. It could be argued that potential applicants will be less likely to work hard in, say, high school if they are aware that their admission to a university depends in part on a random process. I doubt that it will have much of an effect on motivation. The threshold serves as an incentive to motivate students to work up to the threshold standards. Probabilistic selection and uncertainty do not dampen people's motivation to pursue risky opportunities when there is some chance of a payoff. People continue to pursue risky careers—professional sports, entertainment, entrepreneurial business ventures—where chance and random events have a significant influence on success or failure. People also continue to invest in the stock market, despite uncertainty. Most high school students who apply to highly selective private universities realize that random factors will influence their chances of admission; indeed, many college applicants use the strategy of diversification, applying to multiple universities to hedge their bets. Random selection above a threshold may also have unintended educational benefits. Schools would be less inclined to teach to admission tests when scores higher than the threshold have no effect on admission chances. Students might be less inclined to focus narrowly on grades and be more likely to pursue a broader (e.g., liberal arts) educational career.

Others might argue that random selection above a threshold is not fair to the most qualified—those with the highest grades or test scores. Again, this is based on the assumptions that there is agreement on what constitutes merit, that small differences of measures of merit are meaningful, and that there is a tight correspondence between one particular characteristic or measure of merit and future performance. These assumptions are tenuous.

Whenever I present my ideas about random selection above a threshold to people who favor score adjustment to meet affirmative action hiring goals for particular types of minorities, they inevitably raise the following objection. If the threshold is set too high, then too few members of minority group X who, on average, score lower than Caucasians will be included in the pool and thus less likely to be selected. My response is that organizations should set the cutoff at a point that allows them to meet their diversity goals and their goals of admitting students who are competent enough to perform successfully. These goals are not mutually exclusive. Studies of affirmative action programs at elite universities suggest that differences in the qualifications among students from a pool of generally capable students have little effect on productivity outcomes (Bowen & Bok, 1998). The advantage of random selection above a threshold is that it includes members of *all* groups above the threshold, not just those who are members of particular groups that happen to be favored by politicians and administrators.

Tradition, Modification, and Variation in Selection Systems

Three practical implications of an evolutionary perspective for the design of selection systems are: respect for traditional selection practices;

modification of traditional practices when they are mismatched with current conditions; and random selection above a threshold. Taken together, these approaches may seem at odds with one another or even contradictory. There is little respect for tradition in random selection above a threshold. However, these approaches make sense when we place them in context. Traditional practices, such as the interview and the probationary period, are relevant to small groups, groups that are not all that different in size and interaction patterns from the small groups in which humans evolved. In small groups where an individual is selected only occasionally, the individual becomes an integral part of the group. Where an individual will work closely with or be supervised by a specific individual in the group, traditional hiring methods are appropriate. They work when parents hire a baby-sitter, a manager hires an assistant, or a small business owner hires an employee. In circumstances where individuals are hired into work groups, but where hiring occurs frequently and where the groups are embedded into a larger organization, modifications to traditional methods—such as eliminating a portion of interviews or paying recommenders—are appropriate. Situations such as these would include hiring professionals or technicians into large firms. Finally, in contexts where large numbers of applicants are admitted to large organizations on a routine basis and where placement into small groups occurs after they have been selected, random selection above a threshold would be most appropriate. Examples of such situations include admission to universities and the military or hiring large numbers of entry-level employees to large corporations.

NOTES

1. Schmidt and Hunter assert that "productivity [is] probably the most important dependent variable in industrial/organizational psychology" (1983, p. 407). The cult of productivity in industrial psychology has, no doubt, impeded the intellectual growth of the field.

2. This has become a contentious issue in democratic societies characterized by ethnic diversity. Affirmative action has become a much-debated policy—in the United States and India—for dealing with inequalities along racial and ethnic lines. India began a policy of affirmative action in higher education and employment to help redress past discrimination against certain castes, primarily the "untouchables." In ethnically homogeneous societies, such as Japan, affirmative action and diversity are not significant public policy issues. With the rise of feminism in Japan, however, equal opportunity employment for women is becoming a more prominent issue.

3. When I say that a hiring practice "works," I have three things in mind. The practice can be said to work if there is a net advantage to using it, that is, if its net benefits outweigh its net costs. This is, I think, the most acceptable

and evolutionary appropriate definition of "work." Unfortunately, given the complexities of social systems and the various criteria by which one can assess costs and benefits, even this definition does not guarantee consensus. Second, a practice works if it achieves a valued outcome. A third issue is efficiency. A practice works if it is more efficient than other methods. The second and third approaches are simpler than the first, but they have their problems too. A hiring practice may achieve a particular outcome and do so more efficiently than another method, but it may also produce unintended consequences that are dysfunctional. Evaluating the effectiveness of a hiring, or other human resource, practice is a cumulative process that involves using information from a variety of sources based on a variety of criteria.

4. An opposite sort of mismatch is our evolved aversion to bitter foods and swallowing hard objects. This causes resistance to taking modern medicines. We evolved a dislike for bitter-tasting foods because bitter plants are more likely to contain poisons (Profet, 1992) and our aversion to swallowing hard objects is related to the choking reflex. However, some modern medicines, which may be critical to curing some illnesses, may have a bitter taste or come in the form of hard objects (pills). Because of these evolved aversions, people tend to resist taking bitter medicines or swallowing large pills.

5. Much of this discussion of letters of recommendation is from Colarelli et al. (2002).

6. It would be interesting to survey parents of young children and to ask whether they would rely on a valid paper-and-pencil test to select a baby-sitter for their young children. Being primarily concerned about assessing potential harm, it is likely that parents would insist on face-to-face information or at least narrative information from a trusted friend. A slang term used among many interviewers in the United States is "the green tongue." A green tongue refers to odd, inappropriate, or highly unusual characteristics. Some interviewers mention that one objective of interviews is to identify and reject people with a green tongue and that interviews are necessary because paper-and-pencil tests cannot identify green tongues.

7. Agricultural monocultures are notoriously susceptible to disease and blight. If a disease infests a monoculture, it spreads quickly and the entire crop is at risk. On the other hand, diverse ecosystems are more stable and hardy because not all plants are susceptible to the same diseases. Agricultural monocultures tend to be more economically efficient, hence their widespread use. And when conditions can be controlled, they work well. Unfortunately, controlling all relevant disease and weather conditions is difficult. Similarly, psychological monocultures can be efficient and work well when in stable, abundant conditions with minimal competition (March, 1991). However, such conditions are rare.

8. An assessment center is a selection method that uses a combination of paper-and-pencil tests and behavioral exercises.

9. Ultimately, we are all of African origin. The available anthropological evidence indicates that humans originated in Africa.

10. The same is true with the classification of homosexuals. Homosexuals

are often considered important components of diversity programs. However, on what basis should a person be classified as a homosexual? Fewer than 5 percent of males who consider themselves homosexual have had exclusively male sex partners. Most homosexuals are actually bisexual (Baker & Bellis, 1995).

11. The United States Census is now acknowledging mixed racial heritage. The 2000 Census was the first Census in U.S. history to allow people to classify themselves by more than one racial category. People were given a list of six single racial categories and could check all that applied to them. This allowed for 63 racial options. When combined with the Hispanic/non-Hispanic ethnic option, the Census allowed for 126 combinations of race and ethnicity. In previous censuses, people could only check one racial group.

12. Self-reporting is a common method used to classify people into racial or ethnic groups. That is, people classify themselves usually by checking a response on a questionnaire to indicate their race or ethnic group. In Bowen and Bok's (1998) influential study on the impact of affirmative action in selective universities, they used one question to determine race and ethnicity: "Do you consider yourself (1) Black, not Hispanic, (2) Black, Hispanic, (3) White, not Hispanic, (4) White, Hispanic, (5) Asian or Pacific Islander, (6) Native American or Alaskan Native." This widely cited book was based on data from an 18-page questionnaire completed by about 80,000 undergraduate students, and *the most important variable in the study was measured by one multiple-choice question.* The 18-page questionnaire contained no questions about parents' or grandparents' race or questions asking why a person considered himself or herself a member of a particular race or ethnic group.

13. Differences in average scores between minority and majority groups are not regarded as evidence of unfairness (as long as the tests are not culturally biased and the predictive accuracy is roughly equal). Differences in average scores are assumed to reflect true differences on the characteristic measured by the test.

14. To the extent that there is some predictive discrepancy, cognitive ability tests have been found to slightly overpredict for blacks and underpredict for women (Jensen, 1980). Overprediction is to the advantage of blacks in admissions and hiring situations when the majority group regression line is used. Underprediction is to the disadvantage of women when the majority group regression line is used.

15. The range is due to differences in the level of analysis of measurement—whether measuring annual wages, weekly wages, or hourly wages.

16. The benefits of a degree from prestigious universities are due to prestige effects, such as opening more doors, and because they accept more able students (Colarelli, Dean, & Konstans, 1991; Dale & Krueger, in press).

17. African Americans score, on average, about one standard deviation lower than Caucasians on cognitive ability tests. Hispanics score somewhat lower than Caucasians, about .84 of a standard deviation. Asian Americans have slightly higher average IQ scores than Caucasians (Herrnstein & Murray, 1994).

18. The Civil Rights Act of 1991 made bonus points, race norming, and any direct manipulation of test or cutoff scores on the basis of race or ethnicity unlawful.

19. Authur Miller, one of America's greatest playwrights, had such poor high school grades that he was only able to gain admission to the University of Michigan by first attending on a probationary basis (Miller, 2000). "My [high school] academic record (I had flunked algebra three times . . .) was so low as to be practically invisible"(p. 14). The man who developed the technology to sequence the human genome, J. Craig Venter, the former president of Celera Genomics, "barely graduated from high school" (Lemonick, 2000–2001). Venter eventually earned a Ph.D. in physiology and pharmacology from the University of California at San Diego, and his company, Celera, was one of the first organizations to sequence the human genome.

20. Circumstances do exist where core competencies extend beyond skills and abilities. Among management teams and political elites, it is important to include values and ideology among selection criteria. A Republican president would diminish his effectiveness if he or she selected cabinet members who were socialists, even if they were highly skilled in core management competencies. Trust and group problem-solving effectiveness would be diminished (Zand, 1972).

21. There is extensive literature on job analysis in industrial psychology that deals with identifying major and minor dimensions of jobs (Harvey, 1991). Although this literature can be useful, it is highly complex and technical. For most situations, it is unnecessary. I say this based on 15 years of experience in both conducting job analyses and teaching graduate-level courses containing units on job analysis. Thoughtful people with experience in a job or supervising a job can do a perfectly adequate job in identifying the core dimensions of a job through observation, discussion, and common-sense reasoning.

22. Suppose a student with the following characteristics applies for admission to a state university with an affirmative action or diversity program. The student is female; she was born in Brazil; and she lived there until she was six years old. Her parents are both Brazilian citizens; however, the mother was born in Norway and the father in Scotland. The father works for a multinational corporation with headquarters in the United States. After the applicant turned six years old, she lived in various communities in the United States. She holds a Brazilian passport. Placing her in an affirmative action or diversity category would be no simple matter and would involve judgment calls.

23. One can imagine a variety of possible conflicts of interest and how they might play out in setting a threshold. A compromise between top-down testers and diversity advocates might result in different percentages of applicants being randomly selected, depending on how close their scores are to the lower end of the threshold, with a smaller percent being selected the closer the score is to the threshold.

REFERENCES

Aamodt, M. G., Bryan, D. A., & Whitcomb, A. J. (1993). Predicting performance with letters of recommendation. *Public Personnel Management, 22,* 81–90.

Adams, G. A., Elacqua, T. C., & Colarelli, S. M. (1994). The employment interview as a sociometric selection technique. *Journal of Group Psychotherapy, Psychodrama, and Sociometry, 47,* 99–113.

Alexander, R. D. (1987). *The biology of moral systems.* Hawthorne, NY: Aldine DeGruyter.

Anstey, E. (1966). The civil service administrative class and diplomatic service. *Occupational Psychology, 40,* 137–151.

Arenson, K. W. (2000, September 22). California proposal aims to improve college diversity. *New York Times,* p. A–14.

Argyris, C. (1957). *Personality and organization.* New York: Harper.

Arvey, R. D., & Campion, J. E. (1982). The employment interview: A summary and review of recent research. *Personnel Psychology, 35,* 281–322.

Baker, R. R., & Bellis, M. A. (1995). *Human sperm competition.* London: Chapman & Hall.

Bales, R. F., & Slater, P. E. (1955). Role differentiation in small decision-making groups. In T. Parsons and R. F. Bales (Eds.), *Family, socialization and the interaction process* (pp. 259–306). New York: Free Press.

Baron-Cohen, S. (1997). How to build a baby that can read minds: Cognitive mechanisms in mindreading. In S. Baron-Cohen (Ed.), *The maladapted mind: Classic readings in evolutionary psychopathology* (pp. 207–239). East Sussex, UK: Psychology Press.

Berry, M. F. (2000, August 4). How percentage plans keep minority students out of college. *The Chronicle of Higher Education,* p. A48.

Bettenhausen, K., & Murnighan, J. K. (1985). The emergence of norms in competitive decision-making groups. *Administrative Science Quarterly, 30,* 350–372.

Bolster, B. I., & Springbett, B. M. (1961). The reaction of interviewers to favorable and unfavorable information. *Journal of Applied Psychology, 45,* 97–103.

Bowen, W. G., & Bok, D. (1998). *The shape of the river: Long-term consequences of considering race in college and university admissions.* Princeton, NJ: Princeton University Press.

Boyd, R., & Silk, J. B. (1997). *How humans evolved.* New York: W. W. Norton.

Boyer, P. J. (2001, October 22). Man of faith: Can Jesse Jackson save himself? *New Yorker,* pp. 50–65.

Brown, S. H. (1979). Validity distortions associated with a test in use. *Journal of Applied Psychology, 64,* 460–462.

Browne, K. R. (2002). *Biology at work: Rethinking sexual equality.* New Brunswick, NJ: Rutgers University Press.

Bureau of National Affairs. (1988). *Recruiting and selection procedures.* Personnel Policies Forum, Survey No. 146. Washington, DC: Author.

Bush, J. (2000, September 15). Better than affirmative. *New York Times,* p. A-31.

Buss, D. M. (1995). Evolutionary psychology: A new paradigm for psychological science. *Psychological Inquiry, 6,* 1–30.

Cacioppo, J. T., & Berntson, G. T. (1999). The affect system: Architecture and operating characteristics. *Current Directions in Psychological Science, 8*, 133–136—P30.

Campbell, D. T. (1975). On the conflicts between biological and social evolution and psychology and moral tradition. *American Psychologist, 30*, 1103–1126.

Campbell, J. P. (1996). Group differences and personnel decisions: Validity, fairness, and affirmative action. *Journal of Vocational Behavior, 49*, 122–158.

Carter, S. L. (1992). *Reflections of an affirmative action baby*. New York: Basic Books.

Cascio, W. F., Alexander, R. A., & Barrett, G. V. (1988). Setting cutoff scores: Legal, psychometric, and professional issues and guidelines. *Personnel Psychology, 41*, 1–24.

Chagnon, N. A. (1997). *Yanomamö* (5th ed.). Fort Worth, TX: Harcourt College Publishers.

Cohn, A. (1997, November 10). The next great battle over affirmative action. *Time*, pp. 52–55.

Colarelli, S. M. (1996). Establishment and job context influence on the use of hiring practices. *Applied Psychology: An International Review, 45*, 153–176.

Colarelli, S. M., Alampay, M. R., & Canali, K. G. (2002). Letters of recommendation: An evolutionary perspective. *Human Relations, 55*, 315–344.

Colarelli, S. M., & Boos, A. L. (1992). Sociometric and ability-based assignment to workgroups: Some implications for personnel selection. *Journal of Organizational Behavior, 13*, 187–196.

Colarelli, S. M., Dean, R. A., & Konstans, C. (1991). The influence of college characteristics on early career outcomes of accountants. *Canadian Journal of Higher Education, 11*, 24–46. Abstracted in *Higher Education Abstracts* (1992), 28, 234.

Colarelli, S. M., & Dettmann, J. R. (in press). Intuitive evolutionary perspectives in marketing practices. *Psychology and Marketing*.

Coolidge, S. D. (1994, November 10). More accountants are women, but few find room at the top. *Christian Science Monitor*, p. 9.

Cosmides, L., & Tooby, J. (1992). Cognitive adaptations for social exchange. In Jerome H. Barkow, Leda Cosmides, & John Tooby (Eds.), *The adapted mind: Evolutionary psychology and the generation of culture*. (pp. 163–228). New York: Oxford University Press.

Cox, T. (1993). *Cultural diversity in organizations: Theory, research, and practice*. San Francisco: Berrett-Koehler.

Crouse, J., & Trusheim, D. (1986). *The case against the SAT*. Chicago: University of Chicago Press.

Cummins, D. D. (1996). Evidence for the innateness of deontic reasoning. *Mind & Language, 11*, 160–190.

Dale, S. B., & Krueger, A. B. (in press). Estimating the payoff to attending a more selective college: An application of selection on observables and unobservables. *Quarterly Journal of Economics.*

Dunbar, R.I.M. (1996). *Grooming, gossip and the evolution of language.* Cambridge, MA: Harvard University Press.

Executive Office of the President, Office of Management and Budget (2000, December 15). *Provisional guidance on the implementation of the 1997 standards for federal data on race and ethnicity.* Retrieved March 20, 2002, from the World Wide Web: *http://www.whitehouse.gov/omb/inforeg/r&e_guidance2000update.pdf.*

Feingold, A. (1994). Gender differences in personality: A meta-analysis. *Psychological Bulletin, 116,* 429–456.

Fiedler, F. E., & Garcia, J. E. (1987). *New approaches to leadership: Cognitive resources and organizational performance.* New York: John Wiley & Sons.

Friedman, T., & Williams, E. B. (1982). Current use of tests for employment. In Alexandra K. Wigdor and Wendall R. Garner (Eds.), *Ability Testing: Uses, consequences, and controversies* (pp. 99–169). Washington, DC: National Academy Press.

Galbraith, J. R. (1973). *Designing complex organizations.* Reading, MA: Addison-Wesley.

George, J. M. (1996). Trait and state affect. In K. R. Murphy (Ed.), *Individual differences and behavior in organizations* (pp. 145–171). San Francisco: Jossey-Bass.

Ghiselli, E. E. (1956). Dimensional problems of criteria. *Journal of Applied Psychology, 40,* 1–4.

Gillon, S. M. (2000). *"That's not what we meant to do": Reform and its unintended consequences in twentieth-century America.* New York: W. W. Norton.

Hamilton, W. D. (1964). The genetical evolution of social behavior: I and II. *Journal of Theoretical Biology, 7,* 1–52.

Hampshire, S. (2000). *Justice is conflict.* Princeton, NJ: Princeton University Press.

Harris, M. M. (1989). Reconsidering the employment interview: A review of recent literature and suggestions for future research. *Personnel Psychology, 42,* 691–726.

Hartigan, J. A., & Wigdor, A. K. (1989). *Fairness in employment testing: Validity generalization, minority issues, and the General Aptitude Test Battery.* Washington, DC: National Academy Press.

Harvey, R. J. (1991). Job analysis. In M. D. Dunnette and L. M. Hough (Eds.), *Handbook of industrial and organizational psychology* (Vol. 2, pp. 72–163). Palo Alto, CA: Consulting Psychologists Press.

Heilman, M. (1996). Affirmative action's contradictory consequences. *Journal of Social Issues, 52,* 105–109.

Henderson, G. (1994). *Cultural diversity in the workplace: Issues and strategies.* Westport, CT: Quorum Books.

Herrnstein, R. J., & Murray, C. (1994). *The bell curve: Intelligence and class structure in American life.* New York: Free Press.

Hoffman, L. R. (1959). Homogeneity of member personality and its effect on group problem-solving. *Journal of Abnormal and Social Psychology, 58,* 27–32.

Hoffman, L. R., & Maier, N.R.F. (1961). Quality and acceptance of problem solutions by members of homogeneous and heterogeneous groups. *Journal of Abnormal and Social Psychology, 62,* 401–407.

Hoffman, P. (1994, November). The science of race. *Discover, 4.*

Hogarth, R. M. (1980). Beyond discrete biases: Functional and dysfunctional aspects of judgmental heuristics. *Psychological Bulletin, 90,* 197–217.

Holzer, H., & Neumark, D. (2000). Assessing affirmative action. *Journal of Economic Literature, 38,* 483–568.

Hough, L. (1998). Personality at work: Issues and evidence. In *Beyond multiple choice: Evaluating alternatives to traditional testing for selection* (pp. 131–159). Hillsdale, NJ: Lawrence Erlbaum Associates.

Hulin, C. L., Henry, R. A., & Noon, S. L. (1990). Adding a dimension: Time as a factor in the generalizablity of the predictive relationships. *Psychological Bulletin, 107,* 328–340.

Hunter, J. E., Schmidt, F. L., & Judiesch, M. K. (1990). Individual differences in output as a function of job complexity. *Journal of Applied Psychology, 75,* 28–46.

Hyde, J. S., & Plant, E. A. (1995). Magnitude of psychological gender differences: Another side to the story. *American Psychologist, 50,* 159–161.

Jensen, A. R. (1998). *The g factor: The science of mental ability.* Westport, CT: Praeger.

Jensen, A. R. (1980). *Bias in mental testing.* New York: Free Press.

Journal of Career Planning & Employment. (1995, Spring), pp. 37–49.

Judge, T. A., & Higgins, C. A. (1998). Affective disposition and letters of reference. *Organizational Behavior and Human Decision Process, 75,* 207–221.

Kahneman, D., & Tversky, A. (1981, January). The psychology of preferences. *Scientific American,* pp. 160–173.

Klein, K. J., Dansereau, F., & Hall, R. J. (1994). Levels issues in theory development, data collection, and analysis. *Academy of Management Review, 19,* 195–229.

Klein, R. G. (1989). *The human career: Human biological and cultural origins.* Chicago: University of Chicago Press.

Klimoski, R. J., & Strickland, W. J. (1977). Assessment centers—Valid or mearly prescient? *Personnel Psychology, 30,* 353–361.

Klingsporn, M. J. (1973). The significance of variability. *Behavioral Science, 18,* 441–447.

Klitgaard, R. (1985). *Choosing elites: Selecting the "best and the brightest" at top universities and elsewhere*. New York: Basic Books.

Knouse, S. B. (1983). The letters of recommendation: Specificity and favorability of information. *Personnel Psychology, 36*, 331–341.

Kurzban, R., Cosmides, L., & Tooby, J. (1998). Cognitive ontologies: The role of race. Unpublished manuscript, University of Arizona at Tucson.

Lemann, N. (1999). *The big test: The secret history of American meritocracy*. New York: Farrar, Straus & Giroux.

Lemonick, M. D. (2000–2001, December 25–January 1). Gene mapper: The bad boy of science has jump-started a biological revolution. *Time*, pp. 110–113.

Maccoby, E. E. (1998). The two sexes: Growing up apart, coming together. Cambridge, MA: Belknap Press/Harvard University Press.

MacKinnon, D. W., & Hall, W. B. (1972). Intelligence and creativity. *Proceedings, XVIIth International Congress of Applied Psychology* (Vol. 2, pp. 1883–1888). Brussels: Editest.

Malkiel, B. G. (1985). *A Random walk down Wall Street* (4th ed.). New York: W. W. Norton.

Mangan, K. S. (2000, November 24). The unusual rules for affirmative action in medical schools. *Chronicle of Higher Education*, p. A57.

March, J. G. (1991). Exploration and exploitation in organizational learning. *Organizational Science, 2*, 71–87.

McDaniel, M. A., Whetzel, D. L., Schmidt, F. L., & Mauer, S. D. (1994). The validity of employment interviews: A comprehensive review and meta-analysis. *Journal of Applied Psychology, 79*, 599–616.

McWhorter, J. H. (2000). *Losing the race: Self-sabotage in Black America*. New York: Free Press.

Megarry, T. (1995). *Society in prehistory: The origins of human culture*. New York: New York University Press.

Miller, A. (2000). University of Michigan. In Steven R. Centola (Ed.), *Echoes down the corridor: Collected essays 1944–2000* (pp. 14–30). New York: Viking Press.

Moore, R. F. (1996). Caring for identified versus statistical lives: An evolutionary view of medical distributive justice. *Ethology and Sociobiology, 17*, 379–401.

Muchinsky, P. M. (1999). *Psychology applied to work: An introduction to industrial and organizational psychology*. Chicago: Dorsey Press.

Muchinsky, P. M. (1979). The use of reference reports in personnel selection: A review and evaluation. *Journal of Occupational Psychology, 52*, 287–297.

Murphy, K. R., Osten, K., & Myors, B. (1995). Modeling the effects of banding in personnel selection. *Personnel Psychology, 48*, 61–84.

Nisbett, R. E., & Cohen, D. (1996). *Culture of honor: The psychology of violence in the South*. Boulder, CO: Westview Press.

Profet, M. (1992). Pregnancy sickness as adaptation: A deterrent to maternal ingestion of teratogens. In J. H. Barkow, L. Cosmides, & J. Tooby (Eds.), *The adapted mind: Evolutionary psychology and the generation of culture* (pp. 327–365). New York: Oxford University Press.

Ravitch, D. (2000). *Left back: A century of failed school reforms.* New York: Simon & Schuster.

Reich, R. B. (1991). *The work of nations: Preparing ourselves for 21st-century capitalism.* New York. Alfred A. Knopf.

Reskin, B. F., & Roos, P. A. (1990). *Job queues, gender queues: Explaining women's inroads into male occupations.* Philadelphia: Temple University Press.

Rook, K. S. (1987). Effects of case history versus abstract information on health attitudes and behaviors. *Journal of Applied Social Psychology, 17,* 533–553.

Rowe, P. M. (1963). Individual difference in selection decision. *Journal of Applied Psychology, 47,* 304–307.

Sackett, P. R., & Wilk, S. L. (1994). Within-group norming and other forms of score adjustment in preemployment testing. *American Psychologist, 49,* 929–954.

Samuels, D. (2001, September 3). The runner. *New Yorker,* 72–85.

Schmidt, F. L., & Hunter, J. E. (1998). The validity and utility of selection methods in personnel psychology: Practical and theoretical implications of 85 years of research findings. *Psychological Bulletin, 124,* 262–274.

Schmidt, F. L., & Hunter, J. E. (1983). Individual differences in productivity: An empirical test of estimates derived from studies of selection procedure utility. *Journal of Applied Psychology, 68,* 407–414.

Schmidt, F. L., Hunter, J. E., Mckenzie, R. C., & Muldrow, T. W. (1979). Impact of valid selection procedures on work-force productivity. *Journal of Applied Psychology, 64,* 609–626.

Schmidt, P. (2001, December 14). Opposing sides argue their cases in key affirmative-action suit. *The Chronicle of Higher Education,* pp. A24–A25.

Schneider, B. (1996). When individual differences aren't. In K. R. Murphy (Ed.), *Individual differences and behavior in organizations* (pp. 548–571). San Francisco: Jossey-Bass.

Schneider, B. (1987). The people make the place. *Personnel Psychology, 40,* 437–453.

Scott, W. R. (1998). *Organizations: Rational, natural, and open systems* (4th ed.). Engelwood Cliffs, NJ: Prentice Hall.

Selingo, J. (2002, January 11). Critics blast plan to expand class-rank policy in Texas as affirmative-action ploy. *Chronicle of Higher Education,* pp. A29–30.

Sheehan, E. P., McDevitt, T. M., & Ross, H. C. (1998). Looking for a job as a psychology professor? Factors affecting applicant success. *Teaching of Psychology, 25,* 8–11.

Sheppard, R. L., Jr. (1997). Differential item functioning in the Hogan Personality Inventory. Unpublished doctoral dissertation, Central Michigan University.

Shreve, J. (1994, November). Terms of estrangement. *Discover,* 57–63.

Skrentny, J. D. (1996). *The ironies of affirmative action: Politics, culture, and justice in America.* Chicago: University of Chicago Press.

Sowell, T. (1995). *The vision of the anointed: Self-congratulation as a basis for social policy.* New York: Basic Books.

Spaid, E. L. (1993, July 13). Glass ceiling remains thick at companies' top levels. *The Christian Science Monitor,* pp. 9, 12.

Steiner, D. D., & Gilliland, S. W. (1996). Fairness reactions to personnel selection techniques in France and the United States. *Journal of Applied Psychology, 81,* 134–141.

Steward, G. L. (1999). Trait bandwidth and stages of job performance: Assessing differential effects for conscientiousness and its subtraits. *Journal of Applied Psychology, 84,* 959–968.

Sturm, S., & Guinier, L. (1996). Future of affirmative action: Reclaiming the innovative ideal. *California Law Review, 84,* 953–1036.

Sugiyama, M. S. (2001). Food, foragers, and folklore: The role of narrative in human subsistence. *Evolution and Human Behavior, 22,* 221–240.

Tajfel, H. (Ed.). (1982). *Social identity and intergroup relations.* New York: Cambridge University Press.

Taleb, N. N. (2001). *Fooled by randomness: The hidden role of chance in the markets and in life.* New York: Texere.

Taylor, S. E. (1991). Asymmetrical effects of positive and negative events: The mobilization-minimization hypothesis. *Psychological Bulletin, 110,* 67–85.

Toor, R. (2001). *Admissions confidential: An insider's account of the elite selection process.* New York: St. Martin's Press.

Valian, V. (1997). *Why so slow? The advancement of women.* Cambridge, MA: MIT Press.

Van Zelst, R. H. (1951). Job satisfaction and the interpersonally desirable worker. *Personnel Psychology, 4,* 405–412.

Van Zelst, R. H. (1952). Sociometrically selected work teams increase production. *Personnel Psychology, 5,* 175–186.

Van Zelst, R. H. (1952). Validation of a sociometric regrouping procedure. *Journal of Abnormal and Social Psychology, 47,* 299–301.

Vines, G. (1995, July 8). Genes in black and white. *New Scientist,* pp. 34–37.

Webster, E. C. (1964). *Decision making in the employment interview.* Montreal: Eagle.

Wexley, K. N., Alexander, R. A., & Greenawalt, J. P. (1980). Attitudinal congruence and similarity as related to interpersonal evaluations in manager-subordinate dyads. *Academy of Management Journal, 23,* 320–330.

Williams, G. C. (1996). *Plan and purpose in nature.* London: Weidenfeld & Nicolson.

Wolpoff, M., & Caspari, R. (1997). *Race and human evolution.* New York: Simon & Schuster.

Wood, W. (1987). Meta-analytic review of sex differences in group performance. *Psychological Bulletin, 102,* 53–71.

Zand, D. E. (1972). Trust and managerial problem solving. *Administrative Science Quarterly, 17,* 229–239.

CHAPTER 5

Look! We're Modern
Training People

Dear fellow-artist, why so free
With every sort of company,
With every Jack and Jill?
Choose your companions from the best;
Who draws a bucket with the rest
Soon topples down the hill . . .
There is not a fool can call me friend,
And I may dine at journey's end
With Landor and with Donne.
> —William Butler Yeats (*To a Young Beauty*, 1918/1962)

The surest and fastest way to improve is by playing with better players.
> —Faye Young Miller and Wayne Coffey (1992, p. 7)

You play as you practice.
> —Red Auerbach (2000, p. 114)

TRAINING PARADOXES

We admire people who are skillful and people who are educated. Most of us want to become more skillful, want our children to become educated and skillful, and we want better schools and training programs.

Yet, the incessant debates about education and training in the United States reveal a problem: deep uncertainty about how people become educated and skillful. This is why training and education are beset with paradoxes. One paradox is that, although our society makes a national obsession out of the "importance of education" (who gets it, who doesn't, how much money is spent on it, how we compare with other nations), many people become successful despite their lack of educational credentials. Formal education is neither necessary nor sufficient for success in a variety of fields.[1]

Sidney Poitier is an example from the arts. He is one of the great actors and film stars of the twentieth century, yet he did not complete high school. Poitier grew up in poverty in the British West Indies and left school at age 13 (Poitier, 2000). In business, there are numerous examples of successful people in almost every area of business who have no formal education in business. Bill Gates, the founder of Microsoft, is a college dropout. He left Harvard University after two years, when he was barely 20 years old, to found Microsoft (Isaacson, 1997). Yet Gates is one of the richest men in the world with a personal fortune of over $52.8 billion (as of February 2002; Kroll & Goldman, 2002), and Microsoft is one of the most influential corporations in the world. On the low-tech end, Gino Pala, the CEO of Dixon Ticonderoga, dropped out of high school in the eleventh grade. Dixon Ticonderoga is the second largest pencil maker in the United States; it shipped about 2.2 billion pencils domestically in 1998 (Carrns, 2000). There are many others. Andrew Carnegie (the founder and former CEO of U.S. Steel), Dave Thomas (founder and former CEO of Wendy's Hamburgers), Ray Kroc (founder and former CEO of McDonald's Hamburgers), and Richard Branson (founder and former CEO of Virgin Records) did not graduate from high school. Ted Turner (founder of CNN), Steve Jobs (founder and CEO of Apple Computer), Tom Monahan (founder and former CEO of Domino's Pizza), and Michael Dell (founder and CEO of Dell Computer) are all college dropouts.

A recent advertisement in the *New Yorker* Magazine for the MBA program at the Yale School of Management offers a deliciously ironic example of the paradoxical nature of returns from formal education (*New Yorker*, 2001). It featured a bold heading, "Look Who's Coming to the Yale School of Management." Under it was a list of 12 business luminaries, including Warren Buffett, Michael Dell, Rupert Murdoch, George Soros, Jack Welch, two presidents of large nonprofit organizations, and two academics. The connotation of the advertisement was, "You too can be a successful business person if you earn an MBA from the Yale School of Management." I had a hunch that most of these luminaries did not have MBA degrees. So I checked on their backgrounds. Only three had earned an MBA (none from Yale). Perhaps a more suitable title for the ad would be: "Look Who Didn't Attend Yale," or "Look Who Doesn't Have an MBA," or "You Really Don't Need an MBA to Succeed in Business."

A second paradox is the fact that highly skilled performance can come about in areas of the world where modern training methods are generally unavailable. Training is a multibillion dollar industry in the United States that employs all sorts of training professionals with college degrees in education and human resource management. The training industry is obsessed with using what it considers advanced training methods. Many universities in the United States have departments, programs, or courses dedicated to training. These include education departments, human resource management programs in business schools, and industrial psychology programs in psychology departments. Many in the training (and education) industry believe that people who are not exposed to the most advanced training methods and technologies will be left behind. Witness the obsession with computers in the classroom (Cuban, 2001). Yet, despite all the new training technologies and money devoted to the design of effective training programs, people can, and do, learn complex skills without formal instruction. The best example is language (Pinker, 1994). The language skills of the average five-year-old are remarkable. By the time most children reach age five, they have 2,500-word vocabularies and they speak in complete sentences (Health Information Library, 1998). Children learn language by imitating others around them. Despite the ease with which nearly all children learn language, scientists and engineers still cannot make a machine that can recognize, understand, and speak a natural language as well as a five-year-old.

People sometimes learn complex and unusual skills without modern mechanistic training methods. Consider Kenyan long-distance runners. In the mid-1960s, Kenya emerged as a world power in men's middle- and long-distance running.

> No other country compares with Kenyan Olympic success in the men's middle and long distance events since 1968, even considering the fact that Kenya did not compete in the 1976 and 1980 Games. The total medal haul since 1968 is 12 gold, 14 silver, and 8 bronze in the six Olympics Kenya competed in 1968–1996, with at least one gold medal at each Games. (Tanser, 1997, p. 17)

Tanser also points out that, by world standards, Kenya is a poor, underdeveloped country. Its per capita gross domestic product is $1,170 (compared to $27,607 for the United States). There is one TV set for every 106 people, one car for every 180 people. The training of Kenyan runners is low tech. There are few electronic gadgets to monitor runners' heart rates or running form; water and a simple diet are the rule rather than sports drinks, designer diets, and nutritional supplements. Most surprising, some of the most successful track coaches in Kenya had no formal training as coaches or in track and field (Tanser, 1997/1998).

A similar pattern occurs with baseball players from the Dominican Republic. The Dominican Republic is a poor, underdeveloped country on a small Caribbean island. Modern mechanistic training methods, sports psychologists, and high tech training devices do not play a great, if any, role in baseball training there. Yet the "Dominican Republic has produced more professional and major league baseball players than any country apart from the United States, and proportionately more players than any country including the United States" (Klein, 1991, p. 2). No serious student of training can ignore these examples. We must come to grips with the fact that world-class skills can be learned without the presumed benefits of training designed by human resource experts. Such examples illustrate the need for more *reverse engineering* of training—locating proficient people and understanding how they got that way. We need to learn more about how effective systems evolved and what makes them work.

A third paradox is that a nation's wealth, the quality of its universities, and the eminence of its scientists and scholars do not necessarily translate into skilled performance at lower levels. On the one hand, the United States, with an annual gross domestic product of over $9 trillion in the late twentieth century, is the wealthiest country in the world (Central Intelligence Agency, 2000). By many estimates, it leads the world in science and engineering. The United States has produced the most Nobel laureates in science; it produces more Ph.D.s in science and engineering than any country in the world. In 1997, for example, U.S. universities awarded about 27,000 doctoral degrees in science and engineering, twice as many as any other country in the world (National Science Board, 2000). American universities are the envy of the world. More foreign students come to U.S. universities to train in science and engineering than anywhere else in the world (Center for Educational Research and Innovation, 1997). On the other hand, the performance of students in the United States on standardized tests in mathematics tests is middling compared to students in a host of other countries—including those with less wealth, poorer university systems, and less scientific manpower. The Third International Math and Science Study, completed in 1999, found that of 180,000 eight graders in 38 nations, American students were in the middle of the pack (Schemo, 2000). They performed "worse in math and science than students in Singapore, Taiwan, Russia, Canada, Finland, Hungary, the Netherlands and Australia" but did better than students from Iran, Jordan, and Macedonia (Schemo, 2000, p. A1). These results replicated the middling performance of American middle school and high school students found in a similar survey completed four years earlier. In that survey American twelfth graders "lagged far behind students in most other nations in [science and math]" (Schemo, 2000, p. A18). Despite the increased importance of a high school education, the high school completion rate for the country has been static over the last quarter century. The rate fluctuated around 84 percent between 1973 and 1983. There has been a net increase of only 3 percent in the high school graduation rates in the United States in the past 29 years (Kaufman, Alt, & Chapman, 2001). This is not encouraging. On average, a high school diploma in the early twenty-first century does not demonstrate the same level of basic knowledge and skill that it did in the middle of the twentieth century (Ravitch, 2000). These facts also suggest that modern mechanistic training methods do not hold the key to development of ability and skill. Something more basic which does not require inordinate resources is occurring in other countries where students outperform the United States.

A fourth paradox is the training pulpit. Leaders in government and business often speak about the importance of training; "our people are our most valuable resource," they proclaim. Leaders drone on and on about how important it is to invest in training (Gutek, 1991; Ravitch, 2000). Yet, the hard numbers belie that shibboleth. Eighty-nine percent of American corporations offer no formal training to nonmanagement employees (Labor Letter, 1991). Most organizations do not analyze the need for training or evaluate training programs (Saari, Johnson, McLaughlin, & Zimmerle, 1988). American investment and participation in training pales compared to that of many other industrialized countries (Stone, 1991). The per capita expenditure on training among U.S. employers as of 1995 was only $647 (Frazis, Gittleman, Horrigan, & Joyce, 1998).

These paradoxes stem from regarding good training as synonymous with modern training technology, pinning our hopes on modern mechanistic training methods, and ignoring traditional training practices and the social and psychological bases from which they evolved. Something right is going on with traditional training practices. In this chapter, I will describe and critique the mechanistic model of training, present the beginnings of a theory of training based on an evolutionary perspective, and describe approaches to training that are grounded in an evolutionary perspective. First, however, I will define what I mean by training and other key terms used throughout this chapter.

Some Definitions

Training is the systematic acquisition and maintenance of skills and task-specific knowledge. A *skill* is a behavior or mental operation that is instrumental to the performance of a task or set of related tasks. Shooting baskets, using a word processing program, hanging a door, teaching a class, and negotiating a contract are all types of skills. They involve behaviors that produce a particular result (e.g., points in a basketball game, a typed letter, an installed door that opens and closes properly, students who are attentive and who learn something, and an acceptable contract). *Education*, on the other hand, is the systematic acquisition of abilities, general knowledge, and attitudes. An *ability* involves behaviors or mental operations that are instrumental for adapting to a variety of environmental demands. Facility with mathematics, navigation, music, and language are abilities. *Aptitude* is an innate propensity to acquire particular abilities and skills. A person with an aptitude for, say, mathematics has a constellation of genes and experience that happen to be useful for doing mathematics.

Training and education, though related, are not the same thing. The same is true of skills and abilities. Education is about developing abilities and general knowledge, whereas training is about developing skills. Humans are born with some primary abilities, such as counting, navigation, and language. Many of our abilities, however, are *secondary* abilities that require years of education to develop. We do not have an inborn capacity to acquire secondary abilities—such as advanced mathematics, reading, writing, and science—because they are evolutionarily novel (Geary, 1995). Developing complex secondary abilities takes years of learning. Much of this development occurs through years of exposure to kin in the home and to peers. In many societies, it also involves years of schooling. Skills are developed on a foundation of abilities, and most skills take a shorter period to develop than abilities. Because skills are related to specific tasks, the best place to learn skills is the place where one will be performing the particular task, such as the workplace.[2]

Training develops consistency of behavior or outcomes. If we are training checkout clerks in a store to ring up merchandise accurately and quickly and to be friendly to customers, we want the clerks to perform those behaviors consistently. Education, though concerned with consistency on a general level, is also concerned with variability. Education focuses on consistency with respect to general knowledge and principles.

People educated in different countries but in the same subject (for example, biology) can converse with one another about their field and understand each other. However, another goal of education is to create variability—to encourage people to apply their own individual interests and creative talents to general principles. When students write a term paper in a college class, the professor expects each paper to reflect each student's own ideas about the subject matter, though based on a common understanding of general principles. Most colleges and universities expect that their graduating classes are composed of people with a wide variety of talents and abilities who also share a common knowledge of the arts and sciences. However, when students attend a training class, the instructor expects that they will all learn to perform the skill in the same way. Students in a beginning rock-climbing course are all expected to know how to wear a safety harness and tie a rope to the harness in an identical, proper manner.

MECHANISTIC AND TRADITIONAL MODELS OF TRAINING

The mechanistic model of training is a *forward engineering* model. With forward engineering the engineer designs a technology to do something, to achieve a specific goal. Forward engineering begins with a problem and applies principles from science and engineering to develop a new technology or to re-fit existing technologies to solve the specific problem. Forward engineering has worked reasonably well in the hard sciences. It has not worked as well in the social sciences because, as I have argued in Chapter 2, social systems are too complex and loosely coupled to allow even the most meticulously designed interventions to produce consistently intended results.

The mechanistic model of training is an application of forward engineering to training. The model contains three major steps: (1) needs analysis, (2) training design, and (3) training evaluation. Needs analysis is the systematic analysis of where in an organization training is needed and what kind of training is needed. Here is where the goal or problem is identified. Professionals use the methods of social science to determine whether a need for training exists and to propose appropriate training programs (Robinson & Robinson, 1989). Once needs have been identified, the training programs are designed, using social science knowledge to address the problems and goals identified in the analysis. The design of training involves everything that takes place in recruiting trainees and training them. Human resource experts, often in conjunction with managers, play the primary role in training design (Noe, 1999;

Robinson & Robinson, 1989). Finally, using a scientific methodology, experts typically evaluate the training to ensure that adequate data are collected and that the data are interpreted correctly.

Distinctions between Traditional and Mechanistic Training Methods

Most writers on training do not discuss the distinctions between traditional and mechanistic models of training; instead, their focus is on developing, evaluating, and applying mechanistic methods. However, here the concern is with distinctions between the two models. How people view paradigms of training has a significant influence on their expectations for training and how training is designed.

The Characteristics of Traditional Training Methods

Traditional training methods are those that arose *before* the advent of academic psychology, applied social science, and the electronic transmission of information and images. They are methods that humans have used over the millennia to teach skills, primarily to children and young adults. Traditional methods have four characteristics. They involve face-to-face interaction, spoken communication, direct observation, and extended periods of time. Humans evolved in small groups where people gathered information and learned about their physical and social environments from observation and face-to-face interaction. It is highly probable that over our evolutionary history, psychological mechanisms evolved that are receptive to information acquired from conversation and observation and that are efficient when processing those types of information. As a method of training, face-to-face interaction allows continuous and extensive feedback about performance. Instructors can continually monitor the students' execution of skills, their emotional states, their level of motivation, their rate of progress, and their energy level. It also permits regular rewards and punishments. A smile or a frown, a word of praise or criticism, helps to keep students on track and motivated. Face-to-face interactions in combination with verbal instruction and extended periods of practice allow students and instructors to develop a rapport with one another, learn about each other's personalities, and develop a master–student relationship.

People learn by watching and imitating other people (Bandura, 1977; Boyd & Richerson, 1985). It is easier to learn most skills by imitating people who are competent at them than by reading a description of each element of skillful performance. Imitation and observation are key components of the psychological and biological processes that enable children to learn the complex skill of spoken language. Many top athletes train in camps with other top athletes where they are able to watch how superior athletes perform, learn, and train (Tanser, 1997/1998). Watching skillful performers not only allows students to imitate effective performance routines, but it also helps them learn about the habits, motivations, and identities of skillful performers (Lave & Wenger, 1991). Athletes can observe and imitate how other athletes eat, how much they rest and sleep, their level of commitment, how they view themselves, and the intensity of their training.

These are the attributes of traditional training methods. Training methods that embody these attributes include on-the-job training, mentoring and coaching, apprenticeships, and lecture-and-discussion. All of these methods involve, in varying degrees, face-to-face interaction, verbal communication, observation, and extended periods of time. Apprenticeship, mentoring, and coaching typically involve the highest levels of sustained personal contact and indirect benefits.[3] With these three methods, students are in the company of a master or trainer who works closely with them—talking to them, motivating them, and modeling skilled performance. On-the-job training is catch-is-as-catch-can. If students are fortunate enough to be in the company of skilled performers, of people who take an interest in them and provide feedback, then on-the-job training can often embody the best attributes of the traditional methods. Lecture-and-discussion is the least intense of traditional methods. Lectures often are viewed as hopelessly old fashioned and ineffective. However, good lectures and relatively small classes allow face-to-face interaction, ample verbal communication, and observation. Practice and coaching are difficult to provide in a lecture setting. However, good lecturers can engage students personally in discussion, use motivating phrases, and get a sense of how well students are learning. They also demonstrate skills and attitudes that students can imitate—such as organized thinking, logical argument, clear presentation, educated speech patterns and good public speaking skills, concentration, enthusiasm for a subject, civility, and interest in other people's concerns.

Characteristics of Mechanical Training Methods

Mechanical training methods depend on academic or other experts for their underlying rationale and curriculum design. They assume that content has little effect on the nature of training and training design and that training is decontextual. The presumption is that training programs should proceed from formal psychological and educational theories rather than from common sense or ordinary knowledge. Ordinary people—those without specialized knowledge of these theories—are presumed to be unqualified to be involved in the design, execution, or evaluation of training and education. Mechanical training methods should work well, regardless of the content of the training. If the proper information is presented and the correct behaviors are rewarded, just about anything can be learned. Similarly, the context of training—where or how information is delivered—is not too important.

PROBLEMS WITH THE MECHANISTIC TRAINING MODEL

From an evolutionary perspective, the mechanical training model has five significant problems. First, it overemphasizes explicit, rationally derived goals. Second, it does not acknowledge or allow for flexibility and serendipity in the development of training methods and systems, even though these processes are critical in the adaptive learning processes in organizations. A third problem is the assumption that professionally developed training methods are superior to traditional training methods. Fourth, mechanical training ignores how content affects learning. And the fifth problem is that the mechanical model pays little attention to the context in which learning takes place. I view these as problems because they are areas where an evolutionary perspective would add to a more complete understanding of the psychology of training. The first two problems involve the relations between training and the larger social systems in which training programs operate. The last three concern the individual and the psychology of learning.

Failing to Acknowledge Problems with Explicit, Rationally derived Goals

Explicit goals are a core component of the mechanically driven training model. This is why the analysis of training needs is a major emphasis (Gagne, 1962; Goldstein, 1980). The basic logic is that clear goals are necessary for effective training. The outcome that one expects from the training program becomes the basis for evaluating the program. One cannot evaluate a training program unless one first specifies the expected outcomes. A needs analysis generates these goals. "Goals and objectives are the key steps in determining a training environment" (Goldstein, 1993, p. 29).

The Latent Functions of Training

In many cases, it makes perfect sense to develop training goals and to conduct an analysis of needs. Yet, organizations should not conduct training sessions *only* if they meet a clear, explicit goal that was derived from a thorough analysis of training needs. Training programs serve useful functions *other* than those based on the goals derived from a needs analysis. Training programs often have latent functions that are useful. Training programs can serve ceremonial functions that inculcate organizationally appropriate values and norms (Belasco & Trice, 1969; Trice, Belasco, & Alutto, 1969). Requiring that employees or students take particular types of courses signals that these areas of knowledge or skill are highly valued. When an organization requires employees to take courses in creativity and problem solving, this signals the value of creativity and problem-solving skills. Values can also be communicated in ways that are incidental to the stated purpose of the training program. When organizations send employees to training programs, this often signals that the organization cares about the employee (Such, 1997). Spending lavishly or frugally on training also communicates values. Training can function as a signal as to how supervisors regard employees. Employees get an implicit message about how well they are doing if their supervisor sends them to a remedial training program or to a posh seminar for people on the "fast track." Training can also stimulate new ideas and expand employees' networks of potentially useful contacts when they interact with people from different backgrounds during training sessions.

Training programs can also improve skills and abilities *other* than those the training program is explicitly designed to improve (Rauscher et al., 1997). Many parents know that learning one skill often enhances others; therefore they enroll their children in all sorts of lessons in the arts and sports. A recent study of American children found that 64 percent play an organized sport and 36 percent take music, dance, drama, or art lessons (McGrath, 1998). Most parents do not expect their children to become professional musicians, dancers, or athletes, but they understand the importance of these lessons. Childhood lessons are probably a cultural fixture because of the *other* skills, abilities, and attitudes that the lessons develop. Dancing, tennis, violin, piano lessons—in addition to teaching dancing, tennis, violin, and piano—also teach young people about practice, persistence, competition, and so on. Knowing how to practice with the specific intent of improving a particular behavior is useful, regardless of the skill it was learned on (Ericsson & Lehmann, 1996). A young woman who took ice skating lessons as a girl probably learned many things that will stay with her for years after she hangs up her skates: good motor coordination, the importance of being physically fit, knowledge that consistent and deliberate practice will lead to improvement; the realization that there will always be other people more and less talented than herself; the importance of developing a network of associations with peers and experts; the importance of a good teacher; how to compete with and learn from peers; how to motivate oneself to work at a task even when one does not feel like working; and how thinking about one's self (e.g., personal identity, self-esteem, belief in one's abilities) affects learning a skill.

Perhaps managers also have a tacit understanding of the complex relations between training and skills. Although studies show that most managers take a cavalier attitude to training fads and needs analysis (Campbell, 1971; Saari et al., 1988), they may use them at times because they believe that employees will still learn something of value even though the explicit purpose of the training program is questionnable.

Conflicting Goals

An emphasis on a training program's explicit goal can also be problematic because it may compete with other goals. Unfortunately, the mechanical training model does not account for this. It assumes that: (1) goals in organizations are compatible and (2) there is a synchronous hierarchy of goals throughout organizational levels. However, as I argued in Chapters 2 and 3, organizations (and small groups) consist of individuals and units with their own interests and values, and there is inevitably conflict between the values of one unit and those of another. Conflict among goals also occurs in training programs. A goal attached to a training program by one group is likely to be in conflict with what another group believes the goal should be. Similarly, the goals of training programs often do not support larger organizational goals.

Consider the web-based training that is becoming common at many universities. There are multiple interests and goals associated with web-based education in universities (Noble, 1996). University presidents may support web-based courses because they believe that by doing so they are keeping up with change, staying competitive in the marketplace, creating an image of a technologically current institution, and increasing the university's revenue stream by reaching students who cannot physically attend the university. University professors, on the other hand, may oppose the widespread use of web-based education because they believe that students do not perform as well with web courses, it is more difficult to control cheating, and web courses threaten their job security. The university's computer services staff will probably view web-based courses favorably because web courses enhance their power and job security. Undergraduate students in the 18- to 22-age-range may oppose web-based classes because web courses do not give them the opportunity to meet other students and to get personal face-to-face attention and feedback from professors. Adult students, on the other hand, may favor them because they make it easier for them to earn a college degree while working full time and raising a family. Vendors who sell computers and software to universities will be supportive of expanded web-based courses because more web courses mean more sales and larger profits.

Or consider the possibly conflicting training goals of managers and ambitious employees. The employees' goals are to acquire marketable skills and sell them to the highest bidder; this conflicts with the managers' goals of quickly training new employees for work *at their company*. When employees leave a company soon after training, the company is left to foot the training bill. Such conflicting goals may be a reason many companies do not invest heavily in training employees.

Failing to Acknowledge the Importance of Serendipity and Flexibility in Training

A problem with the mechanically driven model is that it is designed to *reduce variation* (Patrick, 1992). Deviations from prescribed methods and techniques that produce intended results are viewed as inappropriate. However, deviations from prescribed training procedures and methods can be beneficial. Rarely is there one best way. Useful training programs can come from sources other than deliberate needs analyses by professional instructional designers. Fads and other forms of imitation inject variation into organizations that may serendipitously prove to be useful. By trying various training methods, including some whose utility has not been proved, organizations increase their chances of hitting upon valuable new methods. Imitation is also adaptive by serving as a source of variation from which efficient new training technologies can develop (Alchian, 1950). New programs sometimes originate through imperfect copies of other programs. Imperfect imitations may unwittingly acquire new attributes that lead to the development of different types of programs. Similarly, an organization may copy a training practice that is not effective in the organization that was using it, but because the context of the imitating organization is different, the practice may turn out to be successful there. Instituting training programs without the formal needs analysis can also be beneficial by cushioning the effects of a changing environment. Organizations that experiment with a variety of training programs are more likely to develop a variety of skills in their employees. Although some of those skills may not be useful at the time they were learned, they may be useful under changed circumstances.

Failing to Acknowledge the Importance
of Traditional Training Methods

Most discussions of traditional training methods are humdrum. The following is typical:

> Before beginning a discussion of the more specific [i.e., expert-developed] instructional approaches, it is important to consider the two most frequently used general [i.e., traditional] procedures—on-the-job training and the lecture method. Valid information about the utility of these two procedures is not readily available. Everyone uses these methods, but they are rarely investigated except when they are employed as a control procedure for research exploring another technique. Even in those cases, the discussion of results centers on the "new" technique. (Goldstein, 1993, p. 227)

However, when discussing new methods, the tone changes from blasé to enthusiastic. Goldstein (1993) is effusive over computer-assisted instruction (CAI), averring that it "has tremendous potential" (p. 245).[4]

One way to think about the relative importance researchers give to traditional training methods is to compare the number of pages devoted to traditional and other (typically high-tech and expert driven) methods in books on training. Goldstein (1993) devotes about 11 percent (five pages) of his chapter on instructional methods to traditional training methods (on-the-job training [OJT], lecture, apprenticeship), and he devotes the remaining 89 percent (41 pages) to other methods (e.g., programmed instruction, CAI, videodiscs, machine simulators). Noe (1999) devotes a little over 10 percent (five pages) of his two chapters on training methods to the traditional methods of lecture, OJT, and apprenticeships. The remaining 90 percent (43 pages) include other methods (such as virtual reality, intelligent tutoring systems, and distance learning). Goldstein and Ford (2002) give 22 percent (9 pages) to traditional methods and 78 percent (about 32 pages) to other methods. Ironically, despite all the ink Goldstein and Ford spill on high-tech training methods, Ford dedicates the book to a pair of decidedly traditional trainers: his parents. Patrick (1992) does not even include the terms *apprenticeship*, *lecture*, and *on-the-job* in the index of his textbook on training, while there are 17 entries under the word "computer." He devotes an entire chapter to computers and training and another chapter to simulations.

Although traditional methods merit meager attention, they are widely used; despite the considerable attention given to mechanical methods, they often do not produce better results than traditional methods. Often, they produce dysfunctional, unintended outcomes (e.g., Ravitch, 2000). Lecture and discussion in the classroom and OJT are still the most widely used training methods. One recent survey found that 94 percent of companies use the classroom method (*Industry Report,* 1997). OJT is more difficult to define and measure. However, if we define OJT as any instance where one employee shows another employee how to perform a task or where an employee learns by observing and imitating a more skillful employee, then OJT is probably used in all organizations. In one attempt to quantify the relative use of OJT, Carnevale (1989) reports that American companies spend $180 billion on OJT but only $30 billion on formal training.

High-tech training methods often result in no greater learning than the lecture method or OJT (Goldstein, 1993). There is little evidence that web-based courses produce more effective learning than traditional methods. Some studies suggest that learners prefer traditional classroom methods and that people may be less inclined to practice new material with web methods (Brown, 2001; Zielinski, 2000). In a sweeping historical survey of the educational methods and movements used in the public schools in the United States in the twentieth century, Ravitch (2000) argues that most of the "new" educational methods introduced in the schools throughout the century *lowered* the overall quality of education and limited high-quality education to only a small proportion of students. She writes:

> If there is a lesson to be learned from the river of ink that was spilled in the education disputes of the twentieth century, it is that anything in education that is labeled a "movement" should be avoided like the plague. What American education most needs is not more nostrums and enthusiasms but more attention to fundamental, time-tested truths. (2000, p. 453)

Failing to Acknowledge the Effects of Content on Learning

Much of the literature on education in the twentieth century was based on assumptions from behaviorism and cognitive psychology. Their influence is evident in the summaries in training textbooks on the "principles of learning" (e.g., Goldstein, 1993; Noe, 1999). The implication, of course, is that training programs are likely to be most effective when they apply these principles. Some of the assumptions of behaviorism and cognitive psychology are valid enough. People are likely to repeat and learn behaviors that are rewarded. They learn by observation, and they are more likely to imitate high-status than low-status individuals. The analysis of tasks has also had an important effect on how psychologists think about training and instructional design—training must focus on *what* is to be learned. Training is more likely to produce desired learning when it emphasizes the tasks embedded in skillful performance (Gagne, 1962). Yet standard principles of learning and training task analysis make two problematic assumptions: *equipotentiality* and the *contiguity principle* (Garcia & Koelling, 1966). Equipotentiality is the concept that "the mechanisms of learning are the same regardless of the stimuli, responses, or reinforcers" (Buss, 1999, p. 25; see also Domjan, 1997). The contiguity principle states that "reinforcement will be more powerful if it is followed closely in time and space (and hence contiguous with) the behavior that is being reinforced" (Buss, 1999, p. 27).

The principle of equipotentiality holds that learning occurs in the same way regardless of the content of what is learned. Yet, common everyday experience as well as experimental evidence indicates that this is not true. Humans learn to like sweet foods much more readily than bitter ones. It doesn't take much experience to acquire a taste for sweet chocolate, whereas it takes a while to acquire a taste for martinis (many people never do). It is difficult to teach most children to eat green vegetables, whereas it takes little effort to teach them to respond favorably to mashed potatoes and apple juice. Elsie Bregman (1934) demonstrated the failure of the equipotentiality principle when she replicated—with minor modifications—John Watson's famous "Little Albert" study. Watson had conditioned a young child, "Albert," to respond fearfully to a white rat by pairing the white rat with a loud noise every time the child saw the rat (Watson & Rayner, 1920). Although the child was not initially afraid of the rat, he soon became fearful of the animal after repeated presentations of the rat were accompanied by a loud noise. Watson claimed that this study demonstrated that people could be conditioned to learn virtually any behavior. Bregman's (1934) study was identical in all respects but one: instead of using a white rat, she paired the loud noises with inanimate objects, such as wooden blocks. Despite numerous attempts with various objects on 15 different infants, none of the infants became fearful of the inanimate objects. This was one of the first studies to suggest that learning rates differ by stimuli.

Scientific research and everyday experience illustrate that the contiguity principle does not always hold. Some associations persist, and persist strongly, even when separated by time and space. Psychologist John Garcia and his colleagues conducted a series of brilliant experiments showing that the contiguity and equipotentiality principles are not universal. Garcia fed rats and then exposed them to radiation, which made the rats sick. Based on this one trial, the rats learned to avoid the food, even though they did not become ill until several hours after they ate it (Garcia, Ervin, & Koelling, 1966). Most people have also had the experience of becoming ill several hours after eating a particular type of food. They then find the smell or sight of the food nauseating for years. Bad stuffing at a Thanksgiving meal put me off stuffing for five years. In another study, Garcia paired visual and auditory stimuli with nausea, but the rats did not learn to avoid the visual and auditory stimuli. Rats, as Buss notes, "seem to come into the world 'pre-programmed' to learn some things easily, such as to avoid foods linked with nausea, but find it extraordinarily difficult to learn other things, such as to avoid buzzers and lights that are linked with nausea" (1999, p. 27). This makes adaptive sense because rats primarily use their sense of taste to hunt for food (Rozin & Kalat, 1971). Birds, on the other hand, rely primarily on vision to hunt for food, and—unlike rats—will develop a food aversion based on the sight of a tainted food (Nicolaus et al., 1983).

As these studies make abundantly clear, each species has its unique nature, and the nature of each species influences how readily it can learn different behaviors. All species seem to learn some things more readily than others. One of my favorite examples of this notion is illustrated by Jared Diamond's (1997) explanation for why so few large animals were domesticated before the twentieth century. Of the world's 148 wild, terrestrial mammals that were candidates for domestication—in terms of availability, size, muscle power, milk, and meat—humans were able to domesticate only 14. The major five are the sheep, goat, cow, pig, and horse; the minor nine are the Arabian (one-humped) and Bactrian (two-humped) camels, llama, donkey, reindeer, water buffalo, yak, Bali cattle, and mithan. A number of major attempts were made in the nineteenth and twentieth centuries to domesticate the moose, zebra, and elk, but they all failed. Why have so few species proven amenable to domestication and others destined to remain wild? Diamond gives a number of reasons, but the major one is that it is hard to train some animals to behave in ways that are contrary to their evolved propensities.[5] The failure in domesticating the zebra is particularly amusing. Other than its stripes, the zebra appears similar to the horse and donkey, and one would think that it would have been an ideal candidate for domestication. However, zebras have a nasty disposition. They have a tendency to bite humans and not let go. Indeed, more American zoo-keepers are injured by zebras every year than by tigers. In addition, zebras are difficult to lasso, "even for cowboys who win rodeo championships by lassoing horses—because of their unfailing ability to watch the rope noose fly toward them and then to duck their head out of the way" (Diamond, 1997, p. 172).

Different species evolved in different niches; thus, they developed abilities that are useful for surviving and reproducing in those niches:

"Learning is part of the adaptive pattern of a species and can be understood only when it is seen as the process of acquiring *skills . . . that are of evolutionary significance* to a species when living in the environment to which it is adapted" (Washburn, Jay, & Lancaster, 1965, p. 1546; emphasis added). A greater capacity to learn evolves when behavioral flexibility is important to survival. When flexibility is important to reproduction, where animals have time to learn, and where the creature can afford the costs of mistakes, natural selection favors the development of more sophisticated learning capacities (Alcock, 1993; Balter, 2002). Learning is a facultative adaptation that adjusts the phenotype to changing conditions in the environment. Children who grow up in a French-speaking household learn to speak French. The capacity to learn a wide variety of behaviors is an evolved characteristic of humans. In contrast, obligate adaptations are traits that do not change in the phenotype as the environment changes. Monarch butterflies or salmon, alas, have not learned to change their seasonal migration patterns to areas that are less polluted and more hospitable—and their numbers are consequently dwindling. Within a species, some behaviors are learned more readily than others are because some behaviors are more adaptive to survival and reproduction than others. People and other animals do not respond to all stimuli in the same manner. They respond differentially to most stimuli depending on the evolutionary context in which the stimuli were encountered and the functional value of differential responses.

Humans, too, have a nature, and therefore it will be easier to train humans to behave in some ways than in others. It is a characteristic of human males to form coalitions with other males to pursue their own advantage (often by aggression) against other coalitions of males. This can be confirmed by even the briefest survey of human warfare and politics. Given this fact, how likely is it that "team-building" training—a staple of management consultants and trainers—will enhance cooperation, foster the acceptance of group goals, and motivate people to work for the good of the whole team? The capacity to learn to read and to do complex arithmetic and mathematics is not part of our human nature (Geary, 1995; Moore, 1996). Therefore, teaching children to read and to perform mathematical calculations requires concerted drill and practice over long periods of time (Geary, 1995). On the other hand, sex is something that is part of human nature, and adolescents and young adults learn it effortlessly and with relish, primarily from peers. Moreover, they often learn about sex despite the best efforts of parents and other adults to prevent them.

As these examples should make clear, the idea that training will work equally well regardless of the content of what is being taught is wrong-headed. We implicitly acknowledge our evolved nature when we do not try to fly unaided like birds or swim vast distances like fish. Yet, many psychologists find it harder to acknowledge our nature when they expect that people will be shaped according to objectives of social interventions. Many mechanistic social interventions do not work (or do not work well) because they are incompatible with our evolved psychological mechanisms (Moore, 1996).

The erroneous assumptions of the SSSM about learning have had a profound impact on social scientists' and laypersons' views of human nature, learning, and training (Tooby & Cosmides, 1992). Many still believe that human beings are highly malleable creatures and that human behavior is largely a function of culture. Other than the capacity to learn and the physical limitations imposed by morphology, human nature is erroneously regarded as highly plastic, shaped by environmental contingencies. Thus, many, if not most, of the differences among people are presumed to be due to differences in their environments—what was available for them to learn through socialization and formal education and training. In this view, almost any behavior can be learned, given the proper environment. Therefore, we can move from an unsatisfactory to a satisfactory state of affairs through a change in socialization or a training program.

Examples of these errors span the twentieth century. Behaviorism is one. It began in the early 1900s, founded by the American psychologist John B. Watson. Behaviorism is a system of psychology concerned only with observed behavior rather than internal mental events. It views events in the environment as the causes of behavior and seeks to understand the processes by which environmental events cause behavior. Behaviorists believe that all behavioral responses are associated with and caused by specific environmental stimuli. Watson's system is completely deterministic: "In a system of psychology completely worked out, given the response the stimuli can be predicted, and given the stimuli the response can be predicted" (Watson, 1913, p. 167). Learning is the central explanatory concept in behaviorism. Convinced that all behavior was the result of learning, Watson made the following boast:

Give me a dozen healthy infants, well-formed, and my own specified world to bring them up in and I'll guarantee to take any one at random and *train* him to become any type of specialist I might select—doctor, lawyer, artist, merchant-chief, and, yes, even beggar-man and thief, regardless of his talents, penchants, tendencies, abilities, vocations, and race of his ancestors. (1924/1970, p. 104; emphasis added)

B. F. Skinner was another prominent behaviorist who was influential from the late 1930s to the early 1970s. Like Watson, Skinner posited a general all-purpose learning mechanism—a general ability to learn based on reinforcement and punishment. Skinner went beyond Watson in the boldness of his assertions about the applicability and benefits of behaviorism. Skinner saw behaviorism as the means to engineer a utopian society, a powerful tool for social engineering. He described a utopian society based on behaviorist principles in a novel, *Walden Two* (Skinner, 1948). Many of society's problems, he argued, could be solved with the proper application of behaviorism.

> What we need is a technology of behavior. We could solve our problems quickly enough if we could adjust the growth of the world's population as precisely as we adjust the course of a spaceship, or improve agriculture and industry with some of the confidence with which we accelerate high-energy particles, or move toward a peaceful world with something like the steady progress with which physics has approached absolute zero. (1972, p. 5)

Parenting and sex differences in social behavior are two topics in psychology riddled by the behaviorist fallacy. Academic and popular psychology regularly announce that parents leave an indelible mark on their children's temperaments and personalities as they train and socialize them. Harris (1999) calls this "the nurture assumption."

> The nurture assumption—the notion that parents are the most important part of the child's environment and can determine, to a large extent, how the child turns out—is a product of academic psychology. . . . It has permeated our culture. . . . It provide[s] the background for almost every bit of child-rearing advice you read in newspapers and parenting magazines or get from your pediatrician. (p. 15)

Learning and the environment are also viewed as the causes of most psychological and social differences between men and women. According to much academic psychology, if we change the environment, learning contingencies, explicit instruction, and role models, men and women can develop virtually identical dispositions and capacities. Some psychologists have gone so far as to suggest that sex differences in preferences for and skills in highly aggressive contact sports, such as football, are largely the result of learning and the environment. Carole Beal believes that, with changes in socialization and training experiences, it is "just a matter of time" before men and women are fully interchangeable among virtually all roles in society (except perhaps bearing children), including military combat and co-educational football (1994, p. 287).

Related to the problem of content-free learning is the failure to distinguish between evolved and acquired abilities, or what Geary (1995) calls primary and secondary abilities. Biologically *primary* abilities are neurocognitive systems that support the acquisition of behaviors found in all cultures. The ability to understand and speak a language is a biologically primary ability, as is the ability to navigate a habitat. The abilities to converse and to navigate have advantages for survival and reproduction: thus, they are found in all people, and are not constrained by cultural differences. Biologically *secondary* abilities are behaviors that have been coöpted from biologically primary abilities. They are neurocognitive systems used for purposes "other than the original evolution-based function" (Geary, 1995, p. 25). Biologically primary abilities are easier to acquire than biologically secondary abilities. Biologically secondary abilities are not found in all cultures. Some secondary abilities, like reading, are more widespread in some cultures than in others, and they are likely to vary to the extent that a culture possesses institutions (e.g., schools) that emphasize the development of those abilities. Reading and geometry involve biologically secondary abilities. Although the ability to read is closely linked with our primary language ability and understanding geometry is linked to our primary habitat navigational ability, the abilities to read and to understand geometry are not observed in all cultures. These abilities are associated with the availability of institutions—such as schools—that teach those abilities. Some biologically secondary abilities are easier to acquire than others. Those that are closer to biologically primary abilities are easier to acquire than those that are not. Euclidean geometry is easier to learn than statistics. There is a fairly direct leap from the biologically primary ability of habitat navigation (the shortest way home is "as the crow flies") to Euclidean geometry (a straight line is the shortest distance between two points). However, there is no such short leap from a biologically primary ability to understanding statistics. Euclid's *Elements* appeared about in 323 B.C., whereas the development of statistics did not occur until the seventeenth and eighteenth centuries.

Failing to Acknowledge the Role of Context in Learning

Context—the physical and social setting in which learning takes place—also influences learning. Hummingbirds learn to make associations more quickly with nectar-laden artificial flowers that shift in location than with flowers that stay in the same location (Cole et al., 1982).

This makes evolutionary sense because hummingbirds are more likely to survive and reproduce if they move from flower to flower in search of food than if they repeatedly go back to the same flower. Similarly, people are more likely to learn certain behaviors in particular contexts when doing so increases the chances of survival and reproduction. Two primary contexts in which most human learning has taken place over our evolutionary history has been the small group and the master–apprentice relationship (Klein, 1989; Lave & Wenger, 1991). For thousands of years our ancestors lived in small hunter-gatherer bands. Face-to-face interaction and narratives were the only sources of information about other people. People learned from direct verbal instruction, observation, and hands-on experience. Children learned the basic tasks of survival and culture from their parents, peers, and adult mentors (Megarry, 1995).

Although the evidence that context is important for learning is clear, textbooks on training routinely ignore it. Training and human resource management texts become giddy over the latest technologies, oblivious to whether these technologies provide contexts in which students learn well.

> [One firm] found that in addition to increasing flexibility, the [computer] interactive method produced more retention of knowledge than classroom instruction. . . . Other firms rely on CD-ROMs to implement their anytime, anyplace approach to training, while others use high-definition television projected onto large theater screens in multiple locations to teach sales techniques. Trainees can grill instructors, join long-distance discussions, and take home workbooks. (Cascio, 1998, p. 269)

Muchinsky also writes approvingly of computers in education:

> Computers are having a profound impact in the field of education at all levels. . . . Computer-aided instruction is changing the very nature of the educational process at the college level. . . . Some universities are now offering entire degree programs to students through this technology. A student can earn a degree from a university without ever having physically attended the university. (2000, p. 184)

Absent from these accolades is any mention of context. The same has generally been the case with earlier learning technologies—cassette tapes, videotapes, and television. In 1952, the Federal Communications Commission set aside 242 television channels for educational purposes. At the same time, the Ford Foundation provided extensive funding for educational television. Today, television, including the Public Broadcasting

System, is an entertainment media, with little educational content. Educational television has some, albeit limited, educational value, but it has certainly not become the educational juggernaut envisioned by its founders and early supporters. As each new medium was introduced, administrators and educational prognosticators read their tea leaves and foresaw the withering away of the flesh and blood teacher. The Holy Grail has been the replacement of teachers with more "efficient," less costly, nonunionized, more docile, harder working, and more predictable machines. This version of the Holy Grail would rise up and seize the imaginations of politicians, educational administrators, and policy sages every time a new educational technology came on the scene (Callahan, 1962; Heinich, Molenda, Russel, & Smaldino, 1996). Instead of replacing teachers, the new technologies end up as tools that teachers occasionally use to supplement instruction (Heinich et al., 1996). It's common to use a video- or cassette tape of Martin Luther King giving his "I Have a Dream" speech to supplement lectures and discussions of the civil rights movement in America. However, watching a video will not, by itself, turn a poor speaker into a good speaker. A good coach and plenty of practice and experience are also necessary.

The best way to learn a language is to live in a country where the language is spoken and only associate with native speakers of that language. The best way to learn Spanish is to live in a Spanish-speaking country with Spanish-speaking locals. Living with the locals will be more effective than cassette tapes, interactive computer programs, and college courses because, over evolutionary history, the human capacity to learn language evolved out of interactions in small groups. This, of course, is still how children learn their primary language—by living and interacting with their family members. Young children whose families move to a country where another language is spoken quickly learn the new language by interacting with other young children. Diplomats, Peace Corps volunteers, employees of multinational corporations, and others who must learn to speak a foreign language fluently typically learn languages through "immersion." This technique has a high degree of ecological validity because it mirrors the conditions under which people have effectively learned languages in the real world over millennia: by interacting over an extended period of time with a group of people. Students attend intensive language classes for a period of several weeks where their only task is to learn the language. In these settings, students are immersed in a group where the only language that is spoken is the language that people are learning. Immersion is consistently more effective than short daily periods of grammar-based lessons (Swain, 1991). It was for this reason that David Maxwell, the president of Drake University and formerly a professor of Russian, got rid of the foreign language departments at Drake. In place of traditional college courses, he advocates immersion-based learning, such as study abroad and internship programs.

> If you want to study French, take a college course. If you want to learn to speak it, take a plane to Paris. But steer clear of American classrooms, Mr. Maxwell suggests, because that's one of the last places on the planet where you'll master French—or German, or Spanish. (Schneider, 2001, p. A14)

Successful learning of any skill—whether speaking French, performing surgery, or playing tennis—is more likely to occur when the learner is with other people who are doing the same thing (Lave & Wenger, 1991).

The presumption (sometimes stated, sometimes not) is that learning can take place in virtually any context, *as long as the right information is presented*. Distance learning is predicated on the assumption that students can learn information presented on a computer screen as well as they do from more traditional teacher-centered methods (lecture and discussion, seminars, tutoring). The idea that learning is fundamentally a function of presenting the "right" information is wrong. Context is fundamental to learning (Glidewell, 1977). The acquisition of knowledge and skills involves more than just presenting the right information. Throughout most of human evolution, people learned from other human beings, not from a cathode ray tube. Even reading, which is taken for granted in industrialized countries, is evolutionarily novel. Although humans emerged about 1.2 million years ago and modern humans about 100,000 years ago, writing was invented only about 3,000 (possibly as much as 6,000) years ago. Widespread literacy has emerged in industrialized nations within the last century. Literacy involves gathering information from a page rather than a speaker and from abstract written symbols rather than vocalizations and behavioral signals. Because the brain has not yet evolved adaptive mechanisms specifically for reading, it takes much work to get children comfortable with written words on a page (Geary, 1995). This is why early literacy is still social, and the social, human context is important to teaching children to read. Parents sit with their children and read to them, pointing to words in books as they read. The social aspect of reading involves ancient mechanisms: vocalization, nonverbal behavior, interaction, parent-child attachment, the child's desire to please the parent, and the bestowal of approval by the parent. It is necessary to coöpt the ancient, adaptive mechanisms of learning socially to facilitate the learning of the evolutionarily novel activity of reading. Instruction via computer, on the other hand, does not do this. There is nothing social about a computer screen. Computerized instruction ignores the social context of learning, focusing completely on content and entertainment value. It does not deal with the fact that reading is not an evolved primary ability and that to learn to read it is necessary to engage and coop primary evolved mechanisms.

SOME CONSEQUENCES OF THE MECHANISTIC MODEL

Obsession with New Methods and Technologies

The fads of social engineers dominated training and education throughout the twentieth century. Social engineers with a mechanical design frame of mind tried to improve training and education practices and use them as instruments to realize utopian visions (Tyack & Cuban, 1995). These fads involved curricular methods and educational technologies. Diane Ravitch's (2000) *Left Back* chronicles the flow of curricular fads in the K–12 public schools. These included a panoply of teaching methods informed by a panoply of educational "movements" throughout the century: "the industrial education movement, the scientific movement, the curricular differentiation movement, the mental-testing movement, the child-centered movement, the mental hygiene movement, [and] the life adjustment movement" (p. 462). In management and industrial training, there is a similar parade of training movements and methods. These include the scientific management movement, the human relations movement, the Theory Y movement, the organizational culture movement, the work team movement, the learning organization movement, the total quality management movement, and so on. Applied psychology has generated various training fads: t-groups, sensitivity training, quality circles, team building, and adventure training, to name a few. Many machines have also been heralded as "important innovations" in training. The boilerplate version of the machines-save-the-kids story regularly appears on the radio or TV and goes something like this. A school district, usually a poor one with underachieving kids, gets a windfall gift of computers or a teacher finds an ingenious way to teach a traditional subject over the Internet. These are greeted with great enthusiasm and a blind faith that the new technology will do wonders for improving how quickly and how much the kids learn. It is also common to hear about a business or university investing millions of dollars in the latest training technology because it will create an economy of scale not available in small classes where one instructor is needed for about every 30 to 100 students. Yet after the dust settles, the promises of the new technology inevitably exceed the reality. Web-based education results in lower levels of motivation and practice (Brown, 2001), and students end up being minimally interested in it (Zielinski, 2000). Greater Internet usage is associated with increased depression and loneliness, a reduction of communication with household family members, and declines in the size of the social circle (Kraut et al., 1998). Even the financial returns of web-based courses are less than expected (Carr, 2001).

The Obsession with Fads

Although fads are part of the human condition and are primarily a result of runaway imitation, one has to wonder why education and training have been so dominated by them. One of the most compelling reasons is that training and education activities are banal.[6] What do you see when you look in on a typical college class? You will see a professor lecturing, writing on a chalkboard, and asking students questions. Students will be answering—some stumbling through, others doing quite well. If you look in on a training session for tennis players, what might you see? Perhaps the coach will be taking students through a series of serving exercises, stopping between each one to critique the students. Students might be returning a series of balls from a serving machine. The instructor might be hitting the ball to students at different spots on the court. The basic activities in training and education—drill and practice—are humdrum, and their effects are often not obvious in the short term. Yet administrators often must demonstrate to their superiors and to politicians that they are making progress and improving education. Therefore, they believe they need to show them something new and exciting in the classroom, something that produces quick, tangible results—something better than the same old unexciting drill-and-practice and lectures that produce less tangible results. So, when a new educational method or a flashy educational technology comes along, administrators and politicians jump on the bandwagon. Computers in the classroom, using the Internet for information about geography—these are concrete, visible, and exciting. Educational technologies, in particular, foster the *illusion* that they are valuable because they have immediate and engaging cause-effect relations. One logs on to the Web, and one immediately gets an effect: information. Novelty is another reason why managers are motivated to use new training methods and technologies, regardless of their value for learning. A new method presents a contrast to the everyday learning that goes unnoticed. Ordinary training and learning are so ubiquitous that some people are rarely aware of it, while flashy new technologies are visible and send a clear signal that training is taking place.

Charles Perrow (1983) explored managers' obsession with modern technologies in the context of the nuclear power industry and other industries that use high-technology systems. He found that managers typically rejected plain, unexciting, but effective approaches to solving problems while favoring flashy high-tech approaches, even though they were less effective. Managers favored technological solutions because technology is visible and impressive to superiors or investors and technological solutions made managers look good in the short term. In addition, some technological solutions can make it easier for managers to centralize power and reduce the skills needed by employees. Although technological solutions are not inherently superior to solutions based on human skill, particularly in complex systems, technology has the same seductive power over educational administrators that it seems to have over industrial and military administrators. Millions of dollars have been spent on distance learning, computers in the classroom, and interactive television, even though there is not much evidence that they offer any educational or financial advantages (Cuban, 2001).[7] University administrators have argued that it is important to develop distance education programs because of the potential for large profits, expanded markets, and educational effectiveness. Yet, as educational researcher John Milam argues, "much of the 'revenue' [gain resulting from distance education] is in being perceived as a leader in the use of technology" (Carr, 2001, p. 43). Selling flashy, educational technologies to K–12 and college administrators is like shooting fish in a barrel.

Two other factors may have also contributed to the profusion of educational gimmicks and fads. Training and mass education were part of the great social engineering movements in the first 70 years of the twentieth century, and therefore the more "scientific" a training program appeared, the greater appeal it would have. Training programs that appeared to be scientific and technologically sophisticated, even if they were no better than traditional methods, had greater appeal because they fit better with the zeitgeist of social engineering. A second reason is that small increases in performance became very important for some segments of society. As the mass media and advances in recordkeeping became commonplace in the twentieth century, so too did information about human performance (e.g., televised sporting events, daily stock quotes of publicly traded companies) and exceptional performance (e.g., faster racing times). In many situations, small improvements could make big differences in outcomes. Increasing performance by just a small amount could make the difference between failure and success for college and professional athletes, top students vying for a place at an elite college or professional school, stock fund managers, bankers in charge of loans, and so on (e.g., Specter, 2002). The growing importance of small differences in performance probably increased the demand for training products that *appeared* to be novel and beneficial. Some actually were beneficial, but many were not (Gladwell, 2001).

Making Training and Education Fun

Making training and education fun has become an increasingly important goal over the past 30 years. In 1973, only about 29 percent of colleges were using teaching ratings to evaluate faculty. However, by 1993, the percent jumped to 86 percent (Seldin, 1993). "Student ratings have become the most widely used—and in many cases, the only—source of information on teaching effectiveness" (Seldin, 1993, p. A40). Ratings ("on a scale of 1 to 5, how much did you enjoy this course?") are also *de rigueur* for evaluating training courses in business and industry. Teaching ratings reflect how students feel about instructors—their emotional reactions to them. As Harvey Mansfield wryly notes, with teaching ratings "the wise are judged according to how well they charm the unwise" (Mansfield, 2001, p. A16).

A study by Ambady and Rosenthal (1993) provides evidence that teaching ratings are influenced by factors other than how much or how well students learn. They found that students' ratings of professors based on viewing *ten-second* video clips of the professors were nearly the same as the ratings from other students who had taken semester-long courses with those same professors. Obviously, if ratings based on a 10-second video clip were similar to those based on a semester-long course, then it is unlikely that course ratings have any connection to the content of the course or how much students learned. Ambady and Rosenthal found that students based their ratings from the video clips primarily on nonverbal expressions signifying expressiveness and warmth (e.g., smiling, hands away from the body). Many of my colleagues lament the fact that deans rarely ask about the content of the course, the structure of the syllabus, or teaching methods when they evaluate their teaching performance. Instead, deans focus on teaching ratings. People with reputations as "good" teachers are those who have high teaching ratings. It is not inconceivable that professors or trainers could be immensely entertaining and warm and teach nothing of value. Their students could learn almost nothing in their courses, but they would still give them high teaching ratings. Why has fun become such an important criterion of teaching effectiveness? One possibility is that training and higher education have become "commodified." Training and, to a large extent, education have come to be regarded as products that are sold on the open market.[8] The "education-as-a-business" zeitgeist tells students that they are "customers" to be pleased rather than students to be educated.[9] Another reason may be the widespread belief in the mechanical design view of education. Many educators and policymakers believe that educational programs can be engineered to meet whatever goals are deemed appropriate. When having fun became a goal, they presumed that whatever was inherently difficult, boring, or repetitive could be engineered out of education and more enjoyable methods could be designed to achieve the same results as drill-and-practice.

Training Needs Analysis Will Remain Rare

A cardinal rule of mechanistic training is that a professional needs analysis is the *sine qua non* of good training. Yet most organizations do not conduct training needs analyses (Saari et al. 1988). Why should this be the case? The reflexive answer of many applied psychologists is that managers are ignorant of the psychological literature on needs analysis (Patrick, 1992). A different explanation may be possible. Needs analysis is not widely used because of the disjunction between the assumptions of the mechanically driven model and the realities of the multiple functions of training, tenuous cause-effect relations in complex social systems, self-interest and organizational politics, unfocused goals, and the importance of skill diversity.

Training needs analyses are not routinely conducted because training serves functions other than teaching new skills based on a rational analysis of needs and goals. Changing a training program based on an analysis that focuses on one set of goals may subvert other goals that training serves. A needs analysis that concluded that the average school day could be reduced by 50 percent if teachers modified their curricula ignores the fact that a major latent function of modern K–12 (and probably college) education is child care. One way to get a handle on the functions of a program is to note the complaints that arise when the program stops. When K–12 teachers go out on strike, many adults complain about the lack of adult supervision for children who are not in school, not about the education that children are missing.

The idea of fine-tuned needs analysis is problematic in large, complex systems because of tenuous cause-effect relations. The presumption behind needs analyses is that the analysis will define a critical problem for which training is the solution. A problem with this line of reasoning is that in large complex systems only rarely will an intervention produce expected effects (Hannan & Freeman, 1989). The relationship between a behavior learned in a training program and organizational effectiveness is inevitably murky. Furthermore, the information that a needs analysis provides is often out of date in situations that change rapidly. By the time a needs analysis is finished, situations have changed and the results are moot.

Self-interest and politics work against needs analyses. It is not in a manager's self-interest to sponsor a needs analysis that will hold her accountable for goals that are beyond her control, and much of what goes into meeting (or not meeting) training goals is beyond a manager's control. Managers may have no control over the motivation and abilities of the trainees, the availability of practice time, and the effectiveness of the training—all of which affect whether a training program will meet its goals. A clearly stated training goal ("employees who take the XYZ training program will improve sales by 15 percent within six months after completing the program") can come back to bite a manager if the goal is not achieved. A vague goal ("sales will improve") is more often in the manager's best interests. Even if a manager was willing to stick her neck out with clear, measurable goals, the politics of conflicting interests can make it difficult for agreement to be reached on goals for a program. People with an interest in the training program may not all have the same interests. Section managers may be interested in goals that cast good first impressions because help managers look good to their superiors (Perrow, 1983). The financial manager may be interested in keeping costs low. Trainees may not want a program at all if they are too busy with work; if they must attend, their primary goal is that the program be short. Training managers may be interested in goals that demonstrate how the training program will help the company's bottom line because this increases the job security of training managers.

People may not be clear about their goals or about the relationship between their goals and "organizational" goals. Managers at a health insurance company may be unclear about whether friendly service is important and therefore whether customer service representatives need training. Friendly service may result in too many successful claims and lower profits; yet unfriendly service has the potential to motivate unhappy customers (with the means and time) to file lawsuits. When people do not have clear goals, needs analyses are unlikely to be accurate. At the other extreme, a needs analysis may be unnecessary because the needs are obvious. If a consultant regularly offends clients because of poor table manners at business lunches, then it is obvious that he needs help with table manners. A sophisticated needs analysis is superfluous.

Finally, a rigid insistence that a formal needs analysis be conducted before a new training program can take place can have the unintended consequences of limiting the diversity of the skills in an organization. Needs analysis reduces variation because it is based on the presumption that the training needs it identifies are sufficient. If training is restricted to courses that have been sanctioned by a needs analysis, then the range of skills within the organization becomes restricted. Limiting the diversity of knowledge and skills is an organizational liability because it limits the capacity to adapt to changing environments.

Needs analyses can be useful, however, in stable environments, in simple situations where there are clear cause-effect links, and where a little improvement makes a big difference.

Formal Training Evaluation Will Remain Rare

Proponents of the mechanically driven model of training also lament the lack of formal evaluation of training (Saari et al., 1988). They claim that it is difficult to know if training works unless there is a formal evaluation of it (Goldstein & Ford, 2002). This assumption is not entirely true. Formal evaluation can kill useful programs. Training programs are likely to serve multiple functions, some of which are intentional and obvious, while others may be unintentional and less visible. Mechanical evaluations, however, typically focus on the intended function, so if the evaluation turns out to be negative it is likely to conclude that the program is worthless. Training programs with multiple functions cannot be adequately evaluated by a single criterion. It is difficult to comprehensively assess the mix of skill, entertainment, ceremonial, and bonding functions of training programs (Trice, Bellasco, & Alutor, 1969). If an omniscient observer could calculate the net costs and benefits of a training program over time, it might be that the ceremonial functions are more beneficial than the improvements in skills that it produces. The various lessons many American children take during childhood—dancing, piano, violin, tennis, drama, horseback riding, and so on—described earlier are a case in point. Of course, one can argue that, regardless of a program's multiple functions, it should nevertheless be evaluated for a specific function. Even so, most parents are unlikely to stop tennis lessons despite their child's slow progress in developing a good backhand if the child is also learning to enjoy the sport, developing practice skills, learning sportsmanship, and meeting new friends. Similarly, managers are not likely to eliminate a program based on an evaluation of a specific function if they know the program serves other valuable functions.

A final reason why the evaluation of training is unlikely to catch on in a big way is because it is frequently superfluous. Training would not have been part of the human condition if formal scientific evaluation procedures were necessary to know whether or not training worked. If fathers taught their sons how to spear fish in hunter-gatherer societies, it would have been obvious after a period of training whether the sons learned how to spear fish. Today, it does not take a formal evaluation for parents to know whether their child's piano lessons are having the desired effect; an executive does not need a formal, scientific evaluation to know whether his subordinates benefited from public speaking lessons.

Formal evaluations of training programs are useful and sensible in some circumstances. It would be sensible to spend the time and money to conduct formal training evaluations when training outcomes are specific, where there is a clear link between skilled behavior and unit goals, and when the outcomes are not already obvious and commonsensical. Evaluations are also advisable when a very small improvement in skilled performance can make a large difference in outcomes and when large numbers of people are involved. In such cases, a professional evaluation may be necessary to detect small differences or to gather outcome information on hundreds or thousands of trainees in diverse locations.

Training (and Education) Are Poor Stepchildren

CEOs or politicians intent on winning the approval of employees or voters inevitably emphasize their commitment to training and education. Few people argue with the old saws about the importance of training and education.

- "People are our most important resource."
- "Teachers are responsible for the future of the country."
- "Give a man a fish, and you feed him for a day; teach him to fish and you feed him for a lifetime."
- "We invest in our people."

Yet if training and education are so important, why are trainers and educators among the lowest paid professionals in the United States? The average starting salary for college graduates in 2000 going into education was $27,278, compared to $48,987 for computer-related fields (National Association of Colleges and Employers, 2001). When corporate budgets get tight, training departments are among the first to be reduced or eliminated (E-Pulse survey, 2001). Most college coaches educate a minuscule number of students; yet coaches receive salaries substantially higher than professors. A recent survey reported that the average annual salary of the head coaches of men's teams in Division I-A, BCS conferences, is $116, 254 (Jacobson, 2001).[10] At the same time, the average salary of full professors ranged from $64,365 at baccalaureate institutions to $89,848 at doctoral institutions (Average Salaries of Full-time Faculty, 2001). That some college coaches earn more than one million dollars a year speaks volumes about educational priorities.

"At last count," the Knight Commission reveals, "some 30 college football and men's basketball coaches are paid $1 million or more a year." Often these coaches are the highest-paid university employees, surpassing even the medical school's thoracic surgeons and the business school's marketing whizzes. In some states, the top coach at the major public university earns more than any other public employee—including the governor. (Finn, 2001, p. 55)

The actual dollars spent on training suggest that it is a low priority in most major corporations. American firms spend, on average, less than $400 per year per worker on training. They spend about 1 to 2 percent of their payroll on training (*Industry Report*, 1997), and they spend more on "coffee breaks, lunch, and other paid rest time for their employees than on formal training" (Office of Technology Assessment [OTA], 1990, p. 129). Sixty percent of the training dollars in the United States are spent by one-half of 1 percent of American employers (OTA, 1990). Relative to many other public and private expenditures, expenditures on education are a low priority. The federal research and development budget for education during fiscal year 2000 was $238 million; for defense it was $ 39,466 million; and the NASA (National Aeronautic and Space Administration) budget was $ 9,242 million (Office of Science and Technology Policy, 2001). The total annual expenditure in the United States on K–12 education is only twice what American children spend on consumer goods. Teen Research Unlimited ("TRU") estimated in its semiannual *Teenage Marketing and Lifestyle Survey* that children from 12 to 19 spent more than $153 billion on consumer goods in 1999 (Federal Trade Commission, 2000); the expenditures on elementary and secondary schools for 1999–2000 were estimated at $389 billion (Snyder & Hoffman, 2001). Young adults under 25 spend more per year on food away from home ($1,569), motor vehicle purchases ($2,628), and apparel ($1,420) than they do on education ($1,257); they spend almost as much on entertainment ($1,091) as they do on education. Education is also a low priority for older adults who are likely to have children who are young adults. Adults from 45 to 54 also spend more per year on food away from home ($2,638), motor vehicle purchases ($3,863), apparel ($2,371), and entertainment ($2,331) than they do on education ($1,146) (Bureau of Labor Statistics, 2000).

The hard numbers illustrate a cruel reality about training and education. Despite a lot of talk about how valuable education and training are, they remain low national and personal priorities. An evolutionary perspective might suggest the following explanation. Because people can learn skills without formal programs, many organizations do not invest large sums of money in them. Humans have been training and learning for thousands of years; training and learning are as natural to human existence as sex. Given the inventory of extraordinary skills that humans have been able to develop over the centuries—from tracking wild animals to producing masterful works of art—it is fair to say that humans are good at training and learning. People inevitably learn skills and can learn them quite well, even in the absence of formal programs. Consider the performance of home-schooled children. As measured by standardized achievement tests, home schooled students learn as much as their publicly or privately schooled peers. Yet the average educational credentials of parents who home-school their children are less than those of the average public school teachers (Lines, 2000). There is rarely one best way to teach a skill. Instructional methods involve a high degree of what economists call "substitutability," that is, the degree to which one input factor can be substituted for another and still produce an equal level of output. If a professional instructor is unavailable, a student can often substitute a parent, friend, or book. The students at St. Patrick's High School in rural Kenya did not have a trained track coach, yet the track program at St. Patrick's has produced phenomenal results. At one time the school had four sub-four-minute milers; its graduates have won Olympic gold medals (Peter Rono and Matthew Birir) as well as the Boston Marathon (Ibrahim Hussein won it three times). The coach during those years was Brother Colm O'Connell who, by his own admission, knew very little about athletics, let alone track and long distance running, when he left his native Ireland to teach at St. Patrick's (Tanser, 1997/1998).[11] In chess, expert coaching appears to be unrelated to successful performance (Charness, Krampe, & Mayr, 1996). This is not to say that some trainers, coaches, or teachers are not better than others. This is not to deny that skilled teachers produce, on average, more learning in students than unskilled teachers do. Nor is this to deny that, in some instances, a master teacher is critical to a student's development of high-level skills (Bloom, 1985). However, people can learn from a variety of different methods, and they can learn without formal training programs.

Utilization Problems Will Continue

Many professionals in HR and industrial psychologists are distressed by the lack of formal training programs in industry (Noe, 1999). *Real* training occurs only when professionals design, conduct, and evaluate it. Yet, many employees gain job skills by observing others, asking questions, reading books and manuals, developing relationships with people who have expertise, and practicing. Employers probably know this and therefore do not regard their own reluctance to invest in formal training as detrimental to employees' development of job skills.[12] Similarly, employees who are motivated to acquire skills are likely to pursue a variety of means to acquire them rather than wait passively for a formal training programs to be offered by his or her employer (Stone, 1991). I can recall one colleague who did exactly this early in his career as a professor. Having had little experience teaching and finding that things were not going well in the classroom, he set out to learn how to be a better teacher on his own. Since the university did not offer training programs for new faculty—I suppose university administrators assumed that faculty could learn how to teach on their own (there's an irony here)—he asked more senior professors with reputations as good teachers for tips on how to teach well. He tape-recorded and videotaped his lectures and seminars and then went back over them, looking for specific instances where he could make improvements. He hired a member of the drama department to coach him on improving his lecturing delivery. He polished his lectures, worked on his delivery, and applied the charm, and so his teaching ratings improved. Over the years, I have found that this is common among motivated teaching assistants and young faculty members. I hear them in the halls or computer rooms chatting with senior professors about how to write exams, how to deal with uninterested students, how to liven up their lectures, and so on. Traditional practices will continue because people will continue to learn by using them.

INDIVIDUAL DIFFERENCES, EVOLUTIONARY PSYCHOLOGY, AND LEARNING

For most of the twentieth century, behaviorism and individual difference (differential) psychology were the dominant views that psychologists used to explain abilities and skills. Each of these perspectives is valid to a point, but they are incomplete. They do not adequately address the evolutionary origins and functions of abilities and skills. To adequately repair or improve a part in a system, we need to understand not only how it works but also its function within the system. If an automobile tire goes flat, the tire can be repaired so that it can hold air again. However, if the person fixing the tire does not understand the *function* of the tire—to enable the car to move smoothly forward and backward—then the repair may not be helpful. If he assumes that the primary function of the tire is to hold the car off ground, then he might repair the tire with a metal bolt that protrudes from the tire. Although the tire could again hold air, it would not roll smoothly. Behaviorism and differential psychology attempt to explain how skills and abilities are acquired and work, but they do not deal with the more basic issue of the function of skills and abilities. As such, attempts to fashion training and educational programs based on assumptions of behaviorism or individual difference psychology are incomplete. An evolutionary perspective provides a better understanding in this regard and will be helpful in improving training programs to develop skills (Geary, 1995).

Behaviorism holds that the human mind is virtually a blank slate and that most behavior is learned. The environment a person is exposed to and her learning history are the primary influences on whatever skills and abilities she develops. According to John Watson, the founder of behaviorism: "There is no such thing as *inheritance of capacity, talent, temperament, mental constitution* and *characteristics*. These things . . . depend on training that goes on mainly in the cradle" (Watson, 1924/1970, p. 94). Behaviorism, as we described at length in Chapter 2, does not deal adequately with the fact that some behaviors are learned more easily than others. People learn to speak their native language more easily than they learn algebra. Most people readily learn to "read" facial expressions, while it takes years of study for children to learn to read a written language. While acknowledging that a few behaviors are instinctual—that is, reflect genetic programs rather than experience—behaviorists regard the acquisition of all other behaviors as independent of evolution and hold that evolution has nothing to do with learning. This is not the case. Different species are predisposed to learn some behaviors more easily than others. That some species acquire more of their behavioral repertoires by learning than other species is evidence that learning is an evolved adaptation: "Learning is not independent of evolution. Instead, learning mechanisms are evolved adaptations to the organism's natural environment. Like any adaptation, they are specialized to solve particular kinds of real-world problems" (Gaulin & McBurney, 2001, p. 130). Behaviorism does not adequately account for the adaptive functions of learning processes. How we learn, what we are predisposed to learn, what is difficult to learn, and the settings that facilitate learning were shaped by natural selection.

Behaviorism also does not deal realistically with individual differences in psychological characteristics. Just as people enter the world with different eye and hair colors, metabolisms, complexions, and potential to grow to a particular height, they come into the world with different constellations of psychological characteristics. Parents who have raised more than one child know this. They would find it difficult to believe that the environment is the cause of most abilities and temperaments. Many parents would agree that children come as "packages," and there is only so much a parent can do to influence a child's abilities and temperament. Siblings demonstrate different talents, often from early on, even though they are raised in the same household, by the same parents, and go to the same schools (Harris, 1999).

The assumptions of individual-difference psychologists about the importance of innate or early-acquired traits go too far in the other direction, however. A basic assumption of differential psychology is that people's genetic differences and early developmental experiences determine their basic abilities and temperamental characteristics. It is presumed that these characteristics are fixed early in life and cannot be changed much by experience. Different ability levels, in turn, influence the ease with which people can acquire different skills. A person with athletic ability will learn athletic skills more readily than someone with little athletic ability. Different levels of personality traits will influence a person's motivation to engage in certain behaviors and activities. A person with an extroverted temperament will be more comfortable in social situations and will be more inclined to spend time learning social skills than someone with an introverted temperament. Ability and personality traits are presumed to place a ceiling on the types and levels of behavior in a wide variety of domains that people can be reasonably expected to acquire.

So far, so good. This is compatible with our argument that a weakness of behaviorism is that it does not sufficiently acknowledge innate individual differences and their effect on learning. The problem is that differential psychology has an excessively mechanistic posture about the significance of individual differences, how they work, and their effects. Although the research shows that the effects of most individual psychological differences are modest and probabilistic, it is not uncommon for individual-difference psychologists to *overstate the significance of small differences* in a characteristic, to *reify* a particular characteristic, and to *overstate the practical significance* of their favorite trait. Schmidt argues that a one-point difference on a psychological test is meaningful:

> Suppose . . . that 100 is a perfect score on a valid test. Let us further consider only two groups of applicants: all those with test scores of 91 and

all those with test scores of 92. Despite the fact that the test score difference is only 1 point between these two groups, in the long run . . . the average job performance of the 92 score group will be somewhat higher than that of the 91 score group. (Schmidt, 1995, p. 167)

Perhaps. If there is a an extremely large group of applicants, if the applicants are equal in all other ways, if no other traits influence performance, and if the IQ-performance correlation does not decrease appreciably over time. If wishes were horses, beggars would ride. Ree and Earles exhibit a severe case of IQ myopia in their implicit recommendation to employers to use only intelligence tests in selecting applicants: "If an employer were to use only intelligence tests and select the highest scoring applicant for each job, training results would be predicted well regardless of the job, and overall performance from the employees selected would be maximized" (1992, p. 88). Ree and Earles seem to be blissfully ignorant of the fact that performing well in most jobs requires characteristics other than intelligence. It is unlikely that the job performance of a Republican politician's staff would be maximized if the politician hired only on the basis of intelligence and ignored the political leanings of job applicants. It is unlikely that the job performance of child care workers would be maximized if the day-care center hired the workers solely on the basis of intelligence, ignoring traits such as patience, humor, and kindness. Apparently, Ree and Earles caught their IQ myopia from from Schmidt and Hunter:

Professionally developed cognitive ability tests are valid predictors of performance on the job and in training for all jobs . . . and . . . the use of cognitive ability tests for selection in hiring can produce large labor cost savings, ranging from $18 million per year for small employers . . . to $16 billion per year for large employers. (Schmidt and Hunter, 1981, p. 1128)

According to Timothy Judge and colleagues, woe to the poor soul who scores low on a test of conscientiousness: "There may be limits to what we can do about the causes of our failures . . . An individual low in conscientiousness may have had his or her career inhibited by being undependable, disorganized, and careless" (1999, p. 647). The implicit message is that people with low scores on favored traits are losers. The early testers were more blunt in their prose. Terman wrote disparagingly of "stupid" college students in an article entitled "Adventures in Stupidity" (1922). Today, testers use more ponderous phrases, such as "predicting performance." The message, however, is the same: people who score higher on Test X are the winners.

The view of differential psychologists that innate ability and temperament mechanically constrain learning and life outcomes does not square with everyday reality. If an ability or personality trait is a *necessary* condition for an individual to absorb training, then it would be extremely unlikely that people with low levels of that ability or characteristic could learn and be successful. Yet, most of us know people who do not "test well" but are successful—much more so than would have ever been predicted by their test scores. Martin Luther King's "Letter from a Birmingham Jail" is widely regarded as one of the most influential pieces of writing on civil rights in the twentieth century, and his "I Have a Dream" speech is regarded as one of the most influential and brilliant speeches of the twentieth century. Yet King scored in the bottom half of test-takers on the verbal portion of the Graduate Record Examination (GRE; Cross & Slater, 1997, p. 12, cited in Bowen & Bok, 1997, p. 277n). A second example is my wife's old high school friend who had a burning desire to become a successful playwright. He studied drama at college, wrote plays, and became involved in the local drama community. After he graduated from college, he worked a day-job and wrote plays at night. Seeking more training, he applied to a graduate program in drama at one of the country's most prestigious universities. Unfortunately, he did not "test well," got low GRE scores, and was rejected by the drama school. Yet he persevered. Over the years he became successful and had a number of plays produced at notable venues. A few years ago, I attended one of his plays that was featured at the Stratford (Ontario) summer drama festival and a year or two later, he won the Pulitzer Prize for drama. At the time he was employed as a professor of drama at a prestigious Ivy League university—the same one that had rejected his application to its drama school 20 years before!

Exceptional performance requires more than innate intelligence or talent. It is common knowledge, as well as firmly established in the research literature, that practice, training, motivation, exposure to role models, and focused goals have a substantial effect on a person's abilities and demonstrated performance. Talent is of secondary importance to deliberate practice in achieving high levels of competency, and most of us know people who, through focused hard work, achieved excellence, regardless of initial abilities. Research by K. A. Ericsson and his colleagues supports the common-sense notion that practice improves performance. Ericsson's findings make a convincing case that deliberate practice is more important than ability for becoming highly proficient in most human endeavors (Ericsson & Lehmann, 1996). In a study of musicians, Ericsson, Krampe, and Tesch-Römer (1993) found that only the amount of deliberate practice differentiated among superior, very good, and average performers. Better performers put in more time practicing. Such studies confirm the maxim among performing artists that the three ways to get to Carnegie Hall are: practice, practice, practice. Other studies have found that training and practice have a considerably greater effect on skilled performance and expertise than initial ability (Bloom, 1985; Saxe, 1988). In a fascinating study, Ceci and Liker (1986) found that expert race handicappers with average IQ scores, but with years of practice, outperformed amateur handicappers with high IQ scores. Indeed, deliberate practice over time produces actual physiological changes (see Ericsson & Lehmann, 1996, pp. 279–280). However, deliberate practice is probably much more important for secondary than for primary abilities. Although it is important for primary abilities, practice may occur more as an incidental result of other activities, such as play (Geary, 2002).

Equifinality and substitutability are important for understanding that ability is only one of many components that affect successful performance. A study by Allison (1977) provides a good example. She found that a given level of student performance in a college-level introductory economics course could be achieved either by increasing the average SAT score of students in the course by 200 points or by substituting the best teachers for the worst teachers. Focusing on one or two characteristics easily measured by tests is an easy way out, and a highly profitable one for test developers, test consultants, and test producers; it is also quite an ego boost for people with "good" test scores themselves or those who are employed by organizations that attract high-scoring applicants. Abilities and temperament are more like rubber bands than steel boxes. Some rubber bands stretch more than others, but they all stretch. We can think of an average IQ as an averaged-sized rubber band and a high IQ as a larger rubber band. However, the average rubber band will stretch to encompass some of the area that the larger rubber band covers.

Testers frequently argue that times are different now, that society and organizations are more complex. People do not have as much time as they did in the past to learn. According to Hunter and colleagues:

> Many organizations today are downsizing and de-layering, dramatically increasing the worker-to-manager/supervisor ratio. . . . Workers have more time and freedom to "think on their feet.". . . The value of having "intelligent" workers (that is, who can be creative and problem solve themselves out of trouble) in these jobs is becoming more apparent to managers and supervisors. (2000, p. 295)

This argument is old wine in new bottles. The testers of the 1920s used the same logic: modern society and organizations are too complex to allow the less intelligent to participate in a meaningful way.

> In 1922, the Army test results were analyzed in *The Atlantic Monthly* by Cornelia James Cannon, who concluded that nearly half the white draft could be considered "morons" and fully 22 percent were "inferior men." The "inferior men . . . are persons who not only do not think, but are unable to think; who cannot help in the solution of our problems, but, instead, become a drag on the progress of civilization. In a crude society, they have a place, may even serve a use. In a society so complex as that which we are developing, they are a menace which may compass our destruction." Common school education, she felt, should be limited to very basic subjects followed by "a pretty rigorous process of selection," so that society would not waste money on "second-rate men." (Ravitch, 2000, p. 141)

If tests are needed now because life is more complex than in the past, then why were they needed in 1922 when life was supposedly less complicated? The absurdity of this argument is evident in another way. For most people, life in primitive societies was more mentally challenging than life in modern societies. In hunter-gatherer societies, people had to continually live by their wits (Diamond, 1997). They did not have the securities afforded by modern society, and they had to regularly deal with the challenges of finding food, warfare and raids, and the elements. Moreover, much of our higher intellectual functioning evolved and continues to be used for the problems of dealing with other people—assessing intent, forming coalitions, dealing with enemies and social hierarchies, and so on (Cummins, 1998; Dunbar, 1996). These are among the most difficult problems humans face, regardless of whether they are living in complex or simple societies.

One of the most destructive effects of rigid thinking about individual differences was that it gave school administrators a justification to restrict a solid academic curriculum to only a small portion of K–12 students (Ravitch, 2000). By the 1960s, it had become conventional wisdom in American education that children's ability to learn was fixed by their IQs. This kept most students out of academically oriented and challenging curricula, from which they, and the country, would have undoubtedly profited. We see the same destructive policies being advocated in the workplace and in universities by social engineers who believe that hiring people who score high on tests is a viable and effective solution to productivity "in a complex society" (Gottfredson, 1997).[13]

The Relevance of Individual Differences to Learning and Training

Variation is a biological fact. Some people are taller or shorter, some are more prone to weight gain, while others are more naturally thin. Some are sociable, others are reticent and shy. Some are gifted in drawing or languages. Some individual differences are heritable—that is, they are passed on genetically from parents to offspring. From the standpoint of training, the interesting questions are not whether individual differences in ability exist or what the ranges of those differences are. The interesting questions are: how relevant are individual differences to learning, and to what extent do training and practice override individual differences?

The relevance of individual differences to training and education is not absolute. Only in certain types of situations does it make sense to focus heavily on individual differences in abilities and temperaments. Individual differences have been only marginally relevant to training throughout most of human history because people were, for the most part, not sorted into schools, jobs, and occupations by ability. Rather, they were more or less born into positions, and they had to learn them regardless of their inborn talents. From what we know of hunter-gatherer societies, people learned skills from their parents and relatives. Skill-training was clan-based in the sense that people in certain clans or from certain families would be responsible for certain functions (e.g., making bows and arrows), and they would pass these skills down to their children. Until the modern era, most skills were learned this way or through guilds. *Given sufficient time and practice, people learned what they needed to, regardless of individual differences.* And people generally had time to practice. That this approach to learning skills has been used and worked reasonably well for thousands of years suggests that there is something fundamental to it. Studies by Bloom, Ceci, and Ericsson bear this out. Given sufficient exposure to information and time to practice, people within a wide range of abilities can develop high levels of expertise at a variety of skills and occupations (Bloom, 1985; Ceci & Liker, 1986; Ericsson, Krampe, & Tesch-Römer, 1993; Saxe, 1988).

The modern world does not have a monopoly on the need for, or people with, high levels of expertise. The great architectural wonders of ancient Egypt and Greece were designed and built by skilled architects and artisans. Skilled wordsmiths of antiquity composed great works of literature, religion, and philosophy. Skilled artists and artisans of antiquity created beautiful sculpture. The great cathedrals of the Middle Ages had to be designed, financed, and built—all of which required highly skilled work from architects, administrators, and artisans. What is new is not the processes by which people acquire skills but the mobility of the modern world. Occupational mobility and frequent job changes are primarily the products of the industrial states of the twentieth century. It is these novelties that have caused training methods to receive so much attention.

There are logical problems with the notion that individual differences are critical to learning tasks or constellations of tasks. The necessity or importance of skillfully performing one set of tasks or another varies by social customs, institutions, and technology. And *social institutions and technologies change much more rapidly than human characteristics*. Human evolution proceeds too slowly for natural selection to sculpt talents for tasks that come and go as technologies and customs change. Computer programming came into being in the second half of the twentieth century with the advent of computer technology. Obviously "computer programming aptitude" did not evolve over millennia; nor did the other aptitudes and traits associated with modern technological and cultural activities. As technology and culture change and create new activities and skill demands, some people will *just happen to have* a greater amount of an evolved trait that also *just happens to be* relevant to the skillful execution of a novel cultural activity. For most of human history and in almost all cultures, people did not care one whit about the ability to swim fast. Inherited traits that would help a person to swim fast (like very large feet) were, therefore, not prized. With the advent of swimming as a competitive sport, a growing number of people actually cared how fast someone could swim. So, people who happened to have big feet and who liked to swim were in luck. The great Australian swimmer and 2000 Olympic medalist Ian Thorpe has exceptionally large feet—he wears a size 17 shoe. His large feet gave him an edge in swimming by making it easier for him to propel himself forward (Magnay, 2000). Spatial ability evolved over millennia because people who had greater degrees of it were more successful at navigation, which is important to hunting and gathering. As technology evolved, spatial ability just happened to be useful for a host of new activities, such as piloting sailing ships, architecture, mechanical engineering, and programming computers.

Another problem associated with making too much of the role of individual differences in learning and training is the multiplicity of human psychological traits. Psychologists have identified literally hundreds of personality traits (many of which can be subsumed within a smaller number of more general traits, such as the Big Five). They have also identified numerous types of mental and physical abilities. How constellations of traits relate to task performance would be an inordinately complex problem if there were only one optimal combination of traits for skillfully performing a task. To take a simplified case, if three ability and six personality traits at two levels of each trait (high, low) were involved, there would be 512 possible combinations of traits. Which one is optimal? Fortunately, this was probably not a serious problem throughout human history because the same outcome can be achieved by a variety of means, by a variety of constellations of traits, and by different behavioral strategies. An evolutionary perspective—while acknowledging the existence of traits—does not make them a focus of training and of efforts to develop skilled performance.[14]

LEARNING AND TRAINING FROM AN EVOLUTIONARY PERSPECTIVE

An evolutionary perspective adds to our understanding of abilities, skills, and learning—and ultimately to education and training. It does not, however, replace classical stimulus-response learning theory from the behaviorist and cognitive traditions. It adds fine-tuning and modifications that enhance learning theory—the influence of content and context on learning, a revised view about the role of individual differences, equifinality in skill development and task performance, and the importance to organizations of a diverse skill base. These new insights also suggest several practical implications for training: tapping evolved mechanisms to make training more enjoyable, the importance of practice, groups and training, modeling skills, and training for novel situations.

When Learning Is Fun and When It Is Not

Acquiring primary abilities and the skills related to them should be relatively easy and pleasurable. Primary abilities are fully developed by the time most individuals become adults. Training will be more enjoyable in adults to the extent that training activities take advantage of primary abilities.[15] Learning biologically secondary abilities and skills will be more pleasurable and successful when training methods utilize neurocognitive mechanisms that are compatible with biologically primary abilities (Csikszentmihalyi, 1990). Coöpting primary abilities will increase the success of training by increasing the pleasure students experience during learning, which in turn will result in lower dropout rates and greater persistence and practice. Spoken language is a primary ability (Pinker, 1994). Training sessions that allow students to talk, to discuss problems and cases, to interact with fellow students, and to tell stories will be more enjoyable than training methods that do not. Coöpting primary abilities also increases success by building on existing, primary abilities. Consider phonics—a highly effective method for teaching children to read, a method that has been used in diverse cultures for centuries (Chall, 1992; Rayner, Foorman, Perfetti, Pesetsky, & Seidenberg, 2001). One reason for its enduring success is that phonics coöpts the primary abilities used in understanding and producing spoken language. Phonics associates symbols with sounds that are common to spoken language.

Unfortunately, we do not have a complete theory of biologically primary and secondary abilities. However, if we consider pan-cultural behaviors along with the literature from developmental psychology, we can suggest several primary abilities besides language: (1) reasoning ability, (2) social ability, (3) moral ability, and (4) kinesthetic ability. It seems reasonably clear that humans have a neurological substrate related to reasoning (problem-solving) ability (Jensen, 1998). People are more engaged and enjoy learning more when they can actively solve problems (Csikszentmihalyi, 1990). Training sessions that build in problems are intrinsically enjoyable because they simulate the primary ability of reasoning. Humans also have biologically hardwired social abilities. Training is engaging when the social interaction in training sessions is pleasant. Recall that students give teachers high ratings when they use friendly non-verbal behaviors, such as smiling (Ambady & Rosenthal, 1993). Cooperation and competition stem from primary social abilities (Colarelli, Alampay, & Canali, 2001). Competitive behavior often ensues when males are placed in a group. Females in groups, on the other hand, are more cooperative, although they compete with one another as well. The human proclivity for sports, contests, and games is universal. Therefore, training activities that engage a sense of competition or cooperation will usually be intrinsically enjoyable. Humans also appear to have an innate sense of morality (Cosmides & Tooby, 1992; Cummins, 1998). They are acutely aware of someone who doesn't contribute his fair share in a group, who reneges on an exchange, and who commits a morally offensive behavior. Thus, training activities that use moral problems are intrinsically interesting. Bringing up affirmative action, the death penalty, income redistribution, and similar topics with strong moral overtones guarantee lively class discussions. Kinesthesis (moving in space, positioning the body for locomotion) is a biologically primary ability (Heinrich, 2001). Training sessions are more likely to be enjoyable when students can be active during training. Anyone who has sat through a day-long training session with little opportunity to get up and move around knows this.

Drill and Deliberate Practice

Engaging primary abilities during training sessions keeps students interested and motivated and provides a strong foundation for the development of secondary abilities and skills. However, because biologically secondary abilities are only tangentially based on innate neurocognitive mechanisms, secondary abilities and skills related to those abilities can be difficult to learn and are not always intrinsically enjoyable. Therefore, learning biologically secondary abilities and skills requires drill-and-practice. There is no easy way to acquire most biologically secondary abilities and skills. Greater levels of skill require greater investments in drill and practice.[16] The work by scholars in a number of disciplines shows that practice, or "time on task," is strongly related to skillful performance. Ericsson and his colleagues have found in repeated studies that the amount of deliberate practice is the primary influence on expert performance. People who perform at expert levels practice more, have a longer history of practice, and practice more consistently than people who perform at less skillful levels (Ericsson & Lehmann, 1996). Benjamin Bloom and his colleagues (Bloom, 1974; 1985) also found that time on task (or practice) is the most important variable in learning in school as well as in reaching high levels of performance in sports, music, the visual arts, and the professions. Harold Stevenson's research on the recurrent differences between Asian and American students in scores on standardized mathematics tests points not to innate differences but rather to the differences in the amount of practice, teaching methods, and parental attitudes (Stevenson, Chen, & Lee, 1993). Asian teaching methods are more focused; they stay on one subject for a longer period of time, and they involve more drill-and-practice than American methods. Asian parents are also more likely than American parents to believe that a student's success at school is due to practice and hard work, whereas American parents are more likely to attribute it to innate talent.[17] Studies by Charles Hulin and his colleagues found that, over a range of abilities and criteria for performance, the relationship between initial ability level and performance decreases over time, so that after about five years initial ability is essentially unrelated to the level of performance (Hulin, Henry, & Noon, 1990). These results are congruent with John Carroll's (1963) thesis that differences in aptitudes or intelligence primarily reflect *differences in learning rates*. Thus, most people, regardless of initial ability, can master most tasks, given sufficient time and practice.[18]

The focus on technologies that has dominated the educational and industrial training fields is misplaced. More important is something more basic: practice. Access to computers, CD-ROMs, and distance learning are likely to do little to teach new or improve existing skills because one cannot practice on a computer. One cannot practice speaking French, playing tennis, doing open-heart surgery, or repairing a dent in a car on a computer. Computers are not good at motivating people to practice. The critical components of effective practice are identifying skills and practicing them in sustained, deliberate ways. Practice is not sexy. Managers, school and university administrators, and politicians gain favorable publicity by introducing visible, high-tech training practices. Vendors can make a lot of money by selling high-tech training gizmos and distance learning packages. It is hard to get promoted or to make money by selling practice. Interestingly, many companies intuitively favor an emphasis on practice. This is implied by their use of on-the-job training (OJT), which turns out to be the most common form of training. American organizations spend between $90 and $180 billion on OJT compared to $30 billion for formal training programs (Carnevale, 1989). Almost all organizations use OJT, whereas only a few use formal training methods (Noe, 1999). Similarly, the training that young people clamor for the most is training that involves real-world experience. Many undergraduate and graduate students seek internships, practica, and field experience, while they tend to be more reserved about classroom instruction.

Training in Groups

For most of human history, people developed abilities and skills in a small group. Within the family group infants learn language, locomotion, what to eat, how to eat, and hygiene from their parents and siblings. Peer groups are a fundamental part of how children and adolescents learn basic developmental abilities and skills. Beginning at about age three, children begin forming play-groups and spend more and more of their time with other children of about the same age. As children near age five, their play-groups become increasingly composed of members of the same sex; this preference for same-sex playmates is a cross-cultural universal (Whiting & Edwards, 1988). Children learn games and sports in groups from other children. The games that young humans play with one another, like the play of other young mammals, helps the young learn abilities and skills that will help them to survive and reproduce in adulthood (Boulton & Smith, 1992). Time spent with other children increases as children grow older and by adolescence, children spend a majority of their waking time with groups of other adolescents (Harris, 1999). The influence of children's peer groups on language learning is also critical (Harris, 1999). This can be seen in a dramatic way when parents and their young children move to a new country where the language is different than their native one. The parents typically speak the language of the new country with an accent characteristic of their native language. Yet, within a short time, usually less than a year, young children are speaking the language of the adopted country with near-perfect fluency, without a trace of the accents of their parents. They pick up the new language primarily from their peers—including the colloquialisms and slang common among young persons (Harris, 1999). The "language gate" in the human brain enables children (up to about the age of 12) to acquire languages with greater ease than adults. I can vividly recall the change in language skills of the young children of my office-mate in graduate school. He was a Venezuelan. With his wife and three children (ages 3, 7, and 11), he temporarily relocated in the United States to complete his Ph.D. studies. He spoke good English with a Spanish accent. His children had never been to the United States, and they spoke no English when they arrived. Within 12 months, his children were speaking fluent English. By the time we had finished our studies—about 30 months later—his children were speaking as though they had lived in New Jersey for their entire lives. Yet he and his wife continued to speak with the same Spanish accent they had when they arrived 30 months earlier. Children's ability to learn languages so easily before the age of 12 is a primary ability. That foreign-language instruction in the United States occurs primarily in high school and college is an example of the failure of educators to make use of biologically primary abilities. If foreign-language instruction were concentrated in the early grades, children in the United States would become considerably more fluent in foreign languages.

In nonindustrialized societies, children learn work-related abilities and skills primarily from participating in same-sex work groups of older children and adults who engage in agriculture, crafts, hunting, and gathering. Whiting and Whiting (1975) carried out extensive observations of children in several nonindustrialized societies. They reported that, by middle childhood, boys were typically placed into groups of older boys and men where they learned to herd large animals. Girls were typically assigned to the task of caring for younger children. This kept them in the company of older girls and women, where they also would learn other gender-specific tasks. Sexual behavior is learned primarily in groups of peers. Among humans and other primates, much of the "how-to" of sexual behavior is learned in groups of peers (Symons, 1979).

Apprenticeships among young adults are common in virtually all societies. Young adults are placed in a work group (e.g., hunting, canoe-building, weaving, making pottery) valued by the larger social unit. New group members go through a period of formal and informal training where they learn from masters, as well as from more experienced students (Lave & Wenger, 1991). Formal training typically includes explicit instruction from masters of a craft and the opportunity for extensive practice on tasks appropriate to the trainee's level of skill. Informal training may include assisting with and observing tasks involved in the craft and informal discussions of work-related topics (Coy, 1989). Although apprenticeship training is commonly associated with skilled crafts and trades, apprenticeships are also common in the sciences and professions (although they are not formally called "apprenticeships"). Gawande (2002) describes how he learned to become a proficient surgeon. His residency training was essentially an apprenticeship—the young surgeon engaged in learning-by-doing under the guidance of experienced masters. Graduate students earning their Ph.Ds typically apprentice themselves to a professor through whom they learn the craft of research.

Throughout human evolutionary history, critically important abilities and skills have been learned in the context of a group. This learning has the following characteristics. People engage in face-to-face interaction in a small group for extended periods of time, for months and often years. New initiates to the group gradually increase the degree to which they participate in tasks. As they learn more, they do more and do more complex tasks. They also gradually increase their social activities, moving from the marginal to legitimate members of the group. A central feature of these group contexts is the *opportunity to practice*. Such groups are what Lave and Wenger (1991) call "communities of practice." The work gets done, but part of it involves practice for new members. Novices work on simple aspects of a project. People with higher-level skills work on the complicated tasks. Working with a group creates identification with the group and its mores. Students gradually learn the lore of the group; they learn its lingo; they become enmeshed in a network of relationships; they become competent; they gain status and identity. As they gain status and form an identity associated with the group—seeing themselves in a particular way—they are more likely to actively acquire and practice skills that are congruent with that identity. If a person sees himself as a master carpenter and if he knows that others see him as such, he is motivated to seek knowledge, skills, and tools that are commensurate with that identity. Apprentice groups also enhance motivation through competition inherent in groups. Even if it is not an explicitly competitive group (like a sports team), people in groups—particularly males—typically become competitive with one another (Colarelli, Alampay, & Canali, 2001). The drive for status and resources motivates people to want to outperform their peers. And to outperform peers, one must practice and acquire superior skills.

Much of human learning is adapted to the small group. From boys learning to herd animals in rural villages to graduate students learning the craft of scientific research in universities, the apprentice group has remained a powerful instrument of human learning. This is due to both sociocultural evolution and to evolved psychological mechanisms that predispose people to associate in groups, to gather information from face-to-face interaction, and to learn by observing and doing. No learning context besides the small group affords all of these features. Web-based courses do not involve face-to-face interaction. Information is transmitted to the learner, but the transmitter is not interacting with the learner. In a lecture or seminar, there is only one master, the instructor. Most students are initiates and therefore do not have more experienced peers to interact with. When it comes to practice, students are on their own.

If people want to enhance their skills, one of the most important things they can do is to join groups where people are engaged in the activity that interests them. Clusters of people engaged in a desired activity generate *situated learning* as newcomers immerse themselves in a context that gives them the opportunity to observe good performance, perform, and practice (Lave & Wenger, 1991). Joining a club has been a tried-and-true way of learning skills. People in the Western part of the United States who are interested in mountaineering and rock climbing join climbing clubs, such as the Mountaineers in Washington or the Colorado Mountain Club. The same is true of bicyclists, runners, bowlers, thespians, and bird-watchers. One common theme that appears to run through the lives of individuals who are accomplished is that they joined groups, usually clubs or similar voluntary associations (Bloom, 1985). Many of Kenya's elite runners spent years as members of running clubs, schools, or military organizations that were magnets for talented long-distance runners (Tanser, 1997/1998). In the Dominican Republic, there are "hundreds of locally organized amateur [baseball] leagues, where most of the young players who go on to play professionally begin their careers" (Klein, 1991, p. 44). Clubs have also been found to be important in developing chess-playing skills.

> Clubs provide players, particularly young ones, with reliable access to organized chess activities, chess lessons, newsletters, and often, a chess library. . . . Clubs also help to socialize players into the serious chess-playing subculture. In Europe, clubs sometimes also have commercial sponsors who can provide financial support to players who represent them

in interclub tournaments. . . . [The] age at which players join a club is one index of when they become serious about chess. (Charness, Krampe, & Mayr, 1996, pp. 61–62)

Clubs are communities of practice. Much of a club's activities involve doing and hence practicing—rock climbing, public speaking, chess, sewing quilts. Many provide a type of apprenticeship. Initiates are peripheral. A club includes people with a variety of skills, ranging from beginners to masters, and newer people learn from more advanced peers and masters. As they become increasingly skilled, they become more central to the club and take up mentoring and leadership roles.

Self-help groups appear to be similar to clubs. Self-help groups are also effective in teaching people the skills and attitudes associated with personal change and "healthy" physical and psychological habits (Lave & Wenger, 1991; Lieberman, Yalom, & Miles, 1973). Some self-help groups can be as effective or more effective than treatment provided by mental health professionals for some maladies. One study lasting eight years and costing $27 million found that participation in Alcoholics Anonymous (AA) was as effective in reducing alcohol consumption as cognitive-behavioral or motivational therapies (Project Match, 1997). Self-help groups are common. AA alone has about 60,000 members, and approximately 100 million Americans, almost one-third of the population, say they have participated in some type of self-help group (Gallup, 1994).

Organizations might want to pay employees' club dues as well as give employees time off to attend club meetings and other functions. Up-and-coming managers could polish their speaking skills by joining Toastmasters International, the public speaking club. Of course, the right type of club may not be available, so another strategy is for organizations to encourage the formation of clubs. If particular skills are needed and seem to be lacking, managers could structure incentives for the development of clubs that focus on those skills. In addition to providing instruction in particular skills, clubs socialize members, develop networks of contact, perhaps provide some competitive atmosphere to motivate skill development, and provide opportunities for practice.

Unfortunately, many organizations do not utilize clubs for training because clubs are difficult for managers to control and because consultants and the training industry cannot make much money from them. Clubs are voluntary and autonomous. Managers are hesitant to encourage activities over which they have limited or no control. They are more comfortable using internal HR departments or external consultants for whose services they pay and whose services they can terminate. No one stands to make much money by encouraging clubs. A huge training and consulting industry thrives on peddling a panoply of "off-the-shelf" training programs. Many human resource professionals make a living as trainers. It is not in their interest to tell managers that employees could learn skills less expensively, and often more effectively, by joining clubs. Similarly, textbooks on psychological treatments authored by clinical psychologists do not recommend that people forego professional therapy and join self-help groups. It is not in professionals' self-interest to direct clients to other means, more common and less expensive, that work as well or better than their services.

Skilled people produce skilled people. People inevitably increase their skill level when they are around others with higher levels of skills than their own. A common thread among many eminent individuals is that they were either born in an area or moved to a location where there was a critical mass of people engaged in the endeavor in which they became eminent (Simonton, 1999). People who seek fame and fortune in the performing arts in the United States gravitate to Los Angeles or New York City. Those who want to become outstanding rock climbers gravitate to the climbing meccas like Boulder, Colorado and Yosemite National Park in California. Many parents know that peers are a significant influence on the type and level of skills their children develop (Harris, 1999). Moving an underachieving child to a school where children do well in school can improve the child's performance. Creating meeting spaces and workrooms where experienced, skilled students can interact with and teach new students can be a very effective way to bring new students up to speed. The graduate students in the programs I teach need to learn how to use the computer, particularly to analyze data. Early in my career the graduate students regularly petitioned the faculty to teach a minicourse on computer use and statistical packages. Rather than teaching the course, the faculty arranged for a slew of computers to be moved into two student workrooms where the students would congregate to do computer work. Inevitably, the new students started learning computer skills from the experienced students by watching and asking questions.

The preference of many employers for on-the-job training suggests an understanding of the importance of peers to skill development. Job rotation—moving people into new jobs and departments—is also a common training method in organizations, and it takes advantage of the dynamic of learning skills from peers. In academia, postdoctoral fellowships, visiting professorships, or sabbatical leaves have similar effects. Postdoctoral fellowships allow newly minted Ph.D.s to work with or in the lab of a senior faculty member at an institution other than where they received their degrees. Fellows spend from one to several years working on their own research as well as that of the senior faculty member who acquired the grant to fund the postdoctoral degree. This experience typically puts the new Ph.D.s in a high-powered university with high-powered faculty, learning the craft of research and writing by performing, practicing, and learning from masters and peers. Visiting professorships involve university faculty members going to another university for a semester or longer. They experience a different setting and may learn new ideas, skills, and strategies. Sabbatical leaves, again common in academia, allow a faculty member, about every seven years, to take a semester or a year off from her regular duties to work on a project of her choice. Many often use the time to conduct research, write, or update their class notes. However, travel to other universities and research institutes is common, and the time faculty spend in other institutions allows situated learning to take place. Similar types of opportunities exist in the military, which regularly sends soldiers to train and work with other units and on educational leaves (Beckwith & Knox, 1983).

Sabbatical leaves, postdoctoral fellowships, and visiting professorships are rare in the world of commerce and industry. Immediate production, profit, share price, and competition with other firms are the driving concerns of commerce and industry. Thus, it is not realistic for key personnel to take six months to a year off to work on a project, work in another firm on a temporary assignment, or invest time and energy in ancillary study. However, organizations can reap the benefits of situated learning by locating a firm in an industry center—Silicon Valley for computers, New York City for finance, Chicago for food commodities, Los Angeles for the movie industry, Nashville for country music. This gives a firm a large pool of *potential* employees who have learned from skillful employees in similar organizations. The inevitable turnover and mixing of people allows firms to acquire people with valuable skills, learned from their previous jobs. The Ford Motor Company decided to move its luxury car division and General Motors its advanced design centers to Southern California for precisely this reason—to take advantage of the concentration of skilled designers and the strong car culture in the area (O'Dell, 2000).

Situated learning, however, presupposes time, interaction, masters, and a group of people who have well-honed skills. This approach is not realistic in situations where people must acquire skills rapidly, where new technologies have rapidly made existing skills obsolete, or where new social structures have isolated old-timers from initiates. Recent laws limiting the number of terms that state legislators can serve have created conditions where it is difficult for effective situated learning to take place in legislatures. In Michigan, the limit is six years. Prior to the term limit law, new legislators learned their trade from old-timers in the state house. Old-timers who were regularly re-elected were repositories of legislative experience. Term limits eliminated them. New legislators could no longer find mentors who would give them the benefit of their years of experience. There was no longer a community of practice to pass on traditions to new members. Thus, to learn new legislative skills, Michigan lawmakers had to rely on short-term training sessions, which the legislature instituted soon after the term-limits were imposed (Bryant, 1989).

The rapid introduction of new technologies creates a similar problem. It is difficult for people to learn how to use a new technology when it first emerges because few people know anything about it. This was a problem Gutenberg faced after he invented the printing press. The only people who knew how to use it were a small community of experienced printers in Mainz, Germany, where Gutenberg lived. However, a quirk of history enabled the printing press to spread rapidly throughout Europe. The city of Mainz was pillaged, thus forcing experienced printers to migrate and set up printing shops in other cities (Geck, 1968). Distance learning is a new technology that was introduced in the late 1990s, and many universities have attempted to develop programs based on it. Yet faculty members were more or less on their own when it came to developing web-based courses because there were no cadres of experienced old-timers who knew anything about web courses. Until a critical mass of experience accumulates, progress with a new technology can only move in fits and starts.

Finally, there is the problem of access. One can benefit from a community of practice only if (1) a community of practice is available, (2) one is admitted to the community, and (3) one has the time and resources to participate. Communities of practices are not available everywhere. There are more skiing clubs in Colorado and Utah than in Illinois and Mississippi. If a community to which one aspires is unavailable, one must pick up and move to where one exists or go without the experience. Even if a community is nearby, gaining access may be problematic. Some communities may have admission criteria that exclude many qualified aspirants. And even if one is admitted, only those with the time and resources to fully participate in a community will benefit from it. People need to devote considerable time—often several years—to an apprenticeship (formal or informal) in a community of practice. In addition, initiates typically exchange their labor for the opportunity to perform.[19] People who cannot make ends meet during an apprenticeship (those with families to support, for example) are unlikely to participate.

Evolutionary Approaches to Training in Novel Situations

Evolution is historical. Therefore, skills that develop over a period of time and are adaptive in a given context are an important part of an evolutionary approach to training. Nevertheless, insights from evolutionary psychology can be useful when there are no cadres of experienced old-timers to teach novices or where skills need to be learned quickly. Training programs should adhere as closely as possible to the evolutionary principles described earlier: face-to-face interaction and the opportunity for observation, modeling, feedback, and extensive practice. When few skilled people are available, training programs can be designed by interviewing those who are skilled and teaching the material to a larger number of trainers. However, this approach can only go so far. Trainers' lack of experience and expertise in the skill itself precludes them from being able to deal with as many problems, questions, and contingencies as old-timers. Peer interaction can partially compensate for trainers' limitations, and it also injects some of the benefits of learning in a group. Talented students will learn faster than others; students who bring different experiences to the class will interpret the material in slightly different ways. By structuring training so that students have the opportunity to interact with one another over an extended period of time, they learn from one another. Particularly when the skills are based on a new technology, and hence there is not a large existing knowledge base, peer interaction is likely to foster incremental learning because each student will contribute from a somewhat different knowledge base that may be useful to others. Creating a "learning hothouse" can also be useful in situations where there is not a base of experience. In a learning hothouse, people who are learning the new skills and technologies are clustered together for extended periods of time. Intensive, focused interaction can accelerate learning and the development of expertise.

At the level of the system, the most important thing an organization can do is to allow many variations in its approach to training. Training systems should teach skills that may be useful as organizations' environments change. All organizations face uncertainty, some more than others. Flexibility and variety in training programs—the skills taught and the methods of teaching—provide a hedge against the uncertainty of changing environments and inevitable new skill requirements (Alchian, 1950; Boyd & Richerson, 1985; Campbell, 1965; Nelson & Winter, 1982). A pragmatic recommendation might be that managers allow, say, 20 percent of annual training hours to be in any area and from any program of their employees' choice. Similarly, encouraging employees to join clubs that foster skills and to pursue interests (regardless of how far afield they may seem) will help build a diverse skill base. Imitation is another useful approach under conditions of uncertainty (Alchian, 1950). Imitating the practices of successful organizations is often adaptive by allowing organizations to appropriate the successful trial-and-error learning of other organizations with less cost. It is also a powerful source of variation from which efficient training technologies can evolve. New programs may originate through imperfect copies of other programs. Sometimes imperfect imitations exhibit new attributes that lead to the development of different types of programs.

In summary, training is paradoxical and prodigious. Over the past century, formal training has become paradoxical because, on the one hand, it is admired and advocated while, on the other hand, the relative investments in it are modest and people can become quite skillful without formal training. The paradoxes associated with training stem from an overregard for training technology, an underappreciation for traditional training practices, and a lack of research on the social and psychological wellsprings of traditional training practices. People have been acquiring ecologically relevant knowledge and skills and passing them on to new generations—and doing so quite well—throughout human history. An evolutionary perspective directs our thinking to the context in which humans typically learned and how the mind responds differentially to different content. It means thinking about how current contexts may or may not be conducive to learning. People generally learn better in groups than in classrooms and better in classrooms than in front of computer screens. It means thinking critically about the models of the mind and learning and the usefulness of those models for the practice of training and education. If the mind were really like a blank slate or a computer, then algebra would be as easy to learn as sex, sex education would have been a success story, and adults would be able to learn languages as easily as children do. This makes evolutionary sense. People are more likely to learn behaviors that have greater survival and reproductive value. An evolutionary perspective allows us to become more attuned to what is easy and difficult to learn, the best places to learn in, and how to structure learning in modern learning environments so that they are most compatible with human nature and the nature of human learning.

NOTES

1. The probability of doing well economically and occupationally increases with a college education. Statistically, there is a relationship between earning a

college degree and economic and occupational success. Yet, as the examples of successful individuals without a college education illustrate, skills and knowledge that contribute to occupational and economic success can be learned elsewhere. Entry into some fields is impossible without appropriate formal education. These are fields in which entry is contingent upon educational credentials (e.g., medicine, law, nursing, K–12 teaching), often mandated by law. In addition, some occupations are difficult to learn anywhere but in universities (e.g., experimental physics, archeology) because essential technology and people with specialized knowledge are located primarily at universities.

2. The idea that schools and universities should teach skills is wrongheaded. Schools should be responsible for developing core abilities—abilities that typically take years to develop and upon which skills can be built. Too much emphasis on teaching skills in schools is misguided because students usually cannot learn the precise skills they will use at a given workplace anywhere but that workplace. Most workplaces do things their own way, and these specialized skills can therefore only be learned in those particular environments. No school can teach all of the nuances of the many workplaces they serve. Businesses that want schools to teach skills are essentially lobbying for corporate welfare—asking schools to do for them what they should be doing for themselves. Certainly, it is the schools' responsibility to provide businesses with good raw material, students who can read and write and perform basic mathematics, but not beyond that. Indeed, one of the major reasons for the problems that have plagued American schools in the twentieth century and today is that they have taught too many skills and in so doing have watered down the teaching of basic abilities (Ravitch, 2000).

3. Most people who earn a Ph.D., even in today's world of high-tech universities, still learn by the age-old apprenticeship method—by interacting extensively with a faculty who serves as the student's mentor. I suspect that this may even be the case for those Ph.D.s who write about the virtues of high-tech training methods.

4. In fairness to Goldstein, he does point out that mechanical methods often do not produce any better results than traditional or on-the-job training methods.

5. According to Diamond, these propensities include diet (carnivores are less efficient to keep than herbivores), growth rate (some species grow too slowly), problems of captive breeding (some potentially useful species are particular about where they have sex), nasty disposition (a propensity to bite or kill humans), tendency to panic (it is difficult to keep a nervous species in captivity), and social structure (species whose social structure involves a well-established dominance hierarchy are easier to domesticate because humans can take over the dominance hierarchy).

6. My good friend, Tom Bertonneau, brought this idea to my attention.

7. During a year of flush budgets and revenue forecasts, many Michigan legislators wanted to add $110 million to K–12 educational appropriations to create a "virtual high school" and to provide all public school teachers with laptop computers (Gregg, 2000).

8. Interestingly, most K–12 schools in the United States do not evaluate teachers on the basis of student ratings. One reason is that K–12 education is (not yet) commodified. By law, all children must attend school, and they have no choice in the matter. In addition, it is still presumed that students are not always happy about learning, but that there is a certain body of knowledge that they must master whether they like it or not.

9. The promotional brochures that colleges send to students typically portray happy students having fun. It would be interesting to look at such brochures over the 75 years to see if the emphasis on fun changed over time.

10. The "BCS" conference is the Bowl Championship conference—the group of conferences in which teams play national football championships. These include the Big Ten, Big 12, Southeastern, Atlantic Coast, Big East, and Pacific 10 conferences.

11. This begs the question, why was Brother O' Connell such a good track coach? According to Tanser:

> Colm [O'Connell] simply watched and learned. "I depended upon what I saw and observed." This Colm recalled was invaluable as it gave him a perception of the athlete instead of athletics. . . . Colm places the credit on the Kenyan mentality. "Kenyans are very responsive to any sort of challenge; it is easy to motivate them. . . . The funny thing is that I haven't the qualifications for the job; I would have never been given the opportunity in England or Ireland." (1997/1998, pp. 108–109)

12. This is commonplace at universities, where new professors are hired primarily on the basis of their academic specialization and potential as scholars. While universities religiously give lip-service to good teaching, teaching future professors how to teach is a minimal to nonexistent component of most Ph.D. programs that offer formal instruction on college teaching. Many new faculty learn how to teach on their own.

13. Kingsley Browne and David Geary both pointed out to me that my critique of IQ and other standardized tests is overly harsh. I plead guilty. I have not gone into detail on the extensive literature that shows that cognitive ability and some personality traits predict a variety of outcomes (Herrnstein & Murray, 1994; Hogan, 1991; Jensen, 1998). This is well known, and it was not my intention to argue that this literature is wrong. The problem is that the relatively *moderate* correlations between IQ or conscientiousness and some outcomes have become reified and viewed myopically. That there is a positive correlation between IQ and income or college grades simply means that in a large sample of people there is a higher probability that more people with higher IQ scores will have higher incomes or grades than those with lower scores. Such statistical relationships can say nothing about how any *particular individual* will do. They do not tell us about other attributes of a person or, in most cases, how those other attributes affect outcomes. Of course, this is less so when dealing with large differences in scores. Yet, because people tend to gravitate to activities and occupations that are consonant with their abilities and interests

(Lancaster, Colarelli, King, & Beehr, 1994), it is rare that applicant pools include many people who would be incapable of performing satisfactorily.

We also do not know much about the mechanisms that lead to skillful performance. Yet, very often testers are all too comfortable making statements about what a person can achieve primarily on the basis of an IQ score. This leads to a certain intellectual, administrative, and ethical laziness—an intellectual laziness because other mechanisms influencing outcomes are glossed over (Simonton, 1999—in particular, pp. 2–7); an administrative laziness because decision makers base admission decisions primarily on one bit of information, a standardized test score; and an ethical laziness because many people are unfairly discriminated against and denied opportunities because of their test scores. Because IQ scores predict school and job performance only moderately (and even less so over the long term), a number of people with scores below the cutoff point would be able to perform as well as people above it, yet they are denied opportunities.

14. There are, however, some evolutionary psychologists who place more emphasis on traits (e.g., Segal & Macdonald, 1998).

15. This is particularly true for children (Geary, 1995). Almost all children enjoy talking and playing games that involve counting (jacks) and elementary navigation (hide-and-seek).

16. An interesting question is why do biologically secondary skills require so much practice? What is the evolutionary reason why they take so much more practice than primary abilities? The adaptive mechanism here may be similar to that in memory. Why are some types of information easily remembered (e.g., threatening events, highly pleasurable events) while others are much more difficult to remember (new words, strings of arbitrary numbers)? Events that have survival and reproductive value are more easily remembered. If the mind remembered everything that was presented to it, it would become cluttered, and it would be difficult for people to distinguish the important from the unimportant. The brain probably evolved to regard events and facts not immediately related to survival and reproduction as important *only when they have been learned through extensive repetition*. The same logic may also apply to learning skills and abilities.

17. This interpretation is further supported by research by Geary and his colleagues in which Chinese and American children and adults were matched on IQ (Geary et al., 1997). When matched on IQ, sixth and twelfth grade Chinese students performed better on math tests than American students. However, older (60- to 80-year-olds) Chinese and American adults, also matched on IQ, did not differ on math tests. Presumably, math education in China a generation ago was not on a par with what it is today. This suggests that the math gap between Chinese and American students is not due to differences in innate ability but to differences in competencies attained through learning strategies and practice.

18. Given the importance of time on task to learning, an important question is, what motivates people to stick with a task until they learn it well?

19. Exploitation of initiates in communities of practice can be a problem. Unethical masters may use initiates for cheap labor while not fulfilling on their end of the bargain to train them.

REFERENCES

Alchian, A. A. (1950). Uncertainty, evolution, and economic theory. *Journal of Political Economy, 58,* 211–22.

Alcock, J. (1993). *Animal behavior: An evolutionary approach* (5th ed.). Sunderland, MA: Sinauer.

Allison, E. (1977). *Educational production function for an introductory economics course* (Discussion Paper No. 545). Cambridge, MA: Harvard University, Harvard Institute of Economic Research.

Allison, P. D., & Long, J. S. (1990). Departmental effects on scientific productivity. *American Sociological Review, 55,* 469–478.

Ambady, N., & Rosenthal, R. (1993). Half a minute: Predicting teacher evaluations from thin slices of nonverbal behavior and physical attractiveness. *Journal of Personality & Social Psychology, 64,* 431–441.

American Association for the Advancement of Science. (2001). *Congressional Action on Research and Development in the FY 2001 Budget*-Table 1. Retrieved July 15, 2001, from the World Wide Web: *http://www.aaas.org/spp/dspp/rd/ca01.pdf.*

Auerbach, R. (2000, December). What I've learned. *Esquire,* 114.

Average Salaries of Full-Time Faculty Members 2000–1. (2001, August 31). *Chronicle of Higher Education,* p. 27.

Balter, M. (2002). What made humans modern? *Science, 295,* 1219–1225.

Bandura, A. (1977). *Social learning theory.* New York: Prentice Hall.

Baron-Cohen, S. (1997). How to build a baby that can read minds: Cognitive mechanisms in mindreading. In S. Baron-Cohen (Ed.), *The maladapted mind: Classic readings in evolutionary psychopathology* (pp. 207–239). East Sussex, UK: Psychology Press.

Beal, C. R. (1994). *Boys and girls.* New York: McGraw-Hill.

Beckwith, C. A., & Knox, D. (1983). *Delta force.* New York: Harcourt Brace Jovanovich.

Belasco, J., & Trice, H. M. (1969, July). Unanticipated returns of training. *Training and Development Journal,* 12–17.

Bowen, W. G., & Bok, D. (1998). *The shape of the river: Long-term consequences of considering race in college and university admissions.* Princeton, NJ: Princeton University Press.

Bloom, B. A. (1974). Time and learning. *American Psychologist, 29,* 682–688.

Bloom, B. A. (Ed.) (1985). *Developing talent in young people.* New York: Ballantine.

Boulton, M. J., & Smith, P. K. (1992). The social nature of play fighting and play chasing: Mechanisms and strategies underlying cooperation and compromise. In J. H. Barkow, L. Cosmides, & J. Tooby (Eds.), *The adapted mind: evolutionary psychology and the generation of culture* (pp. 429–444). New York: Oxford University Press.

Boyd, R., & Richerson, P. J. (1985). *Culture and the evolutionary process.* Chicago: University of Chicago Press.

Bregman, E. (1934). An attempt to modify the emotional attitudes of infants by the conditioned response technique. *Journal of Genetic Psychology, 45,* 169–198.

Brown, K. G. (2001). Using computers to deliver training: Which employees learn and why? *Personnel Psychology, 54,* 271–296.

Bruner, J. S. (1963). Needed: A theory of instruction. *Educational Leadership, 20,* 523–532.

Bryant, W. R., Jr. (1989). Building legislative skills. *The Journal of State Government, 62,* 216–218.

Bryck, I. (2001). *With good sense, dollars will follow.* The University of Massachussets Family Business Center. Retrieved July 15, 2001, from the World Wide Web: *http://www.umass.edu/fambiz/good_sense_dollars_follow.htm*

Bureau of Labor Statistics. (2000). *Consumer Expenditure Survey.* Retrieved March 8, 2002, from the World Wide Web: *http://www.bls.gov/cex/home.htm*

Buss, D. A. (1999). *Evolutionary psychology.* Boston: Allyn & Bacon.

Callahan, R. (1962). *Education and the cult of efficiency.* Chicago: University of Chicago Press.

Campbell, D. T. (1975). On the conflicts between biological and social evolution and between psychology and moral tradition. *American Psychologist, 30,* 1103–1126.

Campbell, D. T. (1965). Variation and selective retention in socio-cultural evolution. In H. R. Barringer, G. I. Blanksten, & R. W. Mack (Eds.), *Social change in developing areas* (pp. 19–49). Cambridge, MA: Schenkman.

Campbell, J. P. (1971). Personnel training and development. *Annual Review of Psychology.* Palo Alto, CA: Annual Reviews.

Carnevale, A. P. (1989, February). The learning enterprise. *Training and Development Journal,* 26–37.

Carr, S. (2001, February 16). Is anyone making money on distance education? *Chronicle of Higher Education,* pp. A41–A43.

Carrns, A. (2000, November 24). Hit hard by imports, American pencil icon tries to get a grip. *Wall Street Journal,* pp. A1, A7.

Carroll, J. B. (1963, May). A model of school learning. *Teachers College Record,* 723–733.

Cascio, W. F. (1998). *Applied psychology in human resource management* (5th ed.). Upper Saddle River, NJ: Prentice Hall.

Ceci, S. J., & Liker, J. K. (1986). A day at the races: A study of IQ, expertise, and cognitive complexity. *Journal of Experimental Psychology: General, 115,* 255–266.

Center for Educational Research and Innovation, Organization for Economic Cooperation and Development. (1997). *Education at a glance: OECD indicators 1997*. Paris: Organization for Economic Co-operation and Development.

Central Intelligence Agency. (2000). *The World Fact Book*. Washington, DC: U.S. Government Printing Office.

Chall, J. (1992). The new reading debates: Evidence from science, art, and ideology. *Teachers College Record, 94*, 315–328.

Charness, N., Krampe, R., & Mayr, U. (1996). The role of practice and coaching in entrepreneurial skill domains: An international comparison of life-span chess skill acquisition. In K. A. Ericsson (Ed.), *The road to excellence: The acquisition of expert performance in the arts and sciences, sports, and games* (pp. 51–80). Hillsdale, NJ: Lawrence Erlbaum Associates.

Colarelli, S. M. (1998). Psychological interventions in organizations: An evolutionary perspective. *American Psychologist, 53*, 1044–1056.

Colarelli, S. M., Alampay, M. R., & Canali, K. G. (2001). Sex composition and influence in small groups: An evolutionary perspective and review of the literature. Unpublished manuscript, Department of Psychology, Central Michigan University.

Cole, S., et al. (1982). Spatial learning as an adaptation in hummingbirds. *Science 217*, 655–657.

Cosmides, L., & Tooby, J. (1992). Cognitive adaptations for social exchange. In J. H. Barkow, L. Cosmides, & J. Tooby (Eds.), *The adapted mind: Evolutionary psychology and the generation of culture* (pp. 163–228). New York: Oxford University Press.

Coy, M. W. (1989). *Apprenticeship: From theory to method and back again*. New York: State University of New York Press.

Cross, R., & Slater, R. B. (1997). Why the end of affirmative action would exclude all but a very few Blacks from America's leading universities and graduate schools. *Journal of Blacks in Higher Education, 17*, 8–17.

Cuban, L. (2001). *Oversold and underused: Computers in the classroom*. Cambridge, MA: Harvard University Press.

Csikszentmihalyi, M. (1990). *Flow: The psychology of optimal experience*. New York: Harper & Row.

Cummins, D. D. (1998). Social norms and other minds: The evolutionary roots of higher cognition. In D. D. Cummins & C. Allen (Eds.), *The evolution of mind* (pp. 30–50). New York: Oxford University Press.

Diamond, J. (1997). *Guns, germs, and steel: The fates of human societies*. New York: W. W. Norton.

Domjan, M. (1997). Behavior systems and the demise of equipotentiality: Historical antecedents and evidence from sexual conditioning. In M. E. Bouton & M. S. Fanselow (Eds.), *Learning, motivation, and cognition: The functional behaviorism of Robert C. Bolles* (pp. 31–51). Washington, DC: American Psychological Association.

Dunbar, R.I.M. (1996). *Grooming, gossip, and the evolution of language*. Cambridge, MA: Harvard University Press.

E-pulse survey. (2001, May). *Training*, 100.

Ericsson, K. A., Krampe, R. T., & Tesch-Römer, C. (1993). The role of deliberate practice in the acquisition of expert performance. *Psychological Review, 100*, 363–406.

Ericsson, K. A., & Lehmann, A. C. (1996). Expert and exceptional performance: Evidence of maximal adaptation to task constraints. *Annual Review of Psychology, 47*, 273–305.

Estimated salaries for new college graduates. (2001). Retrieved July 20, 2001, from the World Wide Web: *http://www.educaid.com/college/salary.htm*

Federal Trade Commission. (2000, September). Marketing violent entertainment to children: A review of self-regulation and industry practices in the motion picture, music recording, and electronic game industries. *Report of The Federal Trade Commission*, Appendix B. Retrieved July 15, 2001, from the World Wide Web: *http://www.ftc.gov/reports/violence/vioreport.pdf*

Finn, C. E., Jr. (2001). The cost of college sports. *Commentary, 112*, 53–57.

Frazis, H., Gittleman, M., Horrigan, M., & Joyce, M. (1998). Results from the 1995 Survey of Employer-Provided Training. *Monthly Labor Review, 121*, 3–13.

Gagne, R. M. (1962). Military training and the principles of learning. *American Psychologist, 17*, 83–91.

Gallup, G. H., Jr. (1994, October). Millions finding care and support in small groups. *Emerging Trends*, 2–5.

Garcia, J., Ervin, F. R., & Koelling, R. A. (1966). Learning with prolonged delay of reinforcement. *Psychonomic Science, 4*, 121–122.

Garcia, J., & Koelling, R. A. (1966). Relation of cue to consequence in avoidance learning. *Psychonomic Science, 4*, 123–124.

Gaulin, S.J.C., & McBurney, D. H. (2001). *Psychology: An evolutionary approach*. Upper Saddle River, NJ: Prentice Hall.

Gawande, A. (2002, January 28). The learning curve. *New Yorker*, 52–61.

Geary, D. C. (2002, May 20). Personal communication.

Geary, D. C. (1995). Reflections of evolution and culture in children's cognition: Implications for development and instruction. *American Psychologist, 50*, 24–37.

Geary, D. C., Hamson, C. O., Chen, G., Liu, F., Hoard, M. K., & Salthouse, T. A. (1997). Computational and reasoning abilities in arithmetic: Cross-generational change in China and the United States. *Psychonomic Bulletin & Review, 4*, 425–430.

Geck, E. (1968). *Johannes Gutenberg: From lead letter to the computer*. Bad Godesberg: Inter Nationes.

Gladwell, M. (2001, December 17). Examined life: What Stanley H. Kaplan taught us about the S.A.T. *New Yorker*, 86–90.

Glidewell, J. C. (Ed.) (1977). *The social context of learning and development*. New York: Gardner Press.

Goldstein, I. L. (1993). *Training in organizations* (3rd ed.). Pacific Grove, CA: Brooks/Cole.

Goldstein, I. L. (1980). Training in work organizations. *Annual Review of Psychology, 31,* 229–272.

Goldstein, I. L., & Ford, J. K. (2002). *Training in organizations* (4th ed.). Belmont, CA: Wadsworth/Thomson Learning.

Gottfredson, L. S. (1997). Why g matters: The complexity of everday life. *Intelligence, 24,* 79–132.

Gregg, B. G. (2000, May 19). House GOP has plan to boost per-pupil spending. *Detroit News. http://detnews.com/2000/schools/0005/19/d02-59364.htm*

Gutek, G. L. (1991). *Education in the United States: An historical perspective.* Boston: Allyn & Bacon.

Hannan, M. T., & Freeman, J. H. (1989). *Organizational ecology.* Cambridge, MA: Harvard University Press.

Harris, J. R. (1999). *The nurture assumption: Why children turn out the way they do.* New York: Touchstone.

Hayek, F. A. (1964). The theory of complex phenomena. In M. Bunge (Ed.), *The critical approach to science and philosophy: In honor of Karl R. Popper* (pp. 332–349). New York: Free Press.

Health Information Library. (2001). *Speech Development in 2–5 Year Olds.* Retrieved July 14, 2001, from the World Wide Web: *http://www. covenanthealth.com/Features/Health/Child/CHIL3085.htm*

Heinich, R., Molenda, M., Russel, J. D. & Smaldino, S. E. (1996). *Instructional Media and Technologies for Learning* (5th ed.). Englewood-Cliffs, NJ: Prentice Hall.

Heinrich, B. (2001). *Why we run: A natural history.* New York: Ecco.

Herrnstein, R. J., & Murray, C. (1994). *The bell curve: Intelligence and class structure in American life.* New York: Free Press.

Hinrich, J., & Gil-White, F. J. (2001). The evolution of prestige: Freely conferred deference as a mechanism for enhancing the benefits of cultural transmission. *Evolution and Human Behavior, 22,* 165–196.

Hogan, R. T. (1991). Personality and personality measurement. In M. D. Dunnette & L. M. Hough (Eds.), *Handbook of industrial and organizational psychology* (Vol. 2, pp. 873–919). Palo Alto, CA: Consulting Psychologists Press.

Hulin, C. L., Henry, R. A., & Noon, S. L. (1990). Adding a dimension: Time as a factor in the generalizability of the predictive relationships. *Psychological Bulletin, 107,* 328–340.

Hunter, J. E., & Hunter, R. F. (1984). Validity and utility of alternative predictors of job performance. *Psychological Bulletin, 96,* 72–98.

Hunter, J. E., Schmidt, F. L., Rauschenberger, J. J., & Jayne, M.E.A. (2000). Intelligence, motivation, and job performance. In C. L. Cooper & E. A. Locke (Eds.), *Industrial and organizational psychology: Linking theory with practice* (pp. 278–303). Oxford, UK: Blackwell.

Industry Report. (1997, October). *Training,* 33–76.

Isaacson, W. (1997, January 13). In search of The Real Bill Gates. *Time,* p. 149.

Jacobson, J. (2001, June 8). Female coaches lag in pay and opportunities to oversee men's teams. *Chronicle of Higher Education*, p. A38.

Jensen, A. R. (1998). *The g factor: The science of mental testing*. Westport, CT: Praeger.

Jensen, A. R. (1980). *Bias in mental testing*. New York: Free Press.

Judge, T. A., Higgins, C. A., Thorenson, C. J., & Barrick, M. R. (1999). The big five personality traits, general mental ability, and career success across the life span. *Personnel Psychology, 52*, 621–652.

Kaufman, P., Alt, M. N., & Chapman, C. (2001, November 15). *Dropout rates in the United States: 2000*. U.S. Department of Education, National Center for Education Statistics (NCES publication No. 2002114). Retrieved February 3, 2002, from the World Wide Web: *http://www.nces.ed.gov/pubs2002/002113.pdf*

Klein, A. M. (1991). *Sugarball: The American game and the Dominican dream*. New Haven, CT: Yale University Press.

Klein, R. G. (1989). *The human career: Human biological and cultural origins*. Chicago: University of Chicago Press.

Kraut, R., Patterson, M., Lundmark, V., Kiesler, S., Mukophadhyay, T., & Scherlis, W. (1998). Internet paradox: A social technology that reduces social involvement and psychological well-being? *American Psychologist, 53*, 1017–1031.

Kroll, L., & Goldman, L. (2002, February 28). The world's billionaires. Retrieved on March 2, 2002, from the World Wide Web: *www.forbes.com/2002/02/28/billionaires.html*

Labor letter. (1991, October 22). *Wall Street Journal*, p. A1.

Lancaster, S. L., Colarelli, S. M., King, D. W., & Beehr, T. A. (1994). Job applicant similarity on cognitive ability, vocational interests, and personality characteristics: Do similar persons choose similar jobs? *Educational and Psychological Measurement, 54*, 299–316.

Lave, J., & Wenger, E. (1991). *Situated learning: Legitimate peripheral participation*. New York: Cambridge University Press.

Lieberman, M. A., Yalom, I. D., & Miles, M. B. (1973). *Encounter groups: First facts*. New York: Basic Books.

Lines, P. M. (2000). Homeschooling comes of age. *Public Interest, 140*, 74–85.

Magnay, J. (2000, August 28). Ian Thorpe's world-record swims this week have electrified Australia. Now he's being talked of as possibly the best ever. Some say the secret of his success is his size-17 feet. *Sydney Morning Herald*. *http://www.geocities.com/Colosseum/Field/8824/tarticles.html40*

Mansfield, H. (2001, December 20). To B or Not to B. *Wall Street Journal*, p. A16.

McGrath, C. (1998, July). Busy teenagers. *American Demographics*, 37–38.

Megarry, T. (1995). *Society in prehistory: The origins of human culture*. New York: New York University Press.

Miller, F. Y., & Coffey, W. (1992). *Winning basketball for girls*. New York: Facts on File.

Miller, G. (2000). Mental traits as fitness indicators: Expanding evolutionary psychology's adaptationism. In D. LeCroy & P. Moller (Eds.), *Evolutionary perspectives on human reproductive behavior* (pp. 62–74). New York: New York Academy of Sciences.

Mineka, S., Davidson, M., Cook, M., & Keir, R (1984). Observational conditioning of snake fear in rhesus monkeys. *Journal of Abnormal Psychology, 93*, 355–372.

Mintzberg, H. (1994). *The rise and fall of strategic planning.* New York: Free Press.

Moore, R. F. (1996). Caring for identified versus statistical lives: An evolutionary view of medical distributive justice. *Ethology and Sociobiology, 17*, 379–401.

Muchinsky, P. M. (2000). *Psychology applied to work: An introduction to industrial and organizational psychology* (6th ed.). Belmont, CA: Wadsworth/Thomson Learning.

National Association of Colleges and Employers. (2001, March). Retrieved February 11, 2002 from the World Wide Web: *http://www.jobweb.com/employ/salary/broadoffers.htm*

National Science Board. (2000). Science & engineering indicators—2000. Arlington, VA: National Science Foundation. Retrieved February 3, 2002 from the World Wide Web: *http://www.nsf.gov/sbe/srs/seind00/pdfstart.htm*

Nelson, R. R., & Winter, S. G. (1982). *An evolutionary theory of economic change.* Cambridge, MA: Belknap.

New Yorker. (2001, June 18 and 25). Look who's coming to the Yale School of Management. *New Yorker*, 68.

Nicolaus, L. K., Cassel, J. F., Carlson, R. B., & Gustavson, C.R. (1983). Taste aversion conditioning of crows to control predation on eggs. *Science, 220*, 212–214.

Noble, D. D. (1996). Mad rushes into the future: The overselling of educational technology. *Educational Leadership, 54*, 18–26.

Noe, R. A. (1999). *Employee training and development.* Boston: McGraw-Hill.

O'Dell, J. (2000, February 25). Ford to move luxury-car unit to Irvine. *Los Angeles Times*, pp. C1, C2.

Office of Science and Technology Policy, Executive Office of the President. (2001, April). *Analytical perspectives: R&D chapter, budget of the United States government, fiscal year, 2000.* Washington, DC: Author. Retrieved July 26, 2002, from the World Wide Web: *www.ostp.gov/html/2002rdbudget/2002fullrdbudget.pdf*

Office of Technology Assessment. (1990). *Worker training: Competing in the new international economy* (OTA-ITE-457). Washington, DC: U.S. Government Printing Office.

Patrick, J. (1992). *Training: Research and practice.* London: Academic Press.

Perrow, C. (1983). The organizational context of human factors engineering. *Administrative Science Quarterly, 28*, 521–541.

Peters, T. (1988). The mythology of innovation, or a skunkworks tale, part II. In M. L. Tushman & W. L. Moore (Eds.), *Readings in the management of innovation* (2nd ed.). Cambridge, MA: Ballinger Publishing Co. Harper & Row Publishers.

Pinker, S. (1994). *The language instinct*. New York: HarperCollins.

Poitier, S. (2000). *The measure of a man: A spiritual autobiography*. San Francisco: HarperCollins.

Project Match Research Group. (1997). Matching alcoholism treatments to client heterogeneity: Project MATCH posttreatment drinking outcomes. *Journal of Studies on Alcohol, 58*, 7–29.

Rauscher, F. H., Shaw, G. L., Levine, L. J., Wright, E. L., Dennis, W. R., & Newcomb, R. L. (1997). Music training causes long-term enhancement of preschool children's spatial-temporal reasoning. *Neurological Research, 19*, 2–8.

Ravitch, D. (2000). *Left back: A century of failed school reforms*. New York: Simon & Schuster.

Rayner, K., Foorman, B. R., Perfetti, C. A., Pesetsky, D. & Seidenberg, M. S. (2001). How psychological science informs the teaching of reading. *Psychological Science in the Public Interest, 2*, 31–74.

Ree, M. J., & Earles, J. A. (1992). Intelligence is the best predictor of job performance. *Current directions in Psychological Science, 1*, 86–92.

Robinson, D. G., & Robinson, J. C. (1989). *Training for impact*. San Francisco: Jossey-Bass.

Rozin, P., & Kalat, J. (1971). Specific hungers and poison avoidance as adaptive specializations of learning. *Psychological Review, 78*, 459–486.

Saari, L. M., Johnson, T. R., McLaughlin, S. D., & Zimmerle, D. M. (1988). A survey of management training and education practices in U.S. companies. *Personnel Psychology, 41*, 731–743.

Saxe, G. B. (1988). The mathematics of child street vendors. *Child Development, 59*, 1415–1425.

Schemo, D. J. (2000, December 6). 8th graders see success fall off from 4th grade. *New York Times*, pp. A1, A8.

Schmidt, F. L. (1995). Why all banding procedures in personnel selection are logically flawed. *Human Performance, 8*, 165–177.

Schmidt, F. L., & Hunter, J. E. (1981). Employment testing: Old theories and new research findings. *American Psychologist, 36*, 1128–1137.

Schneider, A. (2001, March 9). A university plans to promote languages by killing its languages department. *The Chronicle of Higher Education*, pp. A14–A15.

Segal, N. A., & Macdonald, K. B. (1998). Behavioral genetics and evolutionary psychology: Unified perspective on personality research. *Human Biology, 70*, 159–184.

Seldin, P. (1993, July 21). The use and abuse of student ratings of professors. *Chronicle of Higher Education*, p. A40.

Simon, H. A. (1976). *Administrative behavior* (3rd ed.). New York: Macmillan. (Originally published in 1945.)

Simonton, D. K. (1999). *Origins of genius: Darwinian perspectives on creativity.* New York: Oxford University Press.

Skinner, B. F. (1972). *Beyond freedom and dignity.* New York: Alfred A. Knopf.

Skinner, B. F. (1948). *Walden two.* New York: Macmillan.

Snyder, T. D., & Hoffman, C. M. (2001). Digest of Education Statistics: 2000. *Education Statistics Quarterly, 3.*

Specter, M (2002, July 15). The long ride. *New Yorker,* 48–58.

Stevenson, H. W., Chen, C., & Lee, S. Y. (1993). Mathematics achievement of Chinese, Japanese, and American children: Ten years later. *Science, 259,* 53–58.

Stone, N. (1991, March-April). Does business have any business in education? *Harvard Business Review,* 46–62.

Such, M. (1997). The effects of the amount, helpfulness, likability, transferability, and type of training on multiple measures of commitment. Master's thesis. Department of Psychology, Central Michigan University. Mt. Pleasant, MI.

Swain, M. (1991). French immersion and its offshoots: Getting two for one. In Barbara F. Fred (Ed.), *Foreign language acquisition research and the classroom.* Lexington, MA: Heath & Co.

Symons, D. (1979). *The evolution of human sexuality.* New York: Oxford University Press.

Tanser, T. (1997/1998). *Train hard, win easy: The Kenyan way.* Mountain View, CA: Tafnews Press.

Terman, L. M. (1922). Adventures in stupidity. *Scientific Monthly, 14,* 24–40.

The 2000 ASTD International Comparisons Report. (2000, April). *Training and Development.* Retrieved July 10, 2001 from the World Wide Web: *http://www.findarticles.com/cf_0/m4467/4_54/61949948/p1/article.jhtml2001*

Tooby, J., & Cosmides, L. (1992). The psychological foundations of culture. In J. H. Barkow, L. Cosmides, et al. (Eds.), *The adapted mind: Evolutionary psychology and the generation of culture* (pp. 19–136). New York: Oxford University Press.

Tooby, J., & Cosmides, L. (1990). On the universality of human nature and the uniqueness of the individual: The role of genetics and adaptation. *Journal of Personality, 58,* 17–67.

Trice, H. M., Belasco, J., & Aluto, J. A. (1969). The role of ceremonials in organizational behavior. *Industrial and Labor Relations Review, 23,* 40–51.

Tyack, D., & Cuban, L. (1995). *Tinkering toward utopia: A century of public school reform.* Cambridge, MA: Harvard University Press.

U.S. Department of Education. National center for Education Statistics. (2000) *Dropout rates in the United States: 1999,* NCES 2001–022, by P. Kaufman, J. Y. Kwon, S. Klein, &. C. D. Chapman. Washington, DC: National Center for Education Statistics.

U.S. Department of Justice, Federal Bureau of Prisons. (1998). *A profile of female offenders.* Retrieved July 15, 2001, from the World Wide Web: *http://www.bop.gov/pdf/cpdfem.pdf*

Washburn, S. L., Jay, P. C., & Lancaster, J. B. (1965). Field studies of Old World monkeys and apes. *Science, 150,* 1541–1547.

Watson, J. B. (1924/1970). *Behaviorism.* New York: W. W. Norton.

Watson, J. B. (1913). Psychology as the behaviorist views it. *Psychological Review, 20,* 158–177.

Watson, J. B., & Rayner, R. (1920). Conditioned emotional reactions. *Journal of Experimental Psychology, 3,* 1–14.

Whiting, B. B., & Edwards, C. P. (1988). *Children of different worlds: The formation of social behavior.* Cambridge, MA: Harvard University Press.

Whiting, B. B., & Whiting, J.W.M. (1975). *Children of six cultures.* Cambridge, MA: Harvard University Press.

Yeats, W. B. (1962). *Selected poems and two plays of William Butler Yeats.* (M. L. Rosenthal, Ed., updated ed.). New York: Collier Books.

Zielinski, D. (2000, March). Can you keep learners online? *Training,* 64–75.

Conclusion

Tyranny is the absence of complexity.

—André Gide

The evolution of complex societies [is among] . . . the deepest puzzles
of the social sciences.

—Peter J. Richerson and Robert Boyd (1999, p. 253)

It would seem that the elaborate organization of a honeybee colony
is an *incidental* consequence of each individual's efforts to maximize
its own genetic success.

—George C. Williams (1996, p. 50; emphasis added)

Human resource interventions are designed by humans, implemented by
humans, and exist in human systems. As such, they reflect human propensities and human beliefs about human nature and social systems; they
are also subject to the uncertainties, self-interests, and conflicts endemic
to complex social systems. Unfortunately, many human resource interventions developed throughout the twentieth century reflect an unrealistic view of human nature and social systems. They reflect the erroneous
view that humans are passive receptacles of culture and that, therefore,
changing cultural inputs can readily change human behavior. They reflect the erroneous view that humans come prepackaged with levels of
master traits and that, therefore, matching people with jobs can readily

enhance organizational efficiency. They reflect the erroneous view that organizations operate like machines and that, therefore, deliberate social engineering will lead to intended outcomes. And they reflect the erroneous view that human resource interventions operate independently of context and of the personal interests of people using them and that, therefore, they can be surgically installed in any organization. These erroneous beliefs have in large measure been responsible for the unimpressive record of applied social science in general and of human resource interventions in particular.

An evolutionary perspective offers a more realistic set of assumptions about human nature and about social systems. This perspective provides a realistic basis for designing interventions, and it offers a powerful theoretical framework for understanding people's preferences for particular human resource interventions. People come into the world endowed with psychological mechanisms that are the products of thousands of years of evolution. These mechanisms predispose humans to behave adaptively for the most part in dealing with features of their environment. Simply changing cultural inputs will not inevitably change the responses activated by psychological mechanisms. People are predisposed to respond to other people and to information about other people in ways that enhance their self-interest. Thus, people will continue to use human resource interventions that seem useful to their interests, and they will be reluctant to use interventions that do not—hence, the widespread use in most businesses of the interview, letters of recommendation, and work sample tests and the relatively low use of paper-and-pencil tests. Similarly, interventions that are compatible with psychological mechanisms are more likely to work than those that are not—hence, the success of phonics for teaching reading, drill-and-practice for teaching math skills, and apprenticeships for training skilled craftsmen and professionals; hence, the failure of whole language as a method of teaching reading, the failure of calculators to improve children's math skills, and the failure of the web to educate students and professionals.

An evolutionary perspective also provides a powerful heuristic for understanding how human resource interventions become incorporated into organizational routines, how they operate within organizations, and why some are rejected. Sociocultural evolution offers an eminently more sensible way than mechanical design of thinking about the adoption and use of interventions. As Donald Campbell cogently argued over a quarter of a century ago, the logic of natural selection—variation, selection, and retention—is as applicable to social as to biological phenomena.

Many of the ideas fundamental to the evolutionary perspective—self-interest, status, dominance hierarchies, social exchange, interdependence,

conflict, adaptations, environmental demands, functions, and unanticipated consequences—exist in other theories that populate the landscape
of social and behavioral sciences. Yet these ideas are scattered among
disparate theories and minitheories, with little sense of coherence (Buss,
1995; Scott, 1998). The evolutionary perspective provides a unifying
logic that incorporates many disparate ideas within the social and organizational sciences. It provides a parsimonious approach—natural
selection—for understanding diverse and complex phenomena. Moreover, its underpinnings are rooted in evolutionary biology, which, over
the past 150 years, has been a principal scientific springboard for fundamental discoveries about the nature of life and behavior. On the other
hand, much of the social science theory and research over the past 150
years lacks a unifying theoretical anchor, except perhaps the blank slate.

The evolutionary perspective on human resource management uses
general principles from evolutionary psychology and sociocultural evolution as frameworks for thinking about human nature and organizations and for guidance in the development and use of interventions. Yet
because of its sensitivity to variation, context, and complexity, it does
not propose universal applications, and it emphasizes the importance of
local knowledge. At the level of the individual, research in evolutionary psychology can provide guidance on learning, decision processes, and
preferences for particular categories of stimuli and situations, as well as
an understanding of *why* these processes and preferences exist. This is
helpful for understanding people's reactions to extant interventions and
for anticipating general responses to new ones. Psychological mechanisms limit the range of appeal of interventions. People will prefer interventions that produce immediate, obvious, and concrete results. They
will prefer interventions that use face-to-face or narrative methods rather
than methods that use statistical information to communicate information about people. People will consciously or unconsciously prefer interventions that, first and foremost, appear to advance their self-interest.

Psychological mechanisms constrain possibilities. The closer that the
features of interventions are linked with human adaptations, the more
likely that interventions will produce reasonably adaptive results. People
will learn skills based on primary abilities more quickly than skills based
on secondary abilities. On the other hand, humans have many other
characteristics beyond basic adaptations, and many of them are assembled within individuals randomly—through sexual reproduction's
shuffling of genes, through exposure to different environments, and
through the unique experiences that people encounter while growing up.
Human variability expands possibilities.

So, too, does the fact that interventions operate in complex social systems, with their attendant conflicts, disparate interests, loose connections, and long and multifaceted causal chains. It also reduces our capacity to predict and control behavior. This is bad news for managers who are looking for interventions that will produce specific, intended effects. It is also bad news for social scientists who believe that they can develop such interventions and for those who are laboring under the delusion that the interventions they already developed work like that. And it is bad news for consultants who want to sell neat solutions and quick fixes. The evolutionary perspective's implications at the organizational level are more general and require a greater sense of humility than the implications of the mechanical designers. I have stressed three themes at the organizational level: variability, functional wisdom, and distributed intelligence. Adequate variation in interventions, practices, ideas, and people are an organization's best insurance against the vagaries of the future. Functional wisdom is often embedded in traditional practices that have stood the test of time. Traditional recipes for living have something to tell us. Distributed intelligence guided only by a general framework is a better arrangement for social systems than those based on grand designs. We know that free markets work better than planned economies, yet we cannot know what specific goods and services will emerge. Similarly, organizations that distribute intelligence widely and give people the freedom to use their ingenuity will be more adaptive than those that orchestrate every detail from a master plan. Yet we cannot know precisely what adaptive routines will emerge.

One difficult conceptual issue that requires considerably more work is the duet of evolutionary psychology and sociocultural evolution. Organizations tend to incorporate practices that are functional and these practices exist independently of the particular people who carry them out. On the other hand, people usually behave in their self-interest, and choices based on self-interest derive from psychological mechanisms. How are choices that are functional for individuals connected to practices that are functional for organizations? Are organizational practices the incidental results of people pursuing their self-interest, or do they have an organizational reality of their own? My hunch is that the former is the case. Precisely how much of a role self-interest plays remains debatable, but that it plays a role is without doubt. It is unfortunate that self-interest has not been given its due in the human resource literature.

People respond to interventions based on conscious and unconscious self-interest, and they use interventions based on self-interest. We can no longer afford to maintain the fiction that human resource interventions operate independently of self-interest, operating only for the good of "the organization." How to deal with the role of self-interest in human resource interventions is another question. Some answers are more satisfactory than others. One approach, common among many mechanical designers, is to ignore self-interest; this, of course, is absurd. Another approach is to assume that the anointed know what everyone's best interest is and to allow the anointed to devise structures that severely curtail other people's choices. (Inevitably, the options available to the anointed are the least constrained.) This approach is authoritarian.

An evolutionary perspective on human resource interventions acknowledges that self-interest operates in human resource interventions, just as it does in other areas of human affairs. Human resource interventions are more likely to be effective (1) when they leverage the power of self-interest, (2) when the role of self-interest is transparent, and (3) when they contain systems of checks and balances to curtail the excesses of self-interest. It is particularly important to acknowledge the role of self-interest when advising or otherwise dealing with leaders of organizations (Ludwig, 2002). Leaders, like everyone else, are motivated by self-interest. When leaders push a program that they claim will "benefit the organization," one must always ask *how the program benefits the leader*. It is often more certain that self-interest is lurking just beneath the surface of a leader's pet program than it is that the program will produce its intended effect or that its goals are widely shared or understood. It is not that managers and leaders do not necessarily have insights that will help an organization adapt, survive, and even prosper. Sometimes they do. However, failing to acknowledge the role of self-interest, particularly on the part of leaders and others who wield considerable power, increases the chances that unbridled self-interest will be destructive. Too often leaders attract coteries of sycophants who are unwilling or unable to point out that the primary beneficiaries of a leader's pet programs are the leader and the leader's allies. Interventions that build in transparency and checks and balances are an antidote. Interventions with these characteristics also help to demystify "organizational" interests and goals. They help to show that what passes for organizational goals are in fact the goals of a person or a group of people. I cringe every time I read a passage referring to an *organization's* interests or virtues or pathologies. Sociologists and legal scholars can make a case that organizations have interests. That may be. However, I cringe because so many scholars and laypersons can glibly refer to an organization's interests (or pathologies or virtues) without acknowledging that they stem from decisions and actions of *individuals* and that they are entwined with individual interests. A common thread running through much of the work in industrial/organizational psychology and political science is the attempt to align interests. An evolutionary perspective suggests that you can temporarily align some interests some of the time, but you can never align all interests all of the time. Conflicting interests are the order of the day. Interventions that explicitly acknowledge conflicts of interest have the best chance—however haltingly—of alleviating suffering, making incremental improvements in human well-being, and of improving organizational effectiveness.

Conflicting interests, variation, and change are inevitable in social systems. Thus, it is more appropriate to conceptualize human resource interventions as activities that are part of a process of *continual maintenance* rather than as solutions or best ways to perform a human resource function. As anyone who has ever owned a house knows, if it's not one thing it's another. Routine maintenance is the key to keeping the house functioning. Storms, small animals, wear and tear, and changes in fashion keep homeowners continually tinkering and repairing. A house is never repaired once and for all. Natural selection, too, is a process of continuous maintenance. Environmental change causes continual adaptive pressures; variations continually arise which provide the raw material for adaptations; and selective retention continually culls unhelpful variations and retains helpful ones. In the same vein, organizations never arrive at an ideal state; there is only the process of maintenance throughout the ups and downs of the inexorable life cycle. As any student of history knows, change is constant and all things eventually pass on. Vigilant maintenance and luck can improve the odds, providing a fighting chance to slow down the inevitable.

Because human biology evolves considerably more slowly than culture, some have argued that evolutionary mismatch theory (Crawford, 1998), the inquiry into the correspondence between present conditions and those in which humans evolved, can provide guidance for improving organizations and human well-being. The basic implications of mismatch theory are to align modern social structures more closely with structures common during the EEA and to develop structures that are compatible with evolved psychological mechanisms. Nicholson (1997) argues that organizations will operate more effectively and people will be happier in organizations if managers create structures that resemble the social conditions under which humans evolved. He recommends smaller work groups and more informal interaction. In a similar vein, Buss (2000) argues that mismatches are a cause of human unhappiness in the modern world—mismatches between modern and ancestral environments. He recommends efforts to make the modern environment more compatible with psychological mechanisms that produce happiness—efforts such as strengthening the family, marriage, and deep friendships. He also recommends efforts to keep in check the psychological mechanisms that escalate competition and conflict. Mismatch theory offers a promising framework for interventions, but its promise will always be limited because the genie of culture is out of the bottle. Culture provides a huge array of evolutionarily novel symbols, materials, and structures that stimulate psychological mechanisms. The interaction of culture with ancient psychological mechanisms produces an escalation of novel symbols and materials (Colarelli, 2000). The appeal of cultural symbols and artifacts to ancient mechanisms can be so powerful that they override efforts to counteract their deleterious effects. Witness the appeal of pornography, psychoactive drugs, celebrities, and junk food—cultural creations that derive their appeal from ancient mechanisms (Barkow, 1992; Nesse & Berridge, 1997). Certainly, increased knowledge of psychological mechanisms and the consequences of novel variations can ameliorate deleterious effects. Yet, variation and change are inevitable, and we cannot turn back the clock. Just as some new variations cause problems, other variations provide opportunities and new methods to address problems. We cannot stop the inexorable meandering of evolution. We can, however, tinker and decrease suffering here and there. Increased knowledge is helpful, but it cannot stop change and life cycles.

An evolutionary perspective does not provide human resource practitioners with the comfort of a best way or with the illusion of certainty. This is not its failing; it is its primary strength. Human resource management has for too long been in under the spell of the mechanical design perspective. Consequently it has been unable to meet expectations. By working with a more realistic set of assumptions, the evolutionary perspective is more likely to meet expectations—more modest expectations. I have suggested some evolutionary-based interventions that will help organizations deal more effectively with selection and training. However, more than arguing for specific techniques, I have argued for a way of thinking, a way of looking at organizations and human resource interventions. By shunning best ways and intended effects, it avoids the hubris of the mechanical design perspective. The evolutionary perspective settles, instead, for improving adaptive processes, maintenance, and limited improvement, ever mindful of context and conflict.

REFERENCES

Barkow, J. H. (1992). Beneath new culture is old psychology: Gossip and social stratification. In J. H. Barkow, L. Cosmides, & J. Tooby (Eds.), *The adapted mind* (pp. 627–637). New York: Oxford University Press.

Buss, D. M. (2000). The evolution of happiness. *American Psychologist, 55,* 15–23.

Buss, D. M. (1995). Evolutionary psychology: A new paradigm for psychological science. *Psychological Inquiry, 6,* 1–30.

Colarelli, S. M. (2000). Evolution, the criterion problem, and complexity. *Behavioral and Brain Sciences, 23,* 151–152.

Crawford, C. (1998). Environments and adaptations: Then and now. In C. Crawford & D. L. Krebs (Eds.), *Handbook of evolutionary psychology: Ideas, issues, and applications* (pp. 275–302). Mahwah, NJ: Lawrence Erlbaum Associates.

Ludwig, A. M. (2002). *King of the mountain: The nature of political leadership.* Lexington: The University Press of Kentucky.

Nesse, R. M., & Berridge, K. C. (1997). Psychoactive drug use in evolutionary perspective. *Science, 278,* 63–66.

Nicholson, N. (1997). Evolutionary psychology: Toward a new view of human nature and organizational society. *Human Relations, 50,* 1053–1078.

Richerson, P., & Boyd, R. (1999). Complex societies: The evolutionary origins of a crude superorganism. *Human Nature, 10,* 253–289.

Scott, W. R. (1998). *Organizations: Rational, natural, and open systems* (4th ed.). Englewood Cliffs, NJ: Prentice Hall.

Williams, G. C. (1996). *Plan and purpose in nature.* London: Weidenfeld & Nicolson.

Index

Abelson, Robert, 165
abilities: defined, 250; developing, 301; importance of, 281, 283–84; like rubber bands, 284; primary, 250, 265, 288–89; secondary, 250, 265, 290–91, 303
accountants, 150
acquired tastes, 260
ACT scores, 148–49
adaptations: defined, 56–57; definition of, 95; evolution of, 94; and individual differences, 85; relevance of, 88; social, 57–58
"Adventures in Stupidity" (Terman), 282
affective orientation, 160, 172–73
affirmative action: difficulty of implementation, 216; goals of, 186–87, 216–17, 220; in hiring, 208–9; and lowered expectations, 217; problems of fairness, 211–12, 213, 215; shortcomings of, 209–10
African Americans, 150–51, 211–12, 234
aggregation, problem of, 189

aggression, 55
agricultural revolution, 6, 113
airport security, 173–74
Alcoholics Anonymous, effectiveness of, 295
Alexander the Great, 47, 117
American students, test scores of, 290, 303
analysis, level of, xxi
anoles, sexual development in, 91
antlers, 51
applicants: capacity for harm, 119, 129; effect on the hiring process, 164, 172; meritorious, 230; pool of, 218–19, 228–29; in random selection above a threshold, 225; screening of, 206
apprenticeships, 253, 292–93, 298; learning in, 266; system of, 117–18. See also training
aptitude, 250, 290
Arendt, Hannah, 159
Argyris, Chris, 2, 30
Army Alpha test, 122, 285
Asian students, test scores of, 290

assessment centers, 144–45, 208
assessment of other people, 111–12
auditions, 113, 118
Auerbach, Red, 245
automotive design, 205
aversion, evolved, 233

Bach, Johann Sebastian, 118, 119
Bacon, Francis, 19–20, 29
banality of evil, the, 159
banding, 221
Basalla, George, xvi
baseball players, Dominican, 248, 294
basketball, 135, 194, 195–96
Bayesian Horticulturist, 60–61
Beal, Carole, 79
behavior: changing, 90, 315–16;
    complexity of, 58–59; flexibility
    of, 261–62; learning of, 280;
    nonverbal, 112; samples of, 226;
    sexual, 292; social, 85
behaviorism: assumptions of, 259;
    failures of, 90–91, 263; history of,
    35; views of, 29–30, 79, 279–81,
    315–16
Berrill, Roland, 16–17
Bertonneau, Tom, 301
Bias in Mental Testing (Jensen), 86–87
Big Five personality traits, 161–63,
    174, 287
biological Calvinism, 92
biology and culture, 50, 55–56
Birir, Matthew, 278
Bloom, Benjamin, 290
Bonds, Barry, xxiii, xiv
bonus points in affirmative action, 220
Boos, Amy, 148–49
Boyd, Robert, xvi, 315
Branson, Richard, 246
Breland, Keller and Marian, 90–91
Browne, Kingsley, 302
bureaucrats, selection of, 114–15
Burke, Edmund, 52
business schools, 3–4
Buss, David, 80

byproducts of evolution, 57
Byzantium, 58, 59

California, X percent plan in, 221,
    222–23
Campbell, Donald, xv, 185, 316
Candide (Voltaire), 88
Cannon, Cornelia James, 285
capacity to blunder, 54
capitalism, 7
Carnegie, Andrew, 246
Carroll, John, 290
cats' purr, 89–90
caves, and organizational problems,
    16–17. *See also* Plato
Celera Genomics, 235
change: adaptive, 74; directions of,
    72–73; and natural selection, 74;
    pace of, 287; process of, 73–75;
    randomness of, 70; resistance to,
    xii–xiii, 9, 69–70, 71, 75; and
    uncertainty, 75–76, 75–77
characteristics, 194–95; acquired, xv;
    defined, 187; effect on learning,
    262; measuring, 136–37; stability
    of, 155–56
Chauncey, Henry, 17, 130, 151
cheating, detection of, 215–16
chess, 278, 294–95
child care, xviii, 233, 273, 282
childhood lessons, 255, 275–76
civil rights, 121
clerical errors, 164
clocks, organizations' resemblance
    to, 10, 11–16, 164
clubs, importance of, 294–96, 299–
    300
coaches, salaries for, 276–77
coffee, "regular," 95
college admissions, 158–59, 172, 190
color blindness, 219
Coming of Age in Samoa (Mead), 79
committed submission, 25–26
commonalities between humans, 84
common sense, 21–22, 65

communities of practice, 293, 295, 298

competition, 293–94

complexity: importance of, 315; of modern life, 286–87; problems associated with, 194–96

complex phenomena, 45, 174

computers: access to, xiii; in education, 266, 268–69, 270; skill sets for, 287

Comte, Auguste, 15, 18, 27, 29

Conant, James Bryant, 17, 130

conflict: and justice, 216; in natural selection, 50, 54–55; within organizations, 8, 191–92

conflicts of interest: in college admissions, 193–94; in hiring, 186; legitimate, 194–95; significance of, 151; in systems, 59, 320; in training, 274

Confucianism, 115

Constantine, Emperor of Rome, 2, 3

conscientiousness, 159, 195, 196, 282

conscription, 116–17

contiguity principle, 260–61

continual maintenance, 320

contradictions, problem of, 195

core competencies, 225–26, 227, 235

corporate welfare, 301

corporations, turnover of, 3

craftsmen, and apprentices, 117–18

creativity: and sexual selection, 55; in the workplace, 159, 160

critical mass: of interest, 296, 297; of personality types, 191

cult of productivity, 232

cultural background, 192

cultural selection, 60

culture: importance of, 321; influence of, 78, 86

Culture and the Evolutionary Process (Boyd and Richerson), xv

Darwin, Charles, 6; three postulates of, 50

decision making, 96; rational, 22–23; third party, 17

deep structures, 64

Dell, Michael, 246

denial of action at a distance, 11, 12–14

design: compromises in, 64–65; evolved, 46–47, 50, 54

designer diversity, 210, 221, 222

determinism, 11, 14–16; genetic, 91

Diamond, Jared, 261, 301

differences: importance of, 271–72; individual, 27, 84–85, 214

Discours sur les sciences et les arts (Rousseau), 119

dissatisfaction, as catalyst for change, 160–61, 173–74

distance learning, 266–67, 268, 271, 290–91, 301

diversification, 76

diversity: definition of, 193; ethnic, 232; management of, 209; not preselected, 227–28; psychological, 210–11

diversity gerrymandering, 213, 224

diversity programs: assumptions of, 210; in higher education, 192–93; problems with, 211–12, 216; shortcomings of, 209–10

DNA, 6, 54

domestication of animals, 261

Dominican Republic: baseball in, 248, 294

dropouts, famous, 246

economists, beliefs of, xxi, 95

education, 150; in business, 35; as child care, 273; commodification of, 273; curricular fads in, 269; defined, 250; fun in, 272–73; of human resource departments, 169; quality of, 214; in social sciences, 33–34; status of, 276–79; substitutability in, 278; and success, 246–47, 300–301

effectiveness, 64–65

efficiency, 10, 64–65, 121, 233

Eichmann, Adolf, 159

Eichmann in Jerusalem (Arendt), 159

emergence, 13, 63–64

employment interviews: information gathering in, xvi, 131–32; modifications to, 204–5; usefulness of, 198, 199–200, 201, 202–3

End of History and the Last Man, The (Fukuyama), 36

environment, importance of, 91–92

Environment of Evolutionary Adaptation (EEA), 79–80, 172–73

equal opportunity, 219

equifinality, 284, 288

equipotentiality, 260

eugenics, 94

evolution: by consequences, 51–52; cultural, 56, 59–60; historical, 53, 299; meanings of, 49–50; pace and change of, 53; purpose of, 50; toward complexity, 52–53, 56

evolutionary perspective: assumptions of, 316; defined, xix–xx; ideas of, 50, 94–95; practical applications of, xxii

evolutionary psychology: model, 79–80

experts: importance of, 10–11; knowledge of, 16; role of, 17, 18–19, 22, 28–30; in the testing industry, 166

face-to-face interaction, 317; information from, 134–35, 137, 198, 266; preference for, xvi, 201; in training, 252, 293

fads, 269, 270

fairness: historical approach to, 214–15; perceptions of, 209–10, 211–12; in randomness, 228; in selection plans, 222, 231

fast and frugal heuristics, 141

feedback mechanisms, 52, 150

feet, large, 287

fellowships, 296–97

Fertile Crescent, 50–51

Fisher, R. A., 52

fixed relationships, 64

Florida, Talented 20 Percent plan, 221, 222–23

foreign accents, 292

forward engineering, 251

four Idols, 19

Frederick the Great, 116

Freeman, Derek, 67, 96

Freud, Sigmund, 94

function, defined, 170–71, 187

function, importance of understanding, 279–80

functional wisdom, 46, 50, 186

fun in education, 272–73

gambling theory, 185

Gardner, Howard, 33

Gates, Bill, xiii, 246

Geary, David, 302

geographical diversity, 193

Gide, André, 315

goals: conflict in, 68–69, 154; hierarchy of, 15–16, 152–53, 256; individual, 152; official, 76, 154; organizational, 68–69; over-emphasis on, 254; personal, 156; problems with, 254; scope of, 70, 71–72; setting of, 15; in training programs, 273

graphology, xii, 172

Great Society programs, 32, 90

green tongue, 233

groups: heterogeneous, 191; homogeneous, 192; impact on performance, 149; life in, 88–89; selection into, 113, 232

Guinier, Lani, 109

Guion, Robert, 138

Hale, Matthew, 8

hamburgers, 46–47

Hampshire, Stuart, 216
Handbook of Industrial and Organizational Psychology, xiv–xv, 167, 174
Hannan, John, 67
harm, avoiding, 199, 201–2, 233
Harrison, Jim, 74
Harvard College, admissions to, 192
Hawking, Stephen, 14
Hayek, Friedrich A., 36, 45, 58, 96
Head to Head (Thurow), 2–3
Herrnstein, Richard, 109
hierarchical reductionism, 64
hierarchies: dominance, 112, 134; nested, 64; status, 91
high school grades (GPA): predictor of college performance, 144, 199, 226; as predictor of success, 235
hiring decisions: away from work, 109–10; demonopolizing, 205; emphasis in, 194; evolutionary approach to, 186; framework of, 139–40; group, 141–42; prejudice in, 138; timing problems of, 164
hiring methods: implementation of, 163–65; validity of, 145–46
hiring methods, mechanistic, 110–11; assessments in, 147; assumptions about, 130–31; complexity of, 136–37; decision making with, 139–41; effect of, 165; information gained in, 133, 138; lack of research on, 140; and legal concerns in hiring, 169; outcomes from, 157; premise of, 129–30; premises of, 163–65; presumptions about, 143; reduce variability, 207–8; standardization in, 143; statistical prediction rules (SPRs), 139–40
hiring methods, traditional, 110, 121; beneficiaries of, 128–31; custom and habit in, 128; decision making in, 141–42; effect of, 165; efficacy of, 144–45; information gained in, 133, 137; lack of standardization in, 142–43; in the private sector, 166; and the test of time, 197; use in evaluating risk, 129. *See also* employment interviews; letters of recommendation
hiring procedures: assessment of, 197; components of, 122–23; effectiveness of, 187–88; purpose, 124–28; working, 232–33
historical incrementalism, 50
historical inevitability, 27–28
history, importance of, 5–6
Hogan Personality Inventory (HPI), 161–63
home schooling, 224, 278
homosexuality, 233–34
horses, 89, 90
hubris, xviii–xix, 58
Hulin, Charles, 290
Hull, Clark, 32, 165
human nature, view of, 26–27
human resource management (HRM): activities of, xxii; utilization of, xi–xii, 48–49
hummingbirds, 265–66
Hussein, Ibrahim, 278
hybrid vigor, 55

identity construction, 212
imitation, 61; imperfect, 60, 257, 300; learning by, 252–53, 259; runaway, 270
immigrants, success of, 150
inclusive fitness, 56–57, 92–93
incrementalism, 52
individual attributes, 12–13
individual differences, 281; explanations of, 86; heritability of, 286; and learning, 286–88
individualism, 7, 119, 121
individuals: aggregating, 190–91; proportion of types, 191
industrial psychology, 15
industrial revolution, 7, 119, 120, 122

industry centers, benefits of, 297
inevitability of uncertainty, 77
information: concrete, 133; gathering
  of, 137–39; immediate, 132–33,
  135; negative, 129, 202, 203, 206
inheritance: of characteristics, 280;
  organizational, 62; of position,
  113–14
initiates, exploitation of, 304
injury and illness, occupational, 35
innovations, 67
insect flight, modeling of, 174
instinct theory, 93–94
instruction, verbal, 252
Internet, use of for recruitment, 75
Internet, use of in education, 269–70
internships, 136, 291
interventions, 3; assumptions about,
  49; characteristics of, 36; defined,
  xxii; evaluations of, 72, 73, 76;
  expectations of, 31; HRM, 9–10,
  60, 72; importance of process, 31–
  32; organizational, 4; outcomes of,
  58; psychological, 33; reasons for,
  21, 73; retention of, 62; social,
  32–33; successful, 90; unsuccessful, 52
interviews: employment, 48; functions
  of, 62
invisible hand of the market, 128–29
IQ: and ability to learn, 285, 302;
  and job satisfaction and turnover,
  157–58
IQ myopia, 282

James, William, 94
Jefferson, Thomas, 16, 130
Jensen, Arthur, 86–87
jobs: analysis of, 235; demonstrated
  competence in, 118–19 (*See also*
  auditions); necessity for experience
  in, 146; performance in, 147–48,
  154, 159, 197; proper placement
  of people in, 24, 124–25, 151–52,
  222, 230; rotation of, 296–97;

satisfaction with, and IQ, 157–58;
  tryouts of, 118, 145, 146–47, 166,
  199
Jobs, Steve, 246
Johnson, Lyndon, 90
Judge, Timothy, 282
junk food, 200–201
Just So Stories (Kipling), 89

Kennedy, John F., 219
Kenya, runners in, 247–48, 278, 294,
  302
kinesthesis, 289
King, Martin Luther, writings of, 283
kin recognition, 133–34
Klitgaard, Robert, 192
knife analogies, 78, 80
knowledge: importance of local, 317;
  ordinary, 65–66, 67, 253–54;
  scientific, 9; tacit, 74–75
Kroc, Ray, 246

land, importance of, 113–14
language: acquisition of, 91–92, 262,
  267–68, 291–92; in children, 247;
  immersion in, 267–68; as a
  primary ability, 289; use of, xvii
language gate, 292
Laplace, Marquis de, 14
learning: context in, 265–66;
  importance of content, 260;
  organizational, 75; rate of, 290;
  without skilled teachers, 278
Left Back (Ravitch), 269
leftovers from evolution, 57
legal concerns in hiring, 110, 167–68,
  169, 206–7
letters of recommendation: bias in,
  206–7; inconsistencies among,
  142–43; information gathering in,
  xvi, 118; modifications to, 206–7;
  requirements for, xii; usefulness
  of, 198–99, 201, 202–3; use of,
  xxiii, 47–48; writers of, 203–4,
  206–7

level, 187, 195
Likert, Rensis, 28
literacy, social aspect of, 268–69
"Little Albert" study, 260
long-distance runners, 247–48, 278, 294
lotteries, fairness of, 228
LSAT, 136, 140, 192–93
Lykken, David, 87

Machiavelli, Niccolo, 2, 114
management, scientific, 12, 24
management advice, industry of, 3–4
Mansfield, Harvey, 272
marital compatibility, xviii
Markowitz, H. M., 76–77
Marx, Karl, 18, 25, 27, 91
math, acquisition of, 265
Maxwell, David, 267–68
McDougal, William, 94
McGregor, Douglas, 1, 25, 28
Mead, Margaret, 79, 96
mechanical design, 16–17; assumptions of, 8–9, 30–31, 71; failure of, 32–34; features of, 36; perspective of, 4; view of organizational problems, 10–11
mechanisms: evolved, 89; psychological, 80, 82–84
mechanists, 11–12
Mendel, Gregor, 6
Mensa, 16–17
mental ability, 195
mentoring, 253, 301
method, defined, xxiii
methodological essentialism, 11
microscope analogy, 52
Microsoft, 246
middle class, 7
Milam, John, 271
military organizations: recruitment in, 115–17; testing in, 120–21
Mill, John Stuart, 16, 18
Miller, Arthur, 235

mind: adaptations of, 84; as a blank slate, 79, 263, 280; modular, 79–80
Mineka, Susan, 82
misanthropes, usefulness of, 160
"Misbehavior of Organisms, The" (Breland and Breland), 90–91
mismatch: potential for, 202; problem of, 200–201, 201; theory of, 320–21
Miyazaki, Ichisada, 115
Monahan, Tom, 246
monocultures, 207–8, 233
moods, importance of, 173
Moore, G. E., 88
Moore, Sir Thomas, 19–20
morality, sense of, 289
motivation, 279
Muchinsky, Paul M., 30, 47
Muggenthaler, Liz Von, 89–90
Münsterberg, Hugo: and organizational practices, 29; on prediction, 15; and psychology, 18, 30–31; reductionist spirit of, 12; on self-rating, 147; and testing, 124–25; view of experts, 22, 138–39
Murray, Charles, 109

natural aristocracies, 16–17, 130
naturalistic fallacy, 88
natural selection, 317; evolution by, 50, 74; and learning, 280; no goal of, 92; in organizations, xx
needs analysis, 251–52, 254–55; and training, 273
nepotism, 113–14
New Atlantis (Bacon), 19
noise from evolution, 57, 172–73
nonverbal cues, 134–35
numbers, dealing with, 139
nurture assumption, 264

occupational mobility, 287
occupational specialization, 113
O'Connell, Colm, 278, 302

OD (organizational development).
See organizational development
OJT. *See* on-the-job-training
"On the Conflicts Between Biological and Social Evolution and Between Psychology and Moral Tradition" (Campbell), xv
on-the-job-training, 253, 257–58, 291, 296
operant conditioning, 76, 260–61
ordinary people: judgment of, 138; supposed incompetence of, 16, 20, 129; in training, 253–54
organizational change, 152
organizational culture, 208
organizational development (OD), 9, 71
organizational goals: defined, 154–55; hierarchy of, 152; and hiring goals, 141; supposition of, 131, 319; in training, 274
organizational procedures, 142
organizational values, 255
Organization Man, The (Whyte), 2
organizations: culture in, 26; defined, 34; evolutions if, 27–28; functionality of, 46, 187; institutional memory in, 52; large, 6–7, 35–36, 139; and leaders' self-interest, 319; minority recruitment in, 218–19, 224–25; problems in, 2; sex ratios in, 86–87; similarity to machines, 8–9, 63; skill base in, 288
Origin of Species, The (Darwin), 6

Pala, Gino, 246
Pangloss, Dr., 88
paradox of uncertainty, 77
paradox of utilization, 62
Parsons, Frank, 124–25, 138–39
path dependencies, 65
peacock's tails, 51
peer groups, importance of, 291–92, 299

pencil, evolution of, xvi, 5, 95
perceptions, limitations of, 66
performance: appraisals, xiii–xiv, 48, 160; over time, 226; predicting, 189, 282
Perrow, Charles, 271
personal goals, 150
personality types, mix of within organizations, 191–94
personnel selection methods, 23
Petroski, Henry, xvi, 5, 95
phonics, usefulness of, 289, 316
pigs, training of, 90–91
pilots, people as, 58, 59
plants, domestication of, 50–51
Plato: cave dweller analogy, 10, 16–17, 18; ideal society of, 24, 124–25; on the importance of experts (philosophers), 17–18, 29; theory of forms, 4, 11
Poitier, Sidney, 246
Polybius, 116
Popper, Karl R., 65, 68, 72
positivism, 14–15, 20–21, 21–22, 28, 119
potential, fulfillment of, 25
practice, 245; defined, xxiii; deliberate, 290–91; importance of, 267, 283–84; opportunity for, 293; use of, 270; value of, 255–56, 303
prediction, 14–15, 171–72
preferences, evolved, 200–201
prestige effects, 234
Princeton University, 193
Principles of Scientific Management, The (Taylor), 22
probability, 185
problems: organizational, 35; solving of, 78–79, 289
process, importance of, 31–32
productivity, 31
Programmer Aptitude Test (PAT), 190
promiscuity, sexual, 88
Prussian army, 116
psychological traits, 287–88

psychologists: assumptions of, 281; I/O, xii, 21, 33–34; organizational, 25; perspective of, 49; terminology of, 137

psychology, 8; criticisms of, 87; education in, 33–34; evolutionary, xvi, 77–78

punctuated equilibrium, 53

purpose, defined, 170–71

Pygmalion effect, 148

Pygmalion (Shaw), 148

quality circles, 67

quotas, hiring, 209. *See also* affirmative action

race: differences in, 212; problems of definition, 211–12; self reporting of, 212–13, 227–28, 234

race norming, 220–21

randomness, usefulness of, 230–31

random selection above a threshold, 225–31; advantages of, 227; effect on motivation, 230–31; establishing the threshold, 229–30, 231, 235; and universities, 232

rational choice, 22–23

rational decision making, 60–61

rats, training of, 260–61

Ravitch, Diane, 269

reading, 265

reciprocity, 133–34, 215

recordkeeping, and performance, 271–72

reductionism, 11, 12, 63–64, 91

redundancy, principle of, 137

Reich, Robert, 2–3, 208

reinforcement and punishment, 264. *See also* operant conditioning

relationships, 69

reproductive success, 92–93, 97, 114, 134–35

Republic, The (Plato), 124–25

resegregation, 217

respectful tinkering, 46

restaurants, 46–47, 154

results, immediate and obvious, 166

Richerson, Peter J., xvi, 315

risk: avoiding, 201–2, 203; evaluating, 129

Robert Jordan vs. City of New London, 158

Roman Empire: army of, 116; decline of, 47; selection of soldier in, 170; success of, xix–xx

Rono, Peter, 278

routines, 142

rubber bands, 284

rules of thumb, 60–61

sabbatical leaves, 297

Samoa, 79, 96

Samuels, David, 193

satisficing, 61

SAT scores: for college admissions, xiii, 17; effect of on country, 190–91; justification of, 130; as predictors of performance, 150, 155–56, 217–18; use of, 110–11, 143–44

Schmidt, Frank, 22

Scholastic Aptitude Tests. *See* SAT scores

science, promise of, 7–8

scientific elite, 21–22, 29

Scientific Management (Taylor), 2

scientism, defined, 36

scientists, productivity of, 149–50

score adjustment, 219–21

Scott, W. Richard, 18, 109

segregation by cognitive ability, 208

selection methods: components of, 170; top down, 214; and tradition, 231–32

self-help groups, 295

self-interest: in affirmative action programs, 218; and conflict, 55; and evolved preferences, 202; and fairness, 216; in hiring practices, 109, 128–29, 141–42, 164–65,

self-interest (*continued*)
186, 198; in HRM, xx; interventions using, 317, 318–19; leveraging, 207, 316; and needs analyses, 274; in racial categorization, 213–14; reducing influence of, 204, 229; in systems, 59
self-rating, 147
self-selection, 302–3
serendipity, 71, 254
seven transformations of a candidate (Chinese), 169–70
sex roles, 112–13, 264–65
sexual development, 91, 97
sexual selection, xviii, 51, 55
Shaw, George Bernard, 148
similarity, preference for, 219
Sinclair, Upton, 2
situated learning, 294, 297–98
ski instructors, 225–26, 227
skills: crossover between, 255; defined, 250; diversity in, 275, 299–300; functions of, 279–80; gaining of, 245–46; proportion of, 196; significance of, 261–62; teaching, 301; unavailability of, 299
Skinner, B. F., 29–30, 90–91, 264
slaves and slavery, 6, 114
Smith, Adam, xx, 128–29
snakes, fear of, 80, 82, 88, 96–97
social abilities, 289
Social Darwinism, 87, 92–93
social engineering, 23, 264, 271
social evolution, xv–xvi
social interaction, 65–66
social interventions, defined, 36
social learning, 65–66
social programs, confidence in, 34
Social Programs That Work (Crane), 34
social sciences: applied, 66–67; failures of, 32, 77; history of, 5; progress in, 4; reality of, 69–70; theory, 317

social skills, 111
social systems: complexity of, 251, 284–85; evolutionary perspective on, 58–59
socioeconomic status (SES), 93
Soderini, Piero, 114
Solomon's House, 19–20
Spencer, Herbert, 92–93
staffing as strategy implementation, 125
staffing models, 125–28
Standard Social Science Model (SSSM), 78–79, 85, 86, 90, 262–63
state universities: and X percent plans, 224
statistical prediction rules (SPRs), 139–40
statistical theory, 5
statistics, 76; usefulness of, 76
status, drive for, 293–94
status quo, justification of, 87–88
Stevenson, Harold, 290
stock market, uncertainty of, 231
strategic planning, failure of, 71
structural inertia, 74
student ratings of teachers, 272–73
Study of Sociology (Spencer), 92–93
Sturm, Susan, 109
substitutability, 278, 284
swimming, 287
systems: evolutionary perspective on, 63–65; interdependence of, 52–53; pretty good, 53–54; under-engineered, 54

Taleb, Nassim Nicholas, 185
Taylor, Frederick W.: and organizational practices, 2, 24, 27–28, 29; and psychology, 18; reductionist spirit of, 12; on science, 1; view of experts, 22, 138
teachers: importance of, 278, 284; learning to teach, 279, 302; plans to replace, 267; salaries for, 276–77; student rating of, 272–73, 302

team-building exercises, 262

technique, defined, xxiii

technology: defined, xxii; seduction of, 271. *See also* computers

tennis players, training of, 270

tenure, 135

term limits, problems with, 297–98

testing: educational, 121; in federal agencies, 166–67, 167–68; in Imperial China, 169–70; industry of, 131, 303; military, 120–21, 122; practical, 135–36; psychological, 121–22; in the twentieth century, 119–22

testing well, importance of, 283

test of time, 66–67

tests: ability to predict outcomes, 165–66, 220; British civil service examinations, 120; cognitive ability, 109; computer scoring of, 121; cultural factors in, 150, 220, 234; economic utility of, 168; employment, 48, 147; impartiality of, 122; in Imperial China, 115; IQ, 133; job sample, 199; lack of contact in, 131–32; personality, 67; predictive value of, 147–48, 150, 198, 213; research on, 174; standardized, 115; in the United States, 120, 248–49; use of to avoid litigation, 167–68; validity of, 156. *See also* LSAT; SAT

Texas, X percent plan in, 221, 222, 223–24

Thomas, Dave, 246

Thorndike model of fairness, 213–14

Thorpe, Ian, 287

three postulates of Darwin, 50

Thurow, Lester, 2

time on task, 290

tire repair, 279–80

Toda, Masanao, 45

to do lists, 73–74

traditional procedures, xii; contempt for, xvii–xviii; use of, xiv

training: in affirmative action, 209; defined, 250; in early societies, 286; effective systems of, 248; effect on performance, 284; evaluation of, 275–76; failure of high-tech, 259; flexibility in, 299; functions of, 90, 255, 275; goals in, 254–55, 256–57, 274; in industry, 249, 296; methods of, 48, 62–63, 247, 252–54, 257–58; military, 117; movements in, 269–70; novelty in, 270–71; programs of, 8, 24, 31–33; status of, 276–79; traditional, 249–50, 252, 257–59, 271; utilization of, 279; web-based, 256–57

training pulpit, 249

traits: correlations to performance, 168; defined, 86; evolved, 287; of executives, 161–63; heritability of, 84–85; overstating of small differences in, 281–82; relationship between, 161–63; theory of, 85–86; value of, 159–60

travel, speed of, xix

Turner, Ted, 246

turnover, 159; in industry, 120; and IQ, 157–58; lowering, 31, 72, 195; and mixing of talents, 297

uncertainty, coping with, 75–76

underengineering, 76

Uniform Guidelines on Employee Selection Procedures, 121

unintended consequences: dysfunction caused by, 62; ignoring, 16; from innovations, 10; of interventions, 31, 273–74; of technology, 96

unions, 7

universities: admissions to, 140–41, 192; selective entrance requirements for, 136; tests in admissions decisions, 167

University of Virginia Law School, admissions, 140–41

utility analysis, 13, 23, 49, 171
utilization paradox, 47–49, 129
Utopia (Moore), 19–20
utopias: constructive, 23; jigsaw
    puzzle, 156–57; organizational,
    23–26, 28–30; spray paint, 156–
    57

values: conflict between, 159–60;
    cultural, 67; diversity in, 211;
    identifying, 198; organizational,
    26, 61, 68, 125; social, 60
variability: as a goal of education,
    251; in organizations, 196–97,
    204, 318; value of, 207
variables, hard-to-quantify, 140–41
variation: among employees, 202–3;
    enhancing, 208–9; necessity of, 54,
    67, 70–71, 74, 76–77, 207;
    reduction of in mechanical models,
    257; role in adaptation, 186;
    social, 60; usefulness of, 95, 257
variation-selection-retention, xvi,
    50–52, 60–63

Vegetius, 116
Venter, J. Craig, 235
violence, culture of, 191
visiting professorships, 297
vocational guidance, 138–39

Walden Two (Skinner), 29–30, 264
Ware, Lancelot, 16–17
Watson, James B., 29–30, 79, 260,
    263, 280
whole equals the sum of the parts, 13,
    190
why questions, xv, 94, 167
Whyte, William, 2
Williams, George C., 315
Wilson, Alan, 89, 90
Work of Nations, The (Reich), 2–3

X percent plans, 221–25

Yanomamo people, 82, 139
Yeats, William Butler, 45, 245

zebras, domestication of, 261

About the Author

Stephen Colarelli is professor of psychology at Central Michigan University. He was educated at Northwestern University, the University of Chicago, and New York University. He has written widely on applying an evolutionary psychological perspective to human resource management. He lives in Midland, Michigan with his wife, Margaret, and two children, Catherine and Julia.